GEORGE SAND

ELIZABETH HARLAN

George Sand

YALE UNIVERSITY PRESS　NEW HAVEN & LONDON

Set in FontShop Scala and Scala Sans by Duke & Company, Devon, Pennsylvania.
Printed in the United States of America by R. R. Donnelley, Harrisonburg, Virginia.

Library of Congress Cataloging-in-Publication Data
Harlan, Elizabeth.
George Sand / Elizabeth Harlan.
p. cm.
Includes bibliographical references and index.
ISBN 0-300-10417-0 (alk. paper)
1. Sand, George, 1804–1876. 2. Novelists, French—19th century—Biography. I. Title.
PQ2412.H37 2004
843'.8—dc22
2004010315

A catalogue record for this book is available from the British Library.

The paper in this book meets the guidelines for permanence and durability of the Committee on Production Guidelines for Book Longevity of the Council on Library Resources.

10 9 8 7 6 5 4 3 2 1

What could be more interesting and less well known to common people than the detail, intimacy, the inside of those great lives about which they know only the outward appearance?

George Sand

To my mother, Hortense Kramon Sarot

L'amour maternel n'est qu'un tissu de joies et de chagrins de premier calibre.

George Sand

This cathexis between mother and daughter—essential, distorted, misused—is the great unwritten story. Probably there is nothing in human nature more resonant with charges than the flow of energy between two biologically alike bodies, one of which has lain in amniotic bliss inside the other, one of which has labored to give birth to the other.

Adrienne Rich, Of Woman Born

CONTENTS

PART THREE: MARRIAGE, MOTHERHOOD, AND MISGIVINGS

PART FOUR: THE DAUGHTER'S DEMISE

PART FIVE: WAR AND PEACE

From then on I glimpsed only future struggles against public opinion of which I had never dreamed, and some unimaginably sad dangers whose nature they assumed I would guess, but . . . I guessed nothing at all. Besides, just as I am active in pursuing what appeals to my instincts, so am I lazy in confronting what is hostile to them, and I did not seek to solve the enigma of the sphinx; but something terrible seemed to be in store for me.

WHO WAS George Sand? More than a century before Simone de Beauvoir declared, "It is still across the dreams of men that women dream," Sand not only dreamed of a liberated life, she *lived* it.[1] Born Amandine Aurore Lucile Dupin in Paris in 1804, she grew up to become a successful, prolific, controversial author who left her husband, took lovers, adopted a male pseudonym, fought for and regained custody of her children and possession of her home, founded journals, participated in the political life of her nation, and died shortly before her seventy-second birthday, surrounded by her adoring son, Maurice, his wife and two daughters, and her estranged daughter, Solange.

During the course of Sand's career, she produced more than ninety novels, dozens of novellas, scores of plays, thousands of pages of autobiography, tomes of commentary and criticism, hundreds of articles, numerous travel journals, and a correspondence comprising some twenty thousand extant letters. Balzac, Sarah Bernhardt, Flaubert, Henry Harrisse, Hugo, Marx, Michelet, Napoléon III, and Flora Tristan figure among Sand's celebrated correspondents.

Although she was omitted from the reformulated French literary canon after 1914, the centennial of Sand's death in 1976 catalyzed interest in her life and work, ushering in new editions of her novels and culminating in the long-awaited English translation of Sand's autobiography, *Story of My Life,* and the completion, in the twilight of the twentieth century, of George Lubin's magisterial twenty-six-volume edition of Sand's correspondence. "When finally completed years from now," Curtis Cate wagered in the preface to his 1975 biography, "this monumental task of epistolary concentration may well make George Sand the most meticulously documented woman in nineteenth-century France, if not in French history."[2]

In their own day Alexander Herzen called her "the Joan of Arc of our time." Why, today's reader may wonder, has Sand's life and work resonated so widely? Matthew Arnold's summation is instructive: "The passion of agony and revolt, the consolation from nature and from beauty, the ideas of social renewal—in the evolution of these is George Sand and George Sand's life and power." Diane Johnson emphasizes Sand's masculine capacity to act independently and think rationally: "In fact the singular and most admirable thing about Sand was that she seems to have considered herself a free and responsible moral agent, accountable, and capable of theorizing, like a man." Daniel Hofstadter assigns Sand's importance to her being female: "For if undoubtedly she was a great woman, it is precisely as a *woman*, not as a writer or social reformer, that she is thought to have been great."[3]

However humorously intended, a UPI press release of 2003 signaling "a domestic problem for President Jacques Chirac, whose wife Bernadette is upset at her husband's refusal to honor next year's 200th anniversary of the birth of France's greatest (and most prolific) woman writer, George Sand, with a tomb in the Paris Pantheon" underscores Sand's enduring and controversial cultural acclaim:

> The Left Bank neo-classical monument entombs France's
> great cultural figures including Voltaire, Victor Hugo and
> Emile Zola, but only one woman—scientist Marie Curie. Now
> the President's wife is quietly backing a campaign by French-
> women to honor Amandine-Aurore-Lucile Dupin Dudevant,
> who wrote under the name of Georges [sic] Sand. The problem
> is not that Sand was the Madonna of her day, marketing her
> work by deliberately shocking the public, smoking in the street,
> wearing trousers, and conducting boldly public affairs, one
> with pianist Frédéric Chopin. What really annoys Chirac was
> her role as a passionate socialist and revolutionary in the 1848

uprising that toppled the Orleans monarchy. In France, such resentments endure.[4]

Understanding Sand's tendency toward self-contradiction is helpful in understanding the diversity of opinion that she inspired. In his eloquent description, Matthew Arnold privileges Sand's protean personality: "Not dominated by the past, not devoted to things established, not overoccupied with theology," Sand was "in search of some more free and wide conceptions of human life, and turned towards the future and the unrealized. . . . Her place is with the party and propaganda of organic change. For any party tied to the past, for any party, even, tied to the present, she is too new, too bold, too uncompromisingly sincere." Far from believing that constancy was virtuous, Sand proudly proclaimed her propensity for change: "Human nature is but a tissue of inconsequences, and I do not for a moment believe those who pretend to find themselves always in accord with their selves of yesterday."[5] Sand changed her mind throughout her life, foiling critics fond of categories and frustrating others craving consistency.

Part revolutionary, part reactionary, Sand's paradoxical relationship to feminism is an especially controversial issue. Whereas André Maurois pays homage to Sand as "the voice of woman at a time when woman was silent," Leslie Rabine, among others, faults her for dissociating herself from the suffragists of her day: "She made the freedom of one woman separate from the freedom of other women." Arguing for "separate spheres" of male and female existence, Sand belittled the contemporary women's movement: "It seems that the socialist ladies confuse equality with identity. Men and women can have different functions without this giving women inferior status."[6] True enough, but the functions Sand had in mind fluctuated along a sliding scale of will and whimsy, and although she articulated the belief that woman's place is in the home, it cannot be forgotten that she left her own in order to gain a public voice.

Sand lore is laced with several commonplaces for which she is best known: the taking of a man's name, the topcoat and trousers that she donned, and her much celebrated love affairs. But these features of her life are neither original nor unique. Many women authors of the day took male pseudonyms; other women, including Sand's mother, wore men's clothing to pass in places where women were unwelcome; and love affairs between unwed partners were as ordinary as loveless marriages. Far more revealing than these overdrawn features of Sand storiography is the fact that in 1831, as a young woman of twenty-seven, married and the mother of two small children, Sand ventured forth from her province in central France, established herself as a writer at the epicenter of French culture, and earned her own living. This was and remains a remarkable achievement that prevails even as Sand's literary reputation has waxed and waned. "Very often," Simone André-Maurois observes, "an artist's masterpiece is her life itself."[7]

Barely five feet tall, with the heart rate of an Olympic athlete, Sand displayed strength and stamina out of all proportion to perceived limitations of size and sex. She rode horseback hard and fast across vast stretches of French countryside and hiked high into the mountains of France and Switzerland. By nineteenth-century standards, she traveled frequently and extensively, beginning with her trip at the age of four to and from war-torn Spain, a journey of thousands of miles. Into her seventies she bathed in the Indre River. Among many other tributes, Sand's celebrity was commemorated in her lifetime by a perfume, a writing pen, and a dirigible that bore her name. She also gets credit for turning Balzac on. "I only take the Indian hookah or the Persian narguile," Balzac wrote of his introduction to the water pipe in his *Traité des excitants modernes*. "I owe George Sand the key to this treasure."[8]

Recognition and success may have come early and powerfully, but not without pain and sacrifice. Looking back, Sand reflected: "I had wanted to be an artist; at last I was one. I imagined that I had reached my long-sought goal—independence and mastery of my own life. I had just shackled a ball and chain about my ankle that I had not foreseen." Prone to migraines and bouts of blurred vision, impaired hearing, severe stomach pains, leg and arm cramps that interfered with walking and writing, depression and exhaustion, Sand suffered throughout her life from a series of physical and emotional disturbances. Life for the woman whom Simone André-Maurois refers to as "this event called George Sand" was by no means charmed.[9]

The litany of hostility to which Sand's life and work have been subjected is now legion, with Baudelaire leading the brigade: "She is stupid, she is heavy, she is garrulous; she has as much depth of judgment, as much delicacy of feeling in her moral judgments, as a concierge or a kept woman." In a paroxysm of misogyny, Nietzsche dismissed Sand along with Madame de Staël as "the best involuntary arguments against emancipation and feminine autonomy." Limiting himself to a critique of her novels, Edgar Allan Poe described Sand as "a woman who intersperses many an admirable sentiment amid a chaos of the most shameless and altogether objectionable fiction." Edmond de Goncourt recorded the following anatomical contortion in his journal: "If autopsies had been made of women with original talent, such as Mme Sand . . . they would show genitalia that resemble men's, clitorises that are similar to our penises."[10]

The American journalist Margaret Fuller experienced Sand very differently on a visit in 1846 while traveling as the *Tribune's* foreign correspondent in Europe. "Her whole appearance and attitude, in its simple and ladylike dignity, present an almost ludicrous contrast to the vulgar caricature idea of George Sand," Fuller wrote a friend. "Her way of talking is just like her writing,—lively, picturesque, with an undertone of deep feeling, and the same skill in striking the nail on the head every now and then with a blow. . . . While talking, she *does* smoke all the time her little cigarette. . . . For the rest, she holds her place in the literary and social world of France like a man, and seems full of energy and courage in it. I suppose she has suffered much, but she has also enjoyed and done much, and her expression is one of calmness and happiness."[11]

André Maurois' 1953 biography of Sand helped rescue her from some of the opprobrium that had accumulated since her death three quarters of a century earlier: "It has been too long the fashion to adopt an attitude of irony and condemnation in dealing with her." If hostility toward Sand has not altogether disappeared, the tide has certainly turned, and for some years now we have basked in admiration for the woman whom Lionel Trilling dubbed "a bright sunny genius."[12]

Aurore Dupin was born at the dawn of the Napoleonic Empire. Her father, Maurice Dupin, was related to the last three Bourbon monarchs through his great-grandfather, Frederick Augustus, elector of Saxony and king of Poland; her mother, Sophie Delaborde Dupin, whose father sold birds and ran a billiard parlor, had, to her mother-in-law's despair, already borne (at least) one illegitimate child to another man. Eschewing those who would obscure her humble origins by promoting her aristocratic pedigree, Sand proudly proclaimed in her autobiography: "The blood of kings was mixed in my veins with that of the poor and lowly."[13]

Indeed, her class-crossed life was fraught with conflict and contradiction. When Aurore was four, her father, an officer in Napoléon's army, was thrown to his death by a spirited stallion, leaving the child in the care of his mother, Marie-Aurore Dupin, at her chateau at Nohant, in central France. Soon thereafter, Sand's mother left for Paris, relinquishing her right to raise her daughter in exchange for the stipend with which her mother-in-law bought her off.

Part biography and part mystery, my book is not really a retelling of Sand's life but an exploration of a latticework of lives: those of her grandmother, her mother, her daughter, Solange, and those of Sand's protagonists, whose stories amplify her own.[14] I begin by doing something that is always ill advised, by laying my cards on the table and exposing the central revelation that has propelled this book from its inception more than a decade ago. Writers are invariably warned against tipping their hand too early, and so I have tried countless other ways of beginning, but to no avail. When I attempted in previous drafts to withhold the hypothesis that informs my work and to weave it seamlessly into the narrative, my storytelling became dull and plodding: a clot of anecdotes, events, and details. In a dutiful if superfluous recycling of information, I'd drawn a map but lost the forest for the trees.

I dug deeper and began again, reminded of what Virginia Woolf wrote about moments of being, of her term "cotton wool," to which she likened ordinary existence in which life goes by as though unlived until something jolts one into awareness. "I feel that I have had a blow," Woolf explained. "From this I reach what I might call a philosophy; at any rate it is a constant idea of mine; that behind the cotton wool is hidden a pattern."[15]

Too often, it seems to me, biographies get trapped in cotton wool, chronicling ordinary existence at the expense of life's turning points and epiphanies. As a case in point, Sand biographies tend to retrace her copious literary career without coming to terms with why she wrote compulsively over the course of some sixty years. The question of how is compelling: the mechanics of Sand's literary life, the writing cabinet where she kept a pet cricket, her self-imposed exile from her husband and children to begin a writing career in Paris, the adoption of a male pseudonym, her nocturnal schedule that induced her to leave a lover's bed to begin a new novel in the middle of the night, the cigarettes and chunks of chocolate that sustained her, her extraordinary experiment in literary genre.

But the question of why is essential. Despite occasional paralysis and constant pain in her writing arm, despite recurrent bouts of near blindness induced by fatigue, despite her constant complaint of working like a slave, what made George Sand produce a minimum of twenty manuscript pages nearly every night of her life? With all due respect, writing was the cotton wool of Sand's existence. By her own admission, she wrote the way she sewed a hem. "I still scrawl novels with deplorable ease," Sand told a friend. "The results of this excessive haste are most marked in her earlier writings," the English critic Frederic W. H. Myers observed. "She has not had time to make them short."[16]

Often, Sand couldn't remember what she had written the night before. "As soon as I had finished my first manuscript, it erased itself from my memory," she said of *Indiana*. "I'll be hanged if I know what my novel is about," she declared of *Château des désertes*. "I dreamt it, for I was in a state of somnambulism most of the time." As she prepared yet another manuscript for submission, Sand wrote her editor François Buloz: "You know that with my poor memory I often have to reread each day what I did the day before, which still doesn't prevent me from repeating or leaving things out again." Elsewhere, Sand referred to a "forgetfulness through which my brain has immediately buried the product of its work," and in yet another context, she commented on her propensity for digression: "This is a defect, they say, I still suffer from; I admit I take little notice of present reality, and have today, exactly like when I was four, an insuperable lack of restraint in that genre of creation."[17]

All those letters, diaries, essays, stories, novels, plays, memoirs; those hundreds of tomes consisting of thousands of items containing millions of words: never mind what they stand for to generations of readers and literary critics. (Everything under the sun.) What did they mean to George Sand? What drove her? What was she reaching for? What haunted her? What was she running from? Sand ranks among the most exhaustively investigated and thoroughly reported figures in the annals of biography. Unless these riddles can be unraveled, there's no point to enumerating her much promoted accomplishments, no reason to reiterate the well-established facts of her life.

I acknowledge that before coming to terms with the story that I've finally put forth, I found myself trapped in a tug of war between information and intuition. While basing my account on data and grounding it with documentation, I've chosen to be guided by intuition, by what Virginia Woolf may have meant by what she called a philosophy and attributed to a *blow* "that is or will become a revelation of some order . . . a token of some real thing behind appearances." I believe George Sand sustained such a blow, one that forced her to suspect a fundamental "truth" about her existence that was suppressed by her mother and grandmother and that she herself would spend her life interpreting and encoding. Following Sand's trail, I, too, was jolted into a revelation, which led me to a sense of what lay below the surface of my subject's life. When I stopped accepting at face value its appearance, a comprehensive reading, a hitherto hidden pattern behind the cotton wool of Sand's existence opened up to me.

What if, I came to wonder, an unverified but universally accepted assumption about George Sand's identity was placed in doubt? What if George Sand's ostensible father, Maurice Dupin, was not, in fact, her real father? And what if she herself had come to believe this and lived her life half-suspecting, half-knowing that her paternal lineage was a lie and her legacy an elaborate cover-up concocted by her mother and coerced by her grandmother, each for reasons of her own? And what if this secret that loomed so large as to threaten an entire family's status quo would prove too crucial and the pressure to keep it hidden too great? Sand's grandmother, stressed by ill health and her granddaughter's disaffection, may have been the first to buckle under the strain, and in a shocking and underexamined episode of Sand's biography, Marie-Aurore Dupin may have confessed the truth about Aurore's questionable origin.

Some years later, following Marie-Aurore's death, Sand's mother, volatile by nature and further destabilized by a difficult menopause, also may have reared up in rebellion against the oppressive myth of her daughter's identity, and in an equally underexamined scene, "the counterpart to the confession that I had heard and accepted from my grandmother," Sand tells us in her autobiography, Sophie Delaborde Dupin may also have divulged this truth.[18] Subsequently, Sand spent her life obsessed with the dilemma of her identity: in pursuit, in denial, and ultimately in sublimation of the central truth of her existence.

So powerful was the sway of illegitimate birth and illicit paternity that Sand visited the same destiny upon her daughter, Solange, dubbed by Nicole Mozet "Sand's great failure." Christine Chambaz-Bertrand, who refers to Solange as "the shadow part of George Sand," raises a crucial question: "Why did a generous and compassionate woman treat so harshly a weaker, even if difficult, being?" Unlike most critics who displace the blame for Sand's relationship with her daughter onto deficiencies in Solange, Chambaz-Bertrand probes the mystery that is key to George Sand's life: "The birth secret that haunts George Sand's novels and upset her life—whose daughter am I?—also upset Solange's life—whose daughter is she? For us, it is the source of the mother/daughter relationship, and the story repeats itself from one mother to another, from one daughter to another."[19]

According to Sand, Solange "was raised with love, in a happy, constructive, moral environment which should have made of her a saint or a heroine."[20] Sand's hyperbole notwithstanding, this is not what happened. As successful as Sand was, Solange, whose life reveals a stifled attempt at repetition of her mother's life, was commensurately unsuccessful. Despite her effort to be worthy of her mother, Solange underwent a series of catastrophic failures. Like Sand, Solange was miserably mismarried, but unlike Sand, she never became fully free of her entanglement with her abusive husband. Emulating her mother, Solange wrote novels, but nothing she wrote ever achieved recognition. Like Sand, Solange gave birth to two children, but both of her daughters died in early childhood. Overshadowed and outcast by her mother, vilified by scholars who defend Sand and condemn Solange, the daughter has been constructed in Sand lore and literature not as a Cinderella but as the bête noire of her mother's existence.

For me, this relationship between mother and daughter is emblematic of Sand's struggle with the issue of her own identity. It's curious that while critics have never hesitated to associate Sand's abundant fictions of mother-daughter strife with her real-life relationship with Solange, they've typically refrained from interpreting Sand's many stories about birth confusion and false identity as revelatory of her own lifelong matrilineal preoccupation. Like the trail of bread crumbs left by Hansel and Gretel as they made their way through the forest, clues to the uncertainty and shame that riddled Sand's life are encoded in her writings, which are littered with birth secrets and mistaken identities.

"I must begin by saying outright that I *do* wish to hold back, so as not to distort or disguise, several circumstances in my life," Sand admitted when it came time to write her autobiography, which she tellingly titled *Story of My Life*. "The life I am recounting now was as good as possible, on the surface. The sun shone for me on my children, on my friends, on my work. But the life I am not recounting was clouded with terrible sorrow."

Acknowledging her intention to obscure the full picture of her past, Sand advised her reader: "I have not entitled it 'my memoirs'; it is by design that I chose the words, 'Story of My Life,' in order to convey that I did not mean to tell others' stories without restrictions. . . . Certain personal confidences, whether confessions or justifications, become an assault on the conscience or reputation of another; or else they are incomplete, and for that reason, untrue."[21]

When criticized for the ambiguities in certain of her fictional works, Sand offered as her defense: "It seems to me it's more *artistic* not to lift the veil." And in a preface to her novel *Valentine,* Sand explained, "By a phenomenon that accompanies all deep emotions, moral as well as intellectual, it is what one wishes to reveal most that one dares least bring up in public." Although she never does entirely lift the veil, Sand lays bare her heart's most ardent desire. Designed as much for obfuscation as for revelation, her complex, often torturous plots typically culminate in some form of legitimation: the happy ending, or restitution, that sets right in Sand's fiction what was set asunder in her life.[22]

PART ONE FOUNDATIONS AND FAULT LINES

CHAPTER ONE

Her Father's Daughter

This father, whom I scarcely knew and who remains in my memory
as a shining apparition—this artistic young man and warrior has
remained wholly alive in the flights of my fancy, in the pitfalls of my
constitution, in the features of my face.

WHAT SHINES through most brightly in George Sand's charming, harmonious depiction of coming into the world is her desire to resolve the
conflict into which she was born. Whatever the particulars of her birth
may have been, what she presents in her autobiography is a carefully
crafted composition, a social still life that tells as much about how Sand
wished to interpret the conditions of her birth as it does about the way it
actually occurred:

> I came into the world on July 5, 1804; my father was playing
> the violin and my mother wore a pretty pink dress. It took
> but a minute. I at least had that portion of happiness that my
> Aunt Lucie predicted of not making my mother labor too long.
> I was born a legitimate daughter, which might very well not
> have happened if my father had not resolutely trampled on the
> prejudices of his family; that too was a portion of happiness,
> for otherwise my grandmother might not have taken such lov-
> ing care of me as she later did, and I would have been deprived
> of the small fund of ideas and knowledge which have been
> my consolation through the troubles of my life.[1]

In the tableau that Sand paints, her father, Maurice Dupin, occupies
the foreground and plays his cherished violin, ("the old instrument I still
have, to whose sound I was born").[2] Surprisingly, considering what is taking place, it is the father, not the mother, who contributes the active element to this composition. Although Maurice Dupin had served as an

officer in Napoléon's army, throughout her autobiography Sand emphasizes Maurice's love of music as much as, indeed more than, his love for
the martial arts. In the end, it is not his military prowess but his creative
sensibility that constitutes Sand's self-designated legacy from her father.

Her mother, Sophie Delaborde Dupin, occupies a position on the sidelines of Sand's description, even though it is she who will shortly perform
the central act that motivates the scene's retelling. But Sophie is passive,
sitting pretty in pink, awaiting the birth that happens quickly and seemingly without effort. Sand underscores her active role in her birth. It is
she who spares her mother a long and difficult labor, who relieves her of
the pain of childbirth, who brings her happiness. Assisted only by her father's hands that play over her—a musical midwife—Aurore takes charge
and, in a sense, gives birth to herself, forecasting another, later birth, or
*re*birth, in which she will redeliver herself as George Sand. There's another less spiritual explanation for Aurore's swift, biological birth: before
becoming Maurice Dupin's wife a month short of Aurore's birth, Sophie
had already borne several babies (in all likelihood by several different fathers), preparing the possibility for this one to come with little discomfort.[3]

The role Sand ascribes to her father of "resolutely trampling on the
prejudices of his family" is exaggerated, to say the least. Maurice's way of
dealing with his family, which is to say his mother, was to avoid confrontation at all costs, even to the point of keeping secret his socially undesir-
able marriage and Aurore's birth. "I was born on 12 Messidor," Sand writes
in her autobiography, *Story of My Life*. "My grandmother had no inkling
of it. On the 16th, my father wrote her on a quite different matter." Four
days after Aurore's birth, instead of bearing the unacceptable tidings of
his newly formed family life, Maurice imparted information designed to
please and appease his hypercritical mother: "My request is at the war
office and should be put before the Emperor next week. My name is on
the promotion list." In August mother and son were still at loggerheads.
"According to you, my dear mother," Maurice wrote, "I'm an ingrate and
a madman. . . . Your letter hurts me . . . because you accuse me of having
engineered my own bad luck. . . . If we had been at war longer, I believe
I would have duly won my ranks, but since they have to be won in ante-
chambers, I admit I have no brilliant campaigns to boast of on that score."
Skirting any mention of his wife or daughter, Maurice accused his mother,
"You reproach me for never telling you what's going on inside me. You

are the one who never wishes it! How is it possible, when the minute I open my mouth, you accuse me of being a bad son?"[4]

The emperor turned down Maurice's request for promotion, and he would have to wait another year before rising to the rank of captain. In the meantime, he complained bitterly to his mother about how "other members of our family are rising in the world" and, in particular, how his envied and much resented nephew René Vallet de Villeneuve, who had recently been made chamberlain to Prince Louis, was taking up his functions with a large gold key embroidered on his back.[5] Madame Dupin responded by blaming Maurice for his lack of advancement. The rivalry between René and Maurice, related through their common patriarchal ancestor the marshal de Saxe, is a persistent theme in Maurice Dupin's brief life.

Maurice was far from "resolute" before the prospect of angering his mother. In two separate, unaccompanied visits to the family château at Nohant after his marriage—one for a fortnight soon after the civil ceremony, and the other for a full two months in the fall following Aurore's birth—Maurice could not muster the courage to reveal his secret. It was not until November 1804, after he had returned to Paris from the second visit, that Madame Dupin learned of her son's domestic arrangements from René, who attributed "Maurice's unsuccessful attempts at obtaining a promotion to his persistent attachment to Sophie" and let slip an indiscreet reference to Aurore's birth.[6] Maurice and his mother kept up their correspondence and occasional visits during Aurore's early life, even as Madame Dupin refused to acknowledge her daughter-in-law and launched a campaign to have the marriage annulled.

Sand would have us believe that the situation changed abruptly on a visit Madame Dupin made to Paris sometime during Aurore's infancy. In addition to the description of her birth, Sand also supplied the material for this subsequent scene, which is even more essential to the establishment of her identity, for within it her grandmother Marie-Aurore Dupin acknowledges her namesake as her biological granddaughter. But for this acknowledgment, the life of the individual we've come to know as George Sand would not have been lived.

The crucial scene follows a period of many months which Madame Dupin spent in a frantic attempt to dissolve her son's marriage to Sophie Delaborde. According to Sand:

My father discovered that his mother was in Paris; he understood that she knew everything and put me in charge of pleading his case. Taking me in his arms, he climbed into a cab, stopped at the door of the house where my grandmother had gotten off, won in a few words the good graces of the doorkeeper, and confided me to the care of this woman, who carried out the following errand:

She climbed to the apartment of my grandmama and asked to speak to her on whatever pretext came into her mind. Once in her presence, she talked to her about this and that, and chatting all the while, interrupted herself to say, "Take a look, madame, at the pretty little girl of whom I'm the grandmother! Her wet nurse brought her to me today, and I'm so happy about it that I can't part with her for an instant." "Yes, she looks very healthy and strong," said my grandmother, looking for her box of sweets. And all at once, the good woman, who played her role very well, placed me on my grandmama's knee, who offered me some tidbits and began to look at me with a kind of shock and emotion. Suddenly, she pushed me away, exclaiming, "You're deceiving me, this child isn't yours; she doesn't look like you! I know, I know who she is!"

Frightened by the movement that propelled me from the maternal bosom, it seems I began, not to scream, but to cry real tears, which were very effective. "Come, my poor dear love," the porter lady said, taking me back. "They don't want any part of you here, let's go."

My poor grandmother was vanquished. "Give her back to me," she said. "Poor child, all this isn't her fault! And who brought this little one?" "Your own son, madame; he's waiting downstairs, I'll carry back his daughter to him. Excuse me if I offended you; I didn't realize, I'm just an ignoramus! I thought to give you pleasure, to bring you a nice surprise. . . ." "It's all right, my dear, I don't blame you," said my grandmother. "Go find my son, and leave me the child."

My father climbed the stairs four at a time. He found me on the lap, against the bosom of my grandmama, who was crying as she did her utmost to make me laugh. No one told me what transpired between them, and as I was only eight or nine months old, it is probable that I didn't take note of it. It is also probable that they wept together and were loving to each other some more. My mother, who recounted to me this first adventure of my life, told me that when my father brought me back to her, I had in my hands a beautiful ring with a big ruby that my grandmama had removed from her finger, charging me to place it on my mother's finger, which my father made me observe religiously.[7]

To further authenticate her account, Sand informs her readers in a footnote, "I wear this ring all the time."[8] The emotional logic may be convincing: The event bore such importance that I retain to this day a treasured souvenir of it. But the sequential logic is flawed: I have the (a) ring; therefore the episode took place. As for the rest of the account, it bears the stylistic hallmark of much of Sand's fiction: meticulous narrative detail, motivational mechanics, melodramatic flourish, and the kind of attenuated suspense that relieves the reader of any real sense of doubt about the outcome.

Notably, the sole source of information about this scene of recognition is George Sand, who claims she was told of it by her mother. However, by the time Sand wrote the scene, in the summer of 1848, there was no one around to dispute its veracity.[9] Her mother, father, and grandmother were dead, and the only other potential witness to the event, the porter who ostensibly presented the baby to Madame Dupin, was never identified.

We know that Sand thought little of distorting and even rearranging pieces of her past that interfered with the way she wished to present her life. Half tongue-in-cheek, half serious, Sand's inestimable editor Georges Lubin cautioned, "We know full well it's essential never to believe G.S." Her fellow novelist and much admiring critic, Henry James, also picked up on this characteristic of his subject: "Madame Sand remembers to the point of gratefully—gratefully as an artist—reconstituting. . . . So it could be that the free mind and the free hand were ever at her service. A beautiful indifferent agility, a power to cast out that was at least proportioned to the power to take in, hangs about all this and meets us in twenty connections."[10] With so much acknowledged as questionable in Sand's account of her life, it's remarkable that this crucial episode, based loosely, if indelibly, on apocryphal information, has been universally incorporated as uncontested fact in biographies of George Sand.

In *Chère George Sand,* Jean Chalon provides a typical example of the way biographers have uncontestedly replicated the scene of her grandmother's recognition and Sand's version of her resemblance to her paternal ancestors: "After persistent refusal, she consented to see her granddaughter, who had inherited the beautiful eyes of the Koenigsmark's and the Saxe's, the beautiful eyes of the first Aurore and the first Maurice, the eyes of Maurice, her Maurice. Vanquished by this resemblance, *which irrefutably established her son's paternity* [emphasis added], Madame Dupin de Francueil agreed to attend the couple's religious marriage."[11]

Given Maurice's visits to Nohant (which account for some two months of Aurore's earliest life), his military obligations, his Parisian social life, and his musical career, he could not have spent much time with his new daughter. This lack of contact, however, did not prevent Sand from idealizing her relationship with her absent father. Revealing examples abound in her heavily edited version of his letters. Where Maurice wrote merely "Aurore, my good mother, is very aware of the kiss I gave her on your behalf, she wishes you a good year and good health," Sand liberally embellished: "[Aurore] doesn't say anything yet, but I can assure you that she thinks nonetheless. I do adore this child, a love you must allow me." In reality, Maurice's mention of her in his letters—e.g., "Aurore is doing marvelously," "Aurore wants to leave right away"—consists of little more than a handful of banal references. Despite this, Sand wrote with impunity, "In all his letters, I find a passionate, paternal love that brings me to tears when I read them."[12]

To emphasize her father's connection to her, Sand occasionally went beyond rearranging his words. Among her posthumously published writings collected under the title *Sketches and Hints,* an entry inscribed "Written on my grandmother's album" contains a passage that Georges Lubin believes to have been written by Aurore Dupin in the voice of her father addressing his mother after his death: "After several hours of stormy navigation, I tacked about again! . . . I've made port! Why do you cry, my good mother? We weren't destined to arrive together. . . . You would have waited for me but meanwhile my life wouldn't have been very gratifying for you. But yours will be necessary to me for a long time still. My daughter is she not your own?"[13]

George Sand's preoccupation with her connection to Maurice Dupin endured throughout her life. In February 1836, when she finally won legal separation from her husband, she triumphantly wrote her mother: "I am my father's daughter, and I don't give a damn about prejudice when my heart tells me what is just and brave. If my father had listened to the idiotic and crazy people of the world, I would not have inherited his name. He has left me a great legacy of independence and paternal love."[14]

Although no one has questioned the veracity of Sand's account of her grandmother's recognition of her, it is entirely possible that, like so much else in her version of her life, Sand invented the scene that would establish her unequivocally as the biological daughter of Maurice Dupin. To test its truth, or lack thereof one must examine the life of the protagonist who carries the burden of its action. For, accordingly, it is Marie-Aurore Dupin who wields the power to confer legitimacy upon the future George Sand. Much as the stability of the French state depended on the maneuvers of its military heroes, the stability of the lineage to which George Sand was heir depended largely on the ingenuity and tenacity of her grandmother Marie-Aurore. Whereas the battles of Fontenoy and Marengo conferred glory on Sand's great-grandfather and father, respectively, the lesser-known struggles and conquests of her grandmother required commensurate courage and perseverance. The story of Marie-Aurore de Saxe is essential to an understanding of George Sand's life.

CHAPTER TWO

The Importance of Being Marie-Aurore de Saxe

She who was the soul of my entire development and the key
that so gently opened all the mysterious doors of my childhood
mind. How good and intelligent she was! It consoles me to think
of her all the time, to see her again in my dreams and to forget
that she no longer exists.

MARIE-AURORE was only two years old in 1750 when her illustrious father, Maurice de Saxe, marshal of the French Army, died. Because she
was so young and he had been away on military campaigns during most
of her early years, he could not have made much of an impression on her.
The distance between them was accentuated by her being the illegitimate
daughter of his former mistress Marie Rinteau. Nevertheless, the connection with such a powerful and prominent man was the shaping force
of Marie-Aurore's life.

During the first third of that life, Marie-Aurore waged a battle to gain,
if not legitimacy, then recognition and security within French society. Over
the course of two decades, Marie-Aurore made repeated attempts to be acknowledged officially as the "natural" daughter (the polite French term
for illegitimate) of the marshal de Saxe and to obtain from the French government the financial support to which she was, as such, entitled. Her
education, social position, and livelihood, and ultimately the destiny of
her granddaughter Aurore Dupin depended upon this recognition.

Marie-Aurore's mother, Marie Rinteau, was born into a petit bourgeois
Parisian family in 1730; two years later Marie's sister, Geneviève, was born.
One doesn't pick up the record of their lives again until the pleasure-
seeking marshal de Saxe, between campaigns during the war in Flanders
in the winter of 1747–48, chanced into their father's lemonade shop on
rue Grenéta and took a lively interest in eighteen-year-old Marie. Praised
by one source for her "freshness and appeal of a rose bud" and found by

another to be "remarkable for her unusual precocity," Marie was accused by a third source of "relying on her beauty to please, without contributing much more than an affable, even temper and her readiness to be loved."[1]

An enterprising if morally unscrupulous man, Rinteau accepted a lucrative job managing a storage operation for pillaged war spoils in Flanders. In exchange for this favor from the marshal de Saxe, Rinteau's teenage daughters became chorus girls at the Royal Academy of Music and, along with their mother, were settled in a comfortable apartment on rue du Battoir, conveniently located near the marshal's residence on quai Malaquais. Even though Rinteau was eventually jailed for illicit activities, his stealthy maneuverings began the carefully constructed project of inscribing his descendants in France's social hierarchy.

Although women of the theater were considered morally tainted in nineteenth-century France, dancers and actresses of the eighteenth century enjoyed a privileged position. They were sought out by the socially prominent, who competed for their friendship and attendance at their salons. The Goncourts noted in their study of women of the eighteenth century, "The woman of the theatre isn't subject to bourgeois prejudices. Society, far from being closed to her, seeks her out, strokes her, adulates her, bows down before her intelligence, her gaiety, her spirit." A contemporary of the Goncourts elaborated: "Every young girl, whatever her age, who managed to get into theatre, was accordingly emancipated. . . . This accounts for how, in the eighteenth century, practically all elegant women . . . who have any social standing belong to the theatre, and, consequently, how all women of the theatre were *femmes galantes.*"[2]

To go with their elevated station in life, Marie and Geneviève traded in their family's common name for the more elegant-sounding Verrières, soon to be enhanced by the particle *de*, lending a false aura of aristocracy to these two lowborn women. But a lawyer named Barbier, who frequented the Verrières' salon, was not deceived; without mincing words, he described the sisters in his journal as "two young prostitutes."[3]

When Maurice de Saxe returned from the campaign in Flanders, he discovered that Marie had given birth to a daughter on 20 September 1748, in the Parc-Royal home of a man named Gervais, who delivered her. The marshal's good friend and former aide-de-camp, the marquis de Sourdis, in the presence of Geneviève de Verrières, held the baby during her baptism and chose for her the name Aurore, in memory of the marshal's beautiful mother, the countess de Koenigsmark, mistress of the marshal's father, Augustus II, king of Poland. Marie-Aurore and her father therefore shared the fact of their natural (illicit) births.

Living in a house owned by the marshal de Saxe and having his child did not prevent Marie de Verrières from enjoying a variety of love affairs, including one with a married tax collector named Louis Lalive d'Epinay. When Marie disguised herself in men's clothing to meet him in front of the opera, they were arrested and narrowly escaped imprisonment—only because d'Epinay's father held sufficient sway to get them released from custody. Unlike the nineteenth century, when George Sand was merely flouting social custom by appearing publicly in men's clothing, during her great-grandmother's era cross-dressing was actually against the law.

When the marshal's suspicion and jealousy grew too great, Marie cleverly parlayed her relationship with d'Epinay into an affair between him and her sister. As proof of her innocence, Marie would show the marshal audacious love letters d'Epinay was writing Geneviève. The marshal's romantic interests soon moved on, but not before establishing pensions of ten thousand and two thousand *livres*, respectively, for Marie and her child.

To regain the marshal's interest, Marie took it upon herself to sharpen her acting skills. She hoped that with some coaching from the dramatist Jean-François Marmontel, she could rival one of the favored actresses of the day, Mademoiselle Gaussin, who had drawn much attention to herself in her recent roles of Zaïre and Iphigénie. But behind the desire to secure her relationship with Maurice de Saxe, Marie's bid for a theater career had an entirely other purpose. Shaken by her brush with the police during the d'Epinay affair, Marie was seeking immunity from the oppressive laws of the day. For the first three quarters of the eighteenth century, being a registered member of a royal theater troupe (including the opera and the Comédie Française) exempted a woman from the authority of parents, abusive husbands, and even the police.

Marie's plan vis-à-vis Maurice de Saxe backfired, however, when she and Marmontel fell in love while the former was visiting Saxony and Prussia. When the marshal returned to discover the betrayal, he immediately cut off further support for mother and child. Not long afterward, in November 1750, Saxe, bored by peacetime inactivity and dissipated by dropsy (a form of edema), died at Chambord at the age of fifty-four. Sand would summarily eulogize him in her autobiography: "Maurice de Saxe, victor of Fontenoy, clever and brave like his father, but no less debauched, more knowledgeable in the art of war, also more fortunate and better supported."[4] His last will and testament made no mention of either Marie de Verrières or the daughter she had borne him.

Still young and beautiful, Marie de Verrières had already replaced Marmontel with the much wealthier duke de Bouillon; in addition her attention turned to the problem of gaining official recognition for her daughter. Marie wrote to the marshal de Saxe's niece, the dauphine Marie-Josèphe de Saxe, requesting her support and protection for the two-year-old child. On the condition that Marie de Verrières sacrifice all further contact with the child, the dauphine agreed to assume responsibility for her uncle's daughter. Marie de Verrières accepted this stipulation, and, indeed, until Marie-Aurore de Saxe married at age eighteen, she never set eyes on her mother again. One of the little noted but extraordinary ironies of George Sand's life is the reenactment by her grandmother and mother of a similar arrangement, according to which Marie-Aurore Dupin would raise the child Aurore in exchange for providing her mother, Sophie, with a pension, on condition that she relinquish control of her daughter's upbringing.

The dauphine de Saxe placed Marie-Aurore in the convent of Saint-Cloud, where she remained for the next five years. When she turned seven, her protectress transferred her to Saint-Cyr, the highly prestigious school founded in 1684 by Madame de Maintenon, which admitted on scholarship two hundred and fifty girls who could demonstrate four degrees of nobility. The dauphine's influence was sufficient to exempt Marie-Aurore from this prerequisite.

At Saint-Cyr Marie-Aurore dressed in the school uniform: a white linen bonnet, a brown muslin dress with matching apron bordered by a ribbon in one of four colors—red, green, yellow, or blue—to signal class level. The teaching staff, comprising forty women selected from among former Saint-Cyr students and several dozen sisters of the order, wore black dresses and gold crosses decorated with fleurs de lys and figures of Christ and Saint Louis. The girls rose daily at six, attended mass at eight, attended class until lunchtime and again from two until six, followed by dinner and then bedtime at nine. For the young women of this generation, Saint-Cyr provided the very best education available. Marie-Aurore distinguished herself in this elite company. "Through her grace and goodness, the girl soon charmed her teachers and companions; her keen intelligence, her quick wit soon made her the darling of the famous convent."[5] In this calm, orderly, and rigorous environment, removed from her mother's libertine social world, Marie-Aurore de Saxe's spiritual and intellectual foundation took form.

When students of Saint-Cyr reached the age of twenty and were returned to their parents, they were each granted a dowry of one thousand *écus* and a trousseau befitting their social station. The dauphine, dismayed at the prospect of returning Marie-Aurore to her mother, mobilized an early effort to find a suitable husband for her seventeen-year-old protegée. First, however, the sticky business of Marie-Aurore's lineage had to be cleared up. For Marie-Aurore to attract a suitable husband, the wording of her baptismal certificate had to be changed. She was originally identified, alternatively, as the daughter of a fictitious individual referred to as Jean Baptiste de La Rivière, "bourgeois de Paris," and of Marie Rinteau, "his wife," or as "a natural child of unknown parentage." Neither identification provided adequate credentials for a good marriage; Marie-Aurore therefore petitioned Parlement, requesting that the following designation be inserted after her officially registered name: "natural daughter of Maurice, Count de Saxe, Marshal-General in the Armies of France, and of Marie Rinteau."[6]

Once Parlement complied and her baptismal certificate was reworded, Marie-Aurore was married off to a forty-four-year-old infantry captain named Antoine de Horne. Her mother hosted a sumptuous reception for the bride and groom at the Verrières' country home in what was then the village of Auteuil, on the outskirts of Paris. This was Marie-Aurore's first contact with her mother since early childhood. As a wedding present, Horne received a royal appointment as King's Lieutenant at Schelestadt, a small town in Alsace, where the couple took up residence several months after the wedding.

"Condemned by a strange freak of destiny never to know passion in marriage," Sand would have us believe that the young and inexperienced Marie-Aurore, who married her husband without ever having met him, was put off by his severity and insolence.[7] Her husband, we are told, refrained from spending the wedding night with his bride. We cannot know whether this information is based on one of Sand's many fabrications or if it is a true recounting of what occurred. A compelling possibility is that

Sand's version contains a kernel of truth but takes the liberty of reversing cause and effect. Perhaps the virginal young wife was sufficiently traumatized by what did take place on her wedding night that a sexual standoff was struck in its wake.

What is clear, however, is that two strands that weave their way through George Sand's life and oeuvre come together in this transmission: the suggestion that her grandmother manifested no sexual interest or activity (except for giving birth to an only son, by a subsequent husband thirty-two years her senior), and Sand's recurring preoccupation with the sexual violence done to innocent young women at the hands of abusive and authoritarian men. Although Sand never explicitly draws the conclusion, a relationship between traumatic loss of virginity and subsequent frigidity emerges.

In all events, Marie-Aurore did not have to endure marriage with Antoine de Horne for very long. Arriving in Schelestadt on a Monday, Horne complained of chest pains the following morning, was repeatedly bled (the accepted treatment for a host of illnesses at that time), and by Friday was dead. After only five months of marriage, Marie-Aurore was widowed at the age of eighteen.

What she did next was extraordinary for a woman of her time. She petitioned Louis XV to be retained as lieutenant governor, or commandant, the position her husband had occupied. Her request was viewed as preposterous, and the king turned it down. This particular piece of her grandmother's history must have made an important impression on the future George Sand. Marie-Aurore was swiftly evicted from her official residence in Schelestadt to make way for a newly appointed lieutenant and was once again left with no means of material support.

Because her protectress, the dauphine, was gravely ill and only days away from dying, Marie-Aurore tried re-petitioning the king. Overwhelmed with political problems, Louis XV did not respond, and Marie-Aurore was forced to take refuge in a convent that sheltered indigent widows. The following year she appealed to the war minister, the duke de Choiseul. She wrote a poignant letter recounting the personal hardships she had endured and the impoverished situation in which she was currently living. Once again she was turned down.

In desperation, she wrote Voltaire, who, in addition to priding himself on helping the needy and oppressed, had written a poem commemorating the battle of Fontenoy. Marie-Aurore was calculating that Voltaire would sympathize with the daughter of a victor of this famous battle. He responded eloquently but ineffectually: "I shall soon be going to join the hero, your father, and I shall inform him with indignation of the condition his daughter finds herself in."[8]

After three years of widowhood, Marie-Aurore could no longer afford to remain in the convent. Having exhausted all other options, she finally took shelter with her mother and aunt in their fashionable and lively home in the Chausée d'Antin. Amid the glitter and gallantry of the Verrières' salon and their well-equipped private theater, which attracted some of the most sought-after figures in Paris society, Marie-Aurore's cloistered education received its worldly finish.

Dubbed by a contemporary the "aspasias of the century," the lifestyle of Marie and Geneviève de Verrières was secured through a succession of love affairs resembling, according to one commentator, "the changing facets of a magic lantern."[9] Their Paris town house (the French term is *hôtel particulier*), which boasted a private *salle de spectacles,* and their country home at Auteuil, where an elaborate theater had been installed in the garden, drew the brightest lights of the contemporary *demimonde.* Marie-Aurore displayed genuine talent, starring as Colette in a production of the *Devin du Village (The Cunning Man)*, directed by the critic Jean-François de La Harpe, and her musical gifts were well utilized in opera productions of works by Grétry and Sedaine.

The precarious financial situation of her mother and aunt, which obviously depended on their suitors' generosity, prompted Marie-Aurore once again to plead her case for increased government support. Fortified in 1772 with a doubled pension thanks to her appeal to the new war minister, Louis François de Monteynard, her income was again increased in 1774, this time to three thousand *livres.* The timing was fortunate because Marie de Verrières, still in her forties, died in 1775, leaving her daughter without a home.

Equipped with her expanded allowance, Marie-Aurore was able to select a residence befitting her station. She chose the respectable convent of the Dames du Calvaire, where she willingly spent her entire royal pension of sixteen hundred francs per year on herself and her chambermaid. Serious and contemplative by nature, Marie-Aurore found the cloistered life appealing. Sand would inherit volumes of extracts and quotations culled by her grandmother from her prodigious readings. "She was a woman of great strength of mind, clear sighted, and imbued with the ideals of pride and self-respect," Sand would write of her grandmother. "She was ignorant of coquetry, for she was too gifted to have need for it, and that method of provocation offended her idea of dignified behavior. She survived a very liberal epoch in a very corrupt world without suffering the slightest blemish to her character."[10]

One of the guests who had frequented her mother's and aunt's home while Marie-Aurore was living there was an attractive gentleman in his sixties named Claude-Louis Dupin de Francueil. A tax collector in the central French province of Berry, Dupin also maintained an interest in a cloth mill in the city of Châteauroux. Having recently ended an intimate relationship with Marie-Aurore's aunt Geneviève, Dupin was immediately taken by the engaging niece. An enduring friendship formed between them, and when Marie-Aurore left her mother's house for the convent, she continued to receive frequent visits from Dupin, whom she and her convent friends fondly called papa.

In 1777, twenty-nine-year-old Marie-Aurore and her sixty-one-year-old suitor fled to London, where they were quietly married at the French embassy. The motive behind the English wedding is not certain. It may have been to avoid the scandal of Marie-Aurore's marrying her aunt's former lover. Or it may have been to avoid a church ceremony. "She had no religion," George Sand explained, "other than the one of the eighteenth century, the deism of Jean-Jacques Rousseau and Voltaire."[11]

Marie-Aurore gave birth to Maurice Dupin on 9 January 1778. An only child, the boy lost his father at the age of eight. As sole survivor of Madame Dupin's turbulent past, Maurice was destined to compensate for the losses and deprivations she had suffered. A pretty child with "the fatal charm of the Koenigsmark family, their velvety eyes, their love of music and poetry, their natural sense of style," Maurice was coddled and grew up sickly. When he developed growing pains, his mother ordered bed rest. Inactivity made him so lazy he would ring for a servant to pick up dropped pens and pencils.[12]

When Maurice was nine, Madame Dupin hired a teacher from the Collège Cardinal Lemoine as his tutor. The twenty-six-year-old Jean-François Deschartres, a self-tonsured abbot whose father had made his living burning lime, was a complex and contradictory man. Although loyal to

Marie-Aurore Dupin and her son, Maurice, ca. 1785–86. Anonymous pastel.
(© Photothèque des musées de la ville de Paris)

his mistress and adoring of Maurice, he was nevertheless pedantic, irascible, and tyrannical. Not surprisingly, Maurice took poorly to his lessons.

Dupin de Francueil died three years before the Revolution, leaving his personal estate in radical disarray; his widow and Deschartres would preside over this estate for the duration of their lives. On the eve of the French Revolution, they left the Château Raoul in the rural center of France, where Maurice was raised, and moved with a reduced household staff to an apartment in Paris on rue du Roi-de-Sicile, near the Bastille.

Given her experience of life, Madame Dupin was understandably ambivalent about the political changes that France was undergoing. Despite her sympathy for the Enlightenment views of Voltaire and Rousseau, on which she had been weaned, her allegiance was split between the old and new order. Although linked to the aristocratic ancien régime through her social connections, her education, and her fortune, she had good reason to be disgruntled by the way she had been treated by the reigning powers. She could never forget the frustration of writing petition after petition for support that was only grudgingly granted. From their apartment a thousand yards away, Madame Dupin could hear the cheers that accompanied the taking of the Bastille on 14 July 1789. Even though she approved her servants' participation in this historic event, she felt her family would be safer away from the fray, and so they moved from rue du Roi-de-Sicile toward the boulevards, to an apartment on rue de Bondy.

In spite of her personal decision not to flee France, as many of the endangered aristocrats chose to do at that time, Madame Dupin clandestinely made a "loan" of sixty-five thousand *livres* to a fund for émigré princes, including the count d'Artois, who would later return to France as King Charles X. In light of the revolutionary injunction against retaining valuables, she thought it wise to conceal a silver dinner service and some jewelry, along with proof of her loan, in a hiding place in her apartment. News of this subversive activity was leaked to the Revolutionary Committee, and at the height of the Terror, on 5 Frimaire (25 November) 1793, a search was conducted at the rue de Bondy residence, the valuables were discovered (though not the even more incriminating proof of her loan), and Madame Dupin was arrested and imprisoned in the Convent of the English Augustinians, recently converted to a house of women's detention, on rue des Fossés-Saint-Victor. Fifteen-year-old Maurice and his tutor, who had dropped his self-imposed title of abbot in favor of the more politically correct "Citizen" Deschartres, were left to fend for themselves for the next nine months while Madame Dupin remained imprisoned.

Young Maurice's separation from his mother was painful, and his brief visits with her in the parlor of the convent-*cum*-prison left them both bereft. His sense of helplessness was relieved when Deschartres enlisted his assistance in the risky business of eliminating incriminating evidence. Over the course of two suspenseful nights, they entered a mezzanine space above the second floor of the rue de Bondy apartment, broke official wax seals applied by the revolutionary investigators, and removed and destroyed the undetected documents testifying to the loan to the émigré princes' fund that could have cost Madame Dupin her life.

When a new revolutionary decree banned all "ex-nobles" from Paris, Maurice and Deschartres were forced to take up residence outside the city gates in the suburb of Passy, and visits to the imprisoned Madame Dupin ended. Increasingly anxious, Maurice wrote of his pain in daily letters to his mother: "Exiled! Exiled at fifteen, and for what crime? Oh, if I could have foreseen that they would take such action against relatives of detained persons, I would have had myself imprisoned with you. . . . Oh, my mother, my mother, give me back my mother soon!"[13]

After reporting an otherwise enjoyable excursion with Deschartres in the nearby Bois de Boulogne, Maurice recounted his desolation: "But nothing in the world can console me for not being permitted to see you. It is a gnawing worm that destroys all species of pleasure, even the sight of these charming woods."[14] His mother sent him a chain with a lock of her hair, which Maurice promised to wear around his neck for the rest of his life.

Despite his sadness at his mother's absence, Maurice began to thrive on independence. Away from his mother for the first time, he blossomed. Long walks with Deschartres in the countryside stimulated his appetite and induced undisturbed nights of sleep. "My headache has not come back," he wrote to his mother. "The country air is most healthful, and I haven't heard from my migraines since I have been here." But then in the very next breath, as though guilt would make him snatch back the report of his well-being, Maurice added, "I am very weary. Perhaps I will dream again, as I did last night, that I am with you. That was very sweet; but on awakening, happiness ended."[15] Increasingly, conflict and guilt would characterize Maurice's relations with his mother.

When Maurice came across the baron d'Espagnac's history of his grandfather the marshal de Saxe, he spent hours poring over it. Brimming with excitement, he wrote his mother in prison: "I am reviewing in depth your father's battles, and I have returned to the one at Malpaquet, which is the first, to work through it and learn it by heart. I now know the number of batteries, how many cannon in each, what factor was decisive in winning the battle, the location of the cavalry, the infantry, the encampment, the village, the farm, the forest, the river, the gap opened up by the cannon, and the number of men fallen, etc."[16]

It's no wonder the ardent adolescent was entranced by his namesake's exploits; Maurice de Saxe was thirteen years old when he distinguished himself at Malpaquet. What's more, we learn from Sand's autobiography that "in 1712, at the age of sixteen, he led a cavalry regiment, had another horse shot from under him, and launched three consecutive charges with a regiment that had been virtually destroyed." The impressionable young Maurice confided to his mother, "I play the role of hero in my imagination."[17] Helpless in the face of her captivity, Maurice fueled his fantasies of omniscience through his grandfather's military prowess.

In mounting desperation, Madame Dupin wrote yet another petition, this time to the Revolutionary Committee of Public Safety, imploring them to reunite her with her son. As evidence of her worthiness, she pointed out that she had chosen to remain in France rather than to flee with her fortune. She shored up her argument by citing her support for her servants, who had participated in the taking of the Bastille. But her petition was turned down, and Madame Dupin remained in prison until 27 July 1794, when she was finally released following Robespierre's fall.

In view of the fever pitch the revolutionary aftermath had reached in Paris, Madame Dupin had decided, even before her imprisonment, that it would be safer to relocate in the French countryside. In August 1793 she had purchased an estate at Nohant, which lay between the cities of Châteauroux and La Châtre, a hundred fifty miles south of Paris in the Berry province where the family had lived contentedly before her husband's death. In July 1794, following her release from prison, Madame Dupin, Maurice, Deschartres, two servants, and two dogs moved to the simple but commodious Louis XVI–style manor house. Although only a single tower remained, the original feudal castle dated back to the fourteenth century. Shaded by elms and lime trees, its main entrance opened onto the center of the tiny village of Nohant. In short order the ancient moat was filled in, a vegetable garden was added, and a wall to the south was removed to extend the view. Including the revenue generated by Nohant, which came to somewhat less than four thousand francs a year, Madame Dupin's annual income, diminished by the Revolution, was now less than fifteen thousand francs a year, a fifth of what it had been at the time of her husband's death. But Madame Dupin turned herself into an efficient and frugal estate manager and was able to run Nohant comfortably as well as economically.[18]

To groom him for the life of a well-bred gentleman, rather than the soldier that he eventually became, in autumn 1796 Madame Dupin sent eighteen-year-old Maurice to Paris. The road between Issoudun and Vierzon was filled with deep ravines and broad, rushing streams, and the journey on horseback took him and Deschartres nearly ten days. From Paris, Maurice's letters home overflowed with details designed to appease and delight his anxious mother. He itemized every concert, ballet, and opera that he attended and described the fashionable homes to which he was invited and the elegant people who enthusiastically received him: Madame de Jassaud's pleasure in their reunion, Monsieur le Duc's delight in lunching with him, the magistrate of Frelon's invitation to a dinner for "important people."

Madame Dupin must have found these reports gratifying; with such a solid foundation, surely Maurice was headed for a brilliant place in society. But there is something fatuous in Maurice's exuberant reports: "In short, my dear mother, in me you will see the finest flower of dandyism." He brags about his newly acquired wardrobe—his fashionable hussar boots, stylish trousers, a new frock coat in the latest mode. "I have had my hair attended to; they found it too short, and instead of cutting all of it, they only exposed the ear. They leave the hair long in front and behind to fall over the neckline of one's outfit. The perfection of the dog ear, when it is long enough, is to put some curlers at the ends without letting the hair frizz. As for the plaits and the pigtail, there is nothing to change. May my maid be consoled and expect to see me with my ear showing."[19]

The letters are laced with other childlike references to his maid: "And a thousand hellos to my *stupid* maid"; "A nice strong fisticuff on the head of my maid, and I whiten her face with a powderpuff"; "Tell my maid that my pigtail suffers a lot without her attention; it sends her best regards."[20] Between the lines of these silly remarks lies sexual innuendo. The double entendres in Maurice's messages suggest that there might have been more than mere child's play between him and his maid, of which Madame Dupin surely would not have approved. The visit to the capital may well have been engineered to distract Maurice from untoward temptation at home and to provide him the opportunity to mingle with the right kind of people, to convert him from an immature, spirited youth to the sophisticated, socially adept adult Madame Dupin wanted him to become.

Despite Maurice's internship in a life of leisure and much to his mother's dismay, when the Directoire ordered universal conscription in September 1798, Maurice decided to embark on a military career. Reading of his celebrated grandfather's exploits had no doubt kindled his fervor, and at the age of twenty, in defiance of his mother's wishes, Maurice enlisted in Napoléon's army with the rank of private in the light cavalry.

Soon after Maurice's departure, a servant at Nohant gave birth to his first son. Madame Dupin dismissed the mother, twenty-one-year-old Anne-

Maurice Dupin. Anonymous portrait. (Courtesy C. O. Darré,
Musée George Sand, La Châtre)

Catherine Chatiron, but decided to keep the baby nearby. Especially sensitive, given her own past, to the plight of natural children, and perhaps
to fill the void of the son she missed so desperately, Madame Dupin chose
to oversee the raising of her illicit grandson, who was baptized Pierre
Laverdure but always known as Hippolyte Chatiron. A peasant woman
was found to nurse the baby, and in her letters to Maurice, Madame Dupin
would make veiled references to the progress of the child, discreetly code-
named the "Little House." Hippolyte, who became half brother to the
future George Sand, would retain a place in the family circle throughout
his life.

Maurice's letters home track his slow ascent through the ranks of the
military and unveil a portrait of the spoiled child turned soldier/dandy. He
consoled his mother for his absence by describing the impressive green
dolman and hussar's saber he now wore. To emphasize his manliness, he
told her he had grown a mustache. From a private, he was promoted to
a corporal and then to a general's aide-de-camp. He fought against the

Russians in Switzerland and saw action at Marengo, where Bonaparte's troops defeated the Austrians. But Maurice Dupin's military career was in no way a reprisal of the illustrious marshal de Saxe's. On the contrary, the grandson's progress was obstructed by his preoccupation with the trappings of military glory and by the flirtatious distractions made possible by his new status and social surroundings.

There is constant discussion in Maurice's letters of horses—those he lacks and those he needs—and incessant requests, sometimes veiled and sometimes straightforward, for more and more money to enhance his prospects for advancement, either through the acquisition of costly military costumes or more and better horses to ride. "My general absolutely insists on getting me a horse, and . . . is sending me to the remount depot. . . . I am leaving by coach with my saddle. I expect to come back at a leisurely pace. But this upsets my plans for economy." Once the horse was acquired, additional expenses accrued. "If the idea of seeing me with curry-comb and pitchfork in hand disturbs you," Maurice writes home, "please let me say, to reassure you, that it would be very easy for me, if I wished, to have my horse cared for by one of the general's grooms for six francs a month." In another letter, he compiled a lengthy list of complaints and once again hinted at needing more money and a better horse: "I did not have the wherewithal to remain there [in Brussels], my crowns having been diminished by twenty sous each in Brabant, due to the rate of exchange. Hence I rush to the remount, where I find the damned horse dying from the strangles."[21]

Interspersed with the complaints and demands, Maurice boasted about his successful social life: "Lady Luck, who goes everywhere with me, has shown me a way to keep from being bored." He described two sisters, one "tall, beautiful, friendly; the younger one small, pretty, witty," with whom he was lunching daily and attending the theater. This was followed by a revealing reference to the marshal de Saxe: "I am not far from Fontenoy, and I shall try to push on to there. If my poor devil of a horse can walk, in a few days I should traverse and get acquainted with all those illustrious places where your dying father beat back the enemy and saved France."

Living in the shadow of his grandfather's glory—"if there was ever a country where the marshal's name is popular and everyone knows his slightest accomplishments, it is here"—cannot have been easy on the young, overprotected Maurice, part of whose problem was the hard act he had to follow. Blaming a horse was easier than blaming himself for his setbacks. So when the charming mistress of one General Collin singled out twenty-two-year-old Maurice and lavished him with special favors, the young soldier fell passionately in love. With his rank of first lieutenant, Maurice must have derived extra satisfaction from having outstripped a superior officer in his conquest of the beautiful and beguiling twenty-seven-year-old Antoinette-Sophie-Victoire Delaborde, the woman he eventually married.

Having failed to distinguish himself on the battlefield, Maurice's greatest act of courage may well have been defying his mother: in spite of her persistent protests, he ultimately took Sophie as his wife. Much like his choice to join the military, Maurice's marital choice was clearly an act of rebellion against the mother who loved him too passionately and held on too tightly. Madame Dupin may not have lost her beloved son to battle as she had feared, but she lost the battle to control his destiny. In her rise to respectability, she had done everything possible to distance herself from her own mother, and, indeed, she had emerged from the hallowed halls of Saint-Cyr a member of the French upper class. Having wrested herself with considerable effort from the tainted shadows of the demimonde, Marie-Aurore de Saxe Dupin could only look upon her son's connection with Sophie Delaborde as a giant step backward in her lifelong battle for social acceptability.

On 1 July 1804, a month after her marriage to Maurice, Sophie gave birth to a baby girl. As Sand relates in her autobiography, Maurice decided she would be named Aurore for his mother, and Sophie agreed. But perhaps it was the other way around; it may actually have been Sophie who came up with the idea, which would have been well received by Maurice. Just as Marie-Aurore Dupin had struggled to gain recognition as a respectable member of French society, Sophie would do no less on behalf of the daughter she bore. It would take time, Sophie calculated, but someday Madame Dupin would recognize this child as her granddaughter. In all events, the first naming of the girl who grew up to rename herself George Sand was a cleverly conceived strategy to gain the love and protection of her paternal grandmother.

CHAPTER THREE

Sophie Victorious

One is not only the offspring of one's father, one is also a little,
I believe, that of one's mother. It seems to me that the latter is
even more the case, and that we are attached to the entrails of the
one who gave birth to us in the most immediate, powerful, and
sacred way.

ANTOINETTE-SOPHIE-VICTOIRE Delaborde was born in Paris in July
1773. Sophie, as she came to be called, was the daughter of Antoine-Claude
Delaborde, who ran a billiard parlor and sold birds on the quai de la Mégis-
serie until his death in 1781. Virtually nothing is known of Sophie's mother,
Marie Anne Cloquard, who died in July 1790. "The genealogies of ordinary
people cannot compete with those of the rich and powerful," Sand would
one day observe in *Story of My Life*.[1] After their father's death Sophie and
her younger sister, Lucie, were looked after by their grandparents, Jean-
Georges Cloquard and his wife, Mother Cloquard, "a good and pious
woman . . . a Royalist . . . [who] kept her two granddaughters in mortal
fear of the Revolution." The incongruity between Mother Cloquard's class
origins and political allegiance goes unexplained.

Compensating for the anonymity that history confers on ordinary
people, Sand relates an event that ostensibly occurred when Lafayette announced before the Commune the king's return to Paris following the
Champs de Mars massacre in October 1789. Selected by local plebeian
dignitaries, fifteen-year-old Sophie Delaborde was dressed in white, pow-
dered, crowned with roses, and told: "Little citizeness, you are the prettiest
girl in the district; they're going to make you a heroine; here is Citizen
Collot-d'Herbois, an actor with the Théâtre-Français, who is going to teach
you a verse compliment with gestures; here is a wreath of flowers; we
shall conduct you to the town hall where you will present these flowers

and say your piece to Citizens Bailly and LaFayette, and you will have indeed earned the respect of your country."

Upon receiving the wreath from Sophie, Lafayette is said to have addressed her: "My dear child, these flowers suit your face more than mine." In the crush of the crowd that formed to watch this historic event, Mother Cloquard and little Lucie were separated from Sophie, who was "escorted by a band of patriots." She rejoined her family "in their poor little abode" at the end of the evening, "so well protected and respected that her white dress was not even wrinkled."

Sand uses the blackout that occurs when Mother Cloquard and Lucie lose sight of Sophie "in her moment of triumph" as the occasion to imagine a narrative that inscribes her mother in recorded history. But underlying this intention lies another, more urgent reason why Sand may have created this appealing and respectable portrait of her mother. Records indicate that in 1789, Sophie gave birth to a child by a disreputable man named Claude-Denis Vantin Saint-Charles with whom she was living. Georges Lubin has noted caustically and with his customary tact in such matters: "Certain erasures in the manuscript, which allude to a previous marriage, to the birth of several children, pose many questions which are difficult to answer, Sophie-Victoire having got around a lot, scattering [marriage] certificates in her wake."[2]

Was Sophie actually pregnant at the time the episode with Lafayette took place? Simple arithmetic makes it likely that she was, given that the child she and Saint-Charles produced was three years old at the end of 1793. No record has been found of a marriage between Sophie and Saint-Charles, and Sand's fairy-tale description of the innocent girl honored publicly by Lafayette contrasts dramatically with data revealing that Sophie was pregnant and unwed.

There are other discrepancies in the public and private versions of her mother's life that Sand provides. She states in her autobiography that to support herself, her mother "played minor roles in a little theatre." In a letter to a personal friend, Sand confided: "She was a dancer, less than a dancer, a walk-on on the lowliest Parisian boulevard stage, when the love of a rich man saved her from this fate, only to plunge her into an even worse one." Sand continued: "She did not belong to that industrious working class which gives one nobility among the poor. She was from the transient bohemian underworld."[3] To put it less romantically, Sophie was a woman who exchanged sexual favors for financial support.

At the height of the Terror, Sophie went onstage and sang a seditious song against the Republic, an action that landed her in jail, coincidentally, in the same English convent-*cum*-prison where Marie-Aurore Dupin had been incarcerated for stashing valuables in the wake of the Revolution. In both the Lafayette anecdote and the incident of sedition, Sophie is scripted, leaving an impression of a life molded by outside circumstance. Sand explains that Sophie "only knew that she left prison as she had entered it, without understanding how or why."[4] The political inversions of her life—why, indeed, would Sophie and her family have been anti-Republican? —suggest confusion, passivity, and submission to external forces rather than self-determination.

In her autobiography, Sand imagines Sophie "wandering in the [convent] cloister" and crossing paths with her future husband, the sixteen-year-old grandson of the marshal de Saxe, on a visit to his mother, Marie-Aurore Dupin. The scenario Sand conjures is pure fantasy, and it is highly unlikely such a scene ever took place. But the coincidence that these two women of such disparate class and social circumstance were incarcerated on common ground before their lives became intertwined provides an ironic footnote to Sand's prehistory.

Sophie was released from prison on 14 August 1794. "At this point my mother's life becomes a complete blank for me," Sand wrote, "just as it had vanished from her own recollections." Coercing her mother's willful forgetfulness, Sand suppressed whatever information she may have received. We do know that a decade after giving birth to Saint-Charles' child (of whom there is no further record), Sophie gave birth in 1799, by another father, to a daughter named Caroline, the half sister with whom George Sand maintained a relationship throughout her life. We know further that in 1800, while the mistress of a quartermaster-general named Claude-Antoine Collin, Sophie met and began an affair with Maurice Dupin, who was then stationed in Milan. Sand idealized Maurice's attraction to Sophie: "My father met her when she was already thirty-years-old, and in the midst of quite a disordered life. He had a good heart; he understood that this beautiful creature was still capable of loving."[5] Sophie was actually twenty-seven when the twenty-two-year-old Maurice first met her, and it was no doubt physical attraction rather than magnanimity that drew him to her. General Collin was almost twenty years her senior, and the dashing young junior officer must have compared more than favorably. Maurice's aristocratic pedigree and a logical assumption of attendant wealth may have been persuasive, as well.

Even though Maurice had boasted freely to his mother when he was courting an elegant canoness in Cologne, he waited several months before mentioning Sophie in his letters home. This rankled Sophie, who resented the nervous subterfuge in which Maurice was engaged with his controlling mother. Hadn't she sacrificed a wealthy senior officer to become his mistress? Why wasn't he willing to sacrifice his wretched old mother? Finally, at the end of 1800, just as Napoléon's army was preparing to cross the Mincio River and to march victoriously against the Austrians in Hohenlinden, Maurice got up his nerve and wrote home, "How sweet it is to be loved, to have a good mother, worthy friends, a beautiful mistress, a bit of glory, a fine horse, and enemies to battle!"[6] The not-so-subtle reference to Sophie, sandwiched between other, more acceptable allusions, piqued Madame Dupin's curiosity. Thus began her relentless campaign to undermine Maurice's love affair.

The day after Maurice wrote his mother about Sophie, he was taken prisoner and spent the next two months in captivity and incommunicado. He must have felt as though he was being punished by fate. Meanwhile, Sophie reingratiated herself with the wealthy General Collin and managed to siphon off some money to help Maurice during his internment. After his release, Sophie harped on the sacrifice she had made and the magnitude of his debt to her. When Maurice went on leave to visit his mother at Nohant, Sophie insisted on accompanying him. Still afraid of his mother's anger, Maurice was willing to take Sophie only as far as the neighboring town of La Châtre, where he installed her at the Tête Noire Inn and registered her under the name of Madame Collin.

Madame Dupin became suspicious as her son's absences from Nohant grew increasingly frequent. When she questioned Maurice about his activities, he was dismissive and then defensive. Sensing a subterfuge, Madame Dupin deployed her faithful retainer Deschartres to do some behind-the-scenes sleuthing, and learning of Sophie's whereabouts, she raised a ruckus. Maurice confessed his arrangement with Sophie and, according

Madame Maurice Dupin, née Antoinette-Sophie-Victoire
Delaborde, ca. 1833. Drawing by George Sand.
(© Photothèque des musées de la ville de Paris)

to Sand's version of her father's conduct, implored his mother to look
kindly upon this woman, who had sacrificed security and incurred considerable risk to be with him.

Nothing could have displeased Madame Dupin more. It was one thing
for her son to father an illicit child with a household servant; such dishonor could be disguised by sending the woman away and raising the
child on the side. But Sophie presented a far greater threat: Maurice, who
"had come to feel . . . [for] the first time . . . the effects of a durable passion," was launched on a course leading straight to marriage. Sand would
have us believe that it was not so much her mother's lower-class origin
nor her lack of money and social status that made Madame Dupin despair;
it was, rather, that Sophie's "youth had been delivered up to frightening
hazards," a euphemistic allusion to her former life of prostitution.[7]

Sophie was alone when Deschartres stormed into the Tête Noire Inn
early one morning, awakened her, called her crude names, accused her
of being a gold digger, and threatened to call in the authorities if she didn't

pack her bags and leave immediately. But Sophie hadn't been raised on the streets of Paris and spent time in military camps for nothing. Spewing venom fueled by a vile temper, she told Deschartres that in fact she was not the wife of General Collin but his former mistress and that Maurice, indebted to her for money *she* had loaned *him*, had declared his intention of marrying her. She then shoved Deschartres out the door and slammed it in his face.

The image Sand proudly conjures of this scrappy, streetwise young woman contrasts dramatically with the spectacle encountered by the authorities summoned by Deschartres: "The magistrates crossed the threshold of the Inn . . . and in the lair of the shrew described by Deschartres they discovered only a tiny woman, pretty as an angel, sitting on the edge of her bed, her hair disheveled and her arms bare, weeping."[8] Sand thus casts her mother as strong-willed and self-defensive, on one hand, and as a vulnerable victim of circumstance, on the other. This poignant mélange of filial pride and pity is evident in the conflicting images Sand presents here and elsewhere.

Sophie remained in La Châtre for another ten days before Maurice sent her back to Paris. En route to rejoin his mistress, he wrote his mother, "Even though I had no desire to do so, I told [Sophie] I would be delighted to marry her. Responding like this doesn't mean a thing when one has every intention of doing the opposite." Whether Maurice was genuinely ambivalent or simply lying, he was quite clearly straining under the yoke of his mother's overprotectiveness. "I'm angry, my good mother," he went on, "that I can't have a mistress without it reducing you to despair." He reminds her that she conducted herself similarly when he was seeing a certain Mademoiselle Fontaine and remarks bitterly, "Whatever mistresses I might take in the Berry, you'll react as though I'm going to ruin or dishonor myself."[9] He concludes by declaring that henceforth he will conduct his love life far from home. Under the pressure of his newly developed dependency on Sophie, Maurice was belatedly playing out the role of coddled child turned rebellious adolescent. His mother's mounting hysteria had the not surprising effect of driving him back into the arms of his mistress.

Maurice soon joined General Pierre-Antoine Dupont de l'Etang as aide-de-camp and, between maneuvers, spent his days playing the violin, studying the piano, and waiting for a promotion. Sophie took a job working in a dress shop in Orléans before joining Maurice at his military post in Charleville in 1802. Blatant discrepancies between some of the actual letters Maurice wrote his mother and the falsified (the term, however harsh, is justified), versions that Sand published in her autobiography reveal that he was torn between loyalty to his mother and his attachment to his mistress.

By the fall of 1802, it is clear from the unedited correspondence with Madame Dupin that Maurice was sufficiently ambivalent about his relationship with Sophie that he was attempting to distance himself: "I held out throughout a lot of argument and tears, after which I forced the little Collin [Sophie] to take 60 louis and to take off, but on the brink of leaving she returned them to me, let the coach go and was dead set against leaving. Once again I had to use everything in my power to prevail upon her to go, which took her three days to agree to."[10]

The highly doctored version of this account that Sand published conforms to the idealized portrait of her parents' love affair to which she adheres throughout her autobiography: for example, Sand replaces Maurice Dupin's denigrating reference to "the little Collin" with the elegant and evocative "Victoire":

> You wished it, you demanded it, you placed me between your
> despair and my own, and I have been obedient. Victoire is in
> Paris. I made the decision. I did the impossible, but sending
> her off thus, I certainly had to provide for her well-being. I took
> an advance against my salary from the division paymaster of
> sixty louis, and I insisted she go to work in Paris; as she was
> leaving, she sent me back the money. I ran after her, brought
> her back, and we spent three days together in tears. I spoke
> to her about you and brought her to hope that someday, when
> you got to know her better, you would stop fearing her. She
> resigned herself and left. But exposing oneself to such trials
> may not be the best way to cure oneself of a passion. In a word,
> I'll do for you all that human strength allows, but don't talk
> to me so much about her in the future. I still find it hard to
> answer you with much composure.[11]

Madame Dupin's anguish over her son's relationship with Sophie was exacerbated by the contemporaneous publication of the posthumous memoir of the dramatist Jean-François Marmontel, the lover who had cost her mother their pension when the marshal de Saxe discovered her infidelity. Sand informs us that Marmontel's memoir "recounts with less reserve his relationship with Mlle. Verrières. Although he speaks of the conduct, character, and talent of this young actress with esteem and affection, he goes into some intimate details which would necessarily make a daughter suffer."[12]

And, indeed, Madame Dupin was suffering. It was bad enough that her mother had been the mistress and not the wife of her famous father, but that her mother had sacrificed the pension he provided for their upkeep because of another illicit affair was unforgivable. That Madame Dupin should have to undergo yet again the humiliation of this shameful picture of her past was intolerable. She dispatched an urgent letter to her son enlisting his help in having the compromising passages suppressed. Maurice looked into the matter and wrote a reasoned response: "We're not rich enough, that I know of, to repurchase the published edition and secure that the next one be corrected: even if we were able to do this, it would add even more spice to the copies sold, and sooner or later we would not be able to prevent new editions from being printed that conformed to the first."[13]

Underestimating his mother's traumatic past and how hard she had struggled to overcome the consequences of her own mother's misconduct, Maurice reassured his mother that Marmontel's account wouldn't be nearly as damaging as she feared: "I understand full well that you suffer to hear your mother spoken of so lightly, but how can that affect your life, which has always been so austere, and your reputation, which is so spotless?" But what doubtless rankled Madame Dupin even more was Maurice's implicit defense of Sophie. Surely it was with her in mind that he formulated his cavalier remarks absolving Madame Dupin's mother of blame: "What was true of her was true of many others. Her errors were circumstantial, and her way of accepting them made her loving and kind."[14]

It is questionable whether Madame Dupin would have graciously accepted any woman who won Maurice's heart, but Sophie was particularly unacceptable. When Madame Dupin learned of their marriage, her hard-won victory of respectability was at risk. The past had not only returned to haunt the present; it had cast a somber shadow over the future as well. Adding insult to injury, Maurice had not dared tell his mother of his marriage, and she had had to learn of it thirdhand, in a letter written by his nephew René Vallet de Villeneuve.[15]

Madame Dupin was hardly inexperienced at cleaning up after Maurice. She had already assumed responsibility for his bastard son by the servant he impregnated before joining Napoléon's army. So when she learned that Sophie had borne a daughter and that her son claimed to be the father, Madame Dupin was not nearly as disturbed as when she learned that Maurice and Sophie were officially wed. In the wake of the French Revolution, new laws were promulgated that protected illicit children within a family: "The bastard child gained a place equal to the other children within the institution of marriage, bearing the husband's name and enjoying the right of inheritance."[16]

Mobilizing her considerable experience of petitioning for her rights, Madame Dupin began a persistent campaign to have her son's marriage annulled. In November 1804, she wrote the mayor of the fifth arrondissement, where Maurice and Sophie were living, giving her son's name and his age as twenty-six, his address as 15, rue Meslay, and the name of the woman with whom he was living as Victorine Delaborde. She then demanded to see the documents that legitimized their union despite Maurice's status as a minor. She went on to explain that the woman had been living on rue de la Monnaie, where she kept a hat shop, until last winter, before moving in with her son. "Since living on Rue Meslay, my son has had a daughter by her, who I believe was born in Messidor [July] and registered under the name of Aurore, daughter of M. Dupin and . . ." Madame Dupin's contempt is evident in her pointed reference to Sophie: "this girl, or woman—I do not know which to call her."[17] The French, "Cette fille, ou femme," is far blunter than the English translation conveys; calling a woman "fille" is the equivalent of calling her a slut.

The new Napoleonic Civil Code, instituted the month of Maurice and Sophie's marriage, did, in fact, stipulate that a man had to have reached the age of thirty to marry without parental consent, and even though Maurice was underage, Madame Dupin's interventions were unsuccessful. Sand explained in her autobiography: "What is not possible today then was due to the disorder and uncertainty the Revolution had wreaked concerning relationships. The new legal code left ways open to evade reverential acts. . . . This was a transitional period between the old and new orders, and the wheels of civil law were not turning smoothly."[18]

Sand glosses the story with a report that the lawyers Madame Dupin consulted advised her that in a court of law "the marriage would, nine chances out of ten, be upheld by the judges, that my [Aurore Dupin's] birth certificate attested to my legitimacy, and supposing that the marriage were broken off, the intention as well as the duty of my father would infallibly be to fulfill the desired formalities and contract another marriage with the mother of the child he had intended to legitimize."[19]

After months of failed attempts to foil the marriage, Madame Dupin was cornered. She had no choice but to recognize her son's commitment to Sophie and the child she had borne as his legal heir, albeit only a month after their wedding. The alternative—denouncing Sophie and disowning the child—was unacceptable, for this would have incurred a definitive break with her son and an irreparably tarnished legacy.

Against this backdrop, the scene Sand depicts in which Madame Dupin recognizes the baby Aurore and thereby legitimizes her as her biological grandchild seems contrived. From a psychological point of view, it smacks more of melodrama than of real life. Indeed, Sand immediately follows this scene with information that argues against its veracity: "Some time had still to pass before my grandmother would consent to see her daughter-in-law, but already rumors were spreading that her son had made a 'disproportionate' marriage, and the refusal to receive her necessarily gave rise to some unfortunate inductions against my mother, consequently against my father. My grandmama was alarmed at the damage that her aversion could do her son. She received the trembling Sophie, who disarmed her by her naive compliance and affectionate kisses."[20]

In the scene in which Madame Dupin recognizes the baby Aurore as her biological granddaughter, she transfers a ruby ring from her own hand to the baby's and charges her with placing it on her mother's finger. Such a gesture—a symbolic wedding of mother and daughter-in-law—seems unlikely in view of the delay that reportedly ensued before Madame Dupin was willing to receive Sophie. The gesture also lacks credibility for another, more practical reason: Madame Dupin would surely have been wary of giving an infant an object the size of a ring, which could easily be swallowed. But the gesture, invented or not, serves its author's sentimental purpose of demonstrating her own role as the agent of reconciliation between her grandmother and mother.

What emerges as more credible than the scene of recognition is Sand's sober analysis of her mother-in-law's delayed reception of Sophie. Accordingly, it was neither personal magnanimity nor grandmotherly attachment that motivated Madame Dupin's change of behavior but damaging "rumors" caused by her rejection of her son's wife. Sand is typically vague in dealing with the content of the rumors. We're told only that "unfortunate allegations against [my] mother" and "consequently against [my] father" had been made. Because rumors generally arise when appearance and reality are at odds, these "allegations" no doubt went beyond the obvious issue of class difference. A "disproportionate marriage" would have been a matter of fact rather than of rumor. Besides which, Madame Dupin was not disturbed by the class disparity between her son and his wife. "The lineage afflicts me little, but more so the personal character of the young woman," she had written the mayor of the fifth arrondissement.[21]

But there was another, deeply disturbing rumor that could have arisen in response to Madame Dupin's rejection of the marriage: Sophie, seven years Maurice's senior, had borne previous children out of wedlock, one of whom, Caroline, was conspicuously part of her son's newly formed ménage; the baby born but a month after the marriage might therefore have been fathered by someone other than Maurice. Sand's reluctance to suggest this is surely due to self-protection rather than oversight.

But this omission (playing things down) is trumped by an act of commission (making things up) when Sand reports: "The religious marriage [of Maurice and Sophie] was celebrated under the eyes of my grandmother, after which a family meal officially sealed the adoption of my mother and me."[22] No record of this marriage has ever been found. Sand's intention, here as elsewhere, was to convey a harmonious resolution to family conflict.

CHAPTER FOUR

Spanish Sojourn

It is said that the tears of childhood are nothing. It is not so. They are as bitter as those which flow later.

ON 10 MARCH 1808, Napoléon's brother-in-law, Prince Murat, arrived in Madrid with his aide-de camp, Maurice Dupin, to command the one hundred thousand French troops posted to the Spanish peninsula. By May, separated from the husband on whose support the family depended and eight months pregnant with his second child, Sophie could no longer contain her anxiety. In the past she had chosen to leave Aurore behind in order to join Maurice at his military post; this time Sophie took her along.

The Paris spring was fresh and lovely, the time of year when Caroline and Aurore could play outside unencumbered by heavy winter clothing. The trees along the boulevards were just coming into hazy green leaf, and flowerpots on balconies were brimming with the season's first blooms. Sophie busied herself packing and making preparations. Aurore wanted to take along her favorite doll but decided instead to leave her tucked under the covers for their family friend Louis-Mammès Pierret to watch over while she was gone.

Sand tells us in *Story of My Life* that before departing for Spain, Maurice told Pierret, as he was called, "I commend to you my wife and children, and if I do not return, consider that it is for the rest of your life."[1] The self-conscious rhetoric of this gallant imprecation sounds less likely to have emerged from the mouth of the young Maurice Dupin than from the pen of a mature George Sand reconstructing the past for posterity. Perhaps this was her way of absolving her mother of blame for taking up with Pierret after her father's death.

The decision to journey across the turbulent Spanish countryside while so close to childbirth, and with a tiny daughter in tow, was incautious, to say the least. Sophie's desire to secure the future of her family no doubt compelled such rash behavior. By bringing along Maurice's daughter, Sophie's status as wife and mother would be recognized, and Maurice's obligation to protect them and the new baby would be safeguarded. The illegitimate Caroline was left at home.

Sand conjectured as to her mother's motive for such a dangerous journey: "This was not a very prudent undertaking on the part of my mother, for she was seven or eight months pregnant. She wanted to take me along, and I was still something of an inconvenience. But my father announced a sojourn of some length in Madrid, and my mother had, I believe, some mistrust based on jealousy."[2]

Indeed, from the very beginning, Maurice and Sophie's relationship was marred by jealousy and insecurity, each obsessed with the fear that the other might be unfaithful. From camp in Hagenau, Maurice wrote Sophie soon after Aurore's birth, "Have no fear of infidelity, because for a long time hence I shall only have dealings with the masculine sex." In another letter, posted soon after from Vienna, Maurice hints at his own uncertainty about Sophie's fidelity, "I don't know if you love me, if you're in good health, if Aurore is sad or cheerful, if my wife is still my very own Sophie." In closing, Maurice voiced a desperate plea: "Let no one see you, think only of taking care of our daughter, and I'll be as happy as I can be, far from you."[3] Aurore's existence thus provided insurance against the betrayals that threatened her parents' relationship. However irresponsible, taking Aurore to Spain on the eve of giving birth to another child was motivated by vulnerability and by a desire to solidify her bond with Maurice.

A woman named Madame Fontanier, the wife of a purveyor to the French army stationed in Madrid, offered Sophie two places in the mail coach she had hired for the trip to Spain. Accompanied only by a twelve-year-old groom, the party progressed from the lush, green countryside of France through the increasingly arid landscape of the Basque valleys. The arduous journey was fraught with unsettling impressions and experiences. What at first appeared on the horizon as a group of men brandishing guns turned out to be three mountain bears standing tall and unperturbed along the trail. The Pyrenees, so different from anything Aurore had ever seen, failed to impress so small a child; instead, the claustrophobic enclosure of the mountains intimidated and frightened her.

Presaging Proust and the famed madeleine episode in *A la recherche du temps perdu*, which celebrates the synesthetic bond between memory

Aurore Dupin. Drawing by François Deschartres. (Courtesy Bibliothèque nationale de France)

and sensation, Sand described her impressions of the honeylike smell of bindweed in flower: "This is the first revelation of odor that I remember, and by a chain of memories and sensations that everyone knows but cannot explain, I never smell the flowers of the bindweed without seeing the spot in the Spanish mountains and the edge of the path where I picked them for the first time."[4]

At an inn near the Spanish town of Burgos, the traveling party passed the fleeing Infanta, whose departure on 2 May 1808 launched the Madrid uprising. She was journeying to Bayonne, to her father, the Bourbon king Carlos IV, and to Napoléon, who had promised (but never delivered) the throne to the kingdom of Lusitania in northern Portugal. The pathetic spectacle of the fleeing queen and her daughter made a striking impression on Aurore: "I saw, I don't know where or when, a very dark skinned woman dressed in a white dress in a carriage with a little girl dressed like her and dark skinned like her. There were a lot of people crying. They said it was the queen and that she was in flight." The spectacle of mother and daughter fleeing kindled feelings of sympathy and identification. Even queens and princesses were not immune to uncertainty and hardship. Sand later recorded: "They seemed sad and uneasy. . . . They had neither retinue nor escort. They were fleeing rather than leaving, and I later heard my mother say in a casual tone, 'It's another queen running for her life.'"[5] Sophie must have been thinking of Marie-Antoinette.

Repelled by the sight of a pigeon slaughtered in preparation for dinner, Aurore couldn't eat that night. The death throes of the pigeon were but a prelude to the human slaughter that lay ahead. "The further we advanced along our journey, the more terrible became the spectacle of war."[6] The heat of the Spanish spring intensified as they passed through burned and pillaged villages. At one inn where they stopped, there were only raw onions to eat, and Aurore slept on a table while her mother and Madame Fontanier sat up through the sleepless night.

Two weeks after departing Paris, they finally arrived in Madrid. Sophie and Aurore joined Maurice at the Palace of the Prince of the Asturias, where they occupied a spacious apartment above Prince Murat's sumptuous ground-floor lodgings. The two months in Madrid were the period in which Aurore was closest to her father, a man who had had so little presence in her earliest life but would have so much importance for the duration. Her sense of identification was fortified by a miniature replica of her father's ornamental hussar's uniform, in which she appeared whenever in the presence of Prince Murat.

Whether or not Murat knew that Aurore wasn't actually a boy, he went along with the deception by always referring to the costumed child as his aide-de-camp, Maurice's title in the prince's entourage. In the privacy of their apartment, Aurore would change into another outfit, a black silk dress with a velvet bordered crepe mantilla, a miniature copy of one of Sophie's Spanish gowns. Sand remembered not how it felt to be a little girl dressed up like her mother, but how magnificent her mother looked when she was dressed this way: "Never did a real Spanish woman have such fine tan skin, such velvety black eyes, such small feet, and such an arching waist."[7]

On 12 June, Sophie gave birth to a boy, Louis Auguste. Sophie claimed to have seen the Spanish doctor press his thumbs over the newborn's eyes and mutter, "This one won't see the sun of Spain."[8] She may have witnessed the doctor attempting to readjust a dislocated lens of the baby's eye, and the doctor's comment may simply have been a metaphoric way of reporting that the baby was born blind. But Sophie would cling to her paranoid belief that hostility toward the French had provoked the Spaniard to blind her baby boy. In all likelihood, the baby was born with cataracts or some other congenital defect.

Several conditions resulting in blindness at birth are associated with prematurity, which in the case of Sophie's baby lends itself to a problem that goes beyond the question of the infant's health. If Louis, as he was called, was born premature, he may well have been conceived after Maurice left Paris for Italy on 16 November.[9] Were Sophie to have become pregnant by another man in her husband's absence, her daring journey to Spain would be all the more explicable: she would have had good reason to be desperately insecure about the status of her marriage.

Just hours after the birth, Maurice posted an optimistic letter to his mother back in France: "After long hours of suffering, Sophie gave birth this morning to a big boy who whistles like a parrot. Mother and child are doing marvelously. Before the end of the month the Prince leaves for France; the Emperor's doctor, who took care of Sophie, says she will be able to travel in twelve days with her child. Aurore is fine. I shall bundle the lot into a carriage which I have just acquired for this purpose, and we shall take to the road for Nohant, where I certainly expect to arrive around the 20th of July, in the cool of evening, and stay as long as possible. This thought, my dear mother, fills me with joy."[10]

When Carlos IV abdicated along with his son Ferdinand VII, Napoléon gave his older brother, Joseph, the throne of Spain. This catalyzed a national uprising of the Spanish people in defense of Ferdinand VII. The French were overcome by popular resistance when their troops were surrounded in Baylen on 22 July, and the French army hastily evacuated Spain. For his loyal service during the Spanish occupation, Napoléon rewarded Murat with the throne of Naples, where Maurice was destined to join him after a furlough at home in France.

The six-hundred-mile return journey from Madrid to Nohant was calamitous beyond all anticipation. En route, the coach that Maurice hired to transport his family and their possessions was requisitioned for the wounded, and Sophie, the fragile baby boy, and Aurore were loaded into a baggage wagon filled with sick and injured soldiers. Maurice joined them for portions of the journey when he wasn't riding with his regiment on the Spanish stallion Leopardo that had been given him by Ferdinand VII. Sophie's paranoia about the Spanish was triggered by the gift: "My mother maintained that Ferdinand had given Leopardo to him hoping it would kill him," Sand would recall.[11]

Food was scarce, and their diet, disastrous for the nursing Sophie, consisted for the most part of raw onions, limes, and sunflower seeds. "What I remember best was the suffering, thirst, voracious heat, and the fever I experienced during the whole trip," Sand recorded.[12] When she playfully pinched an officer at a French camp, she was horrified to find that the sleeve where his arm should have been was empty. As a group of soldiers helped themselves to soup from a large mess pot, Sophie encouraged Aurore to join the men in their meal. Only as the child drank the soup in famished draughts did Sophie realize that the concoction consisted of bread, greasy broth, and some blackened candle wicks floating on the surface.

As conditions worsened, the splendor and comfort of Madrid receded like a dream. The wagon stank with filth as it wended its way through burned-out villages, bombarded towns, roads littered with corpses and lined with ditches "where we would seek to quench our burning thirst with a drop of water, only to come upon floating clots of blood. My mother hid her face, and the air was putrid. We were not close enough to these sinister objects for me to realize what they were, and I asked why so many rags had been strewn about. Finally, the wheel hit something which broke with a strange cracking sound. My mother held me down on the floor of the wagon to keep me from looking; it must have been a corpse."[13]

The July heat was oppressive, and if drinking water was scarce, water for washing was out of the question. In Vitoria they came into contact with a servant whose long, black lice-infested hair contaminated Aurore. She and the baby came down with fever and scabies. Blaming herself, Sand reported, "Scabies had begun with me, and I gave it to my brother, then to my mother later on, and to others—sad fruit of war and misery."[14]

Conditions improved as they neared the French border. They recovered their carriage, and there were now clean inns that offered comfortable accommodations and longed-for foods such as cheese and pastry, which they hadn't seen for weeks. In Fuenterrabia, Aurore was finally bathed, but the pleasure of being clean was mitigated by the sulfur that Sophie smeared over her entire body and forced her to swallow rolled in balls of sugared butter to rid her of the lice and scabies. "That taste and odor that I lived with for two months left me with a great repugnance for anything reminiscent of it."[15]

Crossing the French border didn't end their trials. It was Sophie who came up with the whimsical idea of returning by sea to Bordeaux. A "decked launch was hired, the carriage was loaded onto it, and we set out as if we were on a pleasure trip."[16] As the Dupin family, two mates, and a captain pushed off from shore, someone handed Aurore a bouquet of roses, which she clutched and sniffed throughout the crossing to relieve the noxious smell of sulphur.

Just as the launch was approaching its destination, a gust of wind kicked up and drove it onto a reef. As the hold filled with water and the launch began to sink, the terrified Sophie bundled herself and the children into the carriage. In Sand's recollection of the incident, Maurice remained calm and acted with great courage and self-assurance. Shedding his coat and grabbing a shawl with which he strapped the children to his back, he called out to Sophie, "Don't worry. . . . I'll take you under one arm, I'll swim with the other, and I'll save all three of you, you can be sure of that!"[17]

His treasured African saber was the first object he rescued after saving Sophie and the children. Only then did he concern himself with the carriage and the launch, both of which he saved in an effort that lasted several hours and that he directed with "skill and resolution . . . with calm and a rare presence of mind."[18] Aurore watched with awe as her father performed these miraculous feats. The impression of his heroism would never leave her. The rest of the journey was a blur to the feverish and exhausted child rife with lice and scabies. As their coach rolled into the front yard at Nohant, Aurore sat up and took notice of the surroundings that would become home for the rest of her life.

Sophie was exhausted by the excruciating ordeal she and her family had undergone. Her daughter's robust constitution had been challenged almost beyond endurance, and the health of her infant son, who was puny and weak from birth, was seriously compromised by the treacherous pre- and postnatal journeys to and from Spain. The prospect of a reunion with her mother-in-law under these circumstances added to Sophie's misgivings, but Madame Dupin, whose relief in her beloved Maurice's return was beyond measure, took her completely by surprise. She welcomed mother

Château de Nohant. (Courtesy C. O. Darré, Musée George
Sand, La Châtre)

and children with open arms and immediately assumed responsibility for
the care of Aurore, despite her fever and the rash that covered her from
head to toe.

Deschartres, in "knee breeches, white stockings, yellow gaiters, a very
long nut-brown coat, and a bellows cap," examined the children and
confirmed the baby's blindness as well as the diagnosis of scabies from
which both children were suffering.[19] Deschartres' place of importance
in the life of Nohant had grown considerably over the twenty-odd years
of his employment by Madame Dupin, to whom his opinions and services had become indispensable. To his earlier interest in medicine and

surgery he had added agronomy and crop production and had progressed from his position as Maurice's tutor to estate manager. Judging from the frequency of Maurice's deprecatory remarks about his former tutor in letters home to his mother, we can assume that he felt some resentment for the central place Deschartres occupied in the aging Madame Dupin's life.

Having reached safe haven at Nohant, Sophie could finally give herself over to the task that most preoccupied her, tending Louis, whose little life hung in precarious balance from hour to hour and from day to day. Aurore was singled out for special treatment. Her grandmother took her to her own room and, showing no signs of distaste for the child's unsavory condition, spread her out on the finely dressed Louis XV bed in the form of "a chariot with great bouquets of plumes at the four corners." Aurore was struck by her grandmother's unfamiliar style of clothing and coiffure: "She seemed very tall to me, although her height was only five feet. Her pink and white complexion, her imposing air, her invariable costume consisting of a long-waisted brown silk dress with straight sleeves, which she had refused to modify along the dictates of the Empire fashion, her blond wig teased into a tuft on the forehead, her little round bonnet with a cockade of lace in the center."[20]

Aurore readily discerned contrasts between her grandmother and mother, who was dark and small and wore the Empire style of dress rather than the strange ancien régime attire in which her grandmother was clad. Even greater than the difference in their looks and dress was the difference in their behavior. Madame Dupin was measured and reserved, whereas Sophie was spontaneous and even impetuous. "They were really the two extreme types of our sex: one fair, blond, serious, calm and dignified in her behavior, a real Saxon of noble race, with grand manners full of ease and benevolent kindness; the other dark, pale, intense, shy and awkward in the presence of high society, and always ready to explode when the storm raged too forcefully within, a Spanish nature, jealous passionate, angry and weak, mean and good at the same time."[21]

As Aurore lay recovering on her grandmother's bed, a round-faced boy appeared and presented her with a large bouquet of flowers. Her grandmother introduced him simply as Hippolyte, without explaining that this nine-year-old fellow was, in fact, Aurore's half brother, the child code-named the Little House, who had been born to a serving girl and Maurice. Within hours the two children were playing in the garden, and within days Aurore had recovered her natural strength and energy. She and Hippolyte, who introduced her to the haunts of his simple country childhood, became constant companions. Together they indulged in typical childhood pleasures and pranks, slipping sand patties in the oven when no one was looking and lying in wait to see the kitchen staff's startled reaction when they removed the little "cakes" and discovered what they were. In imitation of the battles Napoléon was waging across Europe, Aurore and Hippolyte enacted war games. They dug graves and buried Aurore's dolls and dangled others by their feet from trees.

Madame Dupin had good reason for her about-face toward Maurice's new family. If, indeed, she had taken the measure of her rival and found her wanting, she was wise enough to realize, nevertheless, that Sophie had won rounds one and two of their contest by becoming Maurice's wife as well as the mother of his legitimate children. All of Madame Dupin's attempts to undermine the couple's union had been foiled. Now it was clear that Maurice was committed not only to Sophie but to the family they had created. Rejecting Sophie would mean severing her own bond with Maurice, and this was the last thing in the world Madame Dupin was willing to do.

For Sophie, the trip to Nohant had its own special meaning. At thirty-five, having borne some half dozen children, she was no longer the fresh, young woman who had once been kept by a succession of admirers. With three remaining children (there was also Caroline in Paris) to feed, clothe, and shelter, Sophie was committed to doing everything within her power to remain in her husband's good graces and to secure the approval of his mother. It was, after all, Madame Dupin who dispensed the allowance on which Maurice and his family lived. Without his mother's largesse, Maurice's chances for professional advancement would also be compromised, because to rise in rank, considerable investment had to be made in uniforms, horses, and other trappings by which prestige and progress within the military were measured.

Like many army wives, Sophie entertained dreams of having her husband stay at home with her and the children rather than going off to fight the battles that Napoléon was waging across the European continent. Maurice sometimes imagined this possibility, too, and together the couple dreamed of a life in which she would raise their children and he could pursue a career in music and theater. Such dreams could be fulfilled, Sophie was wise enough to realize, only if Madame Dupin's benevolence and bounty toward her adored son continued.

Knowing, too, that her baby's only chance of survival depended on re-covering her own strength, Sophie did her best to restore herself to good health. She was obsessed with the thought that because of the deprivations of her Spanish diet, her own milk was poisoning the baby. To compensate, she ate well and took lots of fresh air and exercise to increase her appetite. In between nursing, while the baby lay resting in the shade, she cultivated a little garden beneath a pear tree in the corner of the courtyard. Surrounded by her children, with her husband nearby as she cultivated the rich soil of Nohant, Sophie signaled her intention of setting down family roots. But despite the loving care and attention she gave him, Louis was not far-ing well. His eyes remained lifeless, and his expression grew sad. He lost weight, grew pale, and became increasingly listless when he wasn't fretting. "It was in seeing him suffer," Sand later wrote, "that I began to love him. Until then I had not paid much attention to him, but when he lay out-stretched on my mother's lap, so languid and weak that she hardly dared touch him, I grew sad along with her, and I vaguely understood what it means to worry."[22]

On Thursday, 8 September, not yet three months old, the baby died. He was buried the following day in the cemetery at Nohant, and the house-hold, so joyous since the family's return, was suddenly plunged into mourn-ing. Grieved by the baby's death, Maurice now blamed Sophie for her irre-sponsibility in making the trip to Spain. Surely had she remained in Paris, the baby would never have been born frail and blind. For her part, Sophie was distraught by the suddenness with which her baby had been removed from her. She had not had a chance to cradle him in her arms and to pre-pare him for burial as she would have liked. Deschartres had immediately removed Louis from his mother and pronounced him dead; after that, everything happened so fast that even as the child lay buried in his tiny coffin, Sophie could not be certain that he wasn't just in a coma, giving the appearance of death but not dead after all.

Late into the night following Louis' burial, Maurice and Sophie argued and wept, until Maurice agreed with his wife that they had to make certain their son was no longer living. While the rest of the household slept, Mau-rice dressed, found a shovel, and rushed out to the cemetery, where he set about unearthing his son's freshly made grave. When Maurice finally retrieved the lifeless little body, he brought it back to Sophie, who was waiting anxiously in the house. At least she was able to bathe her baby one final time, to rub him lovingly with perfumes, and to swaddle him in her best linen. Unbeknownst to the rest of the household, throughout the night and the following day the couple kept the baby with them, consoling themselves by watching him lie peacefully in his tiny cradle as though he were only sleeping.

The following night, convinced beyond doubt that the child was no longer living, Maurice wrote his name and the dates of his birth and death on a scrap of paper which he sealed with wax between two glass panes and then placed on top of the baby in his coffin. Sophie covered the tiny body with rose petals before the coffin was nailed shut. Rather than returning the coffin to the cemetery where it had been buried, they reburied it at the foot of the pear tree in Sophie's new garden. It wasn't until many years later, when a gardener accidentally came upon the tiny coffin, that the changed location of Louis' grave was discovered.

All the following week, Sophie and Maurice, accompanied by Aurore and Hippolyte, worked on the newly planted garden by the pear tree. Recalling this time with irony years later, Sand wrote of her father: "I remember that he kept bringing wheelbarrows full of earth and grassy turf and that when he went to get these loads, he would put Hippolyte and me into the wheelbarrow, enjoying watching us, pretending he was going to dump us out to see us laugh or squeal, depending on our mood at the moment."[23]

To Aurore and Hippolyte, the digging and planting were part of their play. Deep in grief, Sophie and Maurice were creating a mortuary garden. Unknown to any of them, the baby Louis' death was but a prelude to an even greater catastrophe. A week after the baby died, Maurice left Sophie at home and went to dine at the home of friends in the neighboring town of La Châtre, several miles south of Nohant. Sophie spent the evening anxious and fretting. Maurice had continued to recriminate her for the poor judgment she displayed in traveling to Spain while pregnant. As far as Sophie was concerned, everything about Spain and the Spanish had proved untrustworthy. The surgeon had blinded her baby at birth, and Ferdinand VII had presented Maurice with a high-spirited Spanish stallion, which was a constant concern to her. That particular night, she no doubt voiced her disapproval once again, as Maurice set out in wet weather.

Bereft of her baby, Sophie was deeply depressed. Having nursed Louis until the time of his death, she was also suffering the painful process of suppressing her milk production. The inevitable swing in hormone levels brought on by the sudden cessation of nursing, along with her extreme emotional fragility, added to her vulnerability. As for Maurice, grieved by his son's death and worn down by quarrels with Sophie, he was eager for the company of good friends and for the chance to escape the mournful oppression of Nohant.

On the evening of 16 September, Madame Dupin was treated to a candid display of her daughter-in-law's jealousy. As the night wore on and Maurice did not return, Sophie became increasingly agitated, pacing up and down and threatening to go out into the rainy night to await him on the road from La Châtre to Nohant. Madame Dupin tried to reassure Sophie that Maurice would soon be home, but when Sophie persisted in her anxiety, the older woman gave her some wise, womanly advice. She suggested that Sophie go to bed and get a good night's sleep to repair her complexion, tarnished by tears. Madame Dupin further advised that if Sophie didn't curb her jealous and suspicious behavior, she would risk losing her husband. This last threat must have influenced Sophie, because she finally gave up her plan to go after Maurice and instead went to bed.

After dinner, Maurice took leave of his hosts and set out for home on Leopardo, trailed by his valet, a man named Weber. Rounding a bend in the road lined by a row of poplars, Leopardo shied at a pile of rubble, reared up, and threw Maurice to the ground. With the help of some locals, Weber moved his master to the nearby Lion d'Argent Inn and then galloped on to Nohant to enlist Deschartre's help.

After sending Sophie up to bed, Madame Dupin had spent the evening playing a game of piquet with Deschartres. As midnight neared, she, too, became concerned about Maurice's delayed return and went to bed with an uneasy feeling. When the servant Saint-Jean rushed outside to meet Weber and then to summon Deschartres, Madame Dupin heard the commotion. Sensing that something was terribly amiss, she set out alone in the rain, without a shawl and shod only in the little prunella slippers she wore around the house. By the time Madame Dupin arrived at the Lion d'Argent, Deschartres had already arrived and pronounced Maurice dead. Sand tells us in her autobiography:

At the fatal spot, the end of her desperate errand, my poor grandmother fell, as if suffocated, on the body of her son. Saint-Jean had hurried to hitch the horses to the berlin and come to carry off Deschartres, the body, and my grandmother, who would not be separated from it. It was Deschartres who recounted to me this night of despair, as my grandmother was never able to speak of it. He told me he had suffered everything the human spirit could bear, short of breaking, during that journey where the poor mother, prostrate over the body of her son, made no other sound than a moan like that of the dying.[24]

A superficial report by "medical experts" gave the time of death as eight o'clock and listed apoplexy as the cause, but more likely Maurice died of broken vertebrae in the neck. For the rest of her life, Madame Dupin could not pass the place by the thirteenth poplar where her son had died without covering her eyes with her hands and breaking down in tears.[25]

It was not until six o'clock the next morning that Sophie learned of her husband's death. Aurore was watching her mother dress when Deschartres entered the room without knocking. The awkward old tutor announced that Maurice had had a serious fall from his horse. When Sophie jumped up to go join her stricken husband, Deschartres blurted out, "He is dead!" He then gave a strange, inappropriate laugh, sat down, and convulsed in tears. "My mother fell onto the chair behind the bed. I can see her livid face, her long black hair spread out on her breast, her bare arms which I was covering with kisses; I can hear her rending cries. She was deaf to mine and did not notice my caresses."[26]

A week after burying his son, thirty-year-old Maurice Dupin was laid to rest in the shade of cypress trees in the cemetery at Nohant. When it came time to record in her midlife autobiography the tragic event of her father's death, Sand was in full thrall to her early family romance. Accordingly, her father "had only had time to recognize the sudden, implacable death that had come to snatch him just at the moment his military career was opening before him, brilliant and without obstacle; just at the moment when, after eight years of conflict, his mother, his wife, and his children were at last accepted by one another and united under one roof, and the terrible conflict of his affections was going to cease and allow him to be happy."[27]

This account conspicuously idealizes the era before her father's fall as a time of family bliss that presaged a peaceful, harmonious future. Despite the obvious, unresolved conflicts with which Maurice Dupin's life was beset, Sand would have us believe that but for his untimely death, her family would have lived happily ever after. Sand's wishful thinking notwithstanding, her assertion is hardly substantiated by the reality of the family situation before her father died. In going home to Nohant with Sophie and the children, Maurice was naively hoping for peace and happiness, but instead he found himself in a hotbed of conflict.

What may have seemed like a reconciliation between his mother and wife would most probably not have lasted, given their deep-seated differences. Indeed, in the short span of time before Maurice died, tensions fueled by the hostility Madame Dupin had felt for Sophie all along began to build between husband and wife. By turning against Sophie with recriminations about their son's sickly life and death, Maurice unwittingly served up proof to his mother of his wife's deficiencies. Had he lived on, so surely would have the conflict among mother, son, and daughter-in-law.

Maurice no doubt realized this, too, and his fall from a half-broken stallion on a wet and winding road in the dark of night lends itself to interpretation as an accidental suicide: a desperate man's veiled attempt to resolve conflicting forces within himself. In a paper presented in 1928, the psychoanalyst Helene Deutsch observed: "Maurice's death plainly bears the mark of an unconscious suicide. For what with the nightmare of domestic strife between the two mothers and, above all, Sophie's almost pathological jealousy, he had a great deal to put up with, and his unconscious obviously helped him in this flight into death." If Maurice Dupin managed to avoid death in the field, he finally succumbed to the fire of his personal life. "His heart was split three ways," Sand would later reflect, "between his mother, his mistress and his daughter, and to his distress, the rift could only be reconciled at the price of terrible suffering. He therefore suffered greatly and more than once, losing all hope, sought death on the battlefield."[28]

Pronounced "a brilliant young officer" by one critic, Dupin drew a harsher assessment from another, who argued that "nothing in his life indicates that he would have made a great mark on the world had he lived."[29] Sand herself was caught in conflict over the meaning of Maurice Dupin's life. When it came time to write her autobiography, she spent a third of it on transcriptions of her father's letters to his mother and wife, liberally revising and occasionally rewriting them, always to aggrandize the man and to magnify his love for her.

CHAPTER FIVE

Sophie's Choice

Yes, I must admit the time came when, placed in an unnatural situation between these two affections which by nature should not have conflicted, I was by turns a victim of the opposing sensitivities of these two women and of my own, too often not spared by them.

AURORE WAS TERRIFIED by the black stockings she was forced to wear and referred to them as "legs of death." When other members of the household began to appear in mourning, Aurore asked her mother, "You mean my daddy died again today?"[1] Although unaware that Maurice was his father, Hippolyte cried and screamed at night. The double deaths of the baby and Maurice, coupled with the grief he was witnessing in everyone around him, induced nightmares in the otherwise intrepid nine-year-old child.

The superstitious servants made matters worse by circulating stories that Maurice's ghost had been sighted walking around the house at night in full dress uniform. Exploiting the situation, a thief draped himself in white and, phantomlike, wandered about the courtyard awaiting a propitious moment to enter the house and make off with whatever valuables he might lay hands on. Hippolyte saw the figure and was terrified. Deschartres took matters in hand and threatened to shoot the intruder. Life at Nohant had promised, and then swiftly rescinded, the security that Aurore so sorely needed.

Deep in shock and depression, Sophie developed severe headaches. Departing from her usual active, industrious behavior, she took to spending whole days in bed, a pattern that persisted for years. "I had seen my mother hundreds of times overcome by violent migraines, prostrate on her bed like a corpse, her cheeks pale, her teeth set," Sand recollected.[2] Identifying with her mother's grief, Aurore also developed headaches, which eventually turned into migraines that would debilitate her, too, for the rest of her life during times of severe stress. Profoundly affected by the emotional upheaval she was witnessing, Aurore became dreamy and would sit staring for long spells without talking. The formerly loquacious little girl was rendered dumbstruck by disaster so overwhelming that it was unspeakable.

There were other significant changes in Aurore's behavior. She became willful and acted like a spoiled child, indulging in wild fits of whimsy and throwing tantrums when she was denied what she wanted. Sand would later provide a keen description of how as a child she "acted out" her grief and incomprehension: "I was intensely irritable and not at all in my normal state of mind. I was subject to a thousand fantasies, and I would emerge from mysterious reveries only to demand the impossible. I wanted them to give me the birds which flew in the garden, and I would roll on the ground in rage if they made fun of me; I wanted Weber to put me on his horse (it was not Leopardo, he had been sold immediately), but of course no one was going to let me near any horse."[3]

Sophie's behavior grew increasingly inconsistent. She would scold and hit Aurore with little provocation and then dissolve in tears and remorse for over-reacting. Frightened and insecure, Aurore became submissive: "I was so happy to regain her affection that I would ask her pardon for the smacks she had administered." But Sophie's behavior was nothing short of abusive toward the daughter who would later write, "No matter how she shook me and made me into a little package that could be pushed and tossed onto a bed or an armchair, her adept and supple hands could never bruise me." It's no wonder Aurore became, according to the mature Sand, "the most morose, melancholy, and irascible child imaginable." With psychological acuity well in advance of her times, Sand expressed keen understanding of her response to childhood trauma: "Most often children are obstreperous and capricious only because they are suffering and cannot or will not articulate it."[4]

Madame Dupin devised a scheme that seems to have worked well to ease the strain and loneliness of her granddaughter's grief. She invited the niece of her chambermaid, Mademoiselle Julie, a girl named Ursule, who was eighteen months older than Aurore, to become her grand-daughter's playmate.[5] Dressed in mourning, Ursule was brought to Nohant, where she spent the next several years taking meals with the family and sleeping with Aurore. Despite their different backgrounds, the two little girls became fast friends, forming a bond that lasted for the rest of their lives.

Against this backdrop, Aurore's early education took shape. She was read tales of Madame d'Aulnoy and Perrault, stories from Madame de Genlis, and was introduced to an abridged version of Greek mythology. With Madame Dupin's encouragement, Aurore developed the habit of writing without inhibition, which Sand credits with helping her to better understand what she read as a child. Madame Dupin also gave Aurore music lessons, instilling in her the principles of harmony and an abiding love for music. Often Aurore would sit on the floor below the harpsichord with Madame Dupin's favorite dog, Brillant, listening in rapture as the older woman sang and played from old opera scores. "I would have spent the rest of my life there, so charmed was I by that quavering voice and the shrill sound of the old spinet."[6]

Although Aurore's grandmother was responsible for her early formal education, Sophie's contribution to her child's formation was no less considerable. "My mother was a great artist who had missed her calling for lack of training." With no formal education, Sophie succeeded in learning to read and write and composed letters "in a style so naive and pretty" that they garnered even Madame Dupin's admiration. "Without knowing the notes, [Sophie] had a ravishing voice, light and incomparably pure." Gifted in all sorts of handiwork, she sewed clothes, sketched, deftly repaired broken objects, even tuned the harpsichord. "She dared anything and succeeded at everything." Even the critical Madame Dupin had to acknowledge her daughter-in-law's practical gifts and referred to her as a "household fairy." Commenting on her mother's "ardor and power of concentration," Sand later reflected, "Whatever she began in the morning had to be finished by the next day, even if she had to spend all night on it."[7] Sophie's hardworking example would serve as a model of discipline for the future George Sand.

Sand would fondly remember the enchanted grotto complete with a waterfall that her mother constructed in the garden at Nohant. Aurore, Hippolyte, and Ursule were enlisted, along with a beloved donkey, to bring basket loads of natural materials out of which Sophie fashioned the magical creation about which Sand would later reflect: "I doubt that I experienced greater surprise or admiration when I later saw the great cataracts of the Alps and Pyrenees."[8]

Meanwhile, the tensions were mounting within the family at Nohant. Deschartres' abiding hostility toward Sophie drove a further wedge between the rivalrous widow and her mother-in-law. "He could not forgive my mother for having supplanted him in his would-be influence over the mind and heart of his dear Maurice." Madame Dupin didn't even try to disguise her resentment of Sophie: "She is a devil, a madwoman. She was never loved by my son, she controlled him, she made him unhappy. She does not miss him."[9] On the contrary, Madame Dupin's attachment to Aurore was growing. Having lost Maurice, the dowager was rapidly transforming Aurore into his surrogate.

In retrospect, Sand referred benevolently to Madame Dupin and Sophie as "my two mothers," but a child can have only one mother, and the threat of losing Sophie overwhelmed Aurore with anxiety and fear. "Nature makes no mistakes," George Sand would later write, "and notwithstanding the infinite kindness and boundless generosity of the way my grandmother raised me, I do not hesitate to say that an aging and invalid forebear can never be a mother."[10]

At night she fantasized a battle between two figures emblazoned in medallions on her bedroom wallpaper. The symbolism seems obvious enough: the playful, dancing nymph embedded in nature is associated with Sophie, and the serious bacchante with Madame Dupin. The night-time drama that Aurore imagined reveals the insupportable turmoil she was experiencing:

> In the middle of the night, [the bacchante] detached herself
> from the medallion, slid down the door, became as large as
> a "grown-up," as children say, and crossing to the other door,
> she tried to tear the pretty nymph from her medallion. The
> latter emitted heartrending cries, but the bacchante ignored
> them. She twisted and tore the paper until the nymph detached
> herself and fled to the middle of the room. The other ran after
> her, and the poor dishevelled nymph having leaped onto my
> bed to hide behind the curtains, the furious bacchante moved
> toward me and pierced the two of us with her thyrsus, which
> had been transformed into a sharp lance, and each blow
> inflicted a wound whose pain I felt.[11]

According to Sand, during the summer of 1810 Aurore's charming grand-uncle Beaumont (Madame Dupin's half brother by their common father, Maurice de Saxe) was recruited to help resolve the conflict between the "two mothers." Despite his religious vocation—he bore the title abbot —and the celibacy that (supposedly) attended it, Beaumont had eased into a comfortable and elegant life. "Gentle, liberal, and lenient in behavior," he was viewed by the family as the voice of reason and equilibrium and had managed to win—no mean feat—both Madame Dupin's and Sophie's trust.[12] It was Beaumont who brokered the deal between these two adversaries that established the conditions of Aurore's future. In exchange for a yearly income of one thousand francs, Sophie was bought out of her daughter's upbringing. Instead of raising Aurore, she would move to Paris to care for her other daughter, Caroline. The proviso to the arrangement was cunning and cruel: Sophie must leave Aurore at Nohant to be raised by Madame Dupin.

In a remarkable act of repetition, Madame Dupin had reconstructed her own past. As we have seen, she had been bartered to the dauphine Marie-Josèphe de Saxe, who oversaw her upbringing and paid for her education on the condition that her mother, Marie de Verrières, sever all contact with her. Although future visits from Sophie would be allowed, under no circumstances was she to bring Caroline to Nohant.

Overhearing the negotiations regarding her future, Aurore came to understand that her inheritance from her father would be compromised if her grandmother lost interest in her. "I consequently acquired a great scorn for money before I even knew what it was," Sand recorded, "and also a haunting fear of the wealth with which I was threatened." In response to the imminent loss of her mother, Aurore's attachment to her grew deeper and more desperate. "Whenever I was alone with her," Sand recalled, "I would cover her with kisses and beg her not 'to give me away to my grandmother for money.' "[13] A new era was under way. Aurore's nighttime fantasy of the nymph and bacchante had foretold the future: her mother was excised from her life, and six-year-old Aurore was cast in the role of the replacement child of Marie Dupin's twilight years.

However much Madame Dupin indulged Aurore after Sophie's departure—she lavished her with sweets and praise as she studied her lessons —her efforts were in vain. The contrast between these two very different women became increasingly marked in Aurore's mind, and the pain of separation from her mother reversed whatever positive feelings she might have harbored toward her grandmother. "She commanded respect, and I found it chilling." Even qualities that once worked in her grandmother's favor, such as her evenhandedness, now worked against her as the lonely little girl called up memories of her mother's temperamental ways and longed for the tumultuous emotional and physical intimacy they had shared: "I felt myself physically and morally attached to my mother by a chain of diamond hardness that my grandmother sought in vain to break but that only kept tightening around my chest, to the point of suffocation."[14]

The rules by which Aurore had been raised thus far began to change, and the changes were neither subtle nor gradual. "No longer was I to romp on the floor . . . or talk Berrichon," the regional patois that was spoken in her province. Instead, she was taught to curtsy, reminded constantly of the proper way to carry herself, and was frequently rebuked by her grandmother for walking like a peasant or losing her gloves. Dressed in Madame Dupin's tailored hand-me-downs, Aurore was no longer to set foot in the kitchen or to use the familiar form of address, *tu* and *toi,* when she spoke with the serving staff, who were by now her friends and companions. Her grandmother instituted the use of the formal *vous* when addressing Aurore and frequently reminded her that she was "too big for such things," when the seven-year-old acted childishly. For her part, Aurore was required to address her grandmother in the third person—"Will dear grandmama permit me to go into the garden?"—an even more archaic and formal manner of address than the use of *vous* between family members.[15]

The repressive regime wreaked havoc on the free-spirited little girl. She became outwardly compliant and submissive while living in constant fear of displeasing the person on whose benevolence her future depended. Without her mother's spunk to counterbalance Madame Dupin's "paralytic languor," Aurore was increasingly put off by her grandmother's rigidity. "She feared the heat and the cold, every draft, every ray of sunlight. I had the impression I was being locked into a box with her when she said, 'Have fun quietly.' "[16]

In Madame Dupin's social circle, Aurore was treated with pity and condescension, something she had never encountered before. "Always be good, my poor child," her grandmother's closest friend, Madame de Pardaillan, warned her, "for that will be your only happiness in life."[17] Aurore was learning that outsiders viewed her situation as highly precarious. She would discover that the plot of her mother's life, and consequently her own, was thicker and more problematic than she could yet imagine.

On the eve of her mother's departure for Paris after one of her (infrequent) visits to Nohant, Aurore frantically composed a letter. "How sorry I am that I can't say goodbye to you. You know how very sad I am to leave you. Goodbye, think of me and rest assured I won't forget you." She signed the note "your daughter" and ventured a final wish-fulfilling command: "Leave your reply behind the portrait of old Dupin."[18] She folded the paper carefully, its childish rounded letters wet and smudged with tears, and stuck it behind the portrait of her dead grandfather that hung in her mother's bedroom. The little girl who would grow up to become nineteenth-century France's most celebrated woman writer had just dispatched the first of some twenty thousand letters that would one day be published under the pseudonym George Sand. To signal the letter's presence, which had to be kept secret from the rest of the household, Aurore slung her mother's nightcap over the picture and tucked a note inside instructing her to shake the portrait. Exhausted, she went back to bed, but panic about missing her mother kept her wakeful for hours during the long, painful night before Sophie's departure.

Aurore's anguish was hardly new or unfamiliar, for this was not the first time she had been separated from her mother. Ever since Sophie's first departure, which blurred together with the rest, Aurore had lived in a state of suspense, longing for and dreaming of her mother's return. By now she was supposed to be beyond the tears and tantrums that Sophie's comings and goings inevitably brought on, but as hard as she tried, Aurore was unable to suppress the storm of sadness that welled up within her each time her mother was about to leave.

Earlier in the day she had become hysterical, begging her mother not to go, throwing herself at her mother's feet, rolling on the floor, and sobbing out her secret plan to run away from Nohant to join her in Paris. Alarmed by her daughter's wild fantasies, Sophie explained that she could not afford to remove Aurore from her grandmother's care, that doing so would deprive Aurore of an education, a good marriage, and the generous inheritance that only her grandmother could provide.

To quell her daughter's protestations and endless pleading, Sophie contrived a story. She told Aurore that she was saving to buy a millinery shop in Orléans and that as soon as she could earn enough money to manage without the pension from Grandmother Marie, she would return to Nohant and take Aurore with her. Storm clouds lifted and Aurore turned cheerful again. Relieved and delighted, she happily helped Sophie pack her bags. The sooner her mother was gone, Aurore now reasoned, the sooner she would return to rescue her: "This marvelous plan went to my head. It almost made me hysterical. I jumped around the room, bursting into shrieks of laughter, crying at the same time. It was as if I were drunk."[19]

Hours later, on the eve of Sophie's departure, anxiety returned in full force as Aurore sat up sleepless in bed, listening for her mother's footsteps in the hall outside her room. When the maid Rose finally finished helping Sophie close her trunks, Aurore tiptoed across the hall. With Aurore's letter open in her lap, her mother told her she had second thoughts about the plan she'd outlined earlier. It would be better, after all, for Aurore to forget about her and to grow accustomed to her grandmother. As the sobbing Aurore became breathless, Sophie desperately renewed her promise. But having been retracted once before, the promise had lost its power to appease.

For some time Aurore had been plotting her escape, collecting jewelry and trinkets that she kept wrapped in a cloth and hidden away in a drawer. When the time was right, she would hock her valuables for the trip to Paris, some hundred and fifty miles away. Regardless of the distance, Aurore planned to set out on foot; rejoining her mother would be worth any hardship. As a tiny girl of four, hadn't she endured the horrors of the journey with her mother to and from Madrid?

Now, several years later, Aurore's consuming desire was that her mother take her with her again, that together they return to Paris so Aurore could be reunited with Caroline and her cousin Clotilde and Aunt Lucie Maréchal (Sophie's sister), with whom she had spent her earliest childhood. Memories of playing war games in Aunt Lucie's garden and of riding to market with her cousin in a basket on the back of a donkey hovered in her imagination, although Aurore could never be sure if she actually remembered these things or if she only thought she did because of the many stories her mother had told her on nights when they snuggled together in Sophie's big yellow bed at Nohant. Such nights had recently ended when Grandmother Marie learned about them from the maid.

Madame Dupin said it was unchaste for such a big girl to sleep in her mother's bed and abruptly put an end to it.

As day began to break, the carriage rolled into the courtyard below. Hearing her mother's steps in the hall, Aurore raced across the tiles, threw herself in her mother's arms, and begged to be taken along. Dressed and ready to leave, Sophie would have none of this last-minute drama. She did not want her traveling outfit soiled or creased and reproached Aurore for making the departure more difficult than it had already become. Instead of kindness and reassurance, Aurore was left with grief and searing regret. She had meant to secure her mother's love but instead had made her angry and impatient to leave.

When the carriage rolled away and all hope drained from her exhausted mind and body, Aurore went back to bed. She slept fitfully for a few hours only to reawaken to overwhelming grief. In panic she ran to Sophie's room, threw herself on the unmade bed, and buried her face in the pillow that still bore the imprint of her mother's head. "It seemed like my mother was dead and that silence and darkness would claim this room to which she would no longer return."[20] When Rose entered to make up the room, Aurore lost her chance to retrieve the promised letter. She returned later only to discover that no letter had been left. The blow was devastating, more than her battered ego could bear. Aurore's realization at that moment was even more painful than the separation: her mother's love, she now knew, was not equal to her own.

Sophie was forty-one years old, still beautiful, and very bored. Even though the trip to Paris would take almost twenty hours by mail coach, not including the overnight stop at a dreadful auberge in Orléans, she was pleased to be on her way back to the city and its bustling boulevards. Nohant was hot in summer and cold and drafty in winter, and the only distractions were reading and writing, which held little interest for Sophie. Her mother-in-law was a stern, snobbish woman who made no secret of her contempt for her daughter-in-law.

As the coach rumbled north along the bumpy road, Sophie felt bad about falsely raising Aurore's hopes. The story about opening a millinery shop had simply popped into her mind as a way of calming her down. She realized Aurore took it as a lie and felt betrayed, but it wasn't altogether a lie, not if one counts dashed hopes and dreams. Before marrying Maurice, while he was serving as General Dupont's aide-de-camp in Paris and wait-ing for a promotion, Sophie had taken a job in a dress shop in Orléans. It felt good to be employed at something industrious and respectable, and even though she missed Maurice, the time passed pleasantly. When Mau-rice was posted to Charleville in 1802, Sophie quit her job and joined him, though the dream of having a dress shop of her own some day had been planted in her mind. Sometimes Sophie imagined what life might have been like had she opened a shop instead of following Maurice from post to post. As the carriage lurched along, Sophie became pensive. It wasn't that she didn't love Aurore; it was just that life had not worked out the way she had hoped or expected it would.

PART TWO REVELATIONS AND CONFESSIONS

CHAPTER SIX

Enigma of the Sphinx

I owe . . . my first socialist and democratic instincts to my unusual circumstances: to my birth, which straddles, so to speak, two classes; to my love for my mother, a love thwarted and bruised by prejudices which caused me much suffering before I could understand them. I owe them also to my education, which was by turns enlightened and religious, and to all the contrasts my own life proffered me from the tenderest age. I therefore was a democrat not only because my mother's blood flowed in my veins, but also because of the upheavals this blood of the people caused in my heart and in my existence.

IN *STORY OF MY LIFE,* there are two crucial revelations concerning Sophie Dupin that are among the most traumatic experiences of Aurore's young life. In each incident, one involving Madame Dupin, the other, some five years later, involving Sophie herself, Aurore is confronted with devastating disclosures about her mother's past. Taken together, the two scenes are curiously complementary and serve as symbolic bookends to Aurore's adolescence.

The first scene of confrontation takes place when Aurore is thirteen years old. She has been living with her grandmother in relative isolation at Nohant and is filled with pain and longing for her absent mother. Unable to concentrate on her lessons, she is reprimanded by Julie, a maid in the Dupin household, for being stubborn and temperamental and is put on notice that if she does not mend her ways, her grandmother will send her back to her mother. This is, of course, exactly what Aurore wants most in the world. When Aurore speaks her heart, Julie reports to Madame Dupin, embellishing her account with a malicious flourish: she tells the aging dowager that her granddaughter hates her. Deeply wounded, Madame

Dupin sets up a blockade that lasts for several days: Aurore is not to come to her room, nor to take meals with her, nor to appear in the garden before Madame Dupin retires. For added emphasis, whenever Aurore passes her grandmother's room, she is treated to the clang of an iron bar being drawn across the door.

When the stalemate is finally broken and Aurore is brought before her grandmother, Madame Dupin delivers a diatribe on Sophie's moral misconduct. "Stay on your knees and listen to me carefully," she commands, "because what I am going to say to you, you have never heard before and shall never hear again from my lips."[1] She proceeds to recount the story of Sophie's life.

Sand finds her grandmother's revelation "without pity and without intelligence" and defends her mother on humanitarian grounds: poor people's lives contain "pressures, misfortunes, and fatal decrees that the rich can never understand and so judge only as poorly as the blind judge colors." With this proviso, Sand proceeds to her grandmother's account:

> Everything she said was factually true and rested on circum-
> stances which did not allow the least doubt. But I could have
> been told this terrible story in a way not calculated to destroy
> my respect and love for my mother, and told thus, the story
> would have been a great deal more credible and truthful.
> It would have meant telling everything—the causes of her
> misfortunes; her isolation and misery from the age of fourteen;
> her corruption by the rich, who exist to lie in wait for hunger
> and cast a slur on innocence; and the unpitying rigor of public
> opinion, which allows no going back and accepts no expiation.
> I should also have been told how my mother had redeemed
> her past, how she had loved my father faithfully, and how, since
> his death, she had lived humbly, grieving and retired from the
> world. I know this last point very well, or at least I believed
> I knew it. But they wanted me to understand that, if they were
> telling me all about the past, they were sparing me the present,
> and that there was in my mother's current life some new secret
> they did not want to tell me and that would make me fearful
> for my own future if I went to live with her. Finally, my poor
> grandmama, exhausted by this long recital, beside herself, her

voice hoarse, eyes watery and red, loosed the final and most frightful word—my mother was a lost woman, and I was a blind child who wished to fling herself into an abyss.[2]

Although the implication is clear that Sophie Dupin had lived a life of prostitution, Sand doesn't tell us what her grandmother actually said, only that this assertion is true and verifiable. What we are given instead of Madame Dupin's verbatim revelation is Sand's opinion of how the presentation should have been made (less harshly); Sand's rationalization for Sophie's misconduct (class); Sand's forgiveness of her mother; Sand's contention (invention?) that Sophie had been faithful to her father and lived chastely since his death; and finally, a warning that "some new secret" about Sophie's present behavior could threaten Aurore's future, should she live with her.

If Sand is vague and elusive about the content of her grandmother's disclosure, she is unstinting in her description of its emotional impact: "For me it was like a nightmare; my throat was tight; each word spelled my death; I felt the sweat pour down my brow; I wanted to interrupt, get up and run away, repulse this frightful confidence with horror; I was not able, I was rooted to the spot where I knelt, my head was battered and bowed by this voice that swept over me and withered me like a windstorm. My icy hands no longer held my grandmother's burning ones; I think I unconsciously shoved them from my lips in terror."

Aurore withdraws in silence and encounters Rose, another household servant, who asks if the interview with grandmother is over, to which Aurore responds, "Yes, it's all over forever" and falls to the floor "prey to convulsions of despair." When she regains her composure, she goes downstairs to lunch. "My exercise books were given back to me, I pretended to work, but my tears had been so acrid and burning that my eyelids were raw; I had a terrible migraine; I was not thinking anymore, I was not living, I was indifferent to everything. I no longer knew if I loved or hated anyone. I no longer felt impassioned over anyone or resentful toward anyone. I had what seemed like an enormous burn inside me and a searing emptiness where my heart should have been. I was aware only of a kind of contempt for the whole universe and a bitter disdain for life as it would henceforth be for me; I no longer loved myself. If my mother was detestable and hateful, then I, the fruit of her womb, was, too."

Time goes by and Aurore resumes her routines, but something irrevocable has been lost:

> In effect, I no longer made any plans, I gave up my sweet reveries. No more novel, no more daydreams. Corambé was silent.[3]
> I lived like a machine. The harm was deeper than anyone thought. Being loving, I still loved others. Still a child, I took pleasure in life. But as I have said, I did not like myself anymore, I no longer cared about myself at all. . . . From then on I glimpsed only future struggles against public opinion of which I had never dreamed, and some unimaginably sad dangers whose nature they assumed I would guess, but being simple and incurious by nature, I guessed nothing at all. Besides, just as I am active in pursuing what appeals to my instincts, so am I lazy in confronting what is hostile to them, and I did not seek to solve the enigma of the sphinx; but something terrible seemed to be in store for me if I persisted in leaving my grandmother, and that something, without making me afraid, did take away the charm of utter confidence I had had in building my castles in Spain.

Sand elaborated on the enigma of the sphinx: "'It will be worse than poverty,' they told me, 'it will be shame!' 'Shame for what?' I asked myself. 'Will I blush to be my mother's daughter? Oh, if it were only that! They know quite well that I'll have no part of such cowardly shame.'"

What Sand tells us next is the real revelation, in fact the only revelation that is spelled out in the entire scene, but by introducing it with the simple words "I then imagined," Sand deliberately relegates the revelation to the realm of fantasy rather than reality: "I then imagined, without blaming anything in particular, some mysterious connection between my mother and someone else who might exercise unjust or illegitimate power over me. And then I intentionally abstained from thinking about it. 'We'll see soon enough,' I thought. 'They want me to seek answers; I shall not.'"

What sort of mysterious connection could Aurore have been imagining? Madame Dupin's allegations about Sophie's character and conduct may well have raised the question of Maurice Dupin's paternity. By separating Aurore's fantasy, and her attendant fear of some mysterious connection that would bode poorly for her, from the body of her grandmother's revelation and its emotional impact, Sand creates the impression that the truly bad news was that Sophie was a lost woman, rather than the even worse news that Aurore may not have been Maurice Dupin's biological daughter.

In all events, this allegation is never attributed to Madame Dupin, from whom it may well have come. Given her agenda—to shock the recalcitrant Aurore into gratitude and obedience—it makes sense that Madame Dupin would have raised the question of paternity. For if Aurore had, indeed, been fathered by someone other than Maurice Dupin, she would be at risk of losing the social and economic privileges with which she had been raised. Madame Dupin could well have calculated that this disturbing information would give pause to her rebellious granddaughter who had threatened to leave in order to rejoin her mother.

We know that in the aftermath of Maurice Dupin's death, Sophie left Aurore at Nohant, returned to Paris, and took up with the family friend Pierret. Surely Madame Dupin, sensitive to gossip that could taint the family reputation, was aware of this arrangement. And surely Aurore, without necessarily understanding the nature of the relationship, was also aware from visits to her mother in Paris, that she and Pierret were close companions. Among whatever else Madame Dupin revealed, it is conceivable she saw fit to cross the *t*s and dot the *i*s for her young and impressionable granddaughter by telling her that her mother was connected with a man who had been rumored to be her true father. Were Aurore to break with her grandmother and return to her mother's home, Pierret might lend truth to the rumor by identifying himself as her father. Sand chose her words carefully when she described her childhood fantasy. If not the biological daughter of Maurice Dupin, Aurore was, after all, his legal daughter and legitimate heir. Even if someone else proved to be her father, interfering with her legal status as Maurice Dupin's daughter would surely constitute "unjust" and "illegitimate power."

In the wake of Madame Dupin's revelation, it is not surprising that the adolescent Aurore's attitude and behavior did not improve. "They wished to tie me to another aim that they had shown me, from which I had obstinately turned away," Sand explained as she looked back at that painful passage in her youth. "If I must be forced to inherit this château, those sheaves of corn that Deschartres tallies up again and again, this library where nothing amuses me, and that wine cellar where nothing tempts me, it is no great happiness or lovely fortune!"

Aurore's lack of attention to her studies, to her appearance, and to the social graces that Madame Dupin valued so highly called for a solution. Unable to effect the desired changes at Nohant, unwilling to return Aurore to her mother in Paris, and no doubt recalling her own felicitous experience at Saint Cyr, Madame Dupin decided to send her granddaughter to boarding school. At the Convent of the English Augustinians (by then restored to an institution of learning), she hoped Aurore could receive the training that would enable her to take her place in society.

Although Sand's overt attachment to her identity as Maurice Dupin's daughter would remain intact, her covert conviction that this father-daughter relationship may have been a well-constructed and carefully maintained lie haunted her throughout her life. In a letter to her friend Charles Poncy, written when she was thirty-nine, George Sand's expression of belief in who she was is revealing:

> I appear to have been born into the ranks of the aristocracy;
> I'm connected to the people through blood as much as through
> spirit. I never forgot that plebeian blood ran in my veins, and
> those who have invented charming biographies of me, gratu-
> itously making me into a countess or marquise, speaking
> of my paternal great grandfather the Marshal de Saxe and of
> my great great grandfather the king of Poland, have always
> forgotten to mention my mother the walk-on actress, and my
> grandfather who sold birds. . . . And I thank God for having
> this blood that is warmer than theirs in my arteries. I don't
> feel that I have to make logical and philosophical attempts
> to dissociate myself from this caste that I'm biologically less
> connected to than I am to my mother's womb.[4]

Revelation is followed by reclamation as Sand gives out and then takes back a bit of crucial information. Sand's equivocation that she is more connected to her mother's womb than to her father's class intentionally dulls the bluntness of her preceding assertion that she only appears to have been born into aristocracy and that her connection to her father's ancestors is mere biographical invention. The quality of "now you see it, now you don't" in Sand's message is typical of how she dealt with her ambivalence about her identity. For obvious reasons, she wished to preserve the presumption of her biological connection with Maurice Dupin, and at the same time she constantly struggled with the pressure to come clean. Once again, without renouncing her connection with her father, when it came time to write *Story of My Life,* Sand reprised her ambiguous message to Poncy: "One is not only the offspring of one's father, one is also a little, I believe, that of one's mother. It seems to me that the latter is even more the case, and that we are attached to the entrails of the one who gave birth to us in the most immediate, powerful, and sacred way."[5]

CHAPTER SEVEN

Convent and Conversion

Adolescence is an age of candor, courage, and often unreasonable,
but always sincere and spontaneous, devotion; if age gives us experience and judgement, it takes away this early artlessness, which
would make us perfect beings if we could retain it as we acquire
wisdom.

IT WAS A COLD, damp day in January of 1818 when Madame Dupin deposited Aurore at the Convent of the English Augustinians in Paris. If Aurore harbored hopes that her mother would veto the plan, these were soon
dispelled. Sophie touted the advantages and accomplishments that such
an education would afford, leaving Aurore no alternative but submission.
"I was made to don the uniform of purplish serge, my outfits were put
into a trunk, a hack drove us to Rue des Fossés-Saint-Victor, and after we
had waited a few minutes in the parlor, a door connecting to the convent
was opened and then closed behind us. I was cloistered."[1]

While Aurore joined the other girls in a game of prisoner's base,
Madame Dupin toured the buildings and grounds with the director,
Madame Anne-Mary Canning, and tried to persuade her to place Aurore
in the upper class. Based on the spotty nature of her previous education,
however, it was decided that Aurore would be best off in the lower class.
To ease the transition between life at home and at the convent, Madame
Dupin deceived Aurore into believing that at the end of the winter she
would be returning to Nohant. "Meanwhile she's fitting in because she
believes it will only be until my departure," Madame Dupin wrote her
friend Dr. Decerfz. "I'm fooling her until she adjusts."[2]

Before leaving, Madame Dupin finalized an arrangement with the
administration that was eerily reminiscent of one that had long ago affected
her own life: just as her own mother, Marie de Verrières, was barred from
seeing her after the dauphine Marie-Josèphe de Saxe took charge of her

education, Madame Dupin left instructions that Sophie was not to visit Aurore at school. Aurore would retaliate by refusing invitations to join her cousins the Villeneuves (on her grandmother's side) for outings on leave days. Consequently, while other students came and went between the outside world and the convent, Aurore spent the better part of the next two years "behind the cloister grill." When it came time to say good-bye, Madame Dupin broke down in tears, but Aurore punished her grandmother for abandoning her by remaining calm and dry-eyed.

Accustomed as she was to her easy-going schedule at Nohant, it was difficult for Aurore to arise at 6:00 on wintry mornings that were so cold the boarders had to crack ice in the water basin to wash themselves. Finding her way around the complicated physical plant of the convent—its "collection of buildings, courtyards, and gardens, which made it more of a village than a house"—was a struggle, and the classroom to which Aurore reported was especially unsavory: "My first reaction on entering the lower class was painful. About thirty of us were crammed into a small, low-ceilinged room. The walls were covered with a vile yellow paper the color of egg yolks; the ceiling dirty and pealing [sic]; filthy benches, tables, and stools; a wretched stove which smoked; the stench of henhouse mixed with that of coal; an ugly plaster crucifix. This was where we were to spend two-thirds of the day, three-quarters in winter."[3]

Language was another hurdle, since Aurore knew no English when she arrived. The nuns, who were English, Scottish, or Irish, as were some two-thirds of the pensioners, lodgers, and half of the officiating priests, spoke mostly English, which everyone was required to speak during certain hours of the day. Craving acceptance, Aurore applied herself assiduously to the task of learning English. By her second year, with the help of a novice who tutored her for an hour each day, Aurore was reading Shakespeare and Byron in the original.

The Mother Superior reported to Madame Dupin that her granddaughter was like "still waters." Sand filled out her self-portrait: "Yellow, apathetic, silent, I appeared in class as the calmest and the most submissive person."[4] By spring, when Aurore began cultivating the little plot of land that every lower-class student was assigned, the orderly routines of the cloistered world had become familiar and comfortable.

The social life of the convent was as elaborate as its physical plant. The students fell into one of several well-defined groups, or cliques, such as schoolgirls tend to form. There were the well-behaved, devout students, known as the "sages"; an intermediary group called the "beasts," who didn't take sides and remained neutral; and the group with which Aurore became affiliated, known as the "devils": "I had not taken any stand on entering the convent. I was more inclined to docility than revolt. It was obvious to all that I arrived there without ill humor and without grief; I wished nothing more than to submit to the general discipline. But when I saw that this discipline was so stupid in a thousand ways and so nastily administered, I cocked my hat and resolutely enlisted on the side of the 'devils.'"[5]

One particular devil named Gillibrand, "the most striking figure in the lower class and the most eccentric in the whole convent," attracted Aurore's attention. She formed a fast friendship with this big eleven-year-old Irish girl whose "resonant voice, frank, bold face . . . [and] independent and indomitable character had caused her to be given the nickname 'Boy.'" Along with Gillibrand and a band of other devils, Aurore participated in the communal fantasy of liberating an imaginary female prisoner harbored in the subterranean passageways of the convent. On illicit missions in and among the cellars and subcellars of the buildings, the devils explored the hidden nooks and crannies where the phantom figure they pursued might dwell. The passion with which the girls probed the unknown spaces of the convent, the excitement with which they sought to open up mysterious, hidden, and forbidden places cannot be dissociated from the sexual awakening that Aurore and her adolescent companions were undergoing. Although the girls never did find the imaginary victim of convent lore, they managed to discover, among other delights and surprises, that mint cordial was distilled by a svelte and lively Scottish nun named Sister Teresa in a vast laboratory underlying the cells and classrooms.[6]

In *Literary Women*, Ellen Moers observes: "The celebrated chapters of George Sand's *Histoire de ma vie* [*Story of My Life*] where she tells of her school years are a classic of tomboy literature. . . . Far from being repressed by confinement, Sand discovered during her school years the delights of indoor adventure. . . . And it is appropriately in this context that George Sand digresses most substantially to pay tribute to the influence upon her of Ann Radcliffe's fiction."[7]

The director of the lower class at the convent, Miss D., derived sadistic pleasure from humiliating her students and was hated by the younger

girls: "I do not understand why our nuns . . . had placed at the head of
the lower class a person of repulsive appearance, expression, and bearing,
with language and character to match. Fat, dirty, stooped, bigoted, limited,
irascible, strict to the point of being cruel, sly, vindictive, she was, from
the first look, an object for my moral and physical disgust, as she already
was for all my classmates."[8]

Kissing the ground was part of convent discipline, though the nuns
generally looked the other way as the girls kissed their hands and bowed
toward the floor. But "Miss D . . . pushed our faces into the dust, and might
have crushed them if we had resisted." Aurore retaliated by writing satirical letters recounting "the rigors of the D." to her grandmother, "who in
no way preached submission or wheedling and still less, piety." Although
students were permitted the privacy of sealing letters intended for relatives, the Mother Superior became suspicious when she noticed the number of letters Aurore was sending her grandmother. She broke the seals,
discovered the seditious content, and suppressed the letters. When Madame
Dupin found out, she came to her granddaughter's defense and complained
to the administration. Rather than a reprimand, Aurore received the reward
of promotion to the upper class. Convent life began to improve rapidly:
"The upper classroom was very large; there were five or six windows, several of which overlooked the gardens. It was heated by a good fireplace
and a good stove. Besides, it was early spring. The chestnut trees were
about to bloom, their rosy clusters raised up like candelabras. I thought
I was entering paradise."[9]

With membership in the upper class came a room of Aurore's own,
and even though she was given the worst private cell in the convent, a
sparsely furnished, cramped attic space, she was delighted: "The window
had four small, square panes and looked out on a covered drainpipe that
obstructed my view down to the courtyard. But my view of the horizon
was magnificent. From over the tops of the great chestnut trees in the garden I could see part of Paris. Large tracts of nurseries and vegetable gardens extended around the grounds. If not for the blue line of monuments
and houses that formed the horizon, I could have fancied myself not quite
in the country, but in a large village."

With the consent of the Mother Superior, a student could be assigned
a spiritual mother from among the convent's community of nuns. Not yet
thirty and very beautiful and loving, Sister Marie-Alicia Spiring was the

most sought-after nun in the convent. Desperate for a good mother, during her second year Aurore formed an attachment to Sister Spiring and was adopted as her spiritual daughter. "I needed someone to cherish and place in my thoughts above all other beings; to imagine perfection, tranquility, power, and fairness through that being; to venerate an object superior to me, and to give heartfelt, assiduous worship to something like God or Corambé. This something took on the grave and serene features of Marie-Alicia. She was my ideal, my holy love, my chosen mother."[10]

Aurore was allowed to visit Marie-Alicia's cell each evening following prayers in the chapel. Having not yet broken ranks with the devils, Aurore would confess to a series of misdeeds, and Marie-Alicia would reprimand her for her misbehavior. In an imaginary dialogue, Sand re-created the delicious mix of scolding and forgiveness that reenacted with Sister Marie-Alicia the dynamics of her early relationship with her mother. "Then you don't want to reform?" asked Marie-Alicia when once again she saw Aurore wearing the cap that betokened punishment for misconduct. "I can't yet," responded the child. "Then what are you doing here with me?" her spiritual mother inquired. "I came to have you scold me." "Oh, that amuses you?" remarked Marie-Alicia. "That does me good," replied Aurore. "I don't see it at all," her superior retorted. "So much the better." Aurore informed her; "that proves you love me." And to herself she mused, "Here is a mother who loves me for myself and who argues with me."[11]

During Aurore's second winter at the convent, Madame Dupin spent two months in Paris. Sand would later reflect on visits with her grandmother: "My boarding school manners pleased her no more than my country ways had. I was completely unpolished. I was as distracted as ever. The dancing lessons given me by M. Abraham, former teacher of Marie-Antoinette, had not rendered me at all graceful. . . . I still slouched, moved too abruptly, walked too naturally, and could not bear the thought of gloves or deep curtsies. My grandmama would scold me excessively for these vices."[12]

Madame Dupin's disappointment with Aurore's development was fueled by an ulterior motive; at this late season of her own life, she wished to secure her granddaughter's future by finding her an appropriate husband. In spite of her burgeoning sexuality and the womanly body she was beginning to inhabit, Aurore was still a child at heart. A succession of potential suitors was presented, but Aurore's emotional unreadiness foiled any prospects. She resented spending less and less time with her mother and more and more time with the boring contessas through whose good graces her grandmother was hoping to secure a match. Aurore's leave days became a dismal ordeal, and only back in the convent did she regain her cheerful disposition.

In self-defense, during the summer of 1819, Aurore underwent a religious conversion so powerful that it took her away from her friends, from the enticements of deviltry, from play, from food; in short, from all forms of familiar pleasure. "I needed a burning passion. I was fifteen years old," Sand would later explain.[13] But this was far more than the typical adolescent identity crisis. Aurore needed to change the very terms of her existence, to transform herself into someone who neither derived from her mother nor belonged to her grandmother. She needed nothing less than to forge a new self.

Despite her grandmother's Voltairian disdain, Aurore was enthralled by the passion and poetry of *The Lives of the Saints*. At prayer in the chapel one morning, she glimpsed "the bare, white arm of the Christ" in a painting by Titian. "The sparkle of the glass made that fleeting moment blinding." Another painting "depicted Saint Augustine under the fig tree, with the miraculous ray of light within which was written the famous *Tolle, lege* [Take it, read it], the mysterious words that induced Monica's son to open the Gospel." It was this vision that led Aurore to read the Gospel. "I realized my disorderly existence was nearing an end, that I must enter a new phase."[14]

> I was told, "God is within you, He is beating in your heart, He fills your entire being with His divinity; grace is circulating in you with the blood of your veins!" This complete identification with the Divinity made itself felt in me like a miracle. I literally burned like Saint Theresa, I no longer slept or ate, I walked without perceiving my body's movements; I condemned myself to worthless austerities, since I no longer had anything left to sacrifice, alter, or destroy in me. I did not notice the fatigue of my fast. Around my neck I wore a filigree rosary which scratched me and which I thought of as my hair shirt. I felt the drops of my blood as coolness, a pleasant rather than painful sensation. All in all I was living in a trance, my body was numb, it no longer existed.[15]

In "The Lie," Paul Hamburg provides a description of the anorectic symptomatology that Aurore seems to have been exhibiting: "Refusal of food is the end point in a regressive pathway that protests, 'I do not want, I do not demand, I do not need.' Risking physical death is a desperate measure to preserve an authentic self (Boris, 1984). In this view, starvation is at once a negation of desire, an assertion of absolute mastery, and, paradoxically, a statement of authenticity. The symptom rejects desire because there is no space to want anything; it risks everything to refuse the [grand]mother's all encompassing demand for love. The anorexic says, 'I *want* nothing. I want to *be* nothing, to *need* nothing. Only by not wanting and not needing can I be me.'"[16]

To witness the ritual of solitary worship, Aurore secretly followed one of the nuns into the chapel at prayer time. "By entering illegally, I was retaining my devil's prerogative. It seems rather curious that the first time I chose to enter a church on my own, I did so to show my disobedience and derision. . . . By chance, an old hunchbacked tenant went by, so little and deformed that, in the shadows, she seemed more like a witch hurrying off to her sabbath than a wise virgin. 'Let's see,' I said to myself, 'how the little monster writhes on her bench!'"[17]

Suggestive of sexual ecstasy, Sand's description of the nun's religious passion was followed by the observation that "only at an age when human passions are still silent does such a love of Christ pose no danger. Later on, it gives rise to aberrations of feeling and disturbing fantasies." At fifteen, Aurore had no doubt already begun to experience her sexual awakening. Was the extreme asceticism to which she retreated a form of sublimation to relieve guilt over her arousal, her way of suppressing her own "aberrations of feeling and disturbing fantasies"? By now she was painfully aware, via her grandmother's revelations of her mother's life, of the pitfalls of passion. The juxtaposition "more like a witch than a wise virgin" is revealing of Aurore's nascent conflict about sexuality.

In response to the repressive convent regime, Aurore began to express herself in writing: "We were forbidden to walk about in two's; there had to be at least three of us together at a time; we were forbidden to kiss; there was concern over our innocent letter-writing . . . letters often full of tender, naive charm, the kind of letters we were strictly forbidden to write, as if they had been love letters, but which prohibition served only to make more ardent and more frequent. . . . So I began to write."[18] Aurore tried her hand at a novel that told the story of a couple's awakening love. Instead of a typical romance, her tale resolved by the couple's giving themselves not to one another but to God.

Having withdrawn from her peers, Aurore formed an association with a poor, sickly, uneducated sister of twenty-eight named Hélène, whose job was to clean the church and make the beds. "She was ugly, of a common physical type, marked by freckles on a dull ashen complexion." Taking pity on Hélène, whose strength was sapped by consumption, Aurore helped her on her daily round of chores: "At Nohant, aspiring only to become a worker with my mother, I had despised study as being too aristocratic. In the convent, thinking only of becoming a servant with sister Hélène, I despised study as being too worldly."[19] When Hélène assigned Aurore a cell next door to her own and conferred the name of Marie-Augustine on her, Aurore was overjoyed; she had already resolved to become a lay sister like her friend. Aurore tried to teach Hélène French, but her poor native English needed remediation before she could learn another language.

One evening while crossing the garden, Aurore overheard an argument in the Mother Superior's rooms. She recognized Hélène's voice and enough of what was being said to realize that her friend was protesting against some shameful accusation. What could they have in mind, Aurore wondered, and was she somehow involved in the accusation? "Were they making a crime of our sacred friendship?"[20] Hearing Hélène's words of protest turn suddenly to cries, Aurore realized with horror that her friend was being beaten. Later that night when Hélène returned sick and disheveled, her face streaming with tears, Aurore brought her tea and stayed with her until she finally calmed down enough to fall asleep. Condemned for something unpardonable that she had done and for which she was now to be alienated from the rest of the community, Hélène was shunned by the other nuns.

Aurore continued to neglect food and sleep. She became weak and listless and could no longer concentrate on her lessons. Sister Marie-Alicia was alarmed to see a healthy young girl undergo such a radical transformation. Meanwhile, word of Aurore's religious conversion reached Madame Dupin, who was dismayed by this development. She had placed her granddaughter in the Convent of the English Augustinians not to make a nun of her but to provide her with the education and social graces that would prepare her for a brilliant marriage. She complained to the Mother Superior, who promptly called in the Father Confessor.

Abbé Prémord's response was particularly appropriate for the individual he was counseling. Rather than a harsh rebuke, Aurore was given a wise reprieve and was ordered back to play. No longer was she to spend recreation periods prostrating herself in prayer. Instead, she was required to join the other girls in their games. Aurore "quickly realized . . . it is not really difficult to regain the taste for jump ropes and rubber balls."[21] With exercise and exposure to fresh air, she rapidly regained her natural good health and vigor.

Aurore's immersion in religion, so fraught with torment and self-denial, was followed by a flowering of creativity. Her fellow students were the delighted beneficiaries. "My return to merriment was like a resurrection for the upper class. Since my conversion, deviltry had hardly had a wing to flap." She organized a group of friends who constructed a little theater at the back of the classroom, using folding screens for wings. To dodge the convent's prohibition of girls dressing up as men, Aurore came up with a clever scheme: "I made up a Louis XIII costume which reconciled decency with artifice. We gathered our skirts from below, up to mid-calf, to make breeches; we put on our blouses backwards, shifted and fanned them out over crumpled handkerchiefs that we tucked into the front and sleeves, to make doublets."[22]

Although Molière was forbidden reading, Aurore remembered enough of *Le Malade imaginaire* to devise a scenario, minus the love scenes, which would be acceptable to the authorities. The theatrical production of improvisational comedy skits was so successful that the administration invited the lower class to a performance, and the Mother Superior praised Aurore for her lively inventions.

In February 1820, the assassination of the duke de Berry interrupted the school year. News of the Restoration infiltrated the convent, unsettling the cloistered existence of the students and staff. Aurore, still a Bonapartist sympathizer, which made her a liberal amid the conservative mainstream, found her party accused of fomenting the assassination. That spring, as the aristocratic population of the school was shifting toward the Third Estate and daughters of the bourgeoisie were beginning to enroll, Madame Anne-Mary Canning died after forty-nine years at the Con-

vent of the English Augustinians. In the midst of France's political upheaval, preoccupied by her own declining health, Madame Dupin decided
to withdraw Aurore from the convent and take her back to Nohant. Sand
would recall: "That news hit me like a thunderbolt right in the midst of
the most perfect happiness I had ever felt in my life. The convent had become my earthly paradise."[23]

During the years Aurore was away at school, she progressed from despair and self-loathing in the wake of her grandmother's revelation to
consolation and consolidation. The ease with which Aurore rebounded
from her bout of asceticism suggests that her conversion stood for something other than a genuine religious vocation. Indeed, the adolescent Aurore was seeking a way out of her quandary over her uncertain identity,
and her dalliance with religious devotion was an early experiment in self-
transformation. Her initial identification with the devils and her subsequent experiment in self-denial, complete with anorectic symptomatology,
ultimately gave way to her rebirth as a creative leader. Instead of taking
the veil and being renamed Sister So-and-So, Aurore Dupin would ultimately
settle for a secular form of conversion in which she would rename herself George Sand.

CHAPTER EIGHT

Coming of Age

Fate had decreed that on my seventeenth birthday there would
be a lull in external influences and that for almost a whole year
I would belong entirely to myself, in order to become—for better
or for worse—what I would be more or less for the rest of my life.

THE CONVENT OF THE English Augustinians had provided the most
spiritually enriching experience of Aurore's life, and it was with much regret that she packed her bags and bade her friends and beloved mentors
good-bye. As she rolled away from Paris in Madame Dupin's large blue
calèche and headed south to Nohant, neither of them could know that the
ailing dowager would never return to the capital.

Wrenched from her home away from home, the only neutral territory
she had known, Aurore was soon caught up again in the struggle between
her mother and grandmother. No sooner had Aurore arrived at Nohant
than Sophie announced she would not set foot on the property until her
mother-in-law was dead.

But being back at Nohant brought consolation as well as conflict, as
the almost forgotten pleasures of country living came rushing back. The
Berrichon patois was music to Aurore's ears in contrast to the "hissing
nasality" of British speech at the convent.[1] A fresh dress of pink gingham
replaced her purplish serge uniform, and she was once again allowed to
arrange her hair as she pleased. The variety of the Nohant diet—fowl from
the farm, vegetables from the garden, her favorite freshly baked breads
and cakes from the kitchen—whetted her appetite after the austere, strictly
regulated convent fare, and she began to put on some of the weight she
had lost during her period of abstinence. Aurore's bedroom had been
freshly papered and painted, and sleeping late in her familiar four-poster
bed was among the welcome pleasures to which she returned.

Having passed from girlhood to young womanhood in her years away,

Aurore now had a figure that attracted the attention of local friends and neighbors. Deschartres, who had not seen her since her departure for Paris in November 1817, barely recognized her upon her return. The stodgy old tutor began calling her mademoiselle. Aurore's childhood playmates from the neighborhood had changed, too, and many of them now held jobs working for her grandmother. Cadet had become a valet, and Fanchon was shepherd to Nohant's flock of sheep.

During the summer, Madame de Pontcarré and her daughter, Pauline, a pensioner from the convent, visited for several weeks, during which time the girls put on a play to celebrate Madame Dupin's seventy-second birthday. Hippolyte, home on leave from his tour of duty as a hussar sergeant, taught Aurore to straddle a horse and ride like a man. Her favorite mount became the four-year-old Colette, whom she would ride for the next fourteen years.

Pauline and her mother's departure was followed some weeks later by Hippolyte's return to military service. The long, lonely winter that lay ahead, in the company of only Deschartres and her grandmother, provoked in Aurore longing memories of her busy, structured life at the convent amid beloved friends. In February Madame Dupin sustained a serious stroke that left one side of her body paralyzed. Dr. Decerfz was sent for, but nothing could be done. From this point on, Madame Dupin's health rapidly declined. The gloom and idleness of rural winter weighed heavily on her active and industrious sixteen-year-old granddaughter.

To add structure to her life, Aurore developed a routine of activities that sustained her during the long winter. To remedy her physical complaints—she suffered from pain in her extremities and recurring bouts of the rheumatism that had plagued her at the convent—Deschartres prescribed rigorous exercise. "I became accustomed every morning to riding eight or ten leagues in four hours," Sand later recorded, "stopping at a farm sometimes for a bowl of milk on my way to adventure, exploring the countryside at random, going everywhere—even so-called impossible places—and indulging in endless daydreams."[2]

As Aurore's equestrian skills improved, Deschartres assigned her the job of exercising the estate's colts and fillies. Riding provided not only freedom of movement but the freedom to fantasize, which further fertilized Aurore's active imagination and nurtured a mind that would soon produce page upon page of thoughts. "That dreamy galloping, or that total forgetfulness the spectacle of nature affords us while the horse, left to walk at a slow pace, stops to graze at the bushes without our noticing the slow or fast succession of landscapes, some gloomy, some delightful; the absence of purpose; the yielding to time taking flight; the picturesque gatherings of flocks or migratory birds; the soft noise of the water splashing under the horses' hooves—all that is rest or movement, spectacle for the eye or sleep for the soul on a solitary ride, would surround me and suspend my train of thought and the memory of my sorrows."[3]

The remainder of the day was spent reading aloud and sketching by her ailing grandmother's side. Having lost a firm grasp of her native French grammar in the English-speaking environment of the convent, she now applied herself to relearning the rudiments of her own language. When Madame Dupin retired at ten in the evening, Aurore devoted herself to reading and writing until two or three in the morning. The pattern of working from late in the evening until morning would persist throughout her life.[4]

Aurore's primary spiritual preoccupation concerned her relationship to religion. "For me it was a matter of life and death to find out if . . . I would choose life in the world or the voluntary 'death' of the convent." To pass the February evenings, Aurore read, cover to cover, Chateaubriand's *Génie du Christianisme*. This was, she decided, "a work of art and not of doctrine." She reread the copy of *L'Imitation de Jésus-Christ* that her convent mother, Marie-Alicia, had given her, but this time she responded with aversion: "Jean Gerson's catholicism is anti-evangelical and, taken literally, is a doctrine of abominable selfishness . . . [an] absolute annihilation of the intellect and heart with a view toward personal salvation."[5]

These readings were followed by those of such philosophers as Mably, Locke, Condillac, Montesquieu, Bacon, Aristotle, Leibniz, Pascal, and Montaigne; Aurore ignored her grandmother's injunctions—found in marginal notations—to disregard certain passages. After the philosophers came the poets and moralists: La Bruyère, Bossuet, Pope, Milton, Dante, Virgil, and Shakespeare. Jean-Jacques Rousseau was the highlight of her winter's reading: "I was finally to fall under the spell of his touching reason and fervent logic," Sand would recall. A fusion between "liberality of mind and religious feeling" began to forge itself within Aurore's thinking, leading her toward the ideology of progress, the particular bent that her Christian enthusiasm was to follow thereafter: "While still practicing the

[Catholic] religion, still refusing the break from its formulas interpreted in my fashion, I had left, without my least suspecting it, the confines of its orthodoxy. Unknown to myself, I had broken irrevocably with all its social and political conclusions. The spirit of the Church was no longer in me; perhaps it never had been."

Meanwhile, at Madame Dupin's urging, René Vallet de Villeneuve was looking for an appropriate marriage partner for his much younger cousin. To Aurore's horror, he proposed a fifty-year-old general of the Empire, whose face bore a scar from a saber wound. When Aurore balked, her grandmother came to her defense, and the general's offer was declined. The reprieve from marriage was a great relief and provided Aurore with the time she needed for her development. Toward the end of her life, Sand looked back on this welcome respite and told her friend Gustave Flaubert:

> I wasn't more advanced at seventeen years old than when I
> was a child of six, not even, thanks to Deschartres . . . who was
> all contradiction from head to toe, great teaching and lack of
> common sense; thanks to the convent where I was filled with
> God knows what, since no one believed in anything; thanks
> to a pure Restoration environment in which my grandmother,
> a philosopher, but in the process of dying, left this life no
> longer resisting the monarchist trend. I then read Chateau-
> briand and Rousseau, I went from the Gospel to the *Social
> Contract*. I read the history of the Revolution written by the
> faithful, the history of France written by philosophers, and one
> fine day I strung it all together like a light made of two lamps,
> and I had *principles*.[6]

As Madame Dupin's condition declined, Aurore was left increasingly on her own. Free to come and go as she pleased, she struck up a friendship with the youngest son of a family of ten children who lived in the nearby town of La Châtre. Smart and handsome, eighteen-year-old Stéphane Ajasson de Grandsagne was preparing for a career in science. Home for the summer holidays, he was pleased to have an eager companion with whom he could share his impressive knowledge of biology and osteology. The young friends spent hours alone in Aurore's bedroom examining a skeleton of a little girl lent them by a local doctor. Exactly what was going on behind Aurore's closed door Deschartres could not be sure, but chances are the explorations of anatomy went beyond the books.[7] The young couple's blossoming romance aroused uncomfortable feelings in the crotchety old tutor, who came up with the strategy of cross-dressing Aurore. The idea was inspired by an acquaintance of Deschartres, a neighboring count who dressed his daughter as a boy so she could go out and ride freely.

Male dress may have succeeded in suppressing Deschartres' disquieting sense of Aurore's burgeoning sexuality, but it had a disturbing effect on Madame Dupin, whose memory of her beloved son was painfully rekindled by Aurore's masculinized appearance. Consequently, the cross-dressing was reserved for riding and romping out of doors and for times when Aurore was not in her grandmother's presence. It was not long before Aurore's transformation caused a stir among the locals: "My costume . . . was considered an abomination; the study of skeletons, a profanation; hunting, destructive; study, an aberration; and my relationship with young men—all sons of my father's friends, whom I had continued to treat as childhood chums . . . whose hands I shook without blushing or trembling like a lovesick hen—were deemed effrontery, depravity, what have you."[8]

But Aurore was not deterred in her quest for new adventures. She and Stéphane, who had begun dabbling in the occult, one day rode horseback into church, where they pranced around the altar until a frantic priest chased them out. Their use of the host they had snatched from the communion plate as the object of target practice fueled additional gossip.

Besides consorting with Stéphane and other neighborhood companions, Aurore kept up an avid correspondence with friends from school. Her adolescent letters abound with lengthy, spontaneous descriptions of people and places, anecdotes about beloved pets, details of dresses made and worn, rounds of balls, first flirtations, and developing romances. As one friend married and another died prematurely, Aurore began the epistolary chronicle that she would continue for the rest of her life.

Her letter of 21 July 1821 to her convent friend Emilie de Wismes documents Aurore's foray into dressing as a man. From the charming scene she evokes, no doubt generously embellished by its imaginative author, we learn much about Aurore's feelings and motives:

> Since we are very isolated here and in order to hunt and ride
> I dress as a man, (but in a frock-coat, as we sometimes did at
> the convent), my grandmother lets me ride with a man-servant

who follows me on horseback. You mustn't be scandalized by this. It may seem out of place in Angers, but in the heart of the Berry, the few young women who live here do as I do, only I pass for a *gentleman,* which leads to some very interesting blunders. One day, three leagues from here, in a village where no one knows me, I sent my servant and my horses to eat at the first farm, as I usually do, and I went off to sketch an old gothic castle. This activity intrigued the residents who have no conception of drawing: soon a *lady* comes out of the château and offers to buy it, another *young lady* drops me a curtsy while calling me monsieur, unaccustomed to seeing *men of fashion* in *these parts,* the wench blushed and looked at me with *narrowed eyes* while, assuming a gallant demeanor, I contorted myself in bows, which made a very favorable impression. All the while, my servant was plied with questions: Your master has a job?—Yes. He draws plans?—Yes.—Does he travel a lot?—All the time. He's very young?—Yes. Then how did he manage to get a job so soon?—Because he's wealthy. Oh! I get it, he's an important nobleman [lord] appointed by the government to inspect the province.—You've got it. As I came over, everyone tipped their hat. Would *monsieur* the inspector care to taste the local wine? Would *monsieur* the engineer care to see the stables, the wool? Soon they were treating me as if I were a prefect; in a little while I would have become a governor.[9]

The heady experience of passing as a man will, of course, be repeated many times in the life of George Sand, but what we have here is an early glimpse of some of the rewards gleaned by this youthful experiment in cross-dressing. The implication is clear that being, or in this case passing as, a male, opens doors to otherwise inaccessible places.

Aurore sets her scene by emphasizing the isolation in which she dwells as a female. By donning a man's costume—the frock coat, or redingote—which enables her to ride astride, she breaks out of isolation and into what is configured as a social paradise. We are led to understand, in the tongue-and-cheek tone of Aurore's lively narrative, that it is not so much her drawing (a typically female pursuit) that elicits the interest of the neighbors but her appearing to be a man, complete with all the attendant prerogatives: elegance, which is to say social station; freedom to travel, which represents mobility; wealth, which entails power; and a function or occupation, which confers responsibility. Social station, mobility, power, responsibility: the very privileges that being female precludes. Aurore's account of the magical effects of dressing as a man doesn't end here, however. She goes on to demonstrate with obvious delectation the world that opens up to a young man who arouses erotic interest, who is invited to taste the local wine, to inspect the stables, to examine the wool production, and who is treated with respect worthy of a governor. In short, a man takes pleasure and has importance.

The charm and persuasion with which the young author wrote was not lost on Aurore's peer, who was leading a far more conventional life. "I really envy you, dear Aurore, the pleasure of riding horseback through the fields," Emilie de Wismes wrote back. "I torment my sweet papa so that he will get me a horse, because I dream of myself in a cocked cap. I have wrung a promise from him." Instead of riding, however, Emilie had to settle for a more typically female fate: "Meanwhile, I stride through our immense town gardens on foot . . . where I often go to watch."[10] Emilie waits and watches, while her envied friend gets to go and do.

Interwoven with the account of boyish pleasures and activities is a poignant and nostalgic narrative that repeats the motifs of love, rejection, and betrayal established in Aurore's earliest correspondence with her mother. Aurore now writes her friends with the same longing refrain, blaming them when they don't write often enough, beseeching them not to forget her, establishing a pattern, to prevail throughout much of her adult life, of burdening relationships with the unmet need for love incurred in childhood. "Write me more often and always at length," she implores Emilie. "Remember that I know how to love and that when I do, it is neither lukewarm nor indifferent." Venting the passionate, unbounded, unrequited love that she would feel so often throughout her life, Aurore scolds her friend, "Naughty Emilie, I won't forgive you until I receive a letter from you. . . . You made me so many promises! Oh! how much I resent you for that."[11] Where there was love, there would follow betrayal.

Worn down by lack of sleep from the vigil of tending her dying grandmother, Aurore began to experience serious episodes of depression tinged with suicidal thoughts and fantasies. "The temptation was sometimes so alive, so sudden, so strange that I could certainly attest to the fact that I had fallen prey to a kind of madness. It took the form of an obsession and from time to time bordered on monomania. Water especially attracted me as if by some mysterious charm. I no longer walked anywhere except along the river bank, and no longer thinking about finding pleasant spots, I followed it mechanically until I came to a deep place. Then, motionless on the edge, as if held by a magnet, I felt a feverish gaiety in my head as I said to myself, 'How easy it would be. I'd only have to take one step.'"[12]

One day while riding with Deschartres along the banks of the Indre, Aurore was paralyzed with fear at the prospect of crossing the river. Deschartres was taken aback by her atypical behavior; she had crossed many times before and in deeper water. Impatient, he called for Aurore to press on, and she prodded her horse into the water. "But right in the middle of the ford, a dizziness seized me, my heart leaped, my vision blurred, I heard the fatal Yes roaring in my ears. I reined my horse abruptly to the right and found myself in deep water, racked by hysterical laughter."

Sand credited the faithful Colette with saving her life. Caught in deep water and pulled by the current, the sturdy mare made it safely to the nearest shore. Was Aurore's preoccupation with suicide her way of pursuing her beloved father, of trying to reach him by retracing his own steps? It was surely more than coincidence that while galloping across the countryside one day, Aurore took a fall in the same spot where her father had died thirteen years earlier.[13]

Madame Dupin had rallied during the spring and summer but took a critical turn for the worse in the fall. Although she "was lucid for hours at a time, finally, her beautiful intelligence, her beautiful soul were dead." During the night of 26 December 1821, Madame Dupin awakened Aurore, presented to her a knife with a mother-of-pearl handle (a treasured legacy of Maurice Dupin), and uttered auspicious words that would never be forgotten. "You are losing your best friend," she told her granddaughter before lapsing into a coma from which she would never awaken. Sand described her reaction to her grandmother's death as merely "sad but peaceful."[14] At age seventeen, Aurore was on her own.

Sand makes much of Madame Dupin's parting words, which take on added meaning if we consider the possibility that by the time they were spoken, the two women may have shared a secret covenant contracted in the scene of revelation that took place before Aurore's convent years. Blood may be thicker than water, but in its absence, her grandmother may have been suggesting, the love, loyalty, and protection of a best friend is invaluable.

The night before Madame Dupin's burial, Deschartres took Aurore with him to the cemetery where her grandmother's grave had been freshly dug; alongside was the vault that gave easy access to Maurice Dupin's grave. The old tutor, whose grief was never quelled, opened the coffin and removed Maurice's detached skull, bestowed it with a final good-bye kiss, and encouraged Aurore to do the same. Sand reports having felt no revulsion participating in this macabre ritual. Such a remarkable gesture, recorded for posterity, lays claim to an extraordinary connection. Perhaps this was its purpose.

CHAPTER NINE

Pater Semper Incertus Est

I don't feel that I must give rational and philosophical reasons
for detaching myself from the class to which the blood in my veins
connects me less directly than to my mother's womb.

WITH MADAME DUPIN no longer in her way, Sophie descended on Nohant to protest René Vallet de Villeneuve's role as Aurore's guardian, an
arrangement that had been made before Madame Dupin's death. Increasingly vindictive and irrational, Sophie soon whisked Aurore away to Paris.
Mother and daughter took up temporary residence with Aunt Lucie
Maréchal before moving into Madame Dupin's apartment on the elegant
rue Neuve-des-Mathurins. All that Aurore had been able to take with her
from Nohant were a few books, her chambermaid, and her dog.

Now that they were living together, Sophie mounted a virulent attack
on Aurore, based on gossip she had heard about her behavior in La Châtre.
Sand later described what happened: "She held up a sheaf of correspondence . . . the fabrications of monstrous lies and idiotic delusions. . . . The
little town's bits of garbage had taken hold of my mother's impressionable imagination; they had become so ingrained there as to destroy the
simplest kind of reasoning."[1]

It is ironic that La Châtre was the scene of a debacle that had taken
place years before, when Deschartres had banished Sophie Delaborde
from the inn where she was sequestered while Maurice visited his mother
at Nohant. Perhaps Sophie's attack on Aurore was a recycling of the blame
she herself had suffered as a young woman. Sand, however, rationalized
her mother's behavior as the by-product of a difficult and protracted
menopause: "She was unwell. She was going through a crisis, exceptionally
long and painful in her case, but which never diminished her energy,
courage, or irritability. This active being could not cross the threshold of
old age without a terrible struggle. . . . She had to constantly recharge the

restless atmosphere with new turbulence—changing her lodgings, picking a fight or making up with someone or other, spending a few hours in the country and then suddenly hurrying away, dining in one restaurant and then in another, even redoing her wardrobe from top to bottom each week."[2]

Despite Sophie's cruel and irrational behavior, Aurore's filial allegiance was firm. When René warned her that associating with her mother and Pierret, who had become Sophie's companion since Maurice Dupin's death, would undermine her prospects for a good marriage, Aurore chose to remain with her mother. Enraged, René cut off relations with his cousin for the next twenty years.

Against this backdrop, the scene of Sophie's revelation takes place. "I do not know how I got her to open her heart to me," Sand tells us in her autobiography, "but it was then I learned of all the unhappiness in her life." If Sand found her grandmother's confession "without pity or intelligence," she assures us that Sophie's was made "with simplicity and remarkable dignity."

What is striking about this revelation is that Sand scripts her mother's part, attributing to her the words she ostensibly spoke, even though the scene had taken place a quarter of a century earlier and Sand could not possibly have summoned from memory such a verbatim exchange. Indeed, the language that is attributed to Sophie—crisp, precise, romantic, hyperbolic—sounds, not surprisingly, like Sand's.

Sand describes Sophie's revelation as "the counterpart to the confession that I had heard and accepted from my grandmother," and, indeed, this second scene of revelation is Sand's way of responding to her grandmother's earlier accusation that her mother's life contained a deep, dishonorable secret. Sophie's revelation is effectively designed to dispel the "enigma of the sphinx" introduced by Madame Dupin. Béatrice Didier's commentary is instructive:

> It's a matter of responding to what must have been, in more
> or less dissimulated form, the criticisms George Sand's grand-
> mother leveled at this daughter-in-law whom she accepted only
> begrudgingly. The discomfort with the maternal image, exacer-
> bated by the presence of the paternal pseudo-mother, translates
> on the level of the manuscript itself into the abundant erasures

of passages concerning the mother. I cited one such example (Part I, chap. IV) where the autobiographer asks herself if it's actually true that the impoverished Victoire worked in a theater. What we have here is the writer's defense against the grandmother's case, for at the time of writing, George Sand was very connected with people in the theater and had no reason to accuse actresses of semi-prostitution. An erasure is then crossed out; the rehabilitation of the mother is put off until later in the text. But the very hesitations of the writer show her difficulty in directing the maternal image.[3]

Much as Sand had avoided divulging her grandmother's denunciation of her mother, she does the same with regard to Sophie's self-revelation(s). We are told only that Sophie "wished to initiate me into the secrets of all her misfortunes" and that "she told me more than I wanted to know." Apparently, it was also more than Sand wanted her readers to know; we never do learn what those secrets were. In Sand's rendition of Sophie's revelation, we learn only that her mother was accused of malice and of some unspecified crime for which she refused to accept any guilt: "'After all,' [Sophie] recapitulated, sitting up in her bed, so beautiful with her red madras scarf tied around her pale face illuminated by those big black eyes. 'I don't feel guilty for anything. It doesn't seem to me that I have ever knowingly committed a malicious act. . . . My only crime is to have loved. Ah! If I hadn't loved your father, I'd be rich, carefree, and beyond reproach.'"

The most important message Sand delivers is Sophie's contention that her extraordinary and exclusive love for Maurice rendered her faithful not only in his life but even after his death: "'Oh, I can tell you plainly that if, since my widowhood, I have conducted myself properly, it was not to please those who demand of others what they don't practice themselves. It was because I could no longer do otherwise. I have loved only one man in my life, and after I lost him, I no longer cared about anyone or anything.'"

Even though this declaration defies both truth and logic, Sand was apparently committed to believing it. Although Sand had her own doubts as she wrote about her mother and father's love affair and the conditions of her birth, she nonetheless kept reality at bay while romanticizing and idealizing her parents' relationship. To this effect, she told a friend, "From the day she fell in love with my father, her conduct was exemplary," and in *Story of My Life* she corroborated Sophie's assertion of unfailing fidelity: "She was chaste, no matter what people may have said and thought about her, and her morals were beyond reproach."[4]

Accordingly, Sand informs us that in 1802 when Maurice Dupin was appointed aide-de-camp to General Dupont, Sophie left the dress shop in Orléans where she had been working and joined him at his military post in Charleville. "From this moment," Sand maintained, "they virtually never quit each other and regarded themselves as bound together by a tie that led to several children, of which only one survived several years and died, I believe, two years before my birth."[5]

But there are serious gaps and distortions in this account. It's not true that Maurice and Sophie "virtually never quit each other" from this time —Sand herself provides contradictory information elsewhere in her autobiography—but it is useful to say they never left each other's side if one wishes to create the impression that Sophie was unfailingly faithful to Maurice and that the children she bore were necessarily his.[6]

Although Sand contended that her father "couldn't have doubts as far as [Sophie's] devotion and fidelity were concerned," as we have seen, Maurice's letters to Sophie are laced with jealousy and fear of losing her, testifying to his insecurity about her loyalty. Given Sophie's history as the mistress of several men and the apparent ease with which she bounced from her affair with General Collin into Maurice Dupin's arms, she may at some point have been unfaithful to Maurice as well. We know that Sophie managed to siphon off some money from Collin when Maurice was taken prisoner. How, indeed, did she pull this off if not by the obvious exchange of favors that had gained her Collin's support in the past?

By the end of 1803, Maurice had not received his hoped-for promotion. Madame Dupin was pressuring him to resign from the military and return home. But because war with England was growing more likely, and with it the possibility of his advancing in rank, Maurice remained in the army. Sand contradicts her account of Maurice and Sophie's being constantly together from 1802 on, when she reports that Maurice "spent the first months of the Year XII (the last months of 1803)" with his mother. The first months of the Year XII of the Republican (Revolutionary) calendar begin on 22 September 1803. The last months of 1803, according to the Gregorian calendar, conclude on 31 December 1803. Sand's casual parenthetical insertion would logically lead her mid-nineteenth-century reader (accustomed only to the Gregorian calendar, since the Republican, or Revolutionary, calendar was dropped in 1806), to believe that these two periods overlapped, when in fact they leave a gap that includes the month of October.

From Maurice's letters home, Sand would have realized that according to the Gregorian or common calendar, he remained with his military company until sometime around 22 September, when he went on leave, and that he was back with his company in Paris by 21 November. The several months between 22 September and 21 November fall during the period which Sand tells us he spent on leave, separated from Sophie, at home with his mother at Nohant and visiting the spa at Vichy.

Sand had good reason to pay close attention to this particular moment in her parents' lives, for if she was born on 5 July 1804, as she believed at the time she was writing (and even if she was born on 1 July, as she subsequently discovered), Sand would have realized that she must have been conceived in the fall of 1803. She would have been all the more sensitive to this period of gestation in that her son, Maurice, was born on 30 June 1823, just a few days earlier (albeit many years later) than her own birth at full term on 5 July 1804. It would have been natural for Sand to contemplate the similar time frames of the two pregnancies. Counting back nine months, Sand would have realized that she had to have been conceived in October 1803, at which time, according to her father's letters and her own transcription of them, her parents were not together!

Sand's interest in her father's whereabouts before her birth led her to look further than just his correspondence. Sand began writing *Story of My Life* in the fall of 1847. At the beginning of February 1848, after transcribing several hundred pages of her father's letters, Sand wrote her old family friend Gaston (Auguste) Martineau-Deschenez, who was well placed in the administration of the war ministry, requesting a copy of Maurice Dupin's military records, which were released at the end of the same month. Sand also wrote to her cousin René Vallet de Villeneuve with additional questions about her father's activities. "I'm abreast of everything up until 1808," Sand informed René, noting that she was also writing to a Monsieur de Vitrolles, who had been in contact with her father in Paris as early as 1802. Contrary to what Sand led René to believe, she was, after all, interested in information about her father's whereabouts prior to 1808. This is explicitly confirmed in a letter of 18 February to her son, Maurice, pressuring him to pursue the matter of obtaining her father's military records from his uncle Villeneuve who "should be aware of campaigns my father was on between 1804 and 1808. I'm asking only for that. Be sure to ask for the service records, with which one can be *certain* of the essential facts. Quick, quick, and quick."[7]

The Revolution of 1848 brought the composition of *Story of My Life* to a temporary halt, and when Sand took up her pen again in June 1848, by then in possession of her father's military records, she reopened her memoir with a reprisal of her birth: "I was born a legitimate daughter, which might very well not have happened if my father had not resolutely trampled on the prejudices of his family; that too was a portion of happiness, for otherwise my grandmother might not have taken such loving care of me as she later did, and I would have been deprived of the small fund of ideas and knowledge which have been my consolation through the troubles of my life."[8]

It is true that Sand was born a legitimate daughter, which was determined, as we have noted, by Maurice Dupin's marriage to her mother before her birth. Sand dodges the issue of biological paternity and, in a tactical distraction, dwells, instead, on the education she would have been denied had Dupin not married her mother.

"But while I am on the topic, I must mention a fairly bizarre circumstance," Sand continues casually before dropping a bombshell on the subject of her identity: "It was only two or three years ago that I learned with certainty who I was. I do not know what motives or musings inspired several people, who claim to have seen me *born,* to tell me that, at the time, for family reasons easy to surmise in a secret marriage, I was not legally given my true age. According to their version, I would have been born in Madrid in 1802 or 1803, and the birth certificate that bears my name really belonged to another child who was born after me and died shortly thereafter." Sand softens the blow of such dramatic information by a self-effacing generalization about her nature: "It's true that this is just one example of the habitually natural laziness which I bring to everything that concerns me personally and that I could have died without knowing whether I had lived as myself or someone else, if I had not decided to write my life story and go into great depth at the beginning."[9]

Who could these "several people, who claim to have seen [Sand] born," have been? In the French, Sand underlined "qui prétendaient m'avoir *vue naître*," emphasizing the important role of witness that these individuals played. Aunt Lucie and her fiancé, Amand Maréchal, and, according to information provided by Sand, Pierret were all present at her birth. In the next paragraph Sand embellishes the mystery of who bore testimony to this version of her identity: "When they made me this alleged revelation, they assured me that my relatives would not be truthful to me on this point." Who could the relatives have been who would have denied this version of her birth? Clearly, there are two opposing camps involved in this enigmatic scenario, which leads logically to the most obvious conflictual relationship in Sand's life, the one between her mother and grandmother.

What if, for reasons of inner conflict (wanting both to reveal and to suppress the true story of her birth identity), Sand intentionally reversed the roles of witness to her birth and their adversaries, the family member(s) who would have denied their testimony? What if, for example, the person or persons who claimed to have seen Aurore born had not actually witnessed her birth but by virtue of the knowledge they claimed to have about it were, ironically, acting as though they had been on the scene. This could explain why Sand underlined the words "vue naître," a kind of veiled clue to signal the irony of a witness who was not actually there but claims knowledge tantamount to having been there.

"During that period," Sand continues, "I skimmed my father's correspondence with my grandmother, and an incorrectly dated letter, misfiled in the 1803 collection, confirmed me in my error." The period to which Sand refers is the time when the "alleged revelation" took place. One possibility is that the revelation Sand writes about here was part of the scene with her grandmother in 1817, when Aurore was thirteen. Under the circumstances, it would have been logical for Aurore to have secretly perused her grandmother's papers and the correspondence between Madame and Maurice Dupin.

Interestingly, the incorrectly dated letter was misfiled with letters belonging to the year 1803, which, as we have seen, has special significance for George Sand's identity, for to have been born in July 1804, as Sand ultimately discovers, means she was conceived in the fall of 1803. "When the time came to transcribe this correspondence," Sand continues, apparently referring to the present or close past, "and I could examine it more attentively, this letter found its correct place and no longer deceived me." Such a letter has never actually emerged, but the meaning of the absent (perhaps nonexistent) letter is crucial to Sand's self-presentation: "So, in the end, a set of letters of no interest to the reader, but very interesting for my elucidation on this point—letters I had never organized and never read—finally assured me as to my identity. I was indeed born in Paris on July 5, 1804; I am indeed *myself*, in a word, which can only leave me feeling pleased, because there is always something disturbing in having doubts about your name, your age, and your nationality. So I endured these doubts for about fifteen years, unaware that in several old, unexplored drawers I had the wherewithal to dissipate them entirely."[10]

"Of no interest to the reader," indeed! Why would Sand, who thought nothing of subjecting her readers to hundreds of pages of transcribed letters filled with trivia, claim that her readers would have no interest in the documentation of a subject as crucial as her birth and identity? On the one hand, Sand may have fabricated the existence of such a letter to clear her contested identity of controversy. On the other hand, if the letter existed, it may have undermined the version of her identity that she wished to promote, in which case she would have chosen to suppress it. In any event, by Sand's own account, based on the transcription of her father's letters and her research into his military records, Maurice Dupin could not have been her biological father.

PART THREE MARRIAGE, MOTHERHOOD, AND MISGIVINGS

CHAPTER TEN

Marriage and Motherhood

If destiny had made me pass immediately from my grandmother's control to that of a husband or the convent, it is possible that, always subject to accepted influences, I would never have become myself.

IN THE SPRING OF 1822, at a dinner party at the home of Aurore's uncle Beaumont, Sophie met an engaging couple named Angèle and James Roëttiers Du Plessis, who invited her and her daughter to visit their country home, a Louis XVI villa at Le Plessis-Picard, near Melun. Enchanted by the lushly landscaped park and the acres of meadows grazed by livestock from a neighbor's farm, Aurore immediately felt at home in the Du Plessis family. The feeling of comfort was reciprocal, and what began as a brief visit turned into an extended stay.

Madame Angèle, twenty-seven and prematurely gray, and seventeen-year-old Aurore took an instant liking to each other. "She looked like a boy without behaving like one, while I had been brought up somewhat like a boy though I didn't look like one. But we had between us that rapport that knew nothing of feminine wiles or vanity." James Du Plessis, a captain in the cavalry, was in his forties and balding, "but his round blue eyes twinkled with wit and merriment, and his entire face expressed the goodness and sincerity of his soul." Of the five Du Plessis daughters, only one of whom had been conventionally raised by James' older brother, four dressed as boys and "rushed and swarmed through the most cheerful and clamorous house" Aurore had ever been in.[1] Angèle and James, whom Aurore soon took to calling mother and father, were a happy, caring couple, and the warmth of their family was irresistible to Aurore, starved as she was for domestic harmony.

The ordeal of her grandmother's illness and death, in addition to years of family conflict, had taken a toll on Aurore. The anorexia-like symptoms she had exhibited at the convent had recently recurred, a sign of the desperate battle she was waging against feelings of helplessness and loss of control:

> I had had several attacks of mute anger that caused me terrible harm, after which I had again felt attracted to suicide. This strange malady took different forms in my imagination. This time I had felt the desire to die of hunger and narrowly missed gratifying this wish in spite of myself, because eating took such an effort of my will that my stomach rejected all food; my throat tightened, nothing would go down, and I could not repress a secret pleasure in telling myself that death by starvation would occur without my having had a hand in it. Thus I was very sick when I went to the Du Plessis family, and my melancholy had turned into a kind of stupor. The succession of emotions had perhaps been too much for me at my age.[2]

At the Du Plessis', Aurore was given new clothes, a fine horse, and access to a library and piano, though the most important element of her new home was the acceptance she found there and the chance to linger a bit longer amid the pleasures of her waning childhood:

> My schoolgirl's tastes returned—wild races, laughter for no reason, moving for the love of moving, noise for the sake of noise. Gone were those frantic walks or morbid daydreams of Nohant, those activities into which you throw yourself with frenzy to shake off your grief, that exhaustion in which you would like to lose yourself forever.
>
> It was there that I renounced, once and for all, the dream of the convent. . . . At Le Plessis, I finally understood that I would never be able to live comfortably anywhere but in the fresh air, the open spaces—always the same, if need be, but without constraints on my use of time and without being forced to relinquish the spectacle of the peaceful and poetic outdoors.[3]

Despite the prediction of René's brother, Auguste de Villeneuve, that Aurore's marriage prospects would suffer if she remained with her mother, several respectable offers came her way. Aurore turned them down, however, unwilling "to accept the idea of being asked for in marriage by men who did not know me, had never seen me, and whose only aim, consequently, was to conclude a business transaction."[4]

On a trip with the Du Plessises to Paris, Aurore met the man she would marry while eating ices at Tortoni's after the theater. Angèle caught sight of a "slender young man, rather elegant, with a cheerful face and military bearing." Approaching the group, Colonel Casimir Dudevant seated himself next to Madame Angèle and asked her, in a whisper, who Aurore was. When she introduced Aurore as her daughter, Casimir asked if she was, therefore, his wife, since Madame Angèle had previously promised him the hand of her oldest daughter, Wilfrid. This one, he told Madame Angèle, seems of a more appropriate age. "I accept, if you wish to give her to me," Casimir declared. Several days later, he visited the Du Plessis household and began a casual friendship with Aurore. "He did not court me," Sand reflected later, "which would have endangered our familiarity; it did not even occur to him. An easy camaraderie developed between us, and he would tell Mme. Angèle, who had long been in the habit of calling him her son-in-law, 'Your daughter is a nice fellow,' while I would retort, 'Your son-in-law is a good child.'"[5]

Casimir's prospects were enhanced by the way he approached Aurore directly, gave her time to deliberate, and awaited her decision before authorizing his father to contact her mother with a proposal. This was, of course, a reversal of the courting convention of the times, and this gesture—singularly sensitive and intuitive on Casimir's part—was probably what won him his idealistic bride. By September they were man and wife.

Born on 6 July 1795, and nine years Aurore's senior, Casimir was the illegitimate, or natural, son of Colonel Jean-François Dudevant, a baron of the Empire. Casimir had embarked on a military campaign as a second lieutenant, but when the army was demobilized, he took a law degree in Paris, splitting his time between his father's Paris and country dwellings. As the only child of Colonel Dudevant, Casimir stood to inherit his father's fortune and, according to James Du Plessis, was a very respectable candidate for Aurore's hand. James reassured Aurore, however, that her own fortune was equal to Casimir's, indeed that it would be more considerable for some time, which dispelled her conscientious concern that marriage to Casimir could be construed as materially advantageous to her.

Sophie objected to the marriage and complained that Casimir was

not attractive enough—she took particular exception to his large nose—
and, in a whimsical turn toward snobbery, contrived an obscure objection
to hearsay that Casimir had once worked as a waiter. The contractual
arrangements for the marriage were made, then broken, and then finally
renegotiated. Sophie insisted that Aurore marry under the dotal system,
by which she would retain ownership of the property she brought into
the marriage while relinquishing its income and management to her husband; she would also be legally constrained from selling off any portion
of the property she brought as dowry to the marriage.

Aurore would have liked a different arrangement: "I had urged Casimir
to resist with all his might this conservative property measure which almost always results in the sacrifice of an individual's peace of mind to the
tyrannical immobility of real estate. For nothing in the world would I have
sold the house and garden at Nohant, but certainly a part of the land,
enough to give me an income proportionate to the expenses involved in
maintaining a relatively large residence. I knew that my grandmother had
always been embarrassed by not having ready cash. But my husband had
to concede in the face of my mother's obstinacy."[6] The couple was married
under dotal law on 17 September 1822, first in a civil ceremony and then
in a religious one at the Church of Saint-Louis-d'Antin.

Given her initial reticence about marriage, Aurore may have been
physically as well as emotionally unprepared. The siblinglike quality of
her relationship with Casimir at Le Plessis might have quelled her anxieties
about becoming a wife, misleading her into believing that married life
could continue in the playful vein in which the relationship had begun.
The question of Aurore's sexual initiation is often addressed from the
point of view of a letter Sand wrote years later to Hippolyte on the occasion
of his daughter's marriage: "Make sure that your son-in-law doesn't brutalize
your daughter on their wedding night," Sand admonished her half brother.
"There is nothing as awful as the horror, pain, and disgust of a poor young
girl without experience who gets raped by a brute."[7]

Biographers have tended to read into this warning a gloss on Aurore's
own wedding night, but the abundant expression of youthful, romantic
love to which Aurore gives vent in her early letters to her husband belies
the likelihood that Casimir was initially a brutal or blundering lover. Nonetheless, something does not ring quite right. From the beginning of their
marriage, Casimir spent more time away from Aurore than with her, ap-

Monsieur and Madame Dudevant. Sketch by François Biard.
(Courtesy C. O. Darré, Musée George Sand, La Châtre)

parently preferring to hunt, play cards, drink, and keep company with
other women. Perhaps his young bride was not the sexually responsive
wife and lover he had hoped for. Or possibly he had not chosen her for
this role, in which he continued to cast other players.

The Dudevants spent the winter of 1822–23 at Nohant, where the
snow-covered countryside remained in a deep freeze for weeks. In mid-
December, Aurore wrote her friend Jane Bazouin, announcing that she
was nearly three months pregnant. In spite of the frigid weather, Casimir
spent his days hunting, leaving his newly pregnant wife to tend to the
baby's layette. It would have been good to have her mother's love and support, but Sophie, further embittered by Aurore's marriage, was hostile and
accusatory: "You were married, my daughter, the day your Father was laid
to rest and you celebrated on his holiday, the Sunday of Saint Maurice,
and I believe that your grieving mother was far from your thoughts. Try

to be a better wife, sister, and Mother someday since you are not a good daughter."[8]

By the end of January, Aurore reassured Emilie de Wismes that she was in good health and high spirits, tolerating her condition with minimal discomfort. "I assure you, dear friend, that the inconvenience is not considerable and that there is no sweeter suffering than that which brings a baby." But all was not well, because sometime before 7 February, Aurore was confined to her bed. "They feared that I could miscarry," she wrote Jane Bazouin, "and I couldn't console myself at the thought of giving up becoming a mother. I stayed in bed for a whole month and took a long time regaining my strength, which I had completely lost."[9]

In her autobiography, Sand notes that this "was the first time I had ever been imprisoned for reasons of health" and describes the diversion she devised to relieve the boredom of her confinement:

> The snow was so thick and stayed on the ground for so long
> that the birds were dying of hunger, and allowed themselves
> to be taken in the hand. All kinds were brought to me. My bed
> was covered with a green cloth, fir branches were tied to the
> bedposts, and I lived in this bower, surrounded by chaffinches,
> robins, greenfinches, and sparrows who, suddenly tamed by
> warmth and food, would come to eat out of my hands and re-
> covered from their apathy, they would fly about the room, gaily
> at first, then anxiously, and then I would have the windows
> opened for them. . . . After several hours or days of intimacy
> with me (that would vary according to the species of bird and
> the amount of suffering each had undergone), they would
> demand their liberty.[10]

In spite of her euphoria about being pregnant, Aurore was apparently experiencing misgivings about her marriage. To Emilie, who was considering the prospect of her own marriage with consternation, Aurore acknowledged, "I admit that the conflicts engendered by different tastes and personalities are all too real in most marriages." Aurore's view of wifely obligation was altogether conventional: "When two people marry, one person must give oneself up, abnegate not only one's will but even one's opinions; someone must assume the role of seeing with the eyes of the other, of loving what he loves, etc. . . . What an inexhaustible source of happiness, when you obey in this way the person you love! Each privation is a new pleasure. You sacrifice simultaneously to God and to conjugal love, and you fulfill your obligations and find happiness at the same time. All that remains is to ask yourself if it's up to the man or the woman to adapt to the ways of the other, and since men are all-powerful and are incapable of such attachment, it is we who have to bow down in obedience."[11]

When her pregnancy was close to term, Casimir took Aurore to Paris, where they rented rooms at the Hôtel de Florence on rue Neuve-des-Mathurins, and on 30 June 1823, Aurore gave birth to a healthy baby boy they named Maurice, for her beloved father: "It was the most beautiful moment of my life, when after an hour of deep sleep which followed the terrible pains of that ordeal, I saw, on waking, the little being asleep on my pillow."[12]

Motherhood initially fortified Aurore's attachment to her husband. The family remained in Paris, and in July, during Casimir's first extended absence following the birth, Aurore wrote him: "How sad it is, my good little angel, my dear love, to write you instead of speaking with you, no longer to have you near me, and to think that this is only the first day. How long it seems to me, and how alone I feel! I hope you won't leave me often, because that hurts me very much and I won't get used to it." About the new baby, Aurore added: "I love him even better if that's possible since I no longer have anyone but him to console me." She implored Casimir to write often, to give details of his trip and of his arrival at Nohant, to reassure her of his unending love. "As for me," she wrote pathetically, "I saw no one today, I have nothing new to tell you." In closing, she wished Casimir good night and, reinforcing the impression of a lonely, isolated, and dependent wife held "hostage in the home," announced, "I'm going to bed all by myself and will cry myself to sleep."[13]

In November, Casimir again left for Nohant, leaving Aurore in Paris with the baby and a gift of some birds. Aurore wrote Casimir that the birds had almost escaped one day when someone left the windows open during her absence and that she was now keeping them in a beautiful cage. The image of the caged birds is ominous. The lengthy, beseeching letters to Casimir continued, begging him to return, expressing anguished concern over his well-being, reinvoking Aurore's early childhood relationship with her absent mother, as well as the correspondence between Maurice Dupin and his mother and wife.

Aurore's concern for her husband sometimes reached comic proportions. No doubt recycling her grandmother's and mother's fears about
Maurice Dupin's well-being during military campaigns, when Casimir
caught cold or took a minor fall, Aurore reacted as though he had been
wounded in battle: "Take good care of yourself, be wary of accidents, you
left so sad and with such ominous thoughts that I won't sleep well until
your return. I pray God for you and recommend you to Him with all my
heart and soul."[14]

There seems to be more wishfulness than reality in her fervent feelings
for this man whom she barely knows and who hardly seems worthy of
generating this degree of passion. Because her own parents were wed just
a month before her birth, Aurore was a significant part of their married
life from the beginning. The love nest she attempts to create with Casimir
is doubtless what she imagines her parents' early married life to have
been. Despite his frequent absences, Casimir is depicted in Aurore's correspondence as an attentive and devoted father to Maurice, much as George
Sand would later depict, in reconstructed letters between her parents, her
father's attachment to her.

In late November, Aurore and Maurice returned to Nohant, but things
were not as she had left them. Under Casimir's management, Nohant had
undergone many changes. In spite of some improvements—"there was
more order and less abuse among the servants; the rooms were better
kept, the paths straighter, the courtyard more spacious; the dead trees had
been burned"—Aurore was deeply disappointed. "Practically a whole new
interior foretold a future where nothing of my past joys and sorrows would
fit."[15] She missed the out-of-service horses that had been sold and the old
dogs that Casimir had had killed, especially her pet dog, Phanor.

Aurore nonetheless persisted in idealizing her marriage. In November
she wrote Emilie: "My dear Casimir is the busiest of men, he's forever
coming in, going out, singing, playing with his child; I can barely manage
to get in an hour or two of reading in the evening. But I read somewhere
that in order to be perfectly in love one has to have hearts and beliefs that
match, with opposite tastes and habits. I'm inclined to believe it, and yet
I don't know if I could love my husband more if he were a poet or a musi-
cian. I don't think it would be possible for me."[16] (Aurore could not yet
have imagined that one day in her future life as George Sand she would
fall in love with Alfred de Musset and Frédéric Chopin.)

Slowly, however, the deficiencies of her marriage effected a shift in her feelings. Taking consolation in motherhood, Aurore began to transfer her attachment from Casimir to her son. Still nursing in January, Aurore received a letter from Sophie advising her to curb her maternal zeal: "I think you'd do better, my dear daughter, if you only offered the breast once a night, or not at all, but three times during the day. In the morning your milk is well restored, after dinner take time to digest before going to bed by nine p.m." To Emilie, Aurore confided, "If you could only know how much we are the idolater and the slave of our child," and in her future novel *Mademoiselle Merquem* (1867) George Sand would still give voice to the belief that "woman is born to become a mother. . . . It is in vain that she avoids marriage and abstains from creating a family, for everything is family for her."[17]

By spring of 1824, Aurore was deeply depressed. At breakfast one morning with Casimir, with no particular preamble, she burst into uncontrollable tears. Blaming external circumstances—the tedious life in the Berry—the couple decided that a change of scene was in order, and arrangements were made to spend the summer at Le Plessis. It was good to be back in the company of spirited young people, and Sand would later observe that her nature, since childhood at Nohant and adolescence at the convent, alternated "repeatedly between withdrawn solitude and utter giddiness."[18] At Le Plessis the giddiness returned, but the reprieve was short-lived, and problems within the marriage became more pronounced. Casimir began treating Aurore disdainfully in front of others and intimidating her into succumbing to his will and authority.

As the Du Plessis family prepared for winter in Paris, the Dudevants decided to rent a house outside the capital at Ormesson rather than return to Nohant. "Probably," Sand later reflected, "we were afraid of finding ourselves alone face to face again, with totally different inclinations and characters which could not interrelate."[19] Although the house was not attractive, the surrounding park was lovely. While Maurice played on the grounds, Aurore sat on a bench reading Montaigne's *Essais*. Aunt Lucie and Clotilde were frequent visitors, providing Aurore with much-needed support during Casimir's many absences.

In October, as Charles X succeeded Louis XVIII, the country took up mourning in a nostalgic display of loyalty to the Bourbon dynasty. Aurore, Casimir, and a group of friends attended the lengthy funeral service at

Saint-Denis. A boring oration accompanied by a two-hour-long anthem held the audience in the church hostage from eight in the morning until four in the afternoon. A pageant of princes filed by, bowing and kneeling in tribute to the departed king and his successor in what Sand later described as an "enigmatic pantomime" whose meaning would have required a handbook explaining each movement.[20] The dramatic high point occurred as the heavy lead casket was being lowered into the vault. Amid drum rolls and claps of cymbals, the ropes broke, and the pallbearers lost their footing and were nearly dragged down and crushed. Hungry and tired, some spectators fainted; others wept.

In general, Aurore felt exhausted, and the depression from which she had suffered in the spring before rejoining the Du Plessis family returned in full force. The gardener was becoming increasingly cranky about Maurice's trampling on the lawns at Ormesson, and the Dudevants decided to re-locate to a small, furnished apartment in Paris on rue du Faubourg Saint-Honoré.

Among the first things Aurore did upon her arrival in Paris was to visit her Jesuit confessor, Abbé Prémord, who had helped her through her spiritual crisis at school. Their meeting led her to take retreat at the English convent, where Sister Marie-Alicia offered Aurore support in her new role as a mother and gave permission for Maurice to join her at the convent. The tiny child was passed through a revolving passage used for delivering parcels and was joyously received by everyone, with the exception of Sister Hélène, who had grown angry and bitter in the time since Aurore had left the school. "All is deception and vanity outside the love of the Lord," she told her former friend and ally. "This precious infant is only a puff of air. To give him your heart is to write on sand."[21] Sister Hélène's hostility did not stop there. She pronounced Maurice's high color and his slight cough from a cold likely indications of consumption; thoroughly unsettled by these remarks, Aurore fled with her son, to return only briefly, and by her-self, to bid her beloved mentors good-bye.

CHAPTER ELEVEN

Passion in the Pyrenees

Monsieur hunts with a passion. He kills antelopes and eagles. He gets up at two in the morning and comes back at nightfall. His wife complains of his absence. He does not appear to foresee that a time may come when she will welcome it.

FOR AURORE'S TWENTY-FIRST birthday, the Dudevants headed south in a mail coach to join Jane and Aimée Bazouin, friends from the convent. In response to Aurore's emotional and physical distress, the Bazouin sisters, on a visit to Nohant en route to the Pyrenees, had suggested that she join them on holiday at Cauterets and Bagnères. Before leaving, Aurore wrote her mother, recalling their difficult journey to Spain when she was four years old. "We're going to take a little trip of 140 leagues in one stretch. That's nothing for you who go to Spain the way one goes to Vincennes, but it's a lot for Maurice who will be two tomorrow."[1] You may have been thoughtless about my welfare as a child, Aurore seems to be saying, but not I with my own child. Far from languishing as Sister Hélène had cruelly predicted, Maurice was a happy, robust toddler.

In her letter to Sophie, Aurore inserted a casual reference to her fear of being consumptive: "As for me, I'm fine except for a residual cough and a little spitting of blood now and then." In her autobiography, Sand elaborated: "I was quite unhappy. . . . Besides, I was ill, though perhaps less so than I appeared. I had a persistent cough, frequent palpitations, and some symptoms of consumption. But I have often had a recurrence of this problem, which has always taken care of itself and which I have been obliged to attribute to nerves. At the time of my story I did not think I was nervous, I thought I was consumptive."[2]

On the trip south, Casimir complained about the discomforts of long-distance coach travel. "The traveling bores him; he wants to be there already," Aurore recorded in a journal she was keeping. While passing through Périgueux, Casimir's temper flared, and Aurore took off on foot, wandering in tears through the town's ancient streets before returning to the coach. Despite Casimir's bad mood, the journey brought unexpected excitement: "At last we entered the Pyrenees. Surprise and admiration nearly overwhelmed me. Of these I had only a vague memory which is now reawakening and being filled in; but neither the memory nor my imagination prepared me for the emotions I felt."[3]

As the Dudevants' coach rolled into Cauterets, ten miles north of the Spanish border, the Bazouin sisters were posted on the side of the road, eagerly awaiting Aurore's arrival. "The accommodations are primitively simple and exorbitantly expensive," she recorded in her journal. "The little town, or rather hamlet, is built entirely of unpolished marble. The streams are crystal clear; everything is clean, repaired after each thaw; and the town is full of rather unpleasant society people." The natural beauty of the environment raised Aurore's spirits, and she began to recover her energy for adventure. The Dudevants joined a climbing expedition, and equipped with ropes and ties, Aurore demonstrated impressive skill as she scrambled up the perilous terrain. "The guide told us as we left that for many years he had led foreigners on the Espeluches," she boasted to her mother, "but no woman had scaled the second pitch."[4] Aurore had gained the distinction of being the first.

She soon found an ideal companion in twenty-eight-year-old Zoé Leroy, the daughter of a wealthy Bordeaux wine merchant. The Bazouin sisters disapproved of the rebellious streak that the friendship brought out in Aurore, who chose riding and hiking expeditions with Zoé over the cures and treatments offered at the hotel. While Casimir hunted, Aurore and Zoé explored Luz and Bagnères, discovering snowfields and waterfalls and the haunts of wild bears. The Bazouin sisters found further cause for disapproval when Aurore made the acquaintance of Zoé's young male friend Aurélien de Sèze, a magistrate of the Bordeaux court.

Five years older than Aurore, slim and elegant with dark wavy hair and delicate features, Aurélien was vacationing at Cauterets in the company of his fiancée, Laure Le Hoult, and her family, though this did not prevent the handsome young lawyer from flirting with Aurore. A passionate friendship developed. For his part, Aurélien found in Aurore the spiritual and intellectual peer that his fiancée could never be. For her part, Aurore found herself able to share thoughts and feelings that Casimir could never have understood.

As prelude to his declaration of love, while boating on the Lac de Gaube, Aurélien carved the letters A-U-R into the side of the boat and pointed out the coincidence that these were the first three letters of both of their names. Aurélien took Aurore's lack of response as rejection and withdrew for the next three days. Aurore was desperate to retain Aurélien's affection and confided to Zoé that if he demanded more (meaning physical consummation), she would be willing to give herself to him. When she learned that Aurélien and his fiancée were headed to Gavarnie, she rounded up Casimir and organized their own expedition to the same destination. At a ball in Gavarnie, Aurélien and Aurore managed to steal off by themselves. Aurélien promised he would not pressure her physically, though Aurore would long remember his kissing her neck before they parted. At the end of August they said their good-byes at the grotto of Lourdes, vowing a chaste and eternal love. Soon after, Aurore and Casimir headed to his native Guillery.

The sight of the sandy Gascon countryside dotted with pine and cork oaks and of the modest tiled "shooting-box" of a house in which Casimir's father, the baron Dudevant, lived was sobering. The father and son were constantly off hunting, leaving Aurore on her own. The rich diet of stuffed fowls and foie gras was hard on Aurore's sensitive stomach. But Aurore's mind and heart were brimming with the excitement of her passionate friendship with Aurélien, and she spent the fall conducting the correspondence with Aurélien and Zoé that would soon fill the several hundred pages of *Le Roman d'Aurore Dudevant et d'Aurélien de Sèze*.

This early epistolary foray into autobiography included poignant descriptions of Aurore's childhood, with special emphasis on her emotional deprivation. Characterizing her mother as "persecutor" and herself as "victim," Aurore wrote (in a letter to Aurélien contained within the novel), "I never go back over these causes for resentment. I never tell them to anyone, and until now I didn't believe in the saying that we feel better when we talk about our problems." Indeed, she continued to talk about her problems and made the important discovery that this brought relief: "But to confide my life in you is like taking waters of forgetfulness. I feel that in storing these old memories in your heart I never need to bring them up again or feel bitter about them." Along with reflections on childhood,

Aurore included romantic recapitulations, inspired by Rousseau's *La Nouvelle Héloise* and Madame de La Fayette's *La Princesse de Clèves*, of her chaste but passionate love affair with Aurélien.[5]

In October, Zoé invited Aurore and Casimir to her home in La Brède. When the Dudevants stopped at Bordeaux, Aurélien visited them at their hotel. Casimir stepped out of the room momentarily, and when he returned he discovered Aurore with her cheek pressed against Aurélien's shoulder. Aurore denied any romantic involvement with Aurélien and assured Casimir that she would be faithful to him. Aurore and Aurélien parted after vowing to keep their relationship chaste in order to honor Casimir.

It is tempting to read disingenuousness into Aurore's conduct toward her husband and to characterize Casimir's behavior as boorish and insensitive. The reality, however, seems more nuanced. In November, Casimir left Aurore and Maurice at Guillery and returned to oversee the management of Nohant. Stopping over at Périgueux, he wrote his wife an extremely tender letter in which he apologized for the terrible scene he had caused the summer before as they passed through this town: "So far this has been the worst, saddest trip of my life. . . . I am sadder than ever, this area reminds me of such a painful memory that I can't help but share it with you. . . . Oh, my good friend, how miserable this memory makes me! I wish I could tear it from my thoughts, but I cannot; I recall it almost with pleasure so that it will absolve me of guilt! With all my heart I curse the peevish person who made you so unhappy on that miserable day, I ask for your forgiveness, my good angel, I will improve myself, I will do all in my power to be worthy of you."[6]

The following morning, not having received her husband's note, Aurore wrote him: "Even though you haven't been gone very long, my dear, my good friend, I wish to write you. . . . I cry, I pray to God for you, I feel so lonely. I've become so used to having you care for me. Oh my friend, I can tell you with assurance, with confidence, that the idea of your sorrow, of the hurt that I've caused you, hurts me, too, and how I can think of nothing else."[7]

It appears that they were both trying to save the marriage. If Casimir was willing to assume responsibility for alienating the affections of his wife before their arrival in Cauterets, despite her relationship with Aurélien, Aurore reassured Casimir that she still loved him and wanted to remain faithful to him. To this effect, Aurore set about writing Casimir an elaborate, eighteen-page letter while he was at Nohant. In it she not only confessed, by way of expiation, her affection for Aurélien but exposed problems that had eroded her relationship with Casimir and proposed a plan to rehabilitate their marriage. However naive and misguided the proposal may have been, the sincerity of her effort cannot be doubted.

Unlike the earlier whitewashed accounts of her marriage addressed to Jane Bazouin and Emilie de Wismes, Aurore now delved into the painful incompatibilities that riddled her marriage: "I saw that you didn't like music and I stopped playing because the sound of the piano made you flee," she wrote her husband. "You read only to please me and after several lines you got so bored and tired that the book would fall from your hands. Above all, when we chatted about literature, poetry, or morality, or when you didn't know the authors I was talking to you about you acted as though what I was saying was pure romantic madness."[8]

Aurore explained that her feelings for Aurélien were due to the emotional deprivations of her marriage: "We had no homelife," she blamed Casimir, "none of the gentle fireside conversation which helps pass the time pleasantly. We didn't understand each other. I couldn't spend an hour at home. I felt so horribly empty that I couldn't keep still. I felt it, I suffered from it, and I wasn't aware of it. I didn't want to make my unhappiness worse. It didn't occur to me to accuse you. You were so good, so considerate."[9]

Acknowledging her husband's essential goodness and generosity, Aurore called her own wants and needs "caprices" and blamed herself: "Don't think, Casimir, that I've forgotten, or that I didn't notice that to satisfy all my whims, you ate thirty thousand francs, half of your dowry. I know that thousands of other husbands would have sooner let me die of misery than to spend their money that way."[10]

To explain the sexual impasse of their marriage, Aurore gave a reason for her loss of physical desire. "Your caresses hurt me. I felt hypocritical reciprocating and you felt I was frigid."[11] In spite of all these problems, Aurore still hoped to salvage the marriage. At the end of this lengthy letter, she drew up a list of eight articles that, if Casimir would agree to them, would save their relationship.

1) They would not go to Bordeaux that winter; the wounds were too fresh and it would be asking too much of Casimir to submit to this. Aurore would go wherever her husband chose.

2) Aurore promised never to write Aurélien in secret. But in exchange, Casimir would allow her to write him once every month or so. Casimir would be allowed to read whatever she wrote.

3) In Paris they would take language lessons together. Casimir would study those subjects that interested Aurore. While Aurore sketched and sewed, Casimir would read aloud to her. She would not require him to like music and would practice her piano while he was out on his walks.

4) She would be allowed to write Zoé; Casimir would be allowed to read what she wrote.

5) If they spent the winter at Nohant, Casimir would read many of the books in its library. He would report to Aurore about their content and meaning. "You'll share your reflections and I'll share mine, all our thoughts and pleasures will be in common."

6) There would be no more anger between them. When Casimir lapsed, Aurore would let him know he was hurting her, and he would be kind to her again. He would forgive her the past, which, after all, would enable him to understand her and make her happy.

7) They would be happy and at peace, preoccupied primarily with Maurice's childhood and future education. Casimir would allow Aurore to speak about Zoé and Aurélien. He would even let her send his fond regards to Aurélien in her letters.

8) So that Aurore could retain hope, some time, some year, Casimir would agree to another trip to Bordeaux.[12]

Casimir took seriously Aurore's letter and the eight articles. From the library shelves at Nohant he took down a copy of Pascal's *Pensées* and wrote Aurore: "I am filled with an infinite regret that laziness has prevented me from reading what, so far as I can see, elevates the mind, and teaches one to think and reason correctly." At the end of December, Aurore spent several days hunting at her uncle Beaumont's château de Buzet, while Casimir visited Bordeaux. He was unprepared for the reports he received of the high esteem in which his wife was held by the Bordelais society. "You enjoy a brilliant reputation here. People speak only about your extraordinary powers of intellect. You may imagine how proud I feel. I positively strut." Armed with an English dictionary and a stockpile of books, he vowed, "I have given up shooting. No more will I go out alone. I am going to spend my life at your side."[13] We do not know how far Casimir got with his reading, but at least he expressed good intentions.

Once the couple reunited at Guillery, however, their relationship further deteriorated. Aurore was impatient with Casimir, finding his jokes foolish and his conversation boring. Casimir suffered from feelings of inadequacy and resented being eclipsed by his wife. Nothing had really changed except for Aurore's growing sense of self-confidence.

In January, Aurore accompanied Casimir to Bordeaux and spent time with Aurélien, who was still in love with her. She took pleasure in her power to ignite his passion by a mere look or a gentle touch. Her feelings for him may not have cooled altogether, but she had gained a measure of self-control since their last desperate meetings. Perhaps writing her feelings in her "novel" based on their love affair had helped. Although her passion gradually began to wane, the relationship would continue to provide grist for its heroine's literary mill. In addition to inspiring *Le Roman d'Aurore Dudevant et d'Aurélien de Sèze,* Aurore's first extramarital fling inspired two of her best-known male protagonists: both Raymond, in *Indiana,* and Octave, in *Jacques,* would be endowed with characteristics reminiscent of Aurélien. Spiritually, Aurélien served as a stepping stone in Aurore's development. He provided the foil against which her deep discontent could be exposed and gave her hope that there could be more to life than the boredom and irritation she experienced with Casimir.

At the news of Colonel Dudevant's sudden death in February 1826, Aurore and Casimir rushed to Guillery. Because Casimir was an illegitimate son, Casimir's stepmother was legally entitled to inherit her deceased husband's entire fortune. Casimir received nothing from this cold and ungenerous woman. Aurore's dowry and the revenues from Nohant would continue to provide the sole support for their marriage.

CHAPTER TWELVE

Ready, Set, Go

I felt that my station in life, my small fortune, my freedom to do nothing, my so-called right to give orders to a certain number of human beings—peasants and domestics; in short, my role as heiress and chatelaine, in spite of its modest proportions and imperceptible significance, was contrary to my taste, my logic, and my abilities.

BY SPRING the Dudevants were settling back into the routines at Nohant. The Berrichon countryside felt lonely and bleak after the liveliness of the south. To relieve the tedium, they entertained a constant stream of visitors. The Du Plessis family came and went, staying for several months during the fall and winter and again in the spring of 1827.

In January, Aurore went to Paris for two weeks to visit family and friends and to attend the theater. After being away for two years, she found the capital cold and impersonal. She missed Nohant and longed for Maurice: "I'm racked with memories of my large, cold rooms, of the mud and mire of my village, of my stables and sties, with my son in tow."[1] She had looked forward to seeing her mother and was disappointed that Sophie was away visiting Caroline in Charleville. Aurore wrote her mother to complain about her latest problems: a persistent cough, sleeplessness, inflammation of her face.

The long winter season passed with the customary round of plays, musicales, and balls and was followed by a welcome return to nature and the out-of-doors: "Gentle springtime, the trees and flowers, the lambs that are born by the hundreds are more agreeable to me than dances and theater," Aurore wrote her friend Jane Bazouin. Maurice's fourth birthday was celebrated on 30 June with regional fanfare: "We made a God-awful racket with clocks and rifles to fete him. I gave a superb feed to the whole commune, and we danced the *bourrée* until two o'clock in the morning in the courtyard. They brought in a huge centerpiece of flowers and then danced all around. It made a round of nearly a hundred people. They made so much noise singing and screaming *Vive Madame* and *vive Maurice,* that my son took fright and began to cry."[2]

Letters flew between Nohant and Paris during this period, with Aurore requesting her purveyor, Louis-Nicolas Caron, and others to send news and goods from the capital. Politics and female fashion competed for her attention: "Please take out a subscription for us to the *Journal des Débats* and the *Petit Courrier des Dames,*" Aurore wrote Caron. To her aunt Madame Gondoüin Saint-Agnan, Aurore sent hats to be styled according to the current vogue. "Could you design one with ribbons, fashionable but very simple and a bit reserved." Although she still conformed with conventional fashion in her attire, Aurore was developing an attraction to a bolder, more masculine style: "A woman arrived here fresh from the *capital* with a dress designed as a man's frock-coat (with a bodice) and a crop trimmed with lace, gold buttons just like a boy's. I'm willing to admit that this style was in poor taste and that it didn't strike my fancy. Nonetheless, I know how anyone well bred must submit blindly and respectfully to the imperatives of fashion, and even if the style were to wear a chamber pot on one's head, I would gladly do it as long as it was clean."[3]

By the very next week Aurore was questioning the social symbolism of the way women dress: "Which leads me to philosophical reflections that I wish to share with you. How come a woman, no matter how superior she is by dint of her good judgment and reason (like you and me, for example), makes it her business to wear skirts and pieces of lace cut in certain ways and slashed with certain colors. Why these rather than those and how to explain the importance we place on this, even though we don't attach to it any idea of coquettishness or vanity?"[4]

Below the surface whirl of activity lay unresolved problems within the Dudevants' marriage. Casimir's good intention of complying with Aurore's required "articles" vanished rapidly when put to the test. In theory, Casimir may have agreed to uphold his end of the intellectual consciousness-raising agreement he struck with his wife, but in practice he was spending less time leading the contemplative life and more time carousing with Aurore's half brother, Hippolyte, who had married Emilie de Villeneuve and was living nearby at the Château de Montgivray.

A welcome distraction from domestic conflict came with the political campaign to defeat Joseph de Villèle's ultra-Royalist local government and

Stéphane Ajasson de Grandsagne. Lithograph by Dévéria.
(Courtesy Bibliothèque nationale de France)

to elect the republican candidate François Duris-Dufresne as deputy of La
Châtre. To be closer to the center of political activity, Casimir and Aurore
rented a house in town, giving dinners and holding balls to entertain
potential supporters of the new regime. Aurore's guest list scandalized
the highly stratified La Châtre society by mixing members from its rank
and file.

Living in La Châtre gave Aurore the chance to rekindle old friendships:
Charles Duvernet, who would cofound with her the journal *L'Eclaireur;* a
law student named Alexis Dutheil; tall, blond, blue-eyed Alphonse Fleury,
nicknamed "the Gaul"; and a poet and amateur botanist, Jules Néraud,

"the Madagascan." Aurore and her troop of male buddies reveled in noisy nightly prowls around town, playing Peeping Tom at lovers' windows, and crashing working-class parties where they danced the bourrée. Sometimes Hippolyte would join in the fun, and on more than one occasion he and Aurore rode into La Châtre by moonlight to serenade the sleeping Dutheil beneath his windows.

Romance was in the air, and it was fun being free and flirting with handsome young men. Having enjoyed the attentions of admirers during her time in the Pyrenees and at Bordeaux, Aurore was now enjoying experimenting with her newfound power to provoke passion. She wrote her aunt in Paris: "I'm beginning to feel the deficit of a suitor. Could you execute this commission for me, as well? As long as you're doing things for me, this shouldn't take too much more trouble. Be good enough, dear Aunt, to choose me one as you would choose for yourself. I don't care whether he's brunette, blond, red headed, grey or black haired; just tell me what's in fashion and send me one according to your taste."[5]

As though in response to Aurore's only half-playful request, an old acquaintance suddenly reappeared in her life. In the fall of 1826, Stéphane Ajasson de Grandsagne, who had been studying in Paris, returned home to La Châtre in poor health. It had been five years since Aurore and Stéphane had engaged in scientific (and probably sexual) explorations behind Aurore's bedroom door. "Partly consumptive, partly crazy," Aurore wrote her friend Zoé, "he spent part of his convalescence here." She lovingly described "his hollow cheeks, his distraught eyes, his stooped figure."[6]

Over the next months, Stéphane's name appeared casually but frequently in Aurore's correspondence, particularly in letters to Casimir, usually as part of a list of friends she was seeing at the same time. "Since you left, my friend, I've hardly had a moment to myself. I saw Stéphane, his brother, Jules Néraud, Dutheil, Charles, and Ursule."[7] Showing an open hand was Aurore's strategy for preventing Casimir from interpreting the relationship with Stéphane as anything more than friendship.

By October 1827, Aurore's list of health complaints had grown to include high fever, chills, facial tics, a sore throat, and palpitations, which were becoming more painful and frequent. With Stéphane's encouragement, Aurore went to Paris in December for a medical consultation. She rented rooms in the furnished Hôtel de Florence, on rue Neuve-des-Mathurins, where she had stayed when Maurice was born. Aurore was seen by Augustin-

Jacob Landré-Beauvais, dean of the prestigious Faculté de Médecine, who examined her thoroughly and prescribed "time" as the best treatment for her ailments. She consulted several other specialists who were equally sanguine about her condition. After reporting the findings to Casimir, she informed him that all the coaches were full and that she couldn't say exactly when she would return to Nohant. She casually inserted news that Stéphane might be joining her on the journey home. After almost three weeks in Paris, Aurore returned with a clean bill of health. She also came home pregnant with her second child, a daughter to be born nine months later, leaving little doubt that Stéphane was the father.[8]

The difference between men's and women's roles in the public realm was beginning to arrest Aurore's attention. To the recently reelected Duris-Dufresne, she wrote a letter of congratulations in which she declared, "I'm too much of a woman (I'm embarrassed to admit) to be an ardent partisan of such and such a doctrine." During the July Revolution, as Charles X abdicated the throne to Louis Philippe, Aurore told her son's tutor, Boucoiran, that although she didn't approve of bloodshed, even in the name of freedom, "You are lucky to be a man; for you, anger saves you from grief."[9]

"If I were a man," Aurore told her friend Charles Meure, a deputy from La Châtre, "I would take the trouble to fully express my republican fancy." But being a woman, Aurore contended, spared her the trouble of applying herself seriously to affairs of state:

> As long as I don't wear a beard, I can amuse myself without
> harm by building castles in my mind. I'm so well identified as
> a person of no importance, weak spirited and a bit nuts, I have
> no fear of influencing people around me or of inducing them
> to make dangerous mistakes. A woman is always a woman,
> and don't think that I am complaining. On the contrary, it's so
> convenient! It's so easy to make a novel out of life, to immerse
> oneself in fantasy, to see life through rose-colored glasses, not
> to have common sense, to wage a campaign at leisure and not
> to go to prison for it, not to pit men of one party against men
> of another, not to have on one's conscience these misgivings
> which must plague important men in the midst of their most
> minor mistakes.

Referring in this same self-effacing letter to "my utopia," Aurore expressed her political credo: "I believe we needed a republic (not a bloody tyranny like what we called a republic in the past) but a more generous constitution, more beneficial to the lower class, less exploitable by the advantaged, a regime which could survive us and be compatible with the way we educate our children, which would not be forcibly overturned and reconstructed by them one day at the same cost that we have just suffered."[10]

Because women were barred from positions of real power, Aurore resorted to fantasies of how she would conduct the business of government. She playfully wrote her aunt Gondoüin Saint-Agnan: "I could see very well that a glorious revolution had taken place, but I saw nothing stable, nothing reassuring for the future. This is why I sacrificed my easy-going activities and the peace and quiet of my country life for my country's welfare. Thus I took hold of the reins of government and began by overthrowing the monarchy with its charter and all that goes with it." Aurore was a pacifist, and her plan included a safe haven for Charles X and his family: the fallen king's choice between exile or retirement in France. The disparity between her idealized version of events and reality was dispiriting: "But how surprised and indignant we were when instead of awaiting our advice and instructions, some random power was authorized to proclaim a king, to resurrect the throne and altar practically on the same foundations as the former throne of Louis XVIII, with the single modification of a flag and a couple of words."[11]

In July 1829, Jane Bazouin, who now bore the married title of Countess de Fenoyl, wrote Aurore, whose charming letters containing descriptions of people and places were the delight of her friends, asking for "a volume in prose or verse, a voyage, a novel if you like."[12] Certainly Jane's commission to write something, *anything*, helped catalyze Aurore's discovery of her literary calling. Her response, dismissive though it appears, reveals how seriously she took her friend's coaxing and how excited she was about the prospect of a formal writing project.

In early November, Aurore responded:

Since you put it in my head to write something for you, my
sweet Jane, I can no longer eat or sleep. I would rather die
of consumption than to break my promise and in the middle
of the anguish this project gives me, I feel more and more

committed to overcoming my difficulty, with the result that
you will be forced to think about me the entire time you
are reading my book. But alas! A book! How to go about it?
Where do I start, especially since I'm in the habit of reading
the endings first! Nevertheless, you give me as much freedom as possible; whether it be a novel or a poem, prose or
verse doesn't matter, you tell me. So here I am comfortably
ensconced, I who have only written two good prose passages
in my life. Specifically, a recipe to make plum pudding and
a laundry list, perfectly precise and well drafted.[13]

In December 1830, while searching for something in her husband's
desk, Aurore came across a sealed package addressed to her. Despite the
notice on the cover in Casimir's hand, "To be opened after my death," she
unsealed it and discovered Casimir's last will and testament, which included
a list of nasty accusations about her wifely shortcomings and betrayals:
"Nothing but curses. He collected all his bad moods and anger toward
me, all his reflections on my *perversity,* all his feelings of disdain for my
character, and he left it for me as a token of his tenderness."[14] Obviously,
Casimir had been keeping score.

Aurore initially reacted by threatening to leave Casimir forever, and
the children as well, but upon reflection she came up with a better plan.
She would spend two three-month sojourns a year in the capital and two
three-month stays at Nohant. Out of the allowance of fifteen thousand
francs that Casimir owed her from her dowry, he would provide her with
the sum of two hundred and fifty francs for each month she spent in Paris.
Cornered by her discovery of his hostile will and testament, Casimir readily
complied with his wife's terms.

Aurore wrote Boucoiran, who had left his post as Maurice's tutor, beseeching him to return to Nohant to take charge of her son's education so
she would be able to leave. Once settled in Paris, Aurore would send for
Solange. But before implementing this ambitious plan, she suffered an
immobilizing bout of rheumatism. "If this miserable condition continues,"
she wrote Charles Duvernet, "I implore you to buy me one of those wheelbarrows that haul paraplegics around in Paris."[15] Aurore's mind was made
up; whatever the obstacles, she would not be daunted.

Aurore spent the new year at Nohant preparing for her move to Paris.

"I went out; I walked a lot during the autumn. I drafted a kind of novel that has never seen the light of day." The result was a heavy tome titled "La Marraine" ("The Godmother"), the work produced in response to Jane's commission. Although her writing efforts had not yet yielded what would be her first published work, they had given her the chance to discover her vocation:

> I realized that I wrote quickly, easily, for a long time without
> fatigue; that my ideas, sleeping sluggishly in my brain, awoke
> and became coherent, through deduction, as the pen ran over
> the pages; that in my life of recollection I had often observed
> and understood rather well the personalities that chance had
> paraded before me, and that, consequently, I knew human na-
> ture well enough to depict it; in short, that of all the small tasks
> of which I was capable, literature, properly speaking, was the
> one that offered me the most chance of success as a profession
> and—let us not mince words—was the way to earn my bread.[16]

Aurore would soon leave her husband and her province, even her children for a time, to establish a career in Paris. She would don a cutaway coat and top hat like her male student companions, let lapse her subscription to the *Petit Courrier des Dames*—and with it her compliance with convention. The time had come to invent another way of life.

CHAPTER THIRTEEN

"Our Motto Is Freedom"

I feel myself being reborn and I see a new destiny opening before me. . . . It's something like a faith to which I will consecrate my whole self. The God has not yet descended upon me, but I'm in the process of building the temple, of purifying my heart and my life.

DURING A COLD SPELL in January 1831, Aurore made the three-day journey from Nohant to Paris, facing the trip by mail coach with adventuresome high spirits; her dream of freedom was coming true. "I arrived without incident and well rested," she reported in her first letter home. "The driver covered me like a mail sack with straw and a sheepskin." The only passenger on the journey, Aurore slept stretched across the back seat of the coach, her head propped on a bag filled with three trussed turkeys en route from the provinces to provision a well-fed family of Parisians. "I was tempted to stash one in my overnight pack," she added in her note, playfully displaying her ravenous appetite for the tempting new tastes and experiences that beckoned her to the capital.[1]

Once in Paris, Aurore briefly occupied Hippolyte's apartment on rue de Seine-Saint-Germain, while looking for work and rooms of her own. Blaming her for being unrealistic about the cost of living in the city, her half brother predicted financial and professional failure. Life in the capital was sweetened, however, by the presence of Aurore's new lover, Jules Sandeau, whom she had met the previous summer while he was home from his law studies in Paris. Handsome and fragile, with thick blond curls, Sandeau at nineteen was seven years younger than Aurore. By February they were living together in Jules' modestly furnished rooms on quai des Grands-Augustins. From their windows Aurore gazed out upon the beautiful Pont-Neuf, the towers of Notre-Dame, and the rows of charming seventeenth-century houses that lined the Ile de la Cité.

As before, she was disappointed that her mother was away in

Charleville visiting Caroline. "I thank you, my dear little Mama, for your obvious desire to see me," she wrote sarcastically. "Don't think for a moment . . . that I feel any jealousy whatever toward my sister," she insisted. "Since you want to give Maurice a gift," the crescendo of anger continued, "I don't dare tell you it would be better to give Oscar two instead."[2] Caroline's son, Oscar, was a year older than Maurice. Just as Sophie had favored Caroline over Aurore in their childhood, she was now repeating the cycle with Oscar and Maurice.

Besides sibling rivalry, Aurore was having other problems. "I was eager to get rid of my provincialism and get into the swim of things, to be *au courant* with ideas and customs. I had an urge to do this; I was curious. Except for the most salient books, I knew nothing of the modern arts; I was especially thirsty for theater." But as eager as Aurore was for new experiences, she was blocked at every turn. She would have liked to read but lacked books. Even if she got hold of some, it was winter and very cold, and she could not afford enough logs to keep the fire in her room going all day long. She tried the Mazarine library, but it, too, was unheated. "I would have been better off working in the towers of Notre-Dame."[3] There was also the practical problem of how to get around Paris inexpensively and efficiently:

> I saw my young friends from Berry, my childhood companions, live in Paris with as little as I, and keep abreast of everything that interested intelligent young people. Literary and political events, the excitement of the theaters and the museums, the clubs and the streets—they saw everything, they went every- where. My legs were as strong as theirs, and so were my good little Berrichon feet, which had learned to walk on bad roads, balancing on thick wooden clogs. But on the pavements of Paris I was like a boat on ice. Delicate footwear cracked in two days; overshoes made me clumsy; I wasn't used to lifting my skirts. I was muddy, tired, runny-nosed, and I saw my shoes and clothing—not to mention the little velvet hats—spattered in the gutters, falling into ruin with frightening rapidity.[4]

And so, like the men with whom she kept company, Aurore took to wearing boots. "With those little iron heels, I felt secure on the sidewalks. I flew from one end of Paris to the other. It seemed to me that I could have made a trip around the world." But in addition to footgear, there was the problem of dress. Aurore recalled Honoré de Balzac's admonition: "You can't be a woman in Paris without an income of twenty-five thousand francs."[5]

The wardrobe a woman needed for public events was far too expensive for Aurore on her limited budget, and so she did as Sophie had done while living on a shoestring in Paris with Maurice: she dressed as a man. After all, hadn't Aurore learned to ride and hunt in a smock and gaiters as a girl? Now she would wear a waistcoat of gray cloth with matching trousers and vest, accessorized by the gray hat and wide wool tie of the first-year student. With her ample dark hair cropped short and covered by a top hat, and her slim, petite figure clad in male garb, Aurore found it easy to pass as a man. The poet Auguste Barbier described her as looking "like a young boy dressed as a woman; she was curious rather than pleasant or good-looking."[6]

For Aurore, it wasn't so much a question of male versus female; crossdressing gave her freedom by making her "invisible." She wrote: "I was no longer a lady, nor was I a 'gentleman.' I was jostled on the sidewalk like a thing that got in the way of busy passers-by. I didn't care; I wasn't busy. No one knew me, no one looked at me, no one gave me a second thought; I was an atom lost in the immense crowds. No one said, as they had at La Châtre, 'There's Madame Aurore, wearing the same hat and dress she always wears'; or as they did at Nohant, 'There goes our lady on her big horse. She must be out of her mind to gallop like that.' In Paris, no one thought anything at all about me; they didn't see me."[7]

The Paris of this era was undergoing rapid expansion owing to an influx of provincials who sought work opportunities as the capital developed commercially. From five hundred thousand inhabitants in 1800, the population had surged to one million by 1840. The *grisettes*, a new class of young women named for the standard gray cloth they wore, were arriving in droves from the provinces to provide labor for the rapidly increasing manufacture of crafts and other fine articles. Living on their own, often in the Latin Quarter, the grisettes formed liaisons with young male students, many of whom were also away from home and family for the first time. Their romances, which rarely led to marriage, became the stuff of stories and novels depicting free love and *la vie de Bohème*.[8]

The concept of Bohemianism first emerged in France in the 1830s

Les Deux Promeneurs. Lithograph by Gavarni. (Courtesy
C. O. Darré, Musée George Sand, La Châtre)

and, according to the historian Jerrold Seigel, was characterized by "the
unlimited right of each person to make his (less often her) personal development and interest the motive of his activity. . . . Bohemianism took shape
by contrast with the image with which it was commonly paired: bourgeois
life. . . . Artists, the young, shady but inventive characters all shared—
with the gypsies whose name they bore—a marginal existence based on
the refusal or inability to take on a stable and limited social identity."[9]

The Bohemians wore what they pleased, lived as they chose, and thought
as they wished without regard for bourgeois conventions. Aurore was to
become a key player on the Bohemian scene. In addition to Sandeau, her
circle of close friends included Gabriel Planet, who assembled a Berrichon

group in Paris and offered a heated space where friends could pay a modest fee to read newspapers; the law student and journalist Félix Pyat; Emile Regnault from Bourges, who was studying medicine; and the passionately republican Alphonse Fleury. They gathered in cafés and in one another's apartments, attended theater, visited museums.

It was obvious from the beginning that to survive, Aurore would have to supplement her modest allowance of 250 francs per month. At first she tried her hand at painting and decorating snuff boxes, but this slow, labor-intensive industry taxed her eyes and could hardly produce enough to generate a living wage. In her future novel *Valentine,* Sand would reflect: "Those of us who know little English, drawing and music, those who paint lacquered boxes, do watercolors on screens, make flowers out of velvet, and twenty other useless things . . . what could we do? Only one in twenty of us have any real expertise."[10]

And so Aurore turned her attention toward the developing literary industry. Culture had begun to occupy a new and privileged place in the French capital. As Paris grew, the middle class expanded in size and wealth, the general public gained literacy, and literature (printed matter of all kinds) was in demand. Serialized novels, the daily *feuilletons* that appeared on the bottom half of the front page, accounted for the growing success of newspapers. A bevy of new journals came into existence, and Aurore would be the beneficiary. In *The Double Life of George Sand, Woman and Writer,* Renée Winegarten comments on this phenomenon: "The moment when Aurore entered the Parisian journalistic scene happened to be a propitious one for women in some respects, and not only on account of the notable growth of popular journalism. From the early eighteenth century onward, greater leisure had encouraged an increase in the number of women readers as well as in the number of authors who catered to them."[11]

But literary success did not come without an early setback. Through her friend the deputy François Duris-Dufresne, she gained an introduction to a colleague in the chamber, a novelist named Auguste-Hilarion Kératry. To this sixty-two-year-old, white-haired gentleman who had written a ridiculous story in which a priest violates a woman who appears to be dead, Aurore presented her fledgling novel, "Aimée," written at Nohant. "Make babies, not books," advised Kératry, whom Stendhal dubbed "the biggest charlatan of all our liberal writers, which is saying quite a lot." Although Sand told this story on herself in her autobiography and may have engaged in the kind of fabrication to which she was inclined, Kératry's reaction to the aspiring young woman writer has become part of the canon of Sand legend. From the bedchamber in which Kératry had received her, with his twenty-five-year-old wife reclining under a pink silk comforter, Aurore ostensibly took her leave after firing off the following retort: "Honestly, sir, take your own advice, if you think it so good."[12]

Aurore turned next to an aristocratic Berrichon friend of the Duvernets named Hyacinthe de Latouche, who had just taken over the satirical journal *Le Figaro*, founded in 1826. Latouche was not impressed with "Aimee," but out of loyalty to his deceased friend Maurice Dupin, he offered Aurore a subeditorship on *Le Figaro*. Latouche's home on quai Malaquais was a wonderful place to work. Aurore enjoyed reporting to a professional office and keeping to a nine-to-five schedule like the other "eaglets" on Latouche's staff. She occupied a cozy spot at a desk near the fireplace and was paid seven francs a column for her work. Aurore toiled over multiple drafts of her articles on the precut sheets of paper that were provided so that the length of the finished piece would conform to the allotted space in the published journal. She was giddy with excitement about her newfound vocation: "A writer must see everything, know everything, laugh at everything," she wrote Boucoiran back at Nohant. "Oh, yes, vive la vie d'artiste! Our motto is *freedom*."[13]

Aurore introduced Jules Sandeau to Latouche, for whom the lovers began collaborating on articles published under the sole signature of J. Sandeau. Aurore had agreed to this anonymity partly in response to family pressure: Casimir's stepmother, the baroness Dudevant, was horrified at the prospect of Aurore's publishing under the family name. Sophie, too, had been critical of Aurore's first published pieces, and so the young writer, caught between two disapproving mothers, sought shelter by hiding her authorial identity behind that of her male companion. But Sandeau was given to fits of depression and laziness, which left Aurore with much of the work. Instead of blaming him or becoming impatient with his procrastination, Aurore tended to mother her young lover.

In addition to *Le Figaro*, Aurore contributed to *La Mode*, a royalist publication headed by Emile de Girardin, to the newly founded *L'Artiste*, and to *La Revue de Paris*. She was learning that in order to write as she pleased one day, she must first comply with the requirements of her editors, however capricious and against her own principles. "Staff writer, junior editor;

that's all I am for the moment," she wrote Boucoiran.[14] But the important thing was honing her skills as an observer, which she did in the cafés and at the theater. In the mornings, when she took her coffee across the street from her apartment at the café Conti by the Pont-Neuf, Aurore delighted in watching the locals read the articles she had contributed the day before, puzzling over the thinly veiled political barbs she had directed at well-known personalities and public figures.

In March, Aurore published an anonymous antigovernment article making fun of the administration's police-state mentality. Louis Philippe, the Citizen King, took personal offense, and *Le Figaro* was seized, though the case was soon dropped and the journal was allowed to continue publication. Aurore's ability to pique the interest of the reading public, as well as to confuse and mystify them, conferred a heady sense of power. She had discovered a forum in which to express the rebellious and seditious streak she had inherited from her mother and had given vent to in her days among the English Augustinians. "I have a goal, a task, I admit it, *a passion*. Writing is a violent, practically indestructible drive; when it takes hold of a feeble mind, it can no longer be stopped."[15] She was, characteristically, only half kidding about the feeble mind. A genuine humility attended Aurore's sense of herself as a writer. She knew she was good and getting better, and so she allowed the passionate drive to express thoughts and feelings, however iconoclastic and outrageous, to take over.

Despite Hippolyte's cynicism about managing on her own, Aurore found ways of working around her limited income. The rent for her modest apartment came to three hundred francs a year. In lieu of a servant, a woman caretaker helped Aurore with her housework for fifteen francs a month. Her evening meal was brought in from a local restaurant for a couple of francs a day, and Aurore washed and ironed her own linen underwear. But the relative impoverishment of her surroundings was more than compensated for by the intellectual and spiritual enrichment of her new way of life.

It was in this modest setting that Aurore first received visits from another of Latouche's protégés, the rising literary star Honoré de Balzac, with whom Aurore and Jules shared readings and discussions of their respective works in progress. "How he used to enjoy talking about his creations, telling them to us in advance, making them up as he talked, reading them as drafts or proofs! Naive and as joyous as a child, he asked advice as if we were all children, not listening to the answers, or using them to fight against it, with his obstinate superiority. He would never lecture; he spoke about and for himself alone. . . . He was so marvelous, so dazzling, so lucid, that we said to ourselves, on our way out, 'Oh yes, he really will have the future he dreams of. He understands too well what he is not, not to make a great personality of himself.' "[16]

In late February, eight-year-old Maurice sent his mother a letter with a drawing. "I received your letter yesterday, my dear little child, with a little artilleryman who doesn't resemble you very much at all. You made his shako practically as high as his whole body."[17] Caught up in her passion for self-improvement, Aurore often lost sight of the fact that Maurice (and subsequently Solange) were young and impressionable and in need of her maternal reassurance more than her critical intervention.

She wrote Boucoiran: "I live only for what concerns Maurice, and the news you send me is all the more tender and dear. . . . Oh yes, I suffer when I am separated from my children. I suffer terribly!" In the very next paragraph, Aurore proclaimed her commitment to her work: "I am more than ever resolved to pursue a literary career, despite the distaste I some-times have for it, despite the days of procrastination and exhaustion that interrupt my work, despite the more than modest life I am leading here, I feel that I'm fulfilling my destiny."[18]

Passionate attachment to her vocation was taking precedence over dedication to her children. Hippolyte's criticism stung all the more for the guilt Aurore felt at being away: "The best thing you have done is your son; he loves you more than anyone in the world. Be careful not to blunt this feeling." Aurore would mask the guilt she felt about leaving the chil-dren by rationalizing her reason for writing: "I have children whom I love more than all the rest, and without the hope of being more useful to them someday with my writer's quill than with a homemaker's needle, I would not leave them for such a long time."[19]

In April, on the eve of her departure for Nohant, Aurore was once again (as on the eve of her departure from Paris three months earlier) im-mobilized by a bout of rheumatism. She wrote young Maurice regretting that her return home would be delayed, revisiting upon her son the trauma of her own childhood separation from her mother. Aurore was apparently suffering as much from ambivalence about forsaking her freedom as she was from whatever physical malady had taken hold.

She wrote Casimir several days later, reporting that she was feeling better and would take an extra day en route home to visit the lovely cathedral town of Bourges and the famous Jacques Coeur palace. With the fervor of a young student whose eyes are just opening onto the wonders of the world, she wrote Emile Regnault at length of the exalted experience of viewing for the first time the great Bourges cathedral. Her spiritual and aesthetic sensibilities having been heightened by her sojourn in Paris, Aurore was awed by the splendors of Saint-Etienne: "Do you realize that your cathedral is one of the most beautiful things in the world? Its interior is the most admirable thing I've seen in my life. . . . It's the essence of romanticism, whereas Notre-Dame is classical. Notre-Dame is to gothic monuments what Chateaubriand is to writers, while S[ain]t Etienne is what Victor Hugo is to poets, or else it's Byron and Hoffman[n], Raphael and Salvator, Rossini and Weber."[20]

Back at Nohant, Aurore was overcome with depression. She expressed joy in her reunion with the children but in little else. In mid-April she wrote her friend Charles Meure, "I get into such bad moods that it's impossible for me to show my face, even to those whom I love most in the world." No sooner had she returned home than she became anxious to be off again for Paris. She confided to her mother: "Everything I'm forced to do has become odious to me, everything I do for myself I do with all my heart. . . . To be out alone and to say to myself, 'I'll dine at four or seven just as I wish; I'll stop by the Luxembourg on my way to the Tuileries, instead of the Champs-Elysées, if I so fancy, that's what I'll do.'"[21]

Sophie continued to level attacks on Aurore. She was acting too independently; she was selfish; she was not paying enough attention to home. Hungry for her mother's understanding and approval, Aurore continued to plead her case: "As far as I'm concerned, my dear Mama, the freedom to think and act is the most important right. If one can join with this the little cares of a family, this freedom is infinitely sweeter, but where do you find that? One way of life always undermines the other." Desperate to justify her own independence, Aurore reminded Sophie of what it was like for *her* to be judged and condemned: "You, my dear Mama, you suffered intolerance, false virtue, hypocrites in your own life. Your beauty, your youth, your independence, your happy and easy-going disposition, how much they were counted against you. . . . A tender and indulgent mother who would have opened her arms to you at each difficulty and said, 'Let them condemn you; I forgive you! Let them malign you; I bless you!' What good she would have done you!" Aurore was asking no more for herself than Sophie took years ago: a pension on which to live and the freedom to pursue her heart's desire. "I ask little for myself, the same pension, the same comfort as you." To this formula Aurore added one crucial ingredient: a writing career that would one day render her self-sufficient. "A thousand *écus* a year and I would have enough, factoring in my love of writing and that my pen already brings in a little revenue."

In May, homesick for Paris and filled with nostalgia, Aurore wrote Emile Regnault: "I always find myself dreaming of Paris with its hazy evenings, its pink clouds that hang over the rooftops, and the pretty, tender green willow trees that surround the bronze statue of old Henri, and those poor little slate-colored pigeons who make their nest in the grotesque old masks on the Pont-Neuf."[22] But for her children, she told Regnault, she would not have traded all this even for the verdant Berrichon countryside.

The problem of raising her children persisted; unwittingly, Aurore was imprinting on their lives the same pattern of distress that she had experienced as a child. Before her departure for Paris in the summer of 1831, eight-year-old Maurice took sick. Aurore's response was cavalier: "Maurice was just ill," she wrote Regnault. "That doesn't mean my departure will be delayed. He's fine today and I hope to leave him in perfect health. Poor child. He's terribly upset."[23] She was apparently oblivious to the connection between Maurice's bouts of illness, which were becoming more frequent, and her comings and goings.

Once in Paris, another piece of the old pattern puzzled its way into her relationship with her son. Despite having been hurt by her mother's preference for Caroline, Aurore was instilling in Maurice seeds of jealousy toward Oscar, Caroline's son. "He's no bigger than you even though he's a year older, but he's much stronger. He's very nice and affectionate." She went on to point out the advantages Maurice had enjoyed, provoking the same guilt that Sophie and her grandmother provoked in her when she complained of being kept away from her mother. Educational advantages were invoked as compensation for maternal deprivation. Oscar "is not as advanced as you," Aurore wrote Maurice. "It's not his fault. You've received much more attention than he has. Take advantage of the position you're in, you will be very glad one day to have gotten an education, and you will have the good fortune to be the pride and joy of your mother."[24]

Maurice was not consoled by these rationalizations. Aurore sent him a policeman's costume, which he failed to acknowledge. She wrote him an angry letter: "It brings me much pain to realize that you have forgotten your poor Mama and that you don't want to take a moment away from your play to write me. I asked you to give me news of your sister; you didn't keep your promise, which is not nice and disturbs me very much."[25]

In addition to scolding Maurice when he didn't do what she wanted, Aurore spared him no account of her own health problems, reversing the roles of parent-as-protector and child-as-protected. "All of yesterday I had the most horrible headache. I didn't get up until five in the evening. If I had had you near me you could have taken care of me." In November she became ill again and wrote Maurice a letter racked with fear and guilt about their separation: "I dreamt that you came to see me in Paris and that you had a horrid, torn-up pair of pants with big patches on the back. I called out after you because I thought you were on the balcony and I was afraid of seeing you fall."[26]

In June, as Aurore prepared for her return to Paris, there were more ailments. "I'm afraid of dying in the next month, I'm really scared," she wrote Regnault. "A migraine, a corn on my foot throw me into real terror." In another letter written the same day, Aurore elaborated on her state of mind and body: "It's chronic, my condition. There is always something wrong, when the rheumatism subsides, shooting pains in my heart start up and then there are the headaches, nerves, infinitely protracted constipation and thousands of random little ailments I can't even count and for which I can't be bothered figuring out the cause."[27]

The unknown cause most likely had to do with Aurore's aggravated emotional state. Her pursuit of freedom had its cost; her elaborate array of symptoms and the manner in which they manifested themselves are persuasive evidence of the conflict in which she was caught. Before each displacement between Nohant and Paris, Aurore would experience physical ailments reminiscent of her traumatized response to her mother's comings and goings when she was a child. And with it all, she was unwittingly passing the torch of her own pain to her child.

In May 1831, Aurore wrote Regnault with the requirements for the apartment he would help her find for her stay in Paris the coming summer: "A single room is not enough. . . . If I only have one, I'll run the risk of being blocked . . . or being caught in *flagrant délit*, embracing little Jules.

I would like to have an exit for letting Jules out at any hour, because my husband could show up I won't say out of the clear blue sky, but from the *diligence,* some day at four in the morning without a place to stay and do me the honor of descending on me."[28]

The note is playful and exhibitionistic, demonstrating not only passion in her relationship with Sandeau but sport as well. In mid-July, Aurore and Jules set up housekeeping in the sixth floor garret of a large corner house near the Pont-Neuf, across from the morgue on quai Saint-Michel. A painting by Corot, "View of the Seine Taken from the Pont-Neuf," done in 1833, immortalizes the modest dwelling, the last house on the right with arches, which no longer exists. The three small rooms with a balcony overlooking Notre-Dame, Saint-Jacques-la-Boucherie, and the Sainte-Chapelle were everything Aurore could have wanted: "I had sky, water, air, swallows, rooftop greenery; I did not feel too much part of modern Paris, which would not have suited my taste nor my resources, but more so in the picturesque and poetic Paris of Victor Hugo, the Paris of the past."[29]

In September, Aurore returned to Nohant and Jules to La Châtre. Gustave Papet stood guard below Aurore's window at Nohant to protect the lovers from being surprised during their late-night trysts. "Your name mixed with our kisses, all our thoughts were of you," she wrote Papet the morning after. "And I believe that your devotion, your presence so close by, your concern for our happiness, added to our pleasure." Half boasting, half titillating, she spared Regnault none of the details of their ecstasy: "And that night that he was there, in my room, in my arms, happy, beat, hugged, bitten, moaning, crying, laughing. I don't think we've ever experienced such heights of pleasure. . . . I'm dumbstruck, I'm covered with bites and blows. I can't stand up. I'm wild with joy. If you were there I would bite you until you bled so you could be part of our ecstasy."[30]

Delirious nights of lovemaking alternated with hard days at work on *Rose and Blanche,* a novel on which Aurore and Jules were collaborating. "When one has not spent the morning working," she wrote Duvernet, "there's no pleasure in being free in the evening." For each of the five volumes of *Rose and Blanche,* its authors would be paid 250 francs, plus an additional 500 francs at the end of three months. Aurore was spending ten and twelve hours at her desk, working through the night until six in the morning. At the end of one week, she had completed the first volume. "Work is the great remedy," she wrote Regnault in September.[31] Jules was

George Sand. After a portrait attributed to Courtois.
(Courtesy C. O. Darré, Musée George Sand, La Châtre)

procrastinating, as usual, and producing very little. The finished novel plots the contrasting course of the lives of two young girls, Rose, who grows up to be an actress, and Blanche, who becomes a nun. After being serialized in various journals, it was published in December 1831 under the joint name J. Sand, suggested by Latouche.

Although *Rose and Blanche* was a popular success, Sophie heartily disapproved. Aurore's response was convenient if cowardly. She disowned her part in producing some of the book's more scintillating passages, attributing them to Jules. She assured her mother that the book on which she was now working, which would become her first independently published novel, *Indiana,* would be different. Aurore confided her true feelings about the former work to Duvernet: "I always have the most beautiful plans in the world, but what I'm doing makes me sick at heart. Blanche and Rose are two stupid creatures, the most distasteful and boring composition I can think of."[32]

Sand's early Russian biographer, Wladimir Karénine, disagrees with her assessment and admires the "marked *realism* of George Sand's first great novel":

> It's very possible that if, from the beginning, George Sand hadn't fallen in with the romantics and hadn't been indoctrinated by de Latouche, Sainte-Beuve and others, but had written from her own inspiration without trying out the 'genre sublime' then in vogue, her talent would have taken an altogether different course and would have been more in the manner of Balzac (even though in the same chapters where she speaks of her foray into a literary vocation she herself says that from the start she and Balzac had understood the difference in their literary aspirations and proclivities: she was given to idealizing in the direction of beauty, and he in the direction of the comic or the ugly).[33]

Jules' health took a bad turn in October while he was still at La Châtre, as he began to exhibit symptoms of consumption. Aurore became fearful that their passion could destroy him: "But to know that this love which devours us is killing him little by little, to know that this delirium of happiness enflames his blood and consumes his life! This thought is horrifying. It has tormented me for a very long time, and now it becomes alarming because it is warranted."[34]

Should they remain apart? she wondered in her letter to Regnault. Would six months away from each other be the reprieve that would restore Jules' health? A few days later Aurore was even more agitated about the presumed consequences of their sexual passion: "To feel him become thin and wasted, dying day by day, and to tell yourself that you are killing him, that your caresses are poison, your love a fire that consumes but does not revive, a fire that destroys, that devours, and leaves only ashes, is a terrifying thought."[35]

They resorted to abstinence for three months; Aurore eventually gave in to Jules' passion when it appeared that withholding was causing him more harm than good. She then became fearful that giving in was worse than resisting. "I'm killing him, and the pleasure that I give him is costing

him his life. I am his *peau de chagrin*."[36] Balzac had just produced his novel
of this name, and apparently Aurore savored lending such literary allure
to her personal life. The high romantic theme that lust could destroy a
lover's health was a commonplace of nineteenth-century passion that
would dot the landscape of Aurore's future love affairs.

As for her own health, Aurore was suffering, too. By winter, which
she and Sandeau were spending in Paris, she was taking vapor of digitalis
for stomach pains that were growing worse. Her pulse was weak and her
tongue discolored, but she was happily hard at work on a novel she was
writing by herself.

At year's end, she wrote Maurice from Paris that ill health would prevent her from being with him for New Year's day. She promised him gifts
upon her eventual return and admonished him to be good, to kiss his sister, and to love his mother in her absence.[37]

CHAPTER FOURTEEN

George Sand Is Born

I ask the support of no one, neither to kill someone for me,
to gather a bouquet, to correct a proof, nor to go with me to the
theater. I go there by myself, as a man, by choice; and when I
want flowers, I go on foot, by myself, to the Alps. . . . If ever I
have a name, it will be entirely of my own making.

THE EXCITEMENT ABOUT Aurore's new novel *Indiana* swept over Paris
in spring 1832, at the same time a massive cholera epidemic struck the
capital. For the next six months the deadly disease raged, claiming more
than 18,000 lives from a population of some 650,000. The epidemic
peaked in April, when more than 860 deaths were recorded in one day.
From her window on quai Saint-Michel, Aurore could see corpses being
loaded onto moving vans, stationed like cabs in public places, waiting to
carry off the dead. She contracted mild symptoms, took hot tea, covered
herself with woolen blankets, and was spared. "Cholera struck some first-
floor apartments in our surrounding neighborhoods," Sand later recorded.
"It spread rapidly, climbing from one landing to the next, in our building.
It carried off six people, and stopped at the door of our garret, as if it dis-
dained such puny prey."[1]

The political situation in Paris was chaotic. On 6 June, during the funeral of General Maximilien Lamarque, the republican opposition to Louis-
Philippe's government made itself felt. Aurore had taken Solange with
her to Paris, and as they strolled in the Luxembourg Gardens, they suddenly
found themselves in the midst of the uprising. Solange was terrified by
the thunderous drum rolls of the charging brigade and the panic that
broke loose all around her. When Solange began to scream, Aurore tried
in vain to calm her and then hastily retreated to the city streets, only to
find that frightened storekeepers had barred their doors against the demon-
stration. Mother and daughter ran breathlessly all the way home to quai

Saint-Michel. From the balcony of their apartment, gun blasts could be heard all through the night.

Against the drama of this backdrop, Sand's new novel started circulating. "I finally began *Indiana* without a purpose, without a hope, and without any outline," Sand later wrote of the novel that earned the twenty-eight-year-old author twenty-four hundred francs, along with her reputation as one of the leading writers of the day.[2] Sandeau had rejected her offer to cosign the work, which she wrote in six weeks during February and March while at Nohant.

The story of Sandeau's turning down the opportunity to sign Aurore's new novel has been told so many times that it has become a legend. He was supposedly too modest and had too much integrity to sign a work to which he had not lent his effort. But this explanation does not hold up when one considers Jules' tendency to procrastinate and the likelihood that Aurore had written most of *Rose and Blanche,* which he willingly cosigned. The more compelling reason for his refusal was the content of the new novel. In addition to its unabashed treatment of female sexuality, *Indiana* presented to the French reading public a scathing critique of the institution of marriage. Jules was probably terrified of being associated with such radical views. Aurore, who welcomed the use of an anonymous pseudonym, also must have felt anxiety about exposing herself as the author of such a work.[3]

Hyacinthe de Latouche, editor of *Le Figaro* and an important promoter of aspiring writers, had advised Aurore in the selection of the pseudonym Georges Sand (the *s* would subsequently be dropped in favor of the English spelling of the first name), under which she published the novel. It was a spring evening when Latouche climbed the stairs to Aurore's apartment and began reading the publisher's copy she had just received. The august editor departed peremptorily with the book tucked under his arm, dismissing it as a mere pastiche of Balzac. The next morning he sent Aurore a note rescinding his first opinion and predicting, "You are destined to a success the equal of Lamartine's. . . . Balzac and Mérimée are dead in the wake of *Indiana.*" His reassessment was extravagantly flattering: "Your book is a masterpiece. . . . The simplicity, the brilliance and steadiness of its style instantly place you at the forefront of contemporary writers; no woman writer alive comes close to equalling you."[4]

Balzac was no less impressed. His review in *Caricature* was a rave:

"Here is a book in which truth takes its stand against the fantastic, the modern world against the Middle Ages, intimate drama against the tyranny of the great Historical Manner. . . . Nothing could be more simply written or more delightfully imagined." Gustave Planche extolled the novel in the pages of *La Revue des Deux Mondes* and compared its writer favorably with Madame de Staël. "Doubtless, in the course of time, the author of *Indiana* will acquire a greater skill, but it is much to be wondered whether technical perfection will ever outweigh the boldness of conception which sheer ignorance has made possible."[5]

The new editor of *La Revue*, François Buloz, invited the young author to become a staff contributor, thereby beginning a lifelong association. He offered her four thousand francs a year in exchange for thirty-two pages of copy per week. Aurore eagerly accepted, and along with an advance of fifteen hundred francs for a new novel, which she had received from Ernest Dupuy, the publisher of *Indiana,* she became, overnight, both rich and famous.

What was it about *Indiana* that took the French reading public and critics by storm? It tells the story of a young woman (its eponymous heroine) of Creole origin (whose dark coloring resembles Aurore's) who is unhappily married to a Colonel Delmare (reminiscent of Casimir), forty years her senior. The novel winds its way through Indiana's subsequent love affairs with the rakish cad Raymon de Ramière (who reminds us of the high-minded Aurélien de Sèze) and with her cousin and protector Ralph Brown, with whom the heroine finally flees, not to commit suicide, as they initially contemplate, but to live free from the oppressive constraints of marriage and society on their native island of Mauritius in the valley of Bernica.

In February, Aurore described to Emile Regnault the heroine of her work in progress: "She's the typical woman, weak and strong, exhausted by life yet able to carry the weight of the world, timid in life and bold in battle. . . . This is, I believe, the way women are in general, an incredible mixture of weakness and energy, of grandeur and pettiness, a creature always made up of two opposing natures, sometimes sublime, sometimes miserable, clever at deception, easily deceived."[6]

"No one has failed to point out that *Indiana* was about me and my life," Sand later wrote, protesting, not very credibly, "That is absolutely untrue." In *Literary Women,* Ellen Moers quite correctly observes: "The first impetus to write, in Sand's case, derived as all the world knows from her own marital situation. And the marriage question, from the unhappy wife's point of view, is the theme of *Indiana*." In what has endured as perhaps the most celebrated passage of the novel, Indiana addresses the following impassioned protest to her husband: "I know that I am the slave and you the master. The laws of this country make you my master. You can bind my body, tie my hands, govern my acts. You have the right of the stronger, and society confirms you in it; but you cannot command my will, monsieur; God alone can bend it and subdue it. Try to find a law, a dungeon, an instrument of torture that gives you any hold on it! you might as well try to handle the air and grasp space."[7]

The personal goal that Sand maintained throughout her life of loving freely and fully and being well loved in return is inextricably connected with her pressing social and humanitarian agenda. In her autobiography she looked back at this period of her life and reflected: "Seeing how far my labor was from being able to take care of the needs of the poverty around me, I doubled, I tripled, I quadrupled the dosage of work. . . . I was governed for a long time by this law of enforced labor and limitless charity, as I had once been by the idea of Catholicism, when I forbade myself the games and pleasures of adolescence to devote myself to prayer and contemplation. . . . It was only by opening my mind to the dream of great social reform that I eventually consoled myself for the narrowness and powerlessness of my devotion."[8]

Sand's novel goes beyond the feminist critique of marriage. When Indiana and her cousin Ralph, reconciled in eternal love for each other, retire to Bernica, the first thing they do is upset the colonial status quo by buying the freedom of aging, ailing black slaves. "A day will come when everything in my life will be changed," Indiana declares, "when I shall do good to others, when someone will love me, when I shall give my whole heart to the man who gives me his." Citing this passage, Naomi Schor eloquently defines the unique place Sand's heroine occupies in the fiction of her era: "What sets Indiana apart from other sadomasochistic female protagonists in nineteenth-century French fiction, notably Emma Bovary, her most illustrious descendant, is that in her story the quest for the love ideal is inseparable from an aspiration toward an ideal world. . . . For all her reading of silly women's novels—that is, romances—when Indiana fantasizes, it is not, as Emma later will, about the beautiful people and Paris but rather about freedom for herself and for all her fellow slaves. Her dream of being freed from patriarchal bondage is inseparable from a dream of emancipating the victims of colonialism."[9]

The overarching theme of freedom—personal, social, political, creative, professional—will resound throughout George Sand's life and oeuvre. Here, in her first independently published novel, she sets the stage on which will unfold a ceaseless production of acts and works undertaken on behalf of the principle of freedom to which she remained committed throughout her life.

The story of the George Sand pseudonym has been told many times with various twists. Because of the prevailing belief that books by women would not sell, it had been Latouche's idea that Aurore publish under a male pseudonym. So when Sandeau declined to lend his name to her trailblazing new novel, another male-sounding signature had to be found. Out of this necessity, "G. Sand," followed by "Georges Sand," and finally "George Sand" was born. The name change was, then, a concession to expedience, a pragmatic response not unlike Aurore's dressing as a man.

To maximize the sales potential of *Indiana,* and because the collaborative effort of *Rose and Blanche* had succeeded so well, Latouche was eager to keep the author's signature as similar as possible. He therefore decided to give back to Jules his full name, Sandeau, for future publications and to save for Aurore the tried and tested name of Sand. This exchange is sometimes referred to as the Adam's rib theory of George Sand's name change, in acknowledgment that the female was formed from a broken-off piece of the male. This may have been the case, but it is ironic that the fragment is revered by posterity, whereas Jules Sandeau's name and work have fallen into oblivion.[10] Some twenty-five years after changing her name, George Sand explained in her autobiography that she chose the name George fast and spontaneously, because in the provincial Berrichon dialect that was commonly spoken in the region where Aurore was raised, the word *george,* via the Latin *georgias,* meant "husbandman" or "farmer."

Underlying this association is another, even more intriguing possibility, one that Sand never acknowledged but that, in light of what we know of her trouble-making history as an adolescent, might have unconsciously informed her choice of name. In Berrichon the word *georgeon* means "devil." According to legend, anyone who so much as pronounces or writes the word risks becoming bedeviled. It is easy to imagine the young Aurore, plume in hand, tempting fate by scribbling the first few letters of the taboo word and stopping just short at "George."[11] Perhaps her chosen name was a nod to her days at convent school when she banded with the group known as the "devils." That Sand chose to drop the final *s* of the traditional French spelling of Georges in favor of the English spelling reinforces the association with this earlier adolescent experience.

That Aurore Dudevant wrote under the masculine name George Sand was not unique. The taking of a male pseudonym was a common practice for nineteenth-century women writers. Princess Marie d'Agoult wrote as Daniel Stern; across the English Channel, Mary Ann Evans, partly inspired by Sand's example, would write as George Eliot; and scores of other women writers followed their examples. What distinguishes George Sand's case is that she would ultimately use the pseudonym in private life, virtually eclipsing Aurore Dupin Dudevant. She actually signed her letters G. Sand or George Sand. But beyond even the signing of letters, in itself a self-consciously literary and therefore public-minded gesture, the public persona merged with the private person who eventually came to be known everywhere and by everyone as Madame George Sand. Writing her friend Laure Decerfz in 1832, Aurore proudly announced, "In Paris Madame Dudevant is dead. But George Sand is known as a lively fellow."[12]

The double birth and marriage patronymic, Dupin-Dudevant, was effectively bypassed in favor of the matronymic (female family name) that George Sand founded. Not only her readers but her personal friends, her lovers, even her children, referred to her as George. When it would come time, at mid-century, for her to write her autobiography, she signed it, accordingly, George Sand, and in so doing did what no other woman writer using a male pseudonym had ever done: she became one, or synonymous, with her invented self.

In March 1833, the affair with Jules, who had been working harder on seducing other women than on producing new writing, came to an end. "This error is the last of my life," the twenty-eight-year-old Aurore wrote Regnault, and then with startling shortsightedness resolved, "Between pure friendship and me, there will no longer be any obstacles."[13] The condition from which Jules had been suffering seems to have disappeared; Sandeau outlived Sand and died in 1883 at the age of seventy-two.

Four months earlier, Sand had published her second novel, *Valentine*, which she had written at Nohant, still flush with the success of *Indiana*.

The question of marriage was once again at the top of Sand's agenda as she created an aristocratic heroine who, in her attachment to a man of the people, yearns for both love and social justice in the form of redistribution of property. In addition to propounding her philosophical views, "In *Valentine* Sand begins to do that remarkable landscape painting which so dazzled her English readers, who had not, before Sand, found Nature celebrated in the novel."[14]

This time the young writer was paid three thousand francs. The two novels, along with commissions for short stories from François Buloz, the new editor of *La Revue des Deux Mondes,* earned Sand enough money to take a servant and sublet from Latouche more spacious quarters on quai Malaquais. Her new apartment, which Sand would occupy for the next three years, became known as the "mansarde bleue." It was situated on the fourth floor and overlooked a courtyard and the gardens of the Ecole des Beaux-Arts. "In settling in at Quai Malaquais," Sand recorded in her autobiography, "I thought myself in a palace, so comfortable was Delatouche's garret in comparison with the one I was leaving. It was a little somber even in broad daylight; there were not yet buildings as far as the eye could see, and the big trees in the surrounding gardens made a thick curtain of green, where blackbirds sang and sparrows twittered with the same freedom as in the heart of the countryside. I felt I possessed a retreat and a life conforming to my tastes and needs."[15]

Jules had been entertaining other lovers in an apartment at 7 rue de l'Université, which Sand had leased for him during the summer of 1832 so that she could live and work alone. Even though, on an unannounced visit from Nohant, she had surprised him in the arms of his laundress, the men in Sand's circle of friends, including Latouche, Sainte-Beuve, and Regnault, took Jules' side and turned against Sand when the couple finally parted. And in a letter to his friend Madame Hanska, Balzac spread the vicious and unfounded rumor that Sand had abandoned Sandeau for Latouche.[16]

The reality was quite different. As the love affair wound down, maternalism replaced sensualism. Sand not only paid the bills to cover the outstanding rent on the apartment she and Jules shared on quai Saint-Michel; she provided her former lover and collaborator with funds to travel to Italy, where he went to recover from their broken love affair and from his own creative stalemate, which can hardly be blamed on the writer who had offered him coauthorship of *Indiana*!

As Sandeau's productivity dwindled, Sand's creative output proliferated. With her first writings she had carved out her thematic territory: the renunciation of a society whose bourgeois conventions smother individuality. In December 1832, *La Revue de Paris* published her novella *La Marquise*, which was followed in March 1833 by *Lavinia* in *Les Heures du Soir*, and by *Métella*, which appeared in October 1833 in *La Revue des Deux Mondes*. Aurore Dupin Dudevant had not only adopted a new name; she had met her objective of launching a self-sustaining career. She had neither expected nor intended the other consequence of her new name and vocation: that they would bring her glory and renown.

PART FOUR THE DAUGHTER'S DEMISE

CHAPTER FIFTEEN

A Daughter Is Born

My daughter Solange was born at Nohant in the month of September 1828. When the doctor arrived, I was already asleep and the infant was dressed and adorned with pink ribbons. I had been longing for a girl, and yet I did not experience the same joy as when I had had Maurice.

George Sand

In nature, big animals devour little ones, big trees smother delicate plants born inconveniently in their shadow.

Solange Clésinger-Sand

SAND'S AMBIVALENCE toward her daughter began even before she was born. Indeed, Solange's birth was conditioned very differently from Maurice's, memorialized by Sand as "the most beautiful moment of my life." At his birth, she proudly tied the umbilical knot with a piece of green silk. Although she would subsequently suppress it, Aurore returned guilty and ashamed from the sojourn in Paris with Stéphane during which she became pregnant with Solange. "I'm unworthy of anyone's friendship," she confided in a letter to her friend Zoé Leroy.[1]

The pregnancy was difficult; by April, Aurore had gained too much weight and was suffering from minor complications. In August she wrote her mother, "I'm so huge that everyone thinks I miscalculated and that I'm going to give birth any minute. I doubt it will be sooner than two months from now." Aurore wrote her school friend Jane de Fenoyl five days after giving birth: "I gave birth all alone, and without any other doctor than my husband and Fanchon. I didn't think that I was due yet, and I believe that I delivered early by nearly a month." By the time she wrote her autobiography, Sand had concocted a full-blown cover-up to distract from Solange's illicit birth: "I was afraid my daughter might not live since she was born prematurely as the result of a fright."[2] In fact, Solange was born large and well formed and, by all indications, at full term.

Sand further reports in *Story of My Life* that the day after Solange's birth she overheard her husband making love to the Spanish maid Pépita in the room next door. There is no question that Casimir Dudevant eventually developed a predilection for bedding household servants, but in the absence of any acknowledgment by Sand that she had cuckolded her husband, the chronological juxtaposition of these two events—Solange's birth and Casimir's conspicuous betrayal—seems contrived. Sand may have told this story, which casts her husband in a particularly culpable light, to mitigate her own guilt. The warmth and intimacy of the letter Aurore wrote him when he went to Paris on business shortly after Solange's birth seems unlikely had the episode with Pépita occurred so recently. "Farewell, my dear friend, that's all the news of my activities," Aurore concluded her lengthy report. "Write me about how you're spending your time. I don't think you'll want for activity, especially in the first few days. Have as good a time as possible so that you will soon have had enough fun and will return to us. I send you all my love. Your son does as much. I will write you. Solange is very nice."[3]

In December Aurore wrote her mother, "My daughter has been weaned for a long time because I have no milk." Was the problem purely physical (there had been no problem with Maurice), or were there emotional reasons for Aurore's inability (or lack of desire) to breast-feed her daughter? Although the nursing did not go well, Solange seems to have thrived. In another letter, Aurore boasted, "My daughter is plump as a little chicken." As Solange grew, Aurore obsessed about her becoming too fat. "I would like her to lose a little weight," she wrote of her tiny daughter, "because if she goes on like this, she'll be just like Rabelais' incredible Gargamelle," a peculiar likeness to strike between one's newborn and one of literature's most unbecoming characters.[4]

Since Solange's birth, Aurore and Casimir had been sleeping in separate rooms, and by 1830, the Dudevants were living separate lives. Casimir could come and go as he pleased but could not do as he pleased under Aurore's roof. Pépita was dismissed, and Aurore began taking extended trips. In April, she left Solange at Nohant and took Maurice to Paris, where they lived as guests of her aunt Gondoüin Saint-Agnan. In May, Aurore visited her friends Zoé and Aurélien in Bordeaux, returning to Nohant in June only for Duris-Dufresne's reelection as representative of La Châtre.

Casimir had retained the master bedroom, while Aurore set herself up in her grandmother's boudoir, a small room that overlooked the garden. With only one door, the room could not serve as a pass-through for the rest of the house and therefore provided the privacy that enabled Aurore to take up her writing life. She crammed the tiny space full of books, an herbarium, and her collection of rocks and butterflies. In place of a bed, she made do with a hammock. For a desk she used her grandmother's old armoire which opened like a secretary and served as home to a little cricket who nibbled sealing wax, sipped wet ink, and tracked across her handwriting. Aurore continually had to ward him off so he wouldn't poison himself on these harmful substances.

Aurore established a schedule, developed in her teens when she was tending her ailing grandmother, of working through the night until dawn. She ordered pounds of vanilla flavored chocolate from Paris, snacking on chunks of it through the night as she wrote. She also ordered reams of writing paper and notebooks. "When I say *some*," she wrote her purveyor, "I mean twenty or so." Aurore was obviously planning to fill many pages. The cricket, whom Aurore called Cricri, was crushed when a servant accidentally closed a window on him. Aurore preserved his remains in a flower which she retained as a cherished relic from this transitional period of her life. Cricri's story would eventually be published, marking his keeper's passage from private life to public acclaim.[5]

Solange was not yet two and a half when Aurore left her husband and children for three months to join her lover Jules Sandeau in Paris and begin her writing career. The irregularity of Solange's life extended much further than the illicit nature of her birth. When Aurore returned to Paris in the spring of 1832, she brought along not only her new novel *Indiana*, which was ready to be launched, but her young daughter as well. Despite the cholera epidemic that was sweeping Paris, three-and-a-half-year-old Solange was taken to the capital to live with her still married mother and her lover in a garret on the banks of the Seine. When Aurore's friend Emile Regnault questioned the propriety of this arrangement, Sand made light of his concerns: "Yes, my friend, I'm bringing you Solange and have no fears about any drawbacks to my bachelor lifestyle. . . . She'll sleep under our [Aurore and Jules'] canopy on a little mattress. We'll get up with her at nine o'clock, and since she's three and a half, I guarantee you she'll notice nothing and have no comments or questions or tales to tell."[6]

Once settled in Paris, Aurore wrote home to Maurice, describing with palpable delectation his little sister's behavior: "She shows her backside to passers-by for a strawberry. Every day she becomes more audacious. She frequents cafés with men she knows, orders ice cream, spits in their glasses, wrangles with them, makes scenes which turn the whole place upside down. She's so cute that everyone takes her for walks and plays with her."[7]

Aurore obviously enjoyed playfully pimping her flirtatious little daughter to her friend Emile Paultre: "She is pink as a lady-apple. . . . I will bring her to you soon," and to Emile Regnault, "Where would you find . . . a more beautiful fiancée than Solange, as pink, as white, as round and ingratiating? Provision yourself with pralines, patience, and goodwill. . . . One of her favorite pastimes is to climb on the backs of the men who are in love with her and pluck their whiskers. Let's see if you qualify."[8]

Aurore's gleeful induction of her daughter into such exhibitionistic behavior is all the more surprising in light of her feelings about displaying herself in public: "I was unhappy enough to cry all the times that . . . I was forced away from my snuff-box and made . . . to expose my back and shoulders which I don't know by what ridiculously prudish instinct I never considered as part of the public domain."[9]

Considering the misgivings Aurore had harbored since childhood about her own mother's reputation, and bearing in mind Madame Dupin's denunciation of Sophie during Aurore's adolescence, it's surprising that the latter would promote in her own daughter behavior so rife with sexual innuendo. But Aurore's initial delight at Solange's flirtatiousness didn't last long. Following Solange's first winter in Paris, Aurore's friend Emile Paultre sent a package of treats down to Nohant. Solange's reaction, an obvious extension of behavior that was rewarded by favorable attention in Paris, now caused her mother consternation: "I thank you for everything," she wrote Emile, "especially Solange, who made the funniest face in the world when she received her box of delicacies. She licked it before I had a chance to open it and cried out to everyone: 'It's the little blond, it's my little blond!'. . . . The clouds are less tempestuous and even making generous allowance for her being only four years old, I'm very concerned that she'll retain this bizarre and uneven streak of personality."[10]

Solange Sand. By Mercier. (© Photothèque des musées de la ville de Paris)

When Solange was irascible, Sand punished her by slaps and spankings. When she was unruly, Sand disciplined her by shutting her in a closet. When she rebelled and failed to make progress in her home tutoring, Sand banished her to a pension in Paris. "It was as though her nature found it impossible to submit to the will of other people," Sand would explain, "and I could not get used permanently to breaking down this incomprehensible resistance. So I decided to separate from her for a time."[11]

Sand was fourteen when her grandmother sent her to a convent school in the capital; Solange was six when she was boarded for the first time. In contrast, Maurice, the object of his mother's adoration, was kept home until he was ten. "Maurice . . . keeps me company, goes out with me, sleeps with me. He's my escort and my husband," Aurore wrote her husband in November 1828. She told Jules Boucoiran, who arrived at Nohant to tutor Maurice when he turned six, "He's my funny, naughty little boy, whom I love more than anything in the world, and without whom I would have no happiness."[12]

Solange suffered acutely from separation from her mother. "Dearest Mama," she wrote home during her seventh winter, "I would like you to come on new year's day. I've finished your little basket. I've been waiting for you for a long time. You see that I haven't forgotten you. I will write you often. Farewell, Mama. I give you a thousand kisses."[13] New Year's came and went without a visit, and by March Solange still had not had a chance to bestow upon her mother her precious handmade gift.

Sometimes Sand acknowledged Solange's favorable traits, most often with a disclaimer that despite what was good in her daughter, she lacked something special that attached to her son: "My daughter is passionate, of strong body and soul. Less gracious and gentle than her brother, she is more intelligent and more courageous." Ironically, the qualities Sand singles out in Solange remind us of her own. Sand's pronouncement that "Solange is a lion, a leopard, anything but a lady. I adore her beyond reason" is contradictory, an indication that some force was at work that simultaneously bound and distanced mother and daughter.[14]

The Dudevants' separation trial was scheduled for July 1836, and Sand's lawyer, Michel de Bourges, who was also her lover, advised her to have the children present at the court hearing. Sand promptly dispatched her friend Gustave Papet to retrieve Solange at boarding school and to accompany her on the journey home. Some twenty years later Sand recorded in her autobiography, "At last my unbearable case was called up in Bourges, where I went at the beginning of July, after having gone to Paris for Solange. Once again I wanted to be in a position to take her away in case of defeat."[15] Sand's rearrangement of the actual scenario suggests that she herself regretted deficiencies in her behavior toward Solange.

In August, Sand took the children on a trip to Switzerland to visit Princess Marie d'Agoult and her companion, the composer Franz Liszt. The following fall, Sand published *Lettres d'un voyageur*, which contains an unforgettable portrait of Solange:

> The most beautiful thing I saw in Chamonix was my daughter. You can't imagine how self-assured and spirited this eight-year-old belle was, running wild in the mountains. The child Diana must have been like this when, before she was able to hunt the wild boar in fearsome Erymanthus, she played with young fauns on the pleasant slopes of Hybla. Solange's fair complex-

ion defies weather and sun. Her open shirt reveals her sturdy
chest whose immaculate whiteness nothing can tarnish. Her
long blond hair floats in loose ringlets down to her strong,
supple loins that nothing wearies, neither the short, sharp pace
of the mules, nor races up the steep, slippery slopes, nor the
rocky gradients we have to climb for hours at a time. Always
solemn and fearless, her cheeks blush with pride and vexation
if we try to give her a hand. Strong as a mountain cedar and
fresh as a flower of the valleys, she seems to guess, though as
yet she is unaware of the value of the intellect, that God's finger
has marked her brow and that she is fated, one day, to dominate by moral force those whose physical strength now protects
her. At the glacier of the Bossons she said to me: "Don't worry,
George dear, when I'm queen I'll give you the whole of Mont
Blanc."[16]

But Sand's ambivalence toward Solange lies below the surface of the
Chamonix encomium. Behind the hyperbolic praise lurks anxiety about
Solange's youth and beauty, her extraordinary strength and assertiveness,
and how these attributes would affect the future play of power between
mother and daughter. "Lest anyone doubt the artist's own maternal devotion," writes Shari L. Thurer in The Myths of Motherhood, "the stunning
young artist Marie Elizabeth Vigée-Lebrun, a favorite of the French court
. . . in an outrageously flattering portrait, The Artist and Her Daughter, pictures herself protectively embracing her child, who was five or six at the
time. A mother's blind love shines through in every stroke. Though sentimental, it is a masterpiece. Reportedly, the artist indulged her daughter
excessively, and the child was difficult and spoiled." Like Vigée-Lebrun,
Sand was caught up in the idealization of motherhood inspired by Rousseau
and "the Romantic child of the poets and philosophers."[17]

That Solange actually declared she would give her mother the whole
of Mont Blanc is doubtful, because of both her young age and her insecurity in relation to her mother, to whom she had recently written: "You
tell me my letter is very nice but yours is much lovelier."[18] Despite the
bravado Sand imputes to her daughter, Solange never viewed herself as
having the upper hand.

The portrait in Lettres d'un voyageur proceeds to compare Solange and

Maurice: "Her brother, though five years older, is less sturdy and less daring. Gentle and mild, he instinctively recognizes and admires her superiority; but he knows, too, that kindness is a gift. 'You'll be proud of *her*,' he often says to me, 'but I'll make you happy.'" In the fullness of time, only half the prediction Sand ascribed to Maurice came true: indeed, the son she dubbed "my most perfect creation" would make his mother happy, but Solange would never make her proud. The barb about Solange's lack of "kindness" reveals a significant reservation. In a letter from the same period, Sand disclosed in plain and private prose a more malevolent view of Solange: "My daughter . . . has a terrible character."[19]

Marie d'Agoult must have sensed that trouble was brewing. No doubt based on their sojourn in Chamonix, d'Agoult's testimony to nine-year-old Solange's superior endowment is tinged with foreboding: "Solange is a beautiful girl, admirably proportioned; she is alert, vigorous, graceful, determined. . . . As strong in spirit as in body; a mind which seems suited to learning; a loving heart, a passionate character, indomitable. Solange is destined to a life of absolute good or evil. Her life will be embattled. She will not submit to convention; there will be greatness in her weaknesses, sublimity in her virtues."[20]

In the midst of the Dudevants' legal separation battle and in defiance of a court order, Casimir removed Solange from boarding school and took her to his family's property in Guillery. Well cared for in familiar surroundings, Solange was hardly at peril, yet according to Sand's account, she apparently counted the rescue of her daughter among the heroic highlights of her life. This charming, if self-aggrandizing, account is enhanced for readers who recognize the subprefect of Nérac as the redoubtable Baron Georges-Eugène Haussmann, who would later remap the city of Paris under the administration of Napoléon III:

> I race to Paris. I send off a telegram. I call the police. I get a
> restraining order. I race to the authorities, I stir up trouble, I
> have everything in order, and I depart for Nérac, where I arrive
> on a beautiful morning, fresh as a red herring after three days
> and three nights in a mail coach, accompanied by Mallefille,
> the adventurer, and by Bocage's servant, the tough guy, and
> by Monsieur Génestal's head clerk, the organization man. I
> descend on the sub-prefect, who is Artaud's brother-in-law and

a charming fellow, to boot. The king's solicitor grimaces as he gives me a list of the charges. The police officer, a bit more human, agrees to accompany me with his sergeant and two adorable *private* policemen. I ask for a bailiff in case a summons is needed to break down the door should there be resistance. At the moment of departure a problem arises. The mayor of Pompiey is needed for breaking down doors, and the mayor in question won't respond to our request since he's a friend of Monsieur Dudevant. I coax the sub-prefect, who's very sympathetic, and he climbs in my car with me, the lieutenant, the bailiff, etc., and the rest on horseback. Imagine what an escort! What an outing for Nérac. What astonishment! The town and the surrounding countryside are alerted. Two pathetic mail coaches that were peacefully leaving for the waters in the Pyrenees were requisitioned for my cortege.[21]

Outwitted and outnumbered, Casimir relinquished his contraband when this impressive brigade arrived at Guillery. "Solange was delivered into my hands like a princess at a border crossing," Sand reported. "The following day, I was overcome with desire to revisit the Pyrenees." Riding hard along flood plains and atop precipitous banks through fog, driving rain, and falling snow, Sand and Solange made fifteen leagues in a day and arrived triumphant at the French border. What was Sand thinking when she made this extraordinary sidetrip, which doubtless did more to imperil her daughter than the relatively benign sojourn in Nérac? The dramatic rescue of her daughter seems to have propelled Aurore to retrace the southbound trajectory of her childhood trip through the Pyrenees with her own mother, whose recent death on 19 August 1837 had unleashed unanticipated sorrow: "Misery, despair, bitter tears, I did not know I loved her so much this poor woman," Sand recorded.[22] As though reversing the destiny of the fleeing Spanish Infanta she had glimpsed on the traumatic journey with Sophie during the Spanish uprising, Sand concluded her account of rescuing Solange with the proud proclamation, "As for me, I'm a Spanish princess, in the middle of some revolution."

CHAPTER SIXTEEN

The Author and the Actress

Such a beautiful and simple woman, she didn't learn anything;
she figured it all out. Poor, abandoned, misunderstood, no one took
the trouble to develop her mind or to steer her feelings, which is
why she became so great as soon as she was able to break out;
which is why she is so true, so much herself, so womanly, the great
tragedian!

AS 1832 CAME TO AN END, Sand was filled with excitement about her
newly established publishing career. To her editor Buloz she wrote enthusiastically, "I will be sure to give you an article for February 1st. Until then
I can't pull myself away from my book."[1] She concluded by thanking him
for the recent increase in her salary with La Revue des Deux Mondes.

Professional commitment and success, however, did not come without
personal conflict. Having stayed in Paris through Christmas and New
Year's, Sand had once again disappointed young Maurice, who longed for
his mother's return for the holidays. Back to back with the letter to Buloz,
Sand wrote Maurice a note, accompanied by gifts of picture books, albums,
and a little notebook. "Grow well, work well, play well," she implored her
young son, "and always love your dear old mother who loves nothing in
the world more than you and your sister."[2] In the last line of her letter she
told Maurice she was saving his first scribbling to show him when he was
older—small consolation for a little boy whose mother could not be with
him at the holidays.

On 8 January 1833, Sand signed a contract with the editor Ernest
Dupuy for thirteen hundred copies of her novel in progress—the one that
kept her from completing straightaway her article for Buloz—tentatively
titled *Trenmor*, to be published in a single volume for two thousand francs.
Seven weeks later Sand had produced enough material to fill two volumes
that would eventually bear the name *Lélia* and earn its author the sum of

five thousand francs. The day after signing the contract, Sand wrote a fre-
netic note to Maurice. She apologized for not answering his recent spate
of letters and indulged in one of her increasingly frequent piques of overprotectiveness. Racked by fears and dreams of Maurice coming to harm,
she cautioned him, "Take care not to get sick in this miserable cold weather.
Always keep your feet warm and your throat covered."[3]

As far as her own health was concerned, a close connection between
work and wellness was taking hold in Sand's life. To Emile Regnault she
confided, "It's curious that this irritation [rheumatism] that I've been free
of for six weeks of regular hard work has returned after eight days of recreation, rest, and perfect health."[4] By immersing herself in work, Sand was
learning, she could keep at bay some of the debilitating symptoms that
since childhood underlay her emotionally overwrought existence.

A highlight of the new year was Sand's meeting with the beautiful actress Marie Dorval. Seeing her perform in Hugo's *Marion Delorme* and
Dumas' *Antony,* Sand was overwhelmed by the passion and verve of this
remarkable *comédienne*. In a rush of excitement, she wrote Marie an admiring note asking if she would receive her visit. Marie responded immediately.
Arriving unannounced at the door to Sand's apartment, she "flung her
arms around my neck, out of breath, crying, 'Here I am!' I had never seen
her except on stage, but my ear recognized her voice immediately. She
was better than pretty—she was charming—and so charming was she
that her prettiness was of no consequence. It was not a face, it was a counte-
nance, a soul. She was still slim, and her waist was a supple reed which
always seemed to sway to a mysterious breeze she alone felt. Jules Sandeau
compared her that day to the broken feather which adorned her hat."

Why, Sand wondered aloud to the accomplished actress, had she
deigned to pay her such a visit? Dorval recounted her own experience of
having once written a fan letter to the famous actress Mademoiselle Mars,
who responded with diffidence. "I remembered while reading your letter,"
Marie told Sand, "that, when I wrote mine, I felt like a true artist for the
very first time, and that my enthusiasm was a revelation. I said to myself
you also are, or will be, an artist." It was not long before Sand wrote an
enthusiastic article for the journal *L'Artiste* comparing Marie Dorval with
Mademoiselle Mars. Sand praised Marie for the suppleness, mobility, and
passion of her performances, qualities that, in her estimation, outranked
her celebrated competitor.[5]

Marie Dorval. (Courtesy Bibliothèque nationale de France)

A product of the provincial stage on which her parents played with a roving theater troop, Marie Dorval, born out of wedlock Marie-Thomase-Amélie Delaunay in 1798, spent her childhood in poverty and, in Sand's words, "grew up sickly and strong, pretty and faded, as cheerful as a child, but also as sad and good as an angel condemned to tread the most difficult roads in life." At fifteen she married an actor named Allan who went by the name Dorval, which, in spite of his early death, Marie kept for the rest of her life. Her first success came in the melodrama *Trente ans ou la vie d'un joueur* (*A Lapse of Thirty Years; or The Gambler's Fate*), by Victor Ducange and Prosper Dinaux, in which she gained attention for her natural performance. At the age of thirty-one, she married a journalist and playwright named Jean-Toussaint Merle, while continuing to take a series of lovers, including, most notably, Alfred de Vigny, with whom she conducted a long-lasting and turbulent affair.

Watching Marie bedazzle her eager audiences fueled Sand's passion for her new friend. Reading Sand's writings stirred Marie's feelings for her ardent young admirer. Mutual respect and ambition drew them together. Sincerity, expressivity, pain, and passion—"that which draws suffering to suffering and softheartedness to the edge of heartbreak"—sealed their friendship.[6]

In late January, Sand and Dorval shared a box at the Opéra-Comique. The following day Sand sent her new friend the first letter that has come down to us of the many that the two exchanged. Sand described herself as "slow" and "stupid" and begged Marie to be patient with her. "I feel as though I love you with a rejuvenated heart. . . . If this is a dream like everything else that I've desired in my life, don't dispel it too soon." By June, Sand was even more smitten: "You are the only woman that I love, Marie: the only one for whom I feel admiration and awe."[7]

After theater, the two women would take supper together and then retire to Sand's quai Malaquais apartment, where they talked into the early hours of the morning. They became known around Paris as the "inséparables." Passionate letters flew back and forth between them, while pages of *Lélia*, the new novel on which Sand was working, piled up on her work table. Alfred de Vigny became jealous of his mistress' attentions to her new friend. It bothered him that Sand smoked, wore trousers, and tossed off flirtatious remarks like "take me for your cavalier" in her letters to Marie. He found Sand graceless and crude, "mannish in the way she was built and in the way she spoke, in the sound of her voice and the boldness of her expressions."[8] The late-night meetings, the passionate prose of their letters, and Sand's masculine exhibitionism soon gave rise to allegations of a lesbian love affair.

Gustave Planche confided his concern to Jules Sandeau, still Sand's lover at the time, and wrote Sand a letter warning her of Marie's reputed sexual proclivity for women: "One of my friends who, by dint of his intimacy with J[uliet]te [Drouet] has every reason to believe in her sincerity, informed me that Madame A[llan] D[orval] had the same kind of passion for her that Sappho had for young Lesbians."[9]

The essayist Arsène Houssaye, exercising more than a little fantasy-driven poetic license, played a considerable part in fanning the flames of scandal that surrounded the Sand-Dorval relationship: "Every evening, at midnight, after the *comédienne* had enflamed the hearts of her audience

. . . she would retire to her little room all upholstered in blue where she would find before a lively fire that warmed the tea pot, the strange woman who smoked cigarettes while awaiting her prey. . . . The brunette undid the blond hair. The blond undid the dark hair. And their tresses mingled in their violent embraces. Sappho never spoke so beautifully to the handsome Phaon. . . . The two bacchantes left each other at sunrise, still drunk at dawn with satisfied desire."[10] Surely, Houssaye was inspired by the passage in Sand's new novel where Pulchérie recalls being stirred by the beauty of her sister, Lélia:

> Your thick black hair was sticking to your forehead, its tight
> curls twisting and intertwining, clinging as if endowed with
> life to your neck, velvet with shade and perspiration. I ran my
> fingers through it: your hair seemed to tighten around them
> and to draw me toward you. Tight over your breast, your thin
> white shirt displayed skin tanned by the sun to an even darker
> shade than usual; and your long eyelids, heavy with sleep,
> stood out against your cheeks which were of a fuller color than
> they are today. Oh, how beautiful you were, Lélia! . . . Your
> breast rose and fell as you breathed with a regularity that
> seemed to betoken calm and strength; and in all your features,
> in your posture, in your shape more clear-cut than mine, in
> the darker shade of your skin, and especially in the proud,
> cold expression on your sleeping face there was something so
> masculine and strong that I scarcely recognized you. I felt that
> you looked like the beautiful dark-haired child I had just been
> dreaming of, and trembling I kissed your arm. Then you
> opened your eyes and their expression filled me with an un-
> known shame; I turned away as if I had done something
> shameful. And yet, Lélia, no impure thought had even crossed
> my mind. How did this happen? I was then totally ignorant.
> I was receiving from nature and from God, my creator and
> my master, my first lesson in love, my first sensation of
> desire.[11]

To be sure, a strong component of confidentiality and consolation bound Sand and Dorval, in addition to mutual admiration and similarly passionate personalities. Given the tumultuous nature of both their heterosexual relationships, Dorval's with Vigny and Sand's with Casimir and Sandeau (he and Sand were in the process of breaking up), it is little wonder that the two women took pleasure in a companionship that allowed them to vent their displeasure with their respective partners. But the fact that Sand and Dorval spent frequent late evenings together in no way proves that they shared a physical relationship.

Nor, for that matter, can passionate letters between women friends, which were a commonplace of nineteenth-century correspondence, be invoked as proof of sexual intimacy between epistolary partners. Indeed, Sand's freedom of expression may have been fueled by memories of repression that stemmed from school days at the Convent of the English Augustinians, where "there was concern over our innocent letter-writing . . . letters often full of tender, naive charm, the kind of letters we were strictly forbidden to write, as if they had been love letters, but which prohibition served only to make more ardent and more frequent."[12]

Georges Lubin judiciously notes that "with George Sand friendship often speaks the uninhibited language of love." But not everyone agrees with our interpretation of the Sand-Dorval relationship. In *Vice Versa: Bisexuality and the Eroticism of Everyday Life*, Marge Garber has come to a different conclusion, asserting that along with Queen Christina of Sweden, George Sand was among the "highly gifted women and girls [who are] partly bisexual, partly homosexual," revealing "their maleness by the preference for women or for womanish men."[13]

Although we are not bound to believe everything Sand explained about herself, her reaction to Montaigne's writings on homosexual friendships among the ancients has the ring of authenticity:

From my youth on, indeed from childhood, I had dreamed of the ideal friendship, and I admired enormously those great examples from antiquity, in which I suspected no sexual element. Later on I would learn that they were accompanied by that extravagant or morbid tendency about which Cicero asked: "Quis est enim iste amor amicitiae? [So what is this so-called love between friends?]." This gave me a sort of fright, as did anything that bore the stamp of possible aberration or depravity. I had envisioned heroes so pure, and then I had to imagine them so corrupt and barbaric. Thus, I was overcome with disgust and even great sadness when, at the age when one is permitted to read everything, I understood the story of Achilles and Patroclus, of Harmodius and Aristogiton. It was, in fact, Montaigne's chapter on friendship which brought about my disillusionment, but thereafter that same chapter, so platonic and so ardent, that virile and saintly expression of a sentiment raised to the level of a virtue, became a sort of sacred law that guided my soul.

It's difficult to imagine the person who expressed this kind of aversion feeling free enough to abandon herself to a physical relationship with another woman. Montaigne's influence may have been at work inadvertently in another way. In his writings he had attacked women, relegating them to inferior status compared with men, a stance that had deeply offended Sand as she strove toward a sense of herself as a strong and independent female. In his essay on friendship, Montaigne had written derisively of the female sex: "To tell the truth, the ordinary capacity of women is not sufficient to respond to this exchange, or to the nurturing communion of this sacred bond; nor do their souls seem steady enough to sustain the strain of such a close and lasting knot."[14] Sand had read Montaigne as a young mother in the gardens at Ormesson during the autumn of 1824. By the time she met Marie Dorval, some ten years later, Montaigne's notion of ideal friendship had taken firm hold of her imagination, and the passionate and independent actress provided the opportunity for Sand to effect a friendship between females that emulated the "sacred bond" Montaigne had reserved exclusively for the male sex.

Adding to the Sand-Dorval drama was a missing cache of correspondence that did not surface until the 1950s, when Simone André-Maurois published sixty letters exchanged by the two women. "A heavy sense of mystery enveloped two slender dossiers of inaccessible and notorious letters," notes Simone André-Maurois. "The actress and the novelist, accused of a homosexual friendship, left an impression of having exchanged unchaste letters. A well-known will placed an embargo on a portion of the documents in question. So much silence surrounding a few papers, carefully suppressed for a century, had created and then sustained a *psychose de scandale*. It shall be seen that the documents do not justify this."[15]

But André-Maurois' publication of the extant letters and her arguments were still insufficient to quell debate. According to Jacques-Louis Douchin, author of *George Sand, l'amoureuse,* Sand and Dorval enjoyed a physical relationship in February 1833 (if only briefly). Douchin's assertion relates to a decision by Caroline, Dorval's youngest daughter, who destroyed a portion of the correspondence between Sand and Dorval following her mother's death, in 1849. "Under these conditions," Douchin reasons, "it goes without saying that we obviously only possess the most innocuous letters."[16] The object of Douchin's study being, as it were, George Sand's love life renders his interpretation somewhat biased.

Whatever was going on between Sand and Dorval, it did not prevent Sand from becoming involved in a brief affair with the writer Prosper Mérimée, whose novel *La Double Méprise,* published later that year, took up in fictional form the subject of their tryst. The young, up-and-coming writer (Mérimée was just a year older than Sand) had pressed for an earlier meeting, but Sand put him off, using as a pretext Casimir's visit to Paris with Maurice and a bout of "neuralgia." Mérimée persisted, however, and in April 1833, while attending the opera *Robert le diable,* by the popular contemporary composer Giacomo Meyerbeer, Sand, with Solange in tow, finally spent an evening with Mérimée. As the lengthy opera wore on, the tired little girl fell asleep in Mérimée's arms.

The Sand-Mérimée affair—fiasco is a better word—lasted but a week. Rumor circulated that it was consummated during a carriage ride through Paris and lasted only one night. Sand reported her disappointment to Marie, who repeated it to Dumas, who then attributed to Sand the following declaration: "I had Mérimée last night, and it wasn't much." In July, Sand confided a deeper, rather contradictory interpretation of their encounter: "If P[rosper] M[érimée] had understood me, he would have loved me and won me over, and if I had been able to subjugate myself to a man, I would have been saved, for my freedom gnaws at me and is killing me."[17]

As Marie's busy acting and touring schedule increasingly took her away, Sand's extreme neediness became burdensome, and Marie's affection for Sand began to cool. The more unavailable and unreliable Marie became, the more the unfulfilled love of the little girl Aurore for her transient and inconsistent mother resurfaced. Sand's letters from this period reprise the familiar childhood refrain of bemoaning her mother's prolonged absences. "Why haven't we seen each other for so long?" Sand complained to her new friend. "To love you so deeply and to spend so many days far

from you, Marie, saddens me and makes my heart heavier than usual."
Sand's plaint continued: "But I don't know why, not seeing you, thinking
of you incessantly, reporting to you all my impressions which in spite of
myself I always want to compare with yours, I'm afraid that I'm not worthy of your friendship, as great and noble a woman as you are."[18] By May,
Sand and Dorval were seeing little of each other. The course of their relationship echoes the schoolgirl Aurore's adolescent crush on Sister Hélène,
which had evolved from ecstatic friendship to scandal, culminating in
pain and disillusionment.

In June 1833, *Lélia* was published. After reading it in early August,
Chateaubriand took up pen and paper to communicate his admiration:
"You will be the Lord Byron of France," he predicted with the unequivocal
self-assurance of an already canonized celebrity. "What the devil is this?"
Jules Néraud wrote Sand after reading her new novel. "Where did you get
all that? Why did you write this book? Where does it comes from, where
is it going? I knew you were very dreamy, I believed you were a believer
at the core, but I would never have suspected that you could attach so
much importance to penetrating the secrets of that very large 'maybe' and
to examining from every direction that immense 'question mark' which
you would do better not to worry about any more than I do." He was astonished that such a moody novel had emerged from his adventuresome,
merry-making friend, "who is jolly, who dances the bourrée, who appreci-
ates species of butterflies, who does not despise a pun, who sews fairly
well, and who makes very good jam!"[19]

What was it about *Lélia* that elicited so much bewilderment? Here
was a novel unlike anything Sand had written before. Gustave Planche
declared, "*Lélia* is not the ingenious account of an adventure, nor does it
describe the dramatic development of a passion. It is the reflection of the
present century upon itself, it is the lament of a society in agony." Sainte-
Beuve described it as a "lyrical and philosophical novel."[20]

Instead of a conventional story that turns on plot development, *Lélia*
is composed of five interwoven voices: that of Lélia, the brooding, romantic,
frigid female counterpart of Etienne de Senancour's recent protagonist
Obermann; of the young poet-lover Sténio; of the gambler and stoic Tren-
more, who repents of his past; of the priest Magnus, made mad by frustrated sexual desire; and of the pleasure-seeking courtesan Pulchérie,
Lélia's sister. These voices intermingle in a series of abstract, letterlike

entries (sans dates and place locations), creating a chorus of arguments about spiritual love.

In her preface to the rewritten 1839 version of *Lélia,* Sand explains her conception of the novel: "The characters . . . represent a segment of the philosophical intelligence of the nineteenth century: Pulchérie is epicureanism . . . Sténio, the enthusiasm and the weakness of a time when intelligence climbs very high . . . and falls very low, crushed by a reality without poetry . . . Magnus, the remains of a corrupt or stupefied clergy. . . . As for Lélia . . . [I wanted to] make her the personification . . . of the spiritualism of our age."[21]

When a fragment of *Lélia* was published in *La Revue des Deux Mondes,* it was preceded by the following editorial comment: "[In *Lélia*], exterior events are unimportant. The unfolding of events, the complications, the peripeteia, and the unraveling of this mysterious drama are formed and resolved in the folds of human conscious. *Lélia,* we are confident, will provoke a dazzling revolution in contemporary literature and will deal the final blow to purely *visible* poetry."[22]

Visible poetry was considered literature in which external events condition the action of the narrative, as distinct from the simple term *poetry,* which was used at the time to include fictional forms in general. The journal *L'Europe Littéraire* represented a group of writers, including Victor Hugo and Prosper Mérimée, whose work was associated with visible poetry. "In the other school of 'la poésie intime' at *La Revue des Deux Mondes,*" Isabelle Naginski informs us, "Sainte-Beuve, Senancour, George Sand, and Musset are concentrating on the depiction of solitary, socially indifferent but spiritually active characters. Their novels do not so much paint a colorful world of costumes and objects; rather they insist on probing the intangible states of being and moral maladies of their contemporaries through the themes of reverie and solitude."[23]

Following the publication of *Lélia* in July 1833, the critic Capo de Feuillide wrote two articles for *L'Europe Littéraire* that virulently attacked the book and its author. Feuillide summed up Sand's novel as "prostitution of body and soul." Raving about its "vile and shameful thoughts" and "corrosive pages," he heaped opprobrium on Sand's work.[24] Sand's friend Gustave Planche, of *La Revue des Deux Mondes,* took personal offense and challenged Feuillide to a duel. Although no harm came to either man, the two met and fired upon each other on 27 August in the Bois de Boulogne, an absurd event that was readily assimilated into a feud between the two literary journals. Sand expressed disgust that matters had gotten so out of control.

But while critics concerned themselves with the literary implications and innovations of *Lélia*, the general reading public looked upon the book, according to Naomi Schor, as a "shocking tale of sexual dysfunction."[25] *Lélia* was widely read as a gloss on its author's alleged sexual frigidity. When Lélia laments the frustration she suffers in her lover's arms, readers concluded that this was a description of George Sand's experience:

> Near him I felt a sort of peculiar, delirious longing which originated in the most refined, exquisite forces of my intelligence and thus could not be appeased by any carnal embrace. I felt my breast consumed by an unquenchable fire and his kisses brought me no relief. I would clasp him in my arms with superhuman strength and then fall exhausted beside him, disheartened by my total incapacity to convey my yearning to him. For me, desire was an ardor of the soul which paralyzed the power of my senses before they had even been aroused; it was a savage fury which seized my brain and concentrated there exclusively. My blood would freeze, impotent and thin, before this immense upsurging of my will. Then would have been the moment to die. But selfishly he would never agree to suffocate me, pressing me against his chest; yet therein lay my only hope for sensual pleasure. I hoped at last to know the languors and delights of love while falling asleep in the arms of death.
>
> When he dozed off, satisfied and sated, I would lie motionless and dismayed at his side. Thus I passed many hours watching him sleep. I found him so beautiful, this man! There was such strength and nobility on his peaceful brow! My heart would throb violently next to him; the burning tide of my restless blood would rush to my face; the unbearable tremors would race through my limbs. I seemed to feel again the excitation of physical love and the mounting confusion of carnal desire.[26]

Based on such passages, André Maurois titled his 1953 biography *Lélia: The Life of George Sand*, conflating the life of his subject with the life of her frigid protagonist. Curtis Cate, writing in the 1970s, perpetuated the biographical fallacy that Maurois had established: "*Lélia* . . . was in reality the thinly disguised expression of Aurore Dudevant's intimate despair." Isabelle Naginski observes, "When Flaubert flatly asserts his identity with his heroine ('Madame Bovary, c'est moi'), we automatically resist the possibility. But when Sand just as flatly denies any identity between herself and her heroine ('Lélia, ce n'est pas moi'), we are equally loath to accept her disclaimer."[27]

The debate surrounding the issue of Sand's sexuality begs the question of the nature of female orgasmic response. Because a woman does not come to climax in a particular episode or a specific relationship does not necessarily indicate that she is unable to experience orgasm under other circumstances. Surely the above passage describing a woman's unfulfilled desire resounds with the authenticity of lived experience. But just as surely the passage from a letter we have cited earlier, in which Aurore writes Emile Regnault of a night of passion shared with Jules Sandeau—"I don't think we've ever experienced such heights of pleasure"—persuades us that Sand was capable of achieving sexual satisfaction.[28] Rather than reading Lélia's sexual frigidity literally as an autobiographical marker, it can be understood as the metaphoric equivalent of the moral and spiritual despair to which Lélia and the era she represents were subject. Looking back, Sand wrote of that time in her life and the life of her country:

> And I opened my eyes at a solemn moment in history. The republic dreamed of in July had ended in the massacres of Varsovie and the holocaust of Saint-Merry's cloister. Cholera had just decimated the world. Saint Simonism, which had captured my imagination for a moment, was felled by persecution, and aborted without having once and for all settled the great question of love and, in my opinion, having even sullied it a little. Art too had, by deplorable aberrations, soiled the cradle of its romantic reform. The times were prone to fear and irony, dismay and impudence—some lamenting the ruin of their unstinted illusions, others laughing on the first rungs of a tainted victory; no one believed in anything anymore—some through discouragement, others through atheism. . . . Afflicted by this profound despondency, I wrote *Lélia* in fits and starts.[29]

CHAPTER SEVENTEEN

Sons and Lovers

> To love is of all that we know that which remains greatest and most
> ennobling. . . . May love survive in spite of everything. Our suffering
> can do no more to destroy it than clouds at night can obliterate the
> beauty of the stars.

AT A DINNER PARTY in June 1833, in honor of François Buloz and a group of his authors, twenty-nine-year-old George Sand made the acquaintance of Alfred de Musset. The second son of an aristocratic Parisian family, trim and handsome with wavy blond hair, an aquiline nose, bright blue eyes, and a reputation for womanizing, the twenty-three-year-old Musset was a rising star in the Parisian literary galaxy. His father had died the previous year, leaving Musset emotionally vulnerable despite his newly acquired title of viscount. "His self-infatuation was so mingled with hatred," writes Dan Hofstadter in *The Love Affair as a Work of Art*, "that it may be considered a case of unreciprocated self-love."[1]

George Sand arrived at the gathering, hosted by Florestan Bonnaire, a financial backer of *La Revue des Deux Mondes,* sporting a gem-studded dagger dangling from the cummerbund of a bolero. When Musset asked her what use she made of such a plaything, she told him she wore it in self-defense. The daring, self-styled author of *Indiana* and *Valentine* obviously made a favorable impression on the young poet, as did he on her. By the end of the evening, according to legend, the dagger had disappeared into the folds of Sand's skirt, signaling, symbolically at least, the lowering of Sand's romantic defenses.

In response to the flattering lines Musset wrote to Sand following their meeting, she sent him a copy of *Indiana*. Several days later, Musset wrote her an impassioned, praise-filled poem titled "After Reading *Indiana*"; soon he was sending notes pressing the illustrious author for further meetings. In July, Sand sent him proofs of her forthcoming *Lélia*, which elicited the following response from her enchanted young admirer: "There are in *Lélia* dozens of pages which go straight to the heart with as much honesty and vigor and beauty as *René* or *Lara*. You've gone and become George Sand; otherwise, you would merely have been Madame so and so, scribbling away."[2]

Musset's first declaration of love was made in writing following an afternoon stroll in the Jardin du Roi (now the Jardin des Tuileries). "I have something foolish and ridiculous to tell you," he declared. He then went on to reveal his feelings toward her: "I am foolishly writing it, Heaven knows why, when I should have said it to you, on coming back from this walk. . . . I am in love with you."[3] Sand reciprocated by allowing Musset to read the journal entries that recorded her impressions of him.

The relationship that ensued was at least as literary as it was libidinous; Musset and Sand carried notebooks in which they chronicled virtually every stage of their love affair—as much for posterity as for each other. Henry James showed a keen understanding of this phenomenon, noting that Sand "put a premium on all passion, on all pain, on all experience and all exposure, on the greatest variety of ties and the smallest reserve about them. . . . Say that we are to give up the attempt to understand [such intimate episodes]: it might certainly be better so, and there would be a delightful side to the arrangement. But in the name of common sense don't say that the continuity of life is not to have some equivalent in the continuity of pursuit, the renewal of phenomena in the renewal of notation."[4]

It was Musset's confession of suffering and neediness that attracted Sand the most. At the end of a particularly despairing letter, he wrote, "Farewell, George, I love you like a child," winning Sand's heart with these words. Much as she had responded maternally to Jules Sandeau, Sand now found in the young Musset another irresistibly dependent soul to succor. In spite of his addiction to gambling, alcohol, and prostitutes, Sand finally succumbed to the seductive young poet. Near dawn, at the end of a star-studded evening in early August, during which Musset pleaded on hands and knees for his beloved to save him from his dissolute past, Sand finally gave in. True to form, Musset recorded Sand's submission: "Softly she turned her head; her eyes were full of tears. Her body bent like a reed, her half-opened lips fell on mine, and the universe was forgotten."[5]

After hastily making arrangements for someone to look after Solange at the quai Malaquais apartment, and in spite of the concerns Musset's

Alfred de Musset. Portrait by Charles Landelle. (Courtesy Bibliothèque nationale de France)

family had about the young poet's involvement with an older woman and a celebrity, on 5 August the lovers took leave of stifling hot Paris and traveled up the Seine by riverboat for a week-long stay in the Fontainebleau forest.

There they hiked in the hills and rode horses. Musset sketched, Sand persevered in her writing assignments, and the lovers read aloud to each other. And then something deeply disturbing took place. On an evening hike to the Franchard rock formations, Musset went off to demonstrate an echo phenomenon that he had experienced on previous visits to this same area. Leaving Sand by herself in the gathering darkness, Musset scampered down a ravine to scale a rock ledge on the other side. Sand waited anxiously as time passed, but no sign or sound of her lover came across the expanse of wilderness that separated them. When she finally heard a desperate cry coming from somewhere down below, she raced down the hillside in search of Musset, slipping and sliding through wild terrain as brambles and bushes tore at her dress. At the bottom of the ravine she came upon her lover in a state of wild delirium. Musset had experienced a terrifying hallucination in which he thought he heard a voice uttering an obscene refrain and imagined he saw a drunken, mocking figure staggering toward him. Trembling with terror, in thrall to schizophrenic delusion, Musset recognized the ghostlike face as his own.

Peace returned to the poet by the following day, and the couple's stay at Fontainebleau continued and concluded well enough. They returned to Paris to a whirlwind of critical acclaim, Musset for his recently published poem *Rolla*, Sand for *Lélia*. In addition to literary fame, the couple was greeted by the publicity that accompanies scandal. Rumors were circulating that Sand was engaged in a love affair with Planche as well as with Musset. "That I pass from Planche to Musset before whomever comes next," wrote the fiercely independent Sand to her friend and confessor Charles Augustin Sainte-Beuve, "is of little importance as long as no one claims that my bed receives two men on the same day."[6]

Sand seems to have derived pleasure from the sexual scandal that surrounded her. Rather than dispel reports that Planche was her lover, her response courted ambiguity: "Planche was taken for my lover, but I don't care; I didn't deny it," she wrote Sainte-Beuve. "I told the truth only to my friends: he is not [my lover]. It's very important to me now that people know he's not, just as I'm completely indifferent about whether they believe that he was. You must understand that I can't live intimately with two men who profess to have the same relationship with me; that would not suit any one of the three of us." When Alexandre Dumas fils joined the fray and accused Planche of being Sand's lover, the two men nearly came to blows. A duel was avoided only after Planche agreed to sign a statement that he was not on intimate sexual terms with George Sand.

Given Sand's extreme preoccupation with cleanliness, Planche, who "stank like a sweating porter," would seem an altogether unlikely choice of lover. When he occupied his box at the Théâtre des Français, the two surrounding boxes remained vacant.[7] But Sand was not making a strenuous effort to quell rumors that Planche was her lover. What seems to have mattered most was her assertion of monogamy—what today we would call serial monogamy—to which she claimed rigorous adherence.

In October, Sand finished the novella *Métella,* which she had begun before leaving for Fontainebleau. Setting her story in Florence suggests that she was already considering Italy as a possible travel destination. By November, Sand had resolved to spend the winter in Italy with Musset. The plans for this sojourn constitute nothing short of a carefully constructed getaway plot that Sand single-handedly masterminded. To Casimir she offered health reasons as a pretext for her travels: "I'm going to Italy to spend the winter and to try to cure the rheumatism which is killing me this year." She quickly settled on a convenient rationalization for depositing her daughter at Nohant: "I'm afraid of taking Solange so far away, and I will leave her at Nohant where she'll be best off spending several months." As for Maurice, Sand's good friend Gustave Papet was enlisted to take him from boarding school on his days off, and the tutor Boucoiran was to arrange for occasional visits to Madame Dudevant.[8]

By early December, as the time to leave drew near, the plan changed somewhat; Sand wrote Casimir again informing him that she would be unable to bring Solange to Nohant personally. Instead, she told him that her maid, Julie, would be traveling with Solange and that if Casimir wished, he could meet them in Châteauroux. About these rearrangements Sand declared, "Solange is delighted."

To manage financially, Sand had written her editor Buloz requesting —demanding is a more accurate description—an advance against the work she planned to produce while abroad. "You must give me my five thousand francs on Sunday or else I'll have to give up the trip. . . . So you must give me a definitive answer." In spite of her growing success as an author and her high level of productivity, Buloz continued to dispense monies cautiously, with the effect that tensions mounted between author and editor. "He held my purse strings for ten years," Sand would record in her autobiography, "and in the lives of artists, these strings which open only to give us a few hours of liberty, in exchange for so many hours of slavery, are our very lifelines." Rather than the five thousand francs Sand had requested, Buloz reluctantly agreed to four thousand. The rest would come later, when the promised work was delivered.[9]

Sand wrote her mother in mid-December, informing her of her responsibility for Maurice during her time away. She didn't ask her mother's permission for the arrangements she had already made; she simply outlined them and proceeded on the assumption that her mother would comply. To the mother who had been so unmothering in her own childhood, Sand now expressed gratitude: "Farewell, my dear mother. I thank you a thousand times for your goodness toward me and my children. I feel relaxed about Maurice because you're taking charge of him."[10] But this expression of gratitude, conditioned not by what her mother had yet done but by what she was now constrained to do, was, in reality, more coercive than sincere. Even had Sophie chosen to decline her daughter's "request" to take charge of Maurice, it would have been too late. By the time Sophie received the letter, Sand was well on her way to Italy.

Up to this point Sand had filled her notes to her mother with reports of her poor health. But now, in spite of complaining to her husband about rheumatism, Sand declared, "I leave in good health this evening." In addition to asserting geographic and sexual independence by traveling to Italy with her lover, as well as securing relief from the burden of maternal responsibility, Sand had ingeniously devised a means of deriving vicarious compensation for the deprivations of her childhood. In her subtle but sure manipulation of her mother, is not Sand also taking a bit of revenge? What you neglected to do for me, Sand seems to be saying, you must now do for my child. But this carefully constructed transfer of maternal responsibility only thinly veils the underlying irony of Sand's situation: in her extended absence from her children, she would repeat the pattern of neglect from which she too had suffered as a child.

In a finishing flourish, Sand arranged to have her son's former tutor, who happened (simultaneously) to have been Sand's former lover, close up her Paris apartment and to see that, in her absence, the workmen and servants did not drink her wine.

Remarkably, the letter Casimir sends his wife while she is en route to Italy contains no suggestion of resentment for her departure. On the contrary, it evidences astounding sensitivity, contrary to the impression of Casimir's dullness and debauchery that interpretations of Sand's marriage generally convey:

> I received, my dear friend, your letter dated from Florence
> where you tell me that you're just passing through en route
> to Venice. I'm very pleased to know that your health can't

deteriorate in a country in which the sun has the faculty of curing colds and fevers, but I'm sorry to see that your fantasies of this trip have been disappointed.

You're casting a cool, calm, philosophical eye on the monuments, the sites, and the riches of all kinds that have made so many hearts beat, that have turned so many heads, and prompted so many passionate pages; this is a charming, memorable country, where everyone can find something special and meaningful. You are in the theatre of your father's and our great army's military exploits; you have read your father's letters to your grandmother; you will no doubt pass some battlefield where he risked his life, which he lost near La Châtre. What an important emotional chapter.

As for me, I'm well, Adieu; I wish you bon voyage, good health, etc. etc.[11]

Casimir went on to report on the children, informing his wife that they were well and thriving. "I received news of Maurice. He continues to work well; he has his pockets filled with honors. . . . Chubby little Solange is well, she is enchanted with being here. She works well, her maid is taking good care of her and teaching her to work well; she's marking napkins, and doing little projects which are quite pretty for her age."

Despite her eagerness to be off, Sand was not without misgivings about leaving her children behind, especially her daughter. "I'm sad not to have my daughter with me," Sand acknowledged, "and now that I've arranged not to see her before the month of August, I think of her day and night with incredible thirst and impatience. What is this love that mothers have? It's still a mystery to me. Cares and worries a hundred times sharper than in the love of a lover and yet less joy and transport in the possession. Absence which isn't felt for the first few days and which becomes cruel and burning like a fever the longer it goes on."[12]

Having waited from before dawn, Sand and Musset boarded a steamer on the quai du Rhône in Lyons and departed for Italy early in the morning of 15 December. On the way to Avignon they met Henri Beyle, the consul at Civitavecchia, otherwise known by the pen name Stendhal. "He had a brilliant wit," Sand would later record, "and his conversation recalled that of Delatouche, though less delicate and graceful, but more profound." She described the illustrious author of *Le Rouge et le noir* as "fat, with a very fine physiognomy under a mask of flesh" and summed up his literary talent as follows: "an awkward writer whose story-telling, nevertheless, captured his readers and held them fast." Stendhal predicted that Sand would find Italy boring and devoid of intellectual stimulation, but she dismissed his warnings: "I was going there, as everywhere, to escape the wittiness he believed I craved."[13]

In Genoa, Sand came down with a fever, which she attributed to difficulty in adapting to the Italian climate. "I continued my trip anyway, not exactly ill, but gradually so worn out by tremors, weakness, and drowsiness that I saw Pisa and Camposanto with great apathy. I became indifferent to choosing one direction or another: Rome or Venice were determined by heads or tails. Venice came up heads ten times. I decided to call this fate, and left for Venice via Florence." A fresh attack of fever greeted her in Florence, where she saw, through a dreamlike trance, Cellini's *Perseus* and Michelangelo's square chapel. "At night," she later recalled, "I would dream I was turning into a mosaic, and I carefully counted my little squares of lapis lazuli and jasper."

The lovers crossed the Apennines on a clear, cold night in January, continued on to Bologna and Ferrara, where Sand was too sick to remember what she saw. She rallied slightly crossing the Po, then slept until they reached Venice, where she awoke to find herself "gliding in a gondola and watching, as though a mirage, the lights of San Marco square reflected in the water and the great cut-out forms of Byzantine architecture silhouetted against the immense moon." The lovers arrived in Venice on New Year's day.

Sand's fever, which came and went, was now accompanied by unbearable migraines that kept her in her room at the Albergo Reale (now the Hotel Danieli) for the first two weeks of their stay in Venice. According to Jean Pommier, the Albergo Reale, which was established in 1822 by Giuseppe dal Niel, known as Danieli, was "one of the best Italian inns, in which the magnificently furnished apartments, which even contain Pianoforte, provide the most beautiful views. There are also clear and saltwater pools, as well as well-appointed Gondolas always available to the guests."[14]

By the end of January, having largely regained her health and stamina, Sand wrote Boucoiran a picturesque description of Carnival season, describing the masked and costumed Venetians, the Neapolitan fishermen, and the troops of musicians who paraded on the quays and floated on the canals in festive boats. But while Sand had been convalescing, Musset had been carousing in the bars and cafés of Venice and getting to know the Venetian nightspots. By the end of several weeks he had contracted a venereal disease. After a month of dissolution, he was deathly ill with typhoid fever.

At the beginning of February, Sand called in an Italian physician, Pietro Pagello, to attend Musset. The handsome young doctor, with his dark curly hair and well-chiseled features, had already been called in by the hotel to bleed Sand during a bout of migraine. The day before this first visit, while Pagello was strolling with a friend outside Sand's hotel, he had glimpsed the exotic-looking young woman and inquired who she might be. So when Sand asked him to attend Musset, the attraction between her and Pagello had evidently already begun. Pagello was soon staying on after professional calls for tea and conversation with his patient's mistress. One evening, raging with fever and too weak to protest from his sickbed, Musset saw Sand seated on Pagello's lap, sipping from a common cup. A slew of jealous accusations followed, which Sand vehemently denied. But by the beginning of March she wrote Pagello the following note, testifying to the rapid progress of their relations: "My angel, take courage. I can no longer go out with you. I was very troubled once again today. Alfred was very sad and dear. I see that he no longer dares to get angry about our intimacy, but that it makes him suffer."[15]

In spite of Casimir's glowing report that Maurice "has his pockets filled with honors," the child's own communication was less jubilant. In a dutiful but tepid note, he wrote his mother about New Year's, which he spent shuttling among his two grandmothers and his great-aunt Lucie Maréchal in Paris. Distorting her son's underlying feeling of dissatisfaction about his winter holidays, Sand wrote her mother a much exaggerated account: "My dear mother, I received your letter today at the same time as one from Maurice who tells me he had a lot of fun, that you were very good to him and that he's very happy to go home with you." In the same letter Sand boasted to her mother of her own accomplishments: "I've developed a lot of independence, and despite people's envy my work has been quite successful."[16]

By February the romance between Sand and Pagello had reached a high-water mark. "Born under separate skies," Sand wrote her Italian lover, "we have neither common thoughts nor common language; do we at least have similar hearts?" Fresh from Musset's recent abandonment, as well as previous disappointments in love, Sand sought reassurance that Pagello would be true to her. "At least you won't betray me, you won't make me hollow promises and tell me lies." Idealizing Pagello as she had idealized previous lovers, Sand exclaimed, "Will it be you, will it finally be you, my Pietro, who will make my dream come true? I believe so, and so far you seem as great as God." Surely Sand wasn't anticipating that in just a few months she would tire of the young doctor and eagerly end their brief affair. In love with Pagello, in love with Venice, which she declared "the most beautiful city in the world,"[17] Sand wrote her husband in early March that she would remain another month in Italy. She sent instructions for him to keep Solange and her maid until her return.

By mid-March the cost of remaining at the Albergo Reale had so depleted their finances that Sand and Musset had to seek other lodgings. They relocated in rooms in the calle delle Rasse, but by then their relationship had deteriorated to the point where Musset made plans to return to France. Accompanying him as far as Mestre, Sand bid Musset farewell on 29 March and departed the following day for a week of travel, including a stop at Trevise, with Pagello.

"[Musset] left for Paris without me and I'm going to stay on for several more months," Sand wrote Boucoiran in early April. She blamed Musset's departure on his frail health. "You know the reasons for this separation. Day by day it became more necessary and it would have been impossible for him to make the journey with me without exposing himself to a relapse. His still fragile lungs required complete abstinence, but his nervous irritation made deprivation insufferable for him."[18] This is the same rationalization she had given for her behavior with Jules Sandeau, whose health she ostensibly "protected" by physically denying herself to him. We can only imagine what effect this revelation had on poor Boucoiran, who knew all too well what it felt like to be deprived of his former mistress' ministrations.

En route to Paris, Musset posted a poignant letter to Sand: "This morning I wandered the streets of Geneva, gazing at the shops: a new waistcoat, a beautiful edition of an English book, that's what attracted my attention. I looked at myself in a mirror, I recognized the child I once was. . . . That was the man that you wanted to love! . . . For you to love me, my poor George! That made me tremble. I made you so miserable. . . . I will see it for a long time, my George, your face paled by your vigils leaning over my bedside for eighteen nights. . . . You were mistaken; you thought you were my mistress, you were only my mother; heaven made us for one another. . . . But we were too tightly bound; it was incest that we committed."[19]

Sand's response was caring and protective: "I know that I love you, that is all. But not with this painful thirst to kiss you every moment that I could not satisfy without killing you. But with a fully virile force and also with all the tenderness of feminine love. To watch over you, to save you from all harm, from every adversity, to lavish you with distractions and pleasures, this is what I've needed and missed since I lost you."[20]

Although Sand behaved maternally toward her lovers—"I need to nourish the maternal solicitude that gets used to watching over a tired and needy being"—it was she who craved the love she had never received from her mother. Exalting and idealizing each successive love object, Sand would eventually find herself disappointed and betrayed. As we've seen, after breaking up with Sandeau, she had declared, "This mistake is the last of my life. Between hallowed friendship and myself there will no longer be any obstacle." This time she went even further, lamenting, "My life as a woman is over."[21] By the spring of 1835 the Musset drama had ended, and Sand was spending quiet days at Nohant reading Plato and the Koran.

Musset would later tell a friend that Sand lacked what the French call "griserie." "Real hot sex, you know, what you get with sluts. I insulted her, accused her of not wanting it."[22] Casimir and Sandeau had expressed similar sentiments, and Prosper Mérimée had complained that Sand left their bed to stoke a fire and work on pages of Lélia.

Was Sand sexually inhibited in ways that disappointed her partners? By her own admission, it would seem so. However painfully aware of this she may have been, she nevertheless expressed a highly idealized view of physical love: "Intimacy without love is a loathsome thing to consider. A woman who toys with her husband in order to dominate him is no better than the prostitute who does what she does for her daily bread or the courtesan for her luxury. . . . Once a human being, man or woman, has learned what complete love can be, he or she can never, and even more must never, fall back to the level of pure animality."[23]

Because Sandeau and Musset did not remain abstinent in response to Sand's sexual coolness, her gesture can be seen as more of a retreat than self-sacrifice. In fact, Sand was keenly aware of the heightened sexual frustration that her lovers experienced when she withdrew physically from them, her denial no doubt fueling their ardor rather than quelling it. Unable to gratify her partners fully, ultimately neglected and betrayed by them, Sand may have chosen to respond by withholding sexual favors. Better, perhaps, to exit an affair convincing herself (and others) that her partner's sexual passion for her was still intact than to confront the possibility that her lover had lost interest.

Pagello, however, represented something different. Clearly on the rebound, Sand found in the young Italian doctor a safe haven from the pain and passion of the Musset fiasco. In May she wrote Musset describing the nature of the attraction between her and Pagello: "He treats me like a twenty-year-old woman and puts a halo over my head as though I were a virgin soul. I say nothing to destroy or maintain his mistake. I let myself rejuvenate in this gentle and honest affection. For the first time in my life, I love without passion."[24]

Upon returning to Venice with Pagello, Sand changed residence again, this time taking rooms in Ca' Mezzani, Corte Minello. At the end of April she relocated once again to a house near the Barcaroli bridge. She continued to press Buloz for additional funds. By June she was broke but received money sent by Boucoiran in time for her thirtieth birthday. Pagello recorded the following description of the woman with whom he had thrown in his lot:

> She was a very clever and active homemaker. I lived with her when she was short of money and I was also just a poor beginner in my profession. With a bit of my money she bought material, sewed curtains, a bedspread and covered a sofa and six chairs, kneeling on the floor, with her coat and some nails, with all the adeptness of an experienced artisan. She took care of the cooking and she swore to me that this was one of her favorite pastimes. Then suddenly, leaving her practical chores, she would go to her work table and dash off thirty or so pages . . . and without rereading she would fold, seal and send them off to her editor Buloz. I asked her: but how did you manage to think up what you wrote. And she responded: "While hammering nails!"[25]

"Love of work is my salvation," Sand wrote Hippolyte in March, reflecting on her ability to work in the midst of life's distractions: "I bless my grandmother, who forced me into the habit of work. This habit has become a faculty, and this faculty has become a need. I've gotten to the point of working thirteen hours in a row without getting sick, and on the average without tiring, seven or eight hours a day, whether the result is good or bad."[26]

Despite her serious bout of sickness in January, despite Musset's neglect and betrayal, despite a new and thrilling love affair, Sand's literary productivity for this period is impressive. In a matter of just several months she had written the novels *Secrétaire intime, Léone Léonie,* and half of *André.* The idea for *Léone Léonie,* whose eponymous protagonist was based on Musset, came from the memoirs of Casanova. By May, Sand had completed *André,* a nostalgic story of a young Berrichon girl, as well as the epistolary novel *Jacques,* a meditation on love, passion, and jealousy. In April, Sand wrote Musset, informing him that she had composed a long letter to him that she planned to publish. She asked him to look it over and if he approved, to pass it along to Buloz. It would become the first of the *Lettres d'un voyageur.*[27]

In May, Sand wrote Musset a thoughtful letter about the emotional progress she had made since their parting. "My child, my soul is calming down and hope is returning." By the time she left Venice in July, the second and third *Lettres d'un voyageur* would be written, as well. *Mattéa* was also produced during the Venice sojourn. This novel, set against a backdrop of eighteenth-century Venice, was written as Sand sat drinking coffee on the colorful Piazza San Marco and observing the cosmopolitan Venetian society. "Who would have predicted," Sand later reflected, "that this Venice, where I thought I was passing through as a traveler, without giving it anything of my life and without taking from it anything but a few artistic impressions, was going to take hold of me, of my being, of my passions, of my present, of my future?"[28] In all, more than a quarter of the novels Sand wrote would be set in Italy.

In addition to bringing in much needed income, work for Sand was also an antidote to depression: "It brings me money and consumes much of the time that I would otherwise spend in the 'spleen' to which my bilious temperament inclines me." Among likely sources of Sand's depression, or spleen, as it was known in those times, was her relationship with her children, and in particular with Maurice. In March she complained to Boucoiran: "Seriously, I'm very disturbed by Maurice's silence. It's incredible that he doesn't think to write me and that since my departure I still haven't been able to learn whether he's getting good grades. Make him aware of his oversight and tell him that he's hurting me so much that I no longer want to write him if he doesn't write me more. Make him cry a little bit if necessary." In May she wrote Maurice plaintively: "My child, I'm very sad and very annoyed; why don't you write me? You think no more of me than if you had an evil heart and yet I know you are good and that you love me. What is it then that causes your silence?"[29]

Maurice had, in fact, written her a letter on 12 May, which crossed with hers, though she wouldn't receive it for several weeks. In it he supplies his reason for the silence: "I haven't written you for a long time because I've been waiting for a letter from you before writing back."[30] Rather than send them directly to Maurice, Sand had been routing her communications to him through Boucoiran. Having suffered his mother's absence at Christmas and the New Year, and then again at Easter, Maurice naturally felt angry and abandoned.

In her letter to Maurice, Sand planted suggestions uncannily reminiscent of her past. Echoing the blame her mother laid on her as a child, Sand wrote her son, "I suppose you sometimes go for days without remembering your poor mother on her travels; perhaps you hear bad things about her." And then, echoing her dying grandmother's words to her, Sand continued, "None of this will change the fact that one day you will acknowledge and choose me as your best friend."[31]

Maurice's response was filled with pathos: "You say that I go for days without thinking of my poor traveling mother; I think of you every single day, I hear nothing bad about you." Sand concluded her letter to Maurice with a threat thinly veiled as a challenge: "Let me know if you are competing for prizes and exactly when the awards will be made, so I can arrange to be in Paris at that time. I need to know in advance. It's a long trip, you know."[32] The trip is long and I must inconvenience myself to make it, so you had better make it worth my while, Sand seems to be saying to her young son.

By the end of May, Sand was crazed with anxiety and guilt about Maurice. "I imagine he's dead and I go mad during the nights." She then associated this obsession with her financial situation: "Added to this is the problem of being absolutely broke and without certain basic necessities." On 1 June she wrote Hippolyte of her plans to remain in Venice, giving as her reason the need to earn more money: "I'm still in Venice for two more months, working like a horse to pay for my trip to Italy, which I still owe to my editor but which I'm paying back little by little." Next came the refrain of suffering over separation from her children: "But I'm suffering a lot from being so far from my children for such a long time."[33]

Sophie had blamed her separation from Aurore on the bargain she struck with Madame Dupin: in exchange for a living stipend, Sophie had agreed to remain in Paris and to relinquish care of Aurore. Sand would attribute her continued absence from her own children to her contractual obligation to her editor. When she blamed her son for his silence, when she complained to him of her pain and suffering, when she implored him to remember her and to love and care for her, she effectively reversed the roles of parent and child, reliving her own past deprivation and experiencing it anew in the relationship with her child. "Keep in mind that I am far from you, that I have a thousand qualms, that I awaken sad every morning and go to sleep sad every evening," Sand wrote Maurice in June. "I'm in pain and am exhausted; you know, my child, grownups are rarely happy." Having missed Christmas, New Year's, and Easter, Sand would also miss her son's first communion in June.[34]

She begged Musset, by then back in Paris, to check on Maurice: "Go see my son, tell me how he is, if he remembers my name, if he has a human face. I dream every night that his skeleton is brought to me or his bloodied body." Sand wrote Solange in June that she would join her again in August and, reprising her mother's unfulfilled promise to her, told her daughter, "After that we will never be apart, my dearest." Of course this was a promise that Sand wouldn't keep.[35]

By July, Sand received word from Casimir that Maurice was having problems. She responded defensively: "What you inform me about Maurice's apathy astonishes me since no one has written a word to me about it. . . . If I could have predicted that my absence would be so harmful to him I would not have left Paris, but it's difficult for me to believe that he has reacted so dramatically."[36] By the end of July, equipped with the funds finally received from Boucoiran, Sand was ready to leave Venice with Pagello for the trip back to Paris. She would later compose the following description of the city in which she had experienced so much emotional and physical turmoil:

"Venice was indeed the city of my dreams; all I had imagined was still less than how it actually appeared to me, mornings as well as evenings, in calm, sunny days as well as in the somber reflected light of storms. I loved this city for itself—the only one in the world I could have loved this way, since a city has always had the effect on me of a prison, tolerable only because of my companions in captivity. In Venice, one could be alone for long periods, and one came to understand how, in the time of its splendor and freedom, its children had virtually personified and cherished it, not as a thing, but as a living being."[37]

Passing through Verona, Sand and Pagello stopped overnight in Milan, then continued their journey by way of Lake Maggiore, Domodossola, Brigue, Martigny, Chamonix, Le Montenvers, and Geneva, where they spent several days and nights. They arrived in Paris on 14 August, in time for Sand to attend the awards ceremony at Maurice's school. Despite his mother's high hopes, the child received no academic prizes. At the end of the month Sand left with Maurice and her mother for Nohant. Musset went on to spend the summer in Baden, while Pagello remained in Paris. In a journal entry during the voyage from Italy to France, Pagello made the following notation: "As we advanced, our relations became cooler and more wary. G. S. was a bit melancholy and considerably more detached. It was painful to acknowledge that she was an actress quite accustomed to these deceits."[38]

Musset wrote Sand a farewell letter filled with sadness and best wishes. Testifying to the literary self-consciousness of their love affair, he declared that in spite of his despair, he would not die before completing his book: "Posterity will record our names like those immortal lovers whose names are joined, like Romeo and Juliette, like Héloise and Abeylard."[39] Musset was referring to the *Confession d'un enfant du siècle* (*Confession of a Child of the Century*), his literary immortalization of their love affair that would appear the following year. In it, Sand would be cast as Brigitte Pierson. Octave, the male protagonist, treats her alternatively as an unfaithful lover and as a kept woman. She treats him in the motherly, nurturing way that Sand treated Musset. In the end, they part and eventually forgive each other. Sand was deeply moved when she read it.

In October, when Musset and Sand again met in Paris, stormy romantic relations resumed. By the end of the month Pagello was on his way back to Venice. By mid-November, Sand and Musset had another break. Sand cut off her long hair—the wavy black tresses that Vigny had compared to Raphael's angels—sent some to Musset, and saved the rest to enclose with Musset's last letter in a skull bought specially for this purpose.[40] She sought asylum in Buloz' Paris apartment so that Musset would be unable to track her down.

Delacroix's portrait of the thirty-year-old Sand captures her in partial profile.[41] Her thick, dark hair, cropped short around her oval face, falls just short of the folded ascot at the neck of her signature redingote with velvet lapels. Underneath is a cream-colored blouse that echoes the alabaster cast of her complexion. Sand's head is slightly uplifted, the far side in semishadow, the near side illuminated as though with hope and inspiration as the subject gazes wistfully into the future. The face in this remarkable portrait, neither masculine nor feminine, is deeply human, endowed with a spirituality suggestive of the gathering greatness of this hugely gifted individual. Sand's first sitting with Delacroix marked the beginning of a lifelong friendship.

In January, after relations between Sand and Musset had resumed once again, she wrote him: "Alas, I am slack and flaccid as a broken cord. I'm on the ground, rolling around with my wounded love like a cadaver. ... I'm no longer in love with you, but I will always adore you." They were still together in February, when they attended one of the season's major theatrical events, Alfred de Vigny's *Chatterton*. But the combination of Musset's dissolute behavior, his outrageous jealousy, and his increasingly abusive treatment were more than Sand could bear. "You say that . . . I should slap you when you abuse me. I don't know how to fight. God made me gentle and at the same time proud," Sand wrote him. "Your behavior is deplorable, impossible. . . . The drunkenness, the wine! prostitutes, still, and always! . . . Your insane jealousy about everything, in the midst of everything else! The more you renounce the right to be jealous, the more jealous you become!"[42]

By March 1835, Sand had had enough. She wrote Boucoiran, orchestrating her getaway. He would book her a seat in the mail coach, fetch her bag and leave it at the station, and come for her with the excuse that her mother was ill, without a servant, and in need of her help. To Musset's mother Sand dispatched a gift of a little bird and a note apologizing for having caused her pain. After all, Sand had come to think of Musset as a son, so it was natural to commiserate with his mother over the suffering their love affair had caused.

By May, she reassured Musset of her resilience and encouraged him

George Sand. Print by Henri Thiriat, after Delacroix.
(© Photothèque des musées de la ville de Paris. Photo:
Degraces)

to have faith in his own: "But your heart, your good heart, do not destroy
it, I beg of you. Give your whole heart or as much as you can to every love
of your life, but let it play its part with dignity, so that you can look back
and say as I do, I have often suffered, I have sometimes been deceived,
but I have loved. It is I who have lived and not some artificial being driven
by ego and ennui."[43]

Musset apparently felt sufficiently encouraged to turn his former mistress' words of wisdom to productive literary use. The following familiar
lines turned up in his play *On ne badine pas avec l'amour* (*Don't Fool with
Love*): "One is often deceived in love, often wounded and often unhappy;
but one loves, and when one is on the edge of the grave, one looks back
and says: I have often suffered, I have sometimes been deceived, but I

have loved. It is I who have loved, and not some artificial being driven by ego and ennui."[44]

In her study of Sand's correspondence, Anne E. McCall informs us that "the epistolary exchanges between Musset and Sand were the subject of conflict between the ex-lovers until Musset's death and even afterwards, between Sand and Paul de Musset. . . . George Sand, who admitted her role in certain 'suppressions,' very much wanted the rest to be faithfully transmitted to posterity. To this end, she made several copies which she conferred to good friends; they were supposed to follow specific instructions, defining the terms of a posthumous publication. Ultimately, Sand wanted this correspondence to be deposited in a library."[45]

Although the love affair had ended, the literature it spawned has lived on.

CHAPTER EIGHTEEN

Mother Love

The genius of Chopin is the most profoundly feelingful that has
ever existed. He made a single instrument speak the language of
infinity.

IN THE FALL OF 1836, Sand made the acquaintance of the young Polish
composer Frédéric Chopin at the home of Princess Marie d'Agoult and
Franz Liszt. Having fled Poland at the threat of the Russian occupation,
Chopin arrived in Paris in 1831, the same year Aurore Dudevant went to
the capital to launch her literary career. Among the other distinguished
guests at the soirée were Giacomo Meyerbeer, Eugène Sue, Heinrich Heine,
and a group of Polish exiles associated with Adam Mickiewicz, who would
shortly become a professor at the Collège de France. Although Sand was
immediately taken with Chopin, the relationship got off to a slow start.
"I've made the acquaintance of a great celebrity, Madame Dudevant, known
by the name George Sand," Chopin wrote his parents several days after
their meeting. "But her face doesn't appeal to me at all. There's even something about her that puts me off."[1]

In the spring of 1838, the Dudevants' legal separation was finalized.
The court settlement represented a major victory for Sand, who regained
ownership of Nohant and the custody of Solange (she would later assume
custody of Maurice as well). In April, Auguste Charpentier traveled to Nohant to paint pictures of the family. His splendid portrait of the writer is
well known: the long, lustrous black hair encircling a placid oval face, a
spray of flowers tucked behind one ear, a braided and bejeweled cross in the
V of her handsome black gown. The strange and portentous little portrait
Charpentier painted of Solange is set ominously against the backdrop of
a cloud-covered sky. It shows a young girl's whitened face emerging in
profile from solid black hair and a torso that flow together like a hooded
garment. The impression, unusual in child portraiture, is sinister and severe.[2]

George Sand. Portrait by Auguste Charpentier.
(© Photothèque des musées de la ville de Paris.
Photo: Adreani)

Sand's interest in Chopin, whose reticence had persisted since their meeting of a year and a half earlier, blossomed into pursuit. Frustrated at Chopin's lack of response, she wrote the composer's friend Woyciech (Albert) Grzymala to inquire about the status of Chopin's relationship with Marie Wodzinska, the fiancée he had left behind in Poland. Sand let it be known that if Chopin and Marie were no longer betrothed, she would be interested in taking care of the composer, who was suffering from tuberculosis. Apparently, Sand's altruistic approach impressed Grzymala, whose encouragement helped propel Chopin into a relationship with Sand that would endure for the next nine years. Overcoming one final obstacle, Sand dispatched Maurice and his tutor, Félicien Mallefille, a jealous and assertive young man with whom she had been conducting an affair, on a trip

Solange Dudevant. By Auguste Charpentier. (Courtesy C. O. Darré, Musée George Sand, La Châtre)

to Normandy. Finally, in the summer of 1838, she and Chopin became lovers.[3]

By the fall Chopin's tubercular symptoms had worsened, and the children, who had not fared well through the lengthy ordeal of their parents' separation, were sickly: Maurice with chest pain and palpitations, and Solange with increasingly severe migraines. To escape the inclement French winter (and Mallefille, who was enraged when he discovered his mistress' new love interest), Sand decided that a winter season in Majorca would be in everyone's best interest.

In mid-October, Sand left Paris with Maurice and Solange, and, for the sake of discretion, Chopin followed soon after. At the end of the month, Chopin rejoined Sand and the children in Perpignan. From Port-Vendres they sailed to Barcelona, and from Barcelona to Palma, arriving in the Majorcan capital on 7 November.

Frédéric Chopin. Portrait by Eugène Delacroix. (Courtesy
Bibliothèque nationale de France)

Solange was seasick during the crossing, but once on the island she
fared well. (Maurice claimed that his sister lost her bilious nature by throwing up into the sea.) Indeed, one of the only consolations of the difficult
winter that lay ahead was the dramatic improvement in Solange's disposition. Being back in the family fold and close to her mother was obviously
what Solange had been longing for. In *Mortal Wounds,* Anthony West
makes the following observation about Solange's adjustment to Majorcan
life: "Solange [10] was a remarkable child. . . . She was the one member
of the party who was not considered by the village to be involved in its
wickedness, and she had a free relationship with the village children that
some of them could recall as long as sixty years later. All the evidence suggests that she was the only member of the group who could speak Mallor-
quin and consequently the only one who really knew how it was regarded
by the villagers."[4]

Contrary to expectations, the weather on Majorca was cold and rainy, and, to make matters worse, the islanders responded inhospitably to the strange traveling party (apparently with the exception of Solange) that had descended on them from France. Chopin's consumption aroused fear of contagion, and in short order they were evicted from their first residence and charged by the landlord for the mattresses he felt compelled to burn in their wake. They had no choice but to move far out to the countryside, where they finally found three small rooms among the ruins of an abandoned monastery at Valldemosa.

The Pleyel piano sent down from France finally arrived after being held up in Majorcan customs for many weeks, and despite Chopin's failing health, the intemperate climate, and an inadequate diet owing to scarcity of familiar foodstuffs, Chopin settled down to a remarkably productive winter of work. In addition to the Mazurka in E Minor, op. 41, no. 2, "which he called *Palmejski* in Polish (for having been written in Palma) and which critics hailed for its 'dramatic displays' and 'poetic effect,'" Chopin also produced what may have been the Prelude in D-flat Major, op. 28, no. 15 (the "Raindrop Prelude"); the Prelude in A Minor, op. 28, no. 2; two polonaises (op. 40); Ballade no. 2 in F Major, op. 38; and the Scherzo no. 3 in C-sharp Minor, op. 39.[5] The composer found time, as well, to give Solange her first piano lessons.

In addition to cooking for the family under extremely limited and rustic conditions (household help was difficult to come by), Sand divided her time between exploring the island with the children, giving them lessons, and doing her own writing. Sand would memorialize their sojourn in *Winter in Majorca,* a travelogue she published several years later.[6] The hardships they had endured were turned against the Majorcan people, for whom Sand displayed unmitigated contempt:

> The Majorcan, then, unable to fatten beef, or make use of wool, or milk cows . . . or grow enough wheat to dare eat bread; scarcely bringing himself to cultivate the mulberry and gather silk; having also forgotten the art of carpentry, for which the island was once famous; possessing no horses . . . nor considering it necessary to maintain one single negotiable road or path on the entire island . . . vegetated for a century or more, with nothing whatever to do except tell his beads and patch his

Maurice and Solange Dudevant. By Nancy Mérienne.
(© Photothèque des musées de la ville de Paris.
Photo: Adreani)

breeches, which were in a sorrier state than those of Don Quixote, his prototype in poverty and pride—until the hog arrived to save the situation. Its export was declared legal, and the new era of prosperity began. In centuries to come the Majorcans will call this the Age of the Hog—just as Moslem historians celebrate the age of the Elephant.[7]

Solange's improved disposition earned her a respite from boarding school when the family returned from Majorca in the spring of 1839, during which time she was tutored at home by a Mademoiselle Suez. Solange's menstrual periods, which began in August 1840, a month short of her twelfth birthday, elicited an anxious response from Sand, who immediately dispatched a message to the family doctor: "My daughter has just undergone a normal little crisis, but a bit prematurely, I believe, even though she is well; I would like you to see her, for perhaps some precaution should be taken." Early puberty seems to have been unsettling to Solange, who once again fell into disfavor with her mother. It did not help matters when Solange began referring to Chopin as "sans sexe" and made up the Polish-sounding prefix "testele," which she added to his name. Conceivably, in the close living quarters on Majorca, the sensitive and observant pre-adolescent had become aware that sexual relations between her mother and Chopin had ceased. Marie d'Agoult, who had recorded such a positive impression several years ago, had a very changed opinion of the twelve-year-old Solange: "A plump, rude, rather pretty girl who doesn't say a word."[8]

By fall, displeased with Solange's behavior and with the lack of progress in her home tutoring, Sand enrolled her in the pension Héreau. Maurice remained at home on rue Pigalle with his mother and Chopin. In the spring, still not pleased with Solange's performance, Sand abruptly withdrew her and transferred her as a day student to the pension Bascans. "It's her character that's the problem," Sand explained to the school's headmaster. Unable to control Solange's increasing rebelliousness and frequent "crises de férocité," Sand left Solange behind in Paris to board at the Bascans pension when she returned to Nohant in June with Maurice and Chopin.[9]

"Farewell, dearest Mama; send for me soon and write me to make the time go by," Solange wrote home. She took care to list the loved ones by whom her mother was surrounded in her absence: "Tell Léontine, Luce, my brother, Chopin, my uncle and everyone to write me."[10]

In her frequent letters from the Bascans pension, where Solange would spend the better part of the next three years, she complained of being sick, of suffering, of lacking things she needed, and of being bored. "Imagine a daughter deprived of her mother for whom all the days, hours, minutes seem so long that she's desperate about the time she must spend before seeing her mother again." Solange wrote home. "She can only cry, and crying doesn't console her. Nothing, not work or play, consoles her. She always has tears in her eyes and whenever she hears someone say the word *mother*, she cries and despairs. Truly, if I had to live a long time, I believe I wouldn't last very long."[11]

Sand responded by scolding Solange for not applying herself to her school work and advised her that "people who are bored make boring people." Solange's childlike pleas provide poignant psychological insight into the relationship between boredom and depression. Sand's failure to understand, much less to sympathize with her daughter's pain, is all the more striking in view of Sand's own feelings as a child in the absence of her mother. More disturbing even than Sand's lack of compassion is her tendency to inflict on Solange the conditions of her own painful past. Sand never acknowledged her jealousy and resentment of her half sister, Caroline, who was raised by Sophie in Paris while Aurore was left behind at Nohant. But by reporting the good times she and Maurice were having at home while Solange was far away, Sand subjected her daughter to similar jealousy and resentment toward Maurice, also (though unacknowledged) a half sibling. Solange's response was predictable: "Are you having fun at Nohant?" she wrote her brother. "Are you doing some riding? Are you going fishing and swimming with Pistolet? I confess that this time I'm really jealous."[12]

Sand's litany of complaints multiplied as Solange grew older: she was too lazy, too moody, too stubborn, and, finally, too independent. Sand compiled a list of Solange's defects—"self-love, the need to dominate people, crazy and foolish jealousy"—and sent it to her at boarding school. Increasingly, Sand responded to Solange's feeling of deprivation by accusing her of exaggeration. Twin themes of truth and reality versus distortion and illusion began to emerge in the relationship between mother and daughter. When Solange wrote home that she wasn't getting enough to eat and was hungry and miserable, Sand replied: "Why do you distort the truth?" to which Solange responded: "I don't need to say that I'm no longer a liar because I never was one." Sand wrote the headmistress, Madame Bascans, accusing Solange of inventing stories to explain away her poor school performance: "And then, to excuse herself, she contrives all sorts of little reasons that come so close to lies that if she thinks she's telling the truth, she's totally deluded." Marie de Rozières, whom Sand had hired as Solange's companion, was charged with chastizing Solange for lying: "To listen to her you'd think the pension was Siberia. You mustn't do it in front of Madame Bascans, but since you're in a position to point out the lies this little girl is telling, make it your business to shame her a little bit."[13]

Sand's complaint that Solange was prone to distorting reality is curiously at odds with the evaluation she sent her daughter's headmistress at the end of summer vacation: "Solange's strong suit is the recall of facts.

She combines this with the ability to express herself, and I believe she will be capable of deep understanding, logical analysis, and skillful writing, in a word, of doing good work on the subject of history." Although Sand was referring to Solange's academic qualifications, in fact Solange brought the same gifts of memory, self-expression, understanding, and logic to her personal relationships. But when she applied them to conflicts with her mother, Sand consistently rejected Solange's version of reality; hence, the irony of Sand's observation that "if she's headed in the direction of using her mind, she'll probably do her best to destroy idolatry."[14]

Early in life Solange developed the annoying habit of taking her mother to task for her own lapses of virtue: "Since I saw you calmly write a letter to Madame Perdiguier that would make her cry," fifteen-year-old Solange wrote her mother from boarding school, "I've realized you do the same thing to me." Typically, Sand deflected Solange's attacks by reversing the blame: "Because you've reflected on how coolly I composed a letter to make someone cry, you should have said to yourself that if I wasn't angry while I was writing, I was suffering inside from the hurt caused by proof of ingratitude, and that I wasn't acting spitefully out of annoyance. You're very eager to accuse and condemn, and your judgments respect no one, not even me."[15]

The core of Sand's complaint against her daughter came at the end of the letter: "An intelligent, well-developed person should be able to understand at your age that the true objective is to love something . . . *goodness, beauty, truth,* and someone more than oneself." The message, which would be repeated many times in many different forms, is clear: Solange was not meant to see the world as it was, but rather as her idealizing mother believed it should be seen. Nor, by implication, was Solange meant to see her mother as she was, but rather as an extension of goodness, beauty, and truth. In essence, Sand was applying to her daughter the same romantic formula she applied to her literature. "Art is not a study of positive reality; it's a quest for ideal truth," Sand famously declared in her foreword to *La Mare au diable* (*The Devil's Pool*), one of her rustic novels (*romans champêtres*) in which she presents an idealized picture of peasant life: "See the simplicity. . . . See the sky and the fields, and the trees, and above all the peasants in their goodness and truth."[16]

Solange's existence (as well as the French peasants', for that matter) was *not* so simple; nor was the backdrop against which it was set. Real life and Sand's literature were *not* the same, and among the novelist's great-est frustrations was her inability to press her daughter into the mold in which she instinctually and efficiently cast her characters. This aspect of Sand's *ars poetica* is aptly articulated by Lucienne de Valangis, the central character of her autobiographical novel *La Confession d'une jeune fille* (*The Confession of a Young Girl*): "I wasn't a liar, I was a romantic. What's real didn't satisfy me; I was looking for something stranger and more brilliant in the realm of dreams. I've remained that way: this has been the cause of all my disasters and also perhaps the seat of all my strengths."[17]

Solange's letters home exposed her to yet another complaint of her mother, who frequently critiqued their style and grammar. Coming from a mother who was a celebrated professional author, this criticism was es-pecially frustrating and hurtful. "You reproach me in ways I don't deserve," fifteen-year-old Solange wrote back on one such occasion. "You tell me my style is affected. If it is, which is altogether possible, it's not by inten-tion. Not everyone has your style. You shouldn't reproach mine for not seeming natural, which is probably because it's so natural that it doesn't seem so. You practically accuse me of not loving you."[18]

In the same letter, Solange responded with exuberance to her mother's novel *Mauprat*, which she had just finished reading: "It is enchanting; the most beautiful novel ever written. Edmonde is the most beautiful of your daughters. I am the one who turned out the worst." When Sand wrote back, she turned her daughter's poignant commentary into an object les-son, taking Solange to task for her shortcomings and contrasting her with the novel's virtuous protagonist: "Why did you like the story of Edmée so much? Why do you say that she's *the most beautiful of my daughters*? It's not because she rides horses and has feathers on her hat. It's because she has heartfelt devotion, because she puts her father, her fiancé and her friends before herself. Why do you like her during the trial? It's because she lays herself bare in order to proclaim her affection and the truth. Your reaction indicates that you know there's more to life than indulging oneself from morning until night, than primping and showing off and living en-tirely for oneself."[19]

Waxing metaphoric, Sand concluded: "Perhaps one day you will be-come a veritable Edmée. Until now you are merely *Edmunda sylvestris*, that is a wild flower, a thorny forest plant." Solange-Edmonde is the full name of the heroine of *Mauprat*, which provides a gloss on the name Sand chose

for her first and only daughter: "Sainte Solange, *the beautiful shepherdess,*
let her head be cut off rather than submit to the feudal lord's right."[20] Like
her namesake, the patron saint of Berry, Sand's daughter grew up willful,
proud, and rebellious. Although her fate fell short of the violence of Sainte
Solange's, Solange Sand's life, lived in the shadow of her all-powerful
mother, would go badly awry.

CHAPTER NINETEEN

Liaison Dangereuse

What role should I play? Will I be responsible for my daughter's unhappiness? Will I turn against her the soul's most precious qualities: feeling and fidelity? Is this why I am her mother? And if I were to snuff out this natural feeling that makes us want our children's happiness . . . if I force her choice, won't I be responsible for the evil effects this will have? What a way to exercise one's maternal authority, to place one's daughter between crime and unhappiness!

Choderlos de Laclos, Les Liaisons dangereuses

Art is not a study of positive reality; it's a search for ideal truth, and *The Vicar of Wakefield* was a more useful and healthy book for the soul than . . . *Liaisons dangereuses.*

George Sand

SOLANGE WAS EIGHTEEN YEARS OLD and engaged to Fernand de Preaulx when her mother presented her to the thirty-three-year-old sculptor Jean-Baptiste Auguste Clésinger on 18 February 1847. Over the course of several sittings, Clésinger not only sculpted Solange's bust, he also captured her heart and won her hand. By the end of the month, Solange had called off her engagement to Preaulx, and on 19 May she and Clésinger were married.[1] Despite the broken engagement and precipitous replacement, Sand was decidedly in favor of her daughter's marriage to Clésinger.

In Sand's recounting, the romance takes the form of a fairy tale, with Clésinger cast in the role of Prince Charming and Solange as the Sleeping Beauty whose passion is awakened with a kiss. Reading between the lines, we come up with a different, more malevolent story line: *Les Liaisons dangereuses* comes to mind, with Sand as prime mover in the role of Madame de Merteuil and Clésinger as the nefarious Valmont. The role of

Jean-Baptiste Clésinger. Photo by Nadar. (Courtesy Bibliothèque nationale de France)

the virginal Cécile Volanges ("she knows nothing, absolutely nothing, about what she so desires to know . . . but everything about her suggests deep sensuality"), seduced and abandoned by the cunning Valmont, falls to Solange, who "still has the innocence of a child," Sand wrote Delacroix, "but her senses are so stirred up that at any moment she could become a woman without realizing what's happening."[2] Solange's spurned fiancé Fernand de Preaulx is honorably dispatched by Sand in a flurry of self-congratulatory maternalism, much as Cécile's fiancé, Gercourt, is dispatched by Madame de Volanges. Like the eighteenth-century epistolary novel by Choderlos de Laclos, the intriguing story of Sand's role in Solange's marriage to Clésinger unfolds in the correspondence between the key players.

Sand made Clésinger's acquaintance in March 1846, when the sculptor sent her an exorbitantly flattering letter requesting that she have a look at his statue titled *Mélancolie,* currently on exhibition. "If you find in it a shadow of the austere melancholy of *Lélia*," wrote Clésinger, "you should be pleased, Madame, for it is your work." He offered to dedicate the statue to Sand and asked permission to immortalize in marble her 1842 novel *Consuelo*. Sand gratified the sculptor with her consent. His response was even more effusive than his first letter. "Oh, madame, I didn't think I was worthy of the distinguished honor you do me by this saintly and pious letter, which displays the fullness of your great heart and your beautiful soul."[3]

Impressed by the positive reception Clésinger's work was receiving —in addition to *Mélancolie,* his *Faune enfant,* also exhibited in 1846, was widely acclaimed—Sand wrote him a note of congratulations and invited him to drop by her Paris apartment so that she and Maurice, himself an aspiring artist, could express their appreciation of his work. In February, accompanied by Maurice and Solange, Sand paid a visit to Clésinger in his Paris studio. The following day she received an impassioned note thanking her for her visit: "Madame, I hasten to send you my little *Faune.* It will truly be a celebration for me to present it to you myself and to thank you for your wonderful visit yesterday. My god, how I wish that I could express myself and let you know all that my beating heart is feeling. But I only know how to write it in marble or bronze. Accept, therefore, Madame, the tribute of a young man who is proud to be able to engrave on eternal marble your great name beside his own. To you, madame Sand, the honor of having created and encouraged a young sculptor, who will ask your help and protection again for *La Terre,* the nurturer of men, that I am going to try to reproduce."[4]

Sand eagerly dispatched a reply: "I don't know how to thank you for the beautiful present you have given me. I deserve it only because I have understood it. Come see me soon, so I can thank you personally. I cannot tell you how happy I am to have this masterpiece before my eyes. You will go very far and rise very high and I will always be proud to have appreciated you before the crowd."[5]

Although Clésinger's original intention had been to sculpt Sand's bust, somehow the project grew to include Solange as well. It is not clear if the idea came from Sand or Clésinger, but in either case Sand insisted on paying the sculptor for his work, even though he offered his services for free. Although the letter Clésinger wrote Sand in mid-March has not survived, Sand's reply suggests that it contained a request for Solange's hand in marriage: "Your letter touches me deeply; maternal feeling disposes me very powerfully toward an artist who is so gifted and courageous in his work, but I must have fifteen minutes to chat with you; I have some questions to ask you, and my mature age authorizes this. . . . Would you like me to come to you for the bust a little earlier than usual? I'll come at one o'clock, my children will come to join me at two. In the meantime, if you have nothing to do this evening, come join us informally at home. With heartfelt greetings."[6]

Sand's intimate acquaintances (including Charlotte Marliani, Delacroix, Emmanuel Arago, and most emphatically Chopin) were quick to point out that Clésinger was riddled with debt, was prone to drink, and had abused, impregnated, and abandoned a recent mistress. Troubled by these allegations, Sand saw fit to question Clésinger directly. However the sculptor responded when they met, Sand's doubts were entirely dispelled. "I assured myself that Clésinger was in every way a man of impeccable credentials," Sand told Charlotte Marliani.[7] Fortified by the endorsements of his friends Jules Dupré and Théodore Rousseau, Sand gave Clésinger permission to pursue Solange.

The last of nine children of the sculptor Georges-Philippe Clésinger, Jean-Baptiste Auguste Clésinger was born in Besançon in 1814. When young Auguste, as he was called, showed an aptitude for drawing and sculpting, his father presented him to Charles Weiss, a wealthy patron of the arts, who awarded him a sum of money to study in Rome. Through the good graces of the archbishop of Besançon, Clésinger gained admission to the Vatican, where he studied with the sculptor Bertel Thorvaldsen. But he squandered the year in pursuit of pleasure rather than training and returned to Besançon, where he frittered away more time and ran up debts.

In 1835, Clésinger left France for Switzerland, where he eeked out a living making architectural drawings. When his funds gave out, he joined a military regiment in Melun. His portrait of General Bougault was rewarded by a posting to Paris, which in turn led to an invitation to join the studio of the celebrated artist David d'Angers. Clésinger's letters from this period reveal high hopes and boundless ambition, but unwilling to forgo

George Sand, 1847. Marble bust by Jean-Baptiste Clésinger.
(© Photothèque des musées de la ville de Paris. Photo:
Habouzit)

the independent commissions that David forbid his apprentices, Clésinger
struck out on his own, never again to train with a master.

   Returning to Switzerland, Clésinger picked up work doing portraits
for twenty francs a piece. By 1843, he was back in Paris sharing space with
the artist Jean Petit in a studio on rue de l'Ouest. Clésinger's bust of his
patron, Charles Weiss, won him a series of commissions—an equestrian
statue, the bust of the duke de Nemours, a grouping of Monsieur Aguado's
children—that mark his debut as a recognized sculptor. At the 1847 salon,
which took place while Clésinger was at work on Sand's bust, his *Femme
piquée par un serpent,* much admired among adversaries of the Academy,
became a *succès de scandale.* Théophile Gautier wrote a stunning commen-

dation of a "marble in which pain appears as a paroxysm of pleasure with a lifelike intensity that sculpture has never attained and that will not be surpassed." A future biographer described the powerful effect Clésinger's piece had on the public: "The audacious naturalism of this beautiful creature asleep on a bed of flowers whose grace, suppleness, elegance evoked monuments of Greek art, had a sensational as well as scandalous effect. It created an extraordinary uproar in the world of the arts."[8]

Sand must have been especially intrigued with Théophile Thoré's tribute, which likened the sculptor to the distinguished general under whom Maurice Dupin had served: "He carves a statue the way a soldier goes to battle, in a fit of passion which knows no obstacles, with courage kindled by the unknown. He's the Murat of sculpture."[9]

Sand was at least as impressed with Clésinger's artistic promise as she was with his character ratings. In a letter to her cousin René Vallet de Villeneuve just days before Solange's marriage, she revealed with disarming candor her fantasy of acquiring an artistically promising son-in-law: "Clésinger the sculptor will be the glory of his wife and of me. He will engrave his titles on marble and bronze, which endure as long as parchment pages."[10]

Although her correspondence leaves the impression that Solange's choice of Clésinger evolved independently ("She's in control of everything," Sand wrote Charles Poncy in April), Sand could not have been unaware of the course and conduct of the relationship. Indeed, her enthusiasm seems to have gone beyond mere compliance to actual coercion. It was Sand, after all, who presented Solange to Clésinger and concurred in the plan to have him sculpt her bust. Had she not been willing to leave Solange alone during her sittings with the sculptor, the romance would never have developed. The truth is that Sand worked herself to the bone to bring Solange and Clésinger to the altar. "I'm overwhelmed with fatigue and migraines," Sand wrote René, "for all this hasn't happened so fast without a prodigious amount of determination, activity, and work."[11]

Sand liberally broadcast her endorsement of Clésinger as the ideal match for her temperamental daughter: "Solange is very happy, too, and so am I! Clésinger is a man! He has made her charming, generous, tender and gentle toward me, she, the spoiled child who claimed she wasn't made for love." Sand's enchantment with her future son-in-law seems to have known no bounds: "As powerful as he is, he has a large, receptive heart; he's open to virtuous ideas in spite of certain limitations that have prevented him from considering them. He understands instinctively because he feels things deeply." On the eve of Solange's wedding, Sand's unmitigated optimism about the match culminated in the pronouncement: "I will have in him a true son who will make of my daughter an admirable woman."[12]

Beyond Sand's eagerness to have a talented artist join the family, there was yet another, more covert reason for which she favored the marriage between her daughter and the sculptor: Sand was terrified that left to her own devices, Solange would become sexually promiscuous. Two weeks before the wedding, Sand confided to Delacroix: "This is between us, my dear friend. The fruit is ripe; it's no longer time to worry too much about who picks it. . . . Especially when one is beautiful, eighteen years old, and aroused! I'm becoming terrified that she could fall into the abyss of co-quetry, the only abyss into which I myself have not fallen!"[13]

Sand added her assurance that the sculptor was man enough to rescue Solange from wayward sexuality: "Clésinger is not about to be jerked around. . . . I think he'll handle her well. . . . I think Cl[ésinger] will be very adept at not being cuckolded. He's very sharp and clever. He's skilled at making himself lovable, which counts for something." In closing, Sand implored Delacroix: "Burn this letter, my dear old friend."

The same day, she wrote Arago: "Pray that marriage comes easily to Solange and that her husband is pleased with Solange, so that she won't be too easy in another way. She loves him very much right now, and he is made to be loved. He gains greatly by being known, and it's not only as an artist that he is a man of unusual constitution. One must dig down deep to discover all of him, and there's a great deal there."[14] Below the surface of Sand's remark lies the innuendo that she was personally in a position not only to judge her daughter's character but to assess Clésinger's ability to satisfy her and thereby stave off danger. Is Sand suggesting that she had firsthand knowledge of the sculptor's sexual prowess?

A month before Solange's marriage, Sand wrote Charles Poncy: "My child, there's another delay. But this time rejoice with me, for I am happy! For the past year I've been preoccupied with and overwhelmed by my daughter, who has been living out a serious and strange novel, one day filled with anger and boredom, the next with tenderness and joy. The hero has changed his name and face; the heart of the heroine reverberates with new feelings. Within six weeks she broke off one love affair that hardly affected her to begin another, far more ardent one. She was engaged to the first, whom she sent away and is now marrying the other. It's bizarre, above all it's brazen, but after all it's her right, and fate smiles on her. She has replaced a modest and gentle marriage for a brilliant and ardent one."[15]

Years later, after her mother's death, Solange put an interesting spin on this speculation by a comment she scrawled in the margin of this letter: "A tall story. The person whom Solange was about to marry had conducted an epistolary and passionate relationship for the past year with G. S."[16] Solange's comment, ironically objectified by the use of the self-referential third person and inserted as a posthumous afterthought to her mother's original autograph, underscores Solange's marginalized role in the story of her own marriage.

Sand's meticulous editor Georges Lubin was sufficiently disturbed by the implications of Solange's comment to provide a lengthy and defensive footnote: "Whether true or not, Solange's comment on the autograph is unverifiable. If it's true, it means that she maneuvered the seduction of her mother's lover. If it's false, her behavior is even more egregious. Finally, whether true or false, nothing in this letter warrants the expression 'a tall story,' except for 'I am happy.' For this remark, according to the hypothesis that Solange wasn't lying, proves what? The spirit of sacrifice in a mother who doesn't want to obstruct her child's happiness, and a child who shows her gratitude by sullying the memory of her mother."[17]

With all due respect, Lubin may have gotten this wrong. Sand's "spirit of sacrifice," at the very least, is questionable. Far from sacrificing Clésinger to Solange, Sand served her daughter up to him. Lubin's contention that Solange may have "maneuvered the seduction of her mother's lover" is also questionable. Clearly, it was Sand who, after vetting her prospect, approved Clésinger's pursuit of Solange.[18]

In another footnote, Lubin invokes the maternalism of Sand's note to Clésinger (in which she asks for a meeting to discuss his detractors' allegations), as evidence that she could not have been his lover: "We invite the unsuspecting reader to read this little note attentively, and then to respond 'in all good conscience' to the following question: If, as several gossip mongers have affirmed without proof, G. S. was Clésinger's mistress, would she have written this note? Would she refer to her *mature age*? In a word, would she have reacted in such a way upon receiving a letter which, by all appearances, constituted a request for her daughter's hand in marriage?"[19]

If Sand was, in fact, the driving force behind Clésinger's and Solange's romance, her response is altogether consistent with the possibility that she and Clésinger had been lovers. That she invoked her age and spoke as a mother would speak with a son in no way precludes the possibility that she was, for a time, Clésinger's mistress. Sand specialized in maternal-istic relationships with lovers who were often many years her junior, Mus-set and Chopin notably among them. "I care for him like my own child and he loves me like his own mother," Sand wrote of Chopin to Charlotte Marliani.[20] Indeed, the eleven-year age difference between Sand and Clésinger is trumped by the thirteen-year difference between her and Alexandre Manceau, the lover she would take several years later and retain for fifteen years, until his death, in 1865. Sand not only took young lovers, but she regularly referred to them as "my son" and treated them as a mother treats a child. In fact, Sand savored the incestuous tension in such relationships, which serve as prototype for many of her fictional love affairs between older women and younger men.

If Sand did have sexual relations with Clésinger, it would not have been with the intention of conducting a long-term, intimate relationship. She was still involved with Chopin when she met the sculptor and was committed, if not to the fact, at least to the appearance of unfailing fidelity. To this effect, a week before Solange's marriage, Sand wrote Chopin's friend Gryzmala about her relationship with the composer: "For seven years I've lived as a virgin with *him* and with *others*. I've grown old before my years, and even without effort or sacrifice, so weary was I with incur-able passion and illusion."[21]

Perhaps the lady doth protest too much. It is possible that during the celibate phase of her relationship with Chopin, Sand succumbed to the ardent and seductive Clésinger. His letters abound with the sort of devo-tion and adulation that could conceivably turn the head of a woman in her middle years, a woman whose emotional and physical needs had long gone unsatisfied. What to do, then, with her passionate admirer? Perhaps the gift of her daughter was Sand's way of showing her gratitude. Her effusive and highly public approbation of their marriage would have been a clever way of covering her tracks. Who, after all, would suspect a mother of approving a marriage between her daughter and her own past lover?

One way or another, having taken the measure of Clésinger's sexual as well as artistic prowess, Sand was imbued with the notion that the

sculptor would make a good husband for Solange, who had exhibited uncertainty about her forthcoming marriage to Preaulx. Back in March, Sand
divulged her concerns about Solange's wavering feelings toward Preaulx
to René Vallet de Villeneuve: "In brief, when it came to drawing up the
marriage contract, when everything seemed in order, all of a sudden my
daughter bursts into tears, claims she's too young, is afraid of marriage,
scolds me tenderly for relinquishing my authority over her."[22]

Given Solange's volatility, in addition to her burgeoning sexuality,
which Sand feared could lead to promiscuity, an alternative to the gentle,
uncompelling Preaulx was required. Although Solange clearly expressed
misgivings about her first engagement, it was Sand who engineered its
demise by proposing a six-month separation between the betrotheds.
Rather than reveal her fear about Solange becoming promiscuous to the
socially conservative René, Sand instead emphasized Solange's sexual unreadiness for marriage: "All in all, marriage frightens her; her heart could
have warmed to a fraternal friendship, but her physical feelings are still
dormant; she's unaware of them and unaware of herself and, at the prospect
of a more intimate union than that of the heart, she recoiled in horror. I
don't know if another mother would have believed it her duty to overcome
this natural reserve, this instinctual fear and to bypass it. As for me, I
thought it my duty to acknowledge it as a secret revelation that she wasn't
yet woman enough and that her time had not yet come."[23]

Based on Solange's initial reaction to marriage, this explanation seems
entirely credible. A month after Solange and Clésinger's wedding, Sand
confided her new concerns to Charles Poncy: "[Solange] is pleased with
her husband, but I'm not pleased with her health. Yet another worry, yet
another anxiety, not to speak of those that I'm not mentioning. This crazy
child still had her period on her wedding day. Without saying a word to
anyone, she plunged into cold water to rid herself of it. She succeeded
only too well; she sunk back into the chlorotic and apathetic condition she
was in all last summer."[24]

Apparently, the marriage did not get off to the passionate start Sand
was counting on, and Solange seems to have fallen into depression. Considering that the reports of Solange's enthusiasm for marriage with
Clésinger were circulated by Sand, it is conceivable Solange's eagerness
was exaggerated. Sand herself provides a clue to this effect in a note to
Jules Dupré dated 14 April and dispatched from Nohant: "Our impassioned

sculptor is here. . . . The grand princess has humbled herself to the point of saying yes. . . . She had this yes in her heart for a long time and didn't want to say it so soon."[25]

For the most part, Sand kept at bay whatever doubts she may have harbored about Solange and Clésinger's union, but for some curious reason she dropped her defenses with her publisher, Pierre-Jules Hetzel—perhaps because he was outside the family circle—and indulged in a malicious fantasy of her daughter's fate: "They'll be married in a fortnight. My daughter is as much of a devil as he is. There's no telling which one will devour the other."[26]

That Sand so readily approved Clésinger's pursuit of Solange's hand in marriage is troublesome in light of such an admission and raises questions about the stealth and alacrity with which Sand rushed the marriage along. In a letter to Maurice, posted from Nohant in mid-April, Sand reported on the situation: "Cl[ésinger] has arrived with the resolution and will of Caesar, with a stubbornness that would suffer neither indecision nor delay. It was necessary to say *yes* or *no* within twenty-four hours. It was very brusque. . . . Solange said yes right away, and despite her indecisive character . . . despite my own sense of *reason*, to be sure, it was *clear* that with a man like the sculptor, there was no turning back." Sand implored Maurice to keep the impending wedding secret, lest Chopin interfere, and (despite knowing otherwise) went so far as to imply that Solange and Clésinger had already become lovers: "Not a word to Chopin. This is none of his business, and once the Rubicon is crossed, *ifs* and *buts* can do no good."[27]

On the eve of her daughter's marriage, Sand proclaimed: "The heart of the heroine reverberates with new feelings." In retrospect, Solange's marginalia, "a tall story," can be read as a belated protest against the unreality of her mother's portrayal; her way of sending a message to posterity that it was passion between Sand and Clésinger (their "epistolary and passionate relationship"), and not her own, that drove (and ultimately doomed) her marriage to the sculptor.[28]

Behind other reasons Sand put forth for supporting this marriage lurked another, perhaps dominant motive: she could not wait to unburden herself of her difficult daughter. Frustrated and exhausted by the time and trouble that Solange had cost her, Sand confided to Arago: "For eighteen years I've shouldered total *responsibility* for an existence over which it has never been possible for me, or for anyone else, to exercise the least *author-ity*. . . . It will thus be of great comfort the day when this responsibility passes into someone else's hands."[29]

Despite Sand's enthusiasm for the marriage, she decided to dispense with the usual festivities. The wedding would consist of a brief, private ceremony attended only by family members and a few close friends. "We don't want to have a celebration, however small," Sand wrote Charlotte Marliani in February. "I don't have the means this year, and after the tremendous hardship that we've had to help out with here at home, after the inevitable expense of transferring property for the dowry, I don't know how I'll get through the year without going into debt or killing myself by slave labor."[30]

To René, Sand explained the plans slightly differently: "We're getting married in the strictest secrecy, and in keeping with our usual practice, we're giving to the poor the money which would otherwise have been spent on wedding festivities." The absence of a wedding party for her daughter is all the more remarkable in light of the elaborate celebration Sand had organized for the marriage of Françoise Caillaud, a beloved serving girl who had grown up on the estate. This occasion involved the entire village. "Françoise was married three days ago," Sand wrote Delacroix. "Her wedding lasted three days and three nights, with all the wonderful old-fashioned rituals and activities. I missed you terribly. You would have found so appealing how unimaginably charming and picturesque the whole affair was."[31]

Sand was so enthralled with Françoise's wedding that she was looking forward to the next occasion to celebrate the marriage of a serving girl from the estate: "In a year or two we might have the chance to have you see Luce's wedding," she concluded in her letter to Delacroix. And, indeed, shortly before her daughter was married, Sand gave another domestic worker, Solange Biaud, a festive wedding party at Nohant. Sand sent Hetzel the following description of the event: "We've recently had a wedding which I paid for as well as for the dowry without being ruined, even though my goddaughter considers herself enriched. Sixty peasants, reveling, danc-ing to the sound of their *pibrochs* [bagpipes] like Scotsmen, singing their heads off, and firing pistol shots in every door, this was no small hubbub; but you should have seen it, nevertheless, to get a feeling for the golden age."[32]

Whatever Sand's reasons may have been, when it came to her own daughter's wedding, she made a deliberate choice: Solange's marriage to Clésinger was not to be an occasion for celebration. As it turned out, from a leg injury sustained several days before the wedding, Sand seems to have developed a case of hysterical paralysis and had to be carried to the church at Nohant-Vicq to attend the ceremony.[33] Disavowing responsibility for Solange and Clésinger's marriage—"They would only allow me a passive role," Sand told Hetzel—perhaps paralysis was her way of feigning helplessness, of signaling to those who witnessed the wedding that she could no sooner move herself than she could have prevented her daughter's doom.

Years later, blaming her husband, herself, and fate, Solange provided a poignant coda to her union with Clésinger: "When I was married, I was a spoiled child with no notion, no idea of life. If I had married a worthy, intelligent, strong and gentle man, if I'd been tied to an Ernest [Périgois], I would surely have made the best, the most settled, and perhaps the most bourgeois of wives. Instead, my husband was a scoundrel, a madman, a wild and stupid beast. I was demoralized very young, at my first exposure to life, by this evil and crazy man. I lost my head, I went insane. I started out as a spoiled child and turned into an extravagant, false, absurd being, the work of the sculptor."[34] And of the mother behind the scenes.

CHAPTER TWENTY

Broken Bonds: Solange and Chopin

Life is an endless wound that rarely rests and never heals.

But thank God I'm only a reed, and the wind that breaks the
oak tree bows me down and lifts me up again.

TO LAUNCH A STYLE OF LIFE befitting the image of success, the
Clésingers immediately furnished an expensive apartment. Solange
outfitted herself with a wardrobe worthy of their projected status, and
Clésinger retained a horse, carriage, and coachman, the better to display
themselves on drives about Paris. In just several months, the newly married couple came close to consuming Solange's entire dowry.

On a visit to Nohant in July, the Clésingers pressed their case for financial assistance. Sand declined on grounds of insufficient funds, but this
refusal did not curb their audacity; they suggested, actually demanded,
that she take out a mortgage on Nohant. Sand was infuriated. Under no
circumstances would she jeopardize the family estate she had struggled
so hard to retain.

But there was more at work than financial need in the Clésingers' ap-
palling demand. Word had reached them of the dowry of one hundred
thousand francs against future royalties that Sand had promised her young
cousin Augustine Brault and her prospective husband, Théodore Rousseau,
the landscape painter and friend of Maurice. The couple was to have been
married in the third week of June, but an anonymous correspondent dissuaded Rousseau on trumped-up grounds that with Sand as her accom-
plice, Augustine had deceived him by not acknowledging that she and
Maurice had been lovers. Rousseau fell for the ruse and called off the engagement. It turns out that the letter was sent by Solange.[1]

The story of Sand's adoption of Augustine Brault, a distant cousin
on Sophie Delaborde Dupin's side of the family (they shared a maternal

grandfather, Jean-Georges Cloquard), dates from the summer of 1844, when Sand invited the twenty-year-old young woman to Nohant. "I would like to find a way to keep her with me and to find her a position," Sand wrote Marie de Rozières the following fall.[2]

What was behind Sand's attraction to this obscure relative who had neither courted her attention nor asked for assistance? Like Sand's mother, Augustine's mother, Adélaïde Philbert Brault, had also made her way in life as a prostitute.[3] She had borne a first daughter, as Sophie had borne Caroline, out of wedlock. As the firstborn legitimate daughter of Adèle Philbert and Joseph Brault, whom she married in 1822, Augustine occupied the same position in her family as Sand did in her own. As a child, Sand had been forbidden by her grandmother to see Adèle Brault, and Sand's appropriation of Augustine was in all likelihood a way of reconnecting with the occluded maternal side of her past.

Two years after Augustine's first summer visit, Sand found a way to rescue the "poor little girl" from her mother's tainted life. She offered a stipend to the Braults, who agreed to allow their daughter to live with her. It is doubtful that Sand grasped the irony of her gesture, which replicated her grandmother's barter with Sophie Dupin. But effectively, Sand bought off Augustine's parents in exchange for taking charge of their daughter's future. Sand rationalized the motives for her reclamation project to Hippolyte: "The poor child was very unhappy at home, what with her mother's promiscuity, between us, and her desire to induct the daughter into the same style of life against her will. I had to intervene, and with the father's help I tucked her into a little corner of my apartment, and she's now very happy."[4]

To Augustine's future fiancé, Théodore Rousseau, Sand provided a more personal explanation: "Augustine is as much my child as those to whom I gave birth, more perhaps, for I gave her support which the others didn't need, and I suffered extreme hardship on her behalf." In addition to Sand's compassionate identification with Augustine, the young woman's beauty, docility, and musical talent further endeared her to Sand, who viewed her as a potential marriage partner for Maurice. Indeed, the prospect of a union between the two had sweetened the deal with the Braults, to whom Sand had written following Augustine's visit to Nohant in the summer of 1845: "[Maurice] is only happy at home, at work, and in his reclusive routines. This fortunate disposition suggests that he should find in Augustine all the security, gentleness, pleasure, and simplicity that he desires.

As for me, an *objective* observer, I see that this is the woman who suits him in every way."[5]

But as Sand was well aware, Maurice was in love with her young married friend the singer Pauline Garcia Viardot. By all indications, his feelings were reciprocated, and by the time Augustine came to live with Sand in 1846, Pauline's husband, Louis Viardot, the former director of the Théâtre des Italiens, was complaining about Maurice's frequent visits. Sand had been instrumental in arranging the marriage between Pauline Garcia and Louis Viardot and was understandably displeased by Maurice's interference in their relationship. She was counting on Augustine's presence to wean him from his untoward attachment to Pauline.

Sand was also hoping Augustine's gentle personality would temper Solange's contrariness, or at least that's what she told friends and family. But having complained constantly about Solange's jealous nature, how could Sand truly have thought that adopting and doting upon a surrogate daughter several years Solange's senior would please or appease her? Or was this another ironic, albeit unconscious, act of repetition, an echo of Sand's own childhood drama, in which her mother's preferential attentions to Caroline had left young Aurore feeling jealous and resentful?

Sand's acute awareness of Solange's jealousy (coupled with her hyper-critical response to it) contradicts her professed lack of awareness of its obvious source: her favoritism toward surrogate daughters and her disaffection from Solange. Underlying Sand's treatment of Solange is something that belies its would-be innocence: Sand was capable of inflicting extreme cruelty on her daughter. When Solange was homesick and unhappy at the Bascans pension, for example, Sand sent a letter scolding her for lack of progress in her schoolwork and callously reporting that back at Nohant she was tutoring her serving girl, Luce Caillaud, who was making excellent progress: "I'm giving daily spelling and arithmetic lessons to Luce. She's very bright and pleasant." The taunt was not lost on Solange: "To hurt me more, you tell me you're giving lessons to Luce while I'm in Paris. You're not very nice when you scold me."[6]

Sand's disingenuous response not only strains the bounds of reason, it tampers with Solange's apt perception of reality: "Why are you upset to learn that I'm giving lessons to Lucette? I hadn't even considered that this would have such an effect on you. Is it jealousy? First of all, I don't think you're very interested in my lessons, since you've always resisted them, and I must say that Luce, on the contrary, is a *quick study,* as they say. Besides, it seems to me that if you love this little one, you should be pleased that I'm helping her by teaching her a few things."[7] Rubbing still more salt in Solange's open wounds, Sand concluded by telling her that Luce had become skilled at needlework and was making herself generally useful around the house. To further bait Solange's jealousy—the child was, after all, confined to a pension far from home—Sand included a report of Luce's recent outing with one of the other girls from the estate.

In the case of Pauline Garcia Viardot, whom Sand "adopted" in much the same way she would later adopt Augustine (each was dubbed "the daughter of my heart"), Sand once again absolved herself of responsibility for Solange's resentment. As with Luce's lessons, Sand rapturously reported Pauline's extended visits to Nohant while thirteen-year-old Solange was away at boarding school. She compiled a list of Solange's faults—"self-love, the need to dominate others, crazy and foolish jealousy"—in contrast to Pauline's virtues, which Sand extolled: "Everyone who saw her here, however briefly, adored her immediately, not only for her talent and intelligence, but above all for her goodness, her lack of affectation and her devotion to others."[8]

Sand concluded her scourge with a gratuitous elegy: "If you should become like her one day, I would be the happiest of mothers." How must Solange have felt, having been depicted as the moral antithesis of the inimitable Pauline? The consequence was obvious and inevitable: failing to resemble Pauline, she would fail to make her mother happy. Solange's only recourse was to become the bane of her mother's existence. Exiled, excluded, and enraged, Solange struck back. Trailing behind her mother and Pauline on a visit through the gardens of the Viardots' new home, the forlorn adolescent swung a riding whip back and forth, flailing the heads off flowers that lined the path. Pauline's recollection was quite clearly contaminated by Sand's view of Solange: "What appalled me most was that viciousness, that gross wickedness, so loathsome because it had no rhyme or reason, no other aim except the displeasure of others. It was always like that. Solange practiced evil in the same way some people practiced art, just for the love of it."[9] Psychology rather than morality provides a better understanding: Solange's stormy behavior was due not to the pursuit of evil for evil's sake but to her struggle to emerge from the eclipse of her mother's affection.

Against this backdrop, the relationship between Solange and Augustine Brault quickly and predictably soured. Relegated to satellite status within the family galaxy, Solange must have rankled at being lodged on the ground floor of Nohant, while Augustine was settled within the intimate hub of the bedrooms upstairs, next door to Sand, Chopin, and Maurice. Sand further aggravated matters by referring collectively to Solange and Augustine as "my two daughters" and by dressing Augustine with greater care and expense than her own daughter. It should have come as no surprise that Solange viewed Augustine as an interloper and resented the favors her mother lavished on her.

The prospect of Augustine's marriage to Rousseau and the promise by Sand of a generous dowry was the proverbial straw that broke the camel's back. The letter Solange anonymously sent Rousseau, like her stealthy beheading of Pauline's flowers, was revenge against the mother who denied the daughter she had borne the entitlements bestowed on her daughters of choice.

By the time of the Clésingers' visit to Nohant in July 1847, tensions were running high. Sand had by then divined Solange's role in breaking up Augustine's engagement to Rousseau and was trying to find a new marriage prospect for her young protegée, still sheltered in the family château. Solange's feeling of dispossession was further fueled when she discovered that, in her absence, her childhood bedroom had been transformed into a theater for Maurice. Sand's refusal to mortgage Nohant brought the situation to a climax. Maurice came to his mother's defense, and the violent melodrama that followed marks a turning point in the relationship between Sand and Solange. From that moment on, all hope for reconciliation was dispelled.

As tempers flared, Clésinger raised a hammer to Maurice. Sand slapped Clésinger in the face, and he punched her in the chest. Maurice ran for a pistol and aimed it at Clésinger, but a visiting priest managed to separate the two men before either was harmed. Sand commanded Solange and her husband to leave Nohant and forbade Clésinger ever to set foot on the property again. The Clésingers left, carrying with them the statue of the *Faune enfant* that Clésinger had dedicated to Sand, as well as his *Mélancolie*, which he had given Sand on the occasion of his marriage.

Solange's retaliation was swift and calculating. From the inn at La Châtre, to which the Clésingers had repaired, she contacted Chopin, who sent his carriage and coachman from Paris to collect them. Nothing could have enraged Sand more than having Chopin come to her daughter's assistance. "At times I think . . . that Chopin loves her far more than me, blames me and takes her side," Sand complained to Marie de Rozières.[10]

It is true that Chopin and Solange shared a deep bond. When Chopin's relationship with Sand began in 1838, Solange was ten years old, and by the time of her marriage in 1847, she had spent more time and had more contact with him than with any other man in her mother's life. Chopin gave Solange her first piano lessons. To broaden her literary horizons, he read her passages from Shakespeare. He taught her phrases from his native language, and Solange added endearing Polish suffixes to their names. Often, she sought out Chopin to play pieces for four hands or to engage him in endless rounds of checkers or other games. Letters to her mother regularly included fond greetings and postscripts for Chopin, who frequently visited Solange at boarding school and accompanied her on trips between Paris and Nohant during vacations. Although Sand recognized the purely filial nature of Solange's attachment to Chopin, she blamed Solange for using her seductive wiles to manipulate Chopin into turning against her: "As much as she acts the role of coquette with him now in order to cast herself as victim, I'm sure that she doesn't think of him as a man, and that she has never thought of him as more than a little papa."[11]

As we have seen, Solange was inducted into the role of coquette from early childhood, when she frequented cafés and flirted with her mother's male companions. At the time, Aurore Dudevant found her daughter's seductive behavior, which she encouraged, adorable enough to write home about. In middle age, however, after having been many times disillusioned in love, Sand had a different attitude toward her daughter, now in the full bloom of womanhood. No longer a plaything, Solange had become a rival.

In a letter to her close friend Emmanuel Arago, Sand vented her resentment of the connection between Solange and Chopin: "Thousands of details that have been incomprehensible to me until now and that made me seem alienated—intimacy between them, mysterious intrigues, rages, tender reconciliations, alarm, angry and unjustified complaints—What shall I say, finally? This friend who was so faithful and so blindly devoted (as he told me, and as others told me), here he is making a case against me, doing Solange's bidding, siding with my son-in-law, when he knows that this man attacked me, and that he, the invalid whom I took care of day and night for nine years, can't have dealings with Clésinger at this time without dishonoring himself in my eyes."[12]

Sand's reasoning is somewhat paranoid, given the actual circumstances of her relationship with Chopin. Sand resented Chopin for his parental advice, for his proprietary attitude while she was supporting him. In return for her generosity, Sand felt Chopin owed her his loyalty and support and that his defense of Solange was tantamount to betrayal. The correspondence between Chopin and Sand in which he criticized her for treating her daughter too harshly and for overindulging her son was subsequently destroyed by Sand, who, by her own admission, did not want the record of what passed between them on this subject to survive. Sand had also grown resentful of the burden imposed on her by Chopin's moodiness and poor health: "What an inconvenience for me! I've finally come free of always defending myself against his narrow-mindedness and despotism while trapped in pity and fear that he would die of grief; for nine years in the prime of life I've been chained to a corpse."[13]

Sexual relations between Sand and Chopin had ended during their winter on Majorca. Sand claimed, as she had with other lovers (notably Sandeau and Musset), that she withdrew sexually from Chopin to protect his fragile health, but Chopin complained that he suffered all the more from physical deprivation. There is no evidence that abstinence was either a recommended or an effective form of therapy for consumption, which, paradoxically, is known in certain cases to heighten sexual desire. What is clear is that as Sand's physical attraction to Chopin diminished, she relegated him to the status of another of her children. "I care for him as my child and he loves me as a mother," Sand wrote Charlotte Marliani from Majorca.[14]

But Chopin wanted a lover, not a mother, and he resented Sand's increasing maternalism. He became intensely jealous of rivals (real and imagined) for her sexual favors. Sand would ultimately accuse Solange of masterminding Chopin's defection by fomenting his jealousy with insinuations about Sand's intimacy with Victor Borie, the twenty-seven-year-old editor of L'Eclaireur, and with Maurice's painter friend Eugène Lambert, a longtime resident of Nohant. Sand denied having sexual relations with other men, although she may have taken occasional pleasure on the side. Despite her ardent disavowal, she had done as much (and denied it) with

Pagello, the Italian doctor, while still living with Musset in Venice. In a letter to Leroux, Sand confided that "there are . . . certain infidelities that do not destroy an old love."[15] During the course of her relationship with Chopin, it appears that Sand had a discreet affair with the thirty-three-year-old socialist leader Louis Blanc, as well as with Victor Borie, with whom she would openly conduct an affair after the end of her relationship with Chopin.

For her part, Sand was suspicious of Chopin's bond with Solange, and though convinced he was not well enough to have acted on his desires, she was persuaded he had fallen in love with her daughter. Otherwise, she reasoned, he would not have taken Solange's side after the Clésingers' despicable behavior toward her: "But as far as he's concerned, with this great, exclusive, and imperishable passion that his friends strive to prove to me, and that he was in the habit of *pretending to*, to make this brusque about-face has to be about being passionate toward someone else, or else I'm more of a fool than I thought." Chopin's preoccupation with Solange was more prurient than passionate. In his initial objection to her marriage to the sculptor, Chopin had voiced his concern: "I guarantee you that at his [Clésinger's] next exhibition, in the form of a new statue, the public will be treated to a display of his wife's stomach and bust."[16] But once Solange was married, Chopin lent his support.

When Sand learned that Chopin had come to Solange and Clésinger's aid following their departure from Nohant, she wrote him a letter serving up the ultimatum that he never again mention the Clésingers to her and that he deny them access to their Square d'Orléans apartment—in short, that he renounce them. Chopin declared his loyalty to Solange and refused. In her present state—she was expecting her first child—Chopin believed she was more than ever in need of not only his but her mother's support. Obviously, this response did not sit well with Sand, who posted the last letter she would write to Chopin on 28 July: "You apparently enjoy listening to all that and believing it. I won't deign to take on such a fight; it disgusts me. I would prefer to see you go over to the enemy than to defend myself against an enemy that sprang from my flesh and was nurtured on my milk." Sand concluded by wishing Chopin well: "Farewell, my friend, may you heal quickly from all ills, and I have reason to believe this will happen, and I will thank God for this bizarre dénouement of nine years of exclusive friendship. Let me hear from you from time to time.

It's useless to ever go back over the rest."[17] Sand was startled not to hear from Chopin again and for the rest of her life blamed Solange for his defection.

In her letter to Emmanuel Arago, written in the wake of Solange and Clésinger's July visit to Nohant, Sand relived the shattering events of the recent past and vented a lifetime of anger turned to enmity toward her daughter. "She [Solange] should have known me, appreciated me, understood me, respected and adored me, for . . . I believe I was the best of mothers." A litany of suffering and self-sacrifice, the longest letter of her life (comprising twenty single-spaced, finely printed published pages) is an apology of maternal martyrdom: "I turned myself into her maid, her dressmaker, her driver, her hairdresser, her constant companion, coming in, going out, staying, paying, sewing, working day and night, enslaved by her whims, never knowing how to refuse or to punish."[18]

In her letter to Arago, Sand returns to the theme of sexual abstinence, which she casts as a personal sacrifice undertaken in her idealized mother role: "I gave up everything for my family. You know it! Still young and passionate, I silenced my heart and my feelings, I withdrew into a life of austerity that I always appeared to be living gladly and without regret. . . . It was maternal love that made me willing to undergo this premature immolation of my life as a woman. I wanted to recover the good opinion of a certain milieu, in order that my daughter could blossom fresh and proud in the midst of gentle affections and enlightened esteem. I also wanted all the attention focused on her, I did my best to make myself old and ugly, so she would sparkle beside me like a star over a cloud."[19]

Although Sand's account belies the more complicated reality of her conduct and its motives, it does address a fundamental factor in her relationship with Solange: the simultaneity of (and disparity between) Sand's physical decline and Solange's sexual coming of age. Quite clearly, Sand regretted the former, but despite her disavowal, she also regretted the latter and responded with trepidation to Solange's becoming a woman. And though there is truth in Sand's assertion that maternal love caused her to suppress her sexuality, it was motherly love for Chopin, not Solange, that elicited this sacrifice. And this love, too, ultimately turned to maternal martyrdom: "I still love him as my son even though he has been most ungrateful to his mother." As Sand confronted the future without Chopin, she would celebrate her freedom: "I will be able to start living again, me, whom he has been killing with pin pricks for nine years. How I shall work and run around and sleep! And take pleasure in thinking and talking."[20]

Arago would respond sympathetically to Sand in her hour of need, coercing her hostility toward Solange and advising Sand to stay the course of her rejection: "Your break with Solange and her husband must be a serious break." Chopin, on the other hand, disapproved of Sand's behavior, which he described in a Christmas letter to his sister Ludwicka following the dramatic events of the past summer: "Meanwhile she is now in the strangest paroxysm of motherhood, playing the part of a juster and better mother than she really is; and that is a fever for which there is no remedy in the case of heads with such an imagination, when they have entered into such a quagmire."[21]

Chopin's analysis of Sand's relationship with him and Solange is without compunction: "It seems as if she wanted, at one stroke, to get rid of her daughter and of me, because we were inconvenient; she will correspond with her daughter; so her maternal heart, which cannot do without some news of her child, will be quieted, and with that she can stifle her conscience. She will believe that she is just, and will pronounce me an enemy for having taken the side of her son-in-law (whom she cannot endure only because he has married her daughter; and I did all I could to prevent the marriage). A strange creature, with all her intellect! Some kind of frenzy has come upon her; she harrows up her own life, she harrows up her daughter's life."[22]

Sand's troubles were far from over after dismissing her daughter and son-in-law from Nohant. On the heels of Rousseau's broken engagement with Augustine, Sand was under duress to find her another suitable husband. The eventual replacement proved unacceptable to Augustine's parents, who were counting on a more lucrative liaison than the one provided. In April 1848, Augustine married Charles de Bertholdi and went to live in the town of Tulle, where Charles taught drawing at a local pension. The Braults unleashed their anger in a published pamphlet accusing Sand of sacrificing their daughter's reputation and ruining her prospects for a decent marriage.[23] Chopin recorded the embarrassing debacle in a letter to his family:

Her [George Sand's] biography has been printed and sold in
the streets; written and signed by Augustine's father, who com-

plains that she demoralized his only daughter and made her
into Maurice's mistress; that she gave her in marriage, against
the will of her parents, to the first comer, after having promised to marry her to her son. He quotes her own letters. In
short, a hideous business, that is known, today, to all the scum
of Paris. It is vile of the father, but the thing is true. This is
what has come of the kind action which she thought she was
doing, and which I opposed from the first day that girl entered
the house. She should have left her to her parents, not filled
her head with thoughts of her son; who will never marry without money (and even then only if he is coaxed into it, for he
will have enough money himself). He was pleased to have a
pretty cousin in the house. He made his mother put her on
an equal plane with Sol. She was dressed the same; and better
served, because Maurice wished it so. Every time the father
wanted to take her away, it was refused, because Maurice
wished it so. Her mother was regarded as insane, because she
saw things clearly; finally the father began to see. So then
Mme. S. made "une victime" of the girl, who was supposed
to be persecuted by her own parents. Solange saw everything,
and therefore was in the way. . . . The mother found her daughter inconvenient, because she, unfortunately, saw everything
that was going on. Hence lies, shame, embarrassment and
all the rest.[24]

Naturally, Sand cast the same events in altogether different terms:
"Necessarily the Braults' infernal malice, my husband's bad faith and prejudice, the cowardly tales told by a few unfaithful servants who were put out
by the vigilance that Augustine, in her capacity as responsible house-
keeper, was exercising on my behalf within my home, and finally the more
direct and even crueler attacks by a domestic enemy that I shall leave unnamed, succeeded at incriminating, in my midst, my son's conduct, Augustine's virginity, and my ostensible indulgence of their *covert* intimacy."[25]

The "domestic enemy" refers, of course, to Solange. The truth of the
complicated drama of Sand's adoption of Augustine lies, no doubt, somewhere in between the Braults' hotheaded accusations and Sand's counter-
attack. But what Chopin underscores of Solange's role as seer and sayer

Frédéric Chopin. After a daguerreotype made several
months before his death. (Frédéric Chopin Institute, Warsaw.
Courtesy Bibliothèque nationale de France)

is most revealing. As we have seen, Sand resented her daughter for many
reasons, not the least of which was Solange's outspokenness, her insis-
tence on telling her version of the truth even when, or perhaps especially
when, it diverged from her mother's. Sand couldn't bear Solange's cynicism,
which she ascribed to perversity rather than to perspicacity, thereby dismissing Solange's interpretation of events as a product of distortion and lies.

Sand would see Chopin only once again before his death. On 4 March
1848, they passed each other in the stairwell of Madame Marliani's apartment in Paris. In this awkward and unexpected meeting, Chopin informed
Sand that she had become a grandmother. On 28 February, Solange had
given birth to her first child, a daughter named Jeanne-Gabrielle Clésinger.
By the time Sand's note of congratulations reached her daughter, the premature baby had died. "Here I am all alone, stretched out on my bed in
mourning," Solange wrote Madame Bascans, the mistress of her former

pension. "My mother is at Nohant, busy marrying off her adoptive daughter." When Chopin died the following fall, on 17 October 1849, Solange was at his bedside. "I finished growing up under Chopin's piano," she told a friend many years later, "and the magic of his divine music remains in my soul among the fond memories of my childhood, which are few and far between."[26]

The break with Solange marks a watershed in Sand's life. Afterward she told a friend: "I remember Solange's early years, this child that in ways I preferred to my other one, or at least that I spoiled more, this child for whom I had limitless bursts of admiration and idolatry. She was the most beautiful child in the world, the most original, the most intriguing. She frightened me sometimes, and this fear of her precocious intelligence was a new attraction for me. Who could have told me that she would cause me so much suffering?"[27]

Or that she would have cost Sand her relationship with Chopin, whose sympathy was with Solange? "I am sorry that the Daughter, that carefully overcultivated plant, sheltered from so many storms, has been broken in her Mother's hand by a carelessness and levity pardonable perhaps in a woman in her twenties, but not in her forties."[28]

CHAPTER TWENTY-ONE

Collateral Damage and *Lucrézia Floriani*

What worries me most is the part about my mother. Shown at certain periods of her life, her conduct toward me is cruel. Considered
as a consequence of her suffering, of her past life, of her education,
it is excusable.

IN THE SPRING OF 1846, Sand began work on her novel *Lucrézia Floriani,* the story of a forty-year-old woman—the eponymous heroine—who
has retired at the peak of a successful stage career to her country estate,
where she is raising her four children born out of wedlock to three different fathers. As the novel opens, Floriani is visited by a former friend and
theater colleague, Count Salvator Albani, and his companion, Prince Karol
de Roswald. On the eve of their departure, Prince Karol falls gravely ill,
and their stay is extended for several months, during which Lucrézia
nurses him back to health. Despite Karol's initial aversion to his caretaker
for the moral disarray of her past life, the prince falls in love with her, she
reciprocates, and his stay at the Villa Floriani is prolonged indefinitely.
After a period of blissful harmony, Prince Karol's obsessive jealousy over
Lucrézia's past love affairs erodes their relationship, which culminates ten
years later in Lucrézia's death from what amounts to a fatal case of exhausted romance: "In ceasing to love she was to cease to live."[1]

In the preface to her novel, Sand asserts: "People who do not create
works of imagination believe that they are only made out of memories,
and always ask you: 'Whom did you mean to portray?' They are very much
mistaken if they believe it is possible to make a real person into a character in a novel." Nonetheless, beginning with Delacroix, in whose presence,
along with Chopin, Sand first read aloud the manuscript of *Lucrézia Floriani,* readers (with the notable exception of Chopin) have universally divined
in the figure of a common-born woman of Bohemian bent and the aristocratic figure of Prince Karol prototypes of Sand and Chopin. In *Chopin's*

Funeral, Benita Eisler describes Delacroix's astonishment at "the recognizable features of [the novel's] subjects flayed by exposure of their intimate relations. . . . He was 'in agony' for Chopin as they both listened to Sand's low, velvety voice in its hypnotic monotone describe Karol/Chopin's 'stubborn adoration' of Lucrézia, and his progressive derangement, all painted, Delacroix said, in the 'transparency of truth.' "[2] Later that evening, when Delacroix interrogated Chopin about his reaction to the novel, the painter was further amazed that Chopin seemed in no way to have identified with the character of Prince Karol.

Notwithstanding Sand's denial and Chopin's obliviousness to any resemblance between himself and Prince Karol, critics have persisted in interpreting *Lucrézia Floriani* as a roman à clef that tracks the demise of its author's relationship with the physically and emotionally fragile composer. The jacket copy of the English translation published in 1985, dispensing altogether with conjecture, declares definitively: "Lucrézia is actually George Sand, thinly disguised, and viewed with some objectivity by the author, and Prince Karol is Chopin. It is in this novel that Sand reveals their relationship and Chopin's relationship with her children."[3]

There are, to be sure, contemporary autobiographical flourishes in *Lucrézia Floriani* that trigger an association with Sand and Chopin (his jealousies, his criticisms of Sand's handling of her children, and, as Eisler points out, "the six-year difference in ages, the 'German' prince's Polish name; the physical resemblance between the author—small, plump, dark —and her heroine," even Chopin's habit of cracking his knuckles).[4] Yet there is also an echo of a more distant relationship that Sand may have been imagining as she wove her tale of wayward and destructive passion.

In character ("a being so stormy and anarchic, a mixture of things so magnificent and so deplorable") as well as condition ("an actress, a woman without morals, a mother of four children by three men,"), Lucrézia Floriani bears a marked (if critically unremarked) resemblance to Sophie Delaborde Dupin, and Prince Karol shares much in common with Maurice Dupin.[5] The parallels between Sand's fictional inventions and her parents compel a different reading of *Lucrézia Floriani* from those done thus far. And though Sand must not necessarily be taken at her word, this other way of viewing the novel may explain why both she and Chopin seemed genuinely disinclined to associate the story of its protagonists with their own.

The two story tracks—the real-life experience of Sophie and Maurice and the novelized tale of Lucrézia Floriani and Prince Karol de Roswald —are strewn with coincidental suggestions and similarities. We know that Sophie lived with a man named Vantin Saint-Charles, with whom she had her first child out of wedlock; in the novel we learn that Lucrézia has borne an illicit child to a man named Vandoni. (Another previous lover is named Saint-Gély.) And this just for starters. Lucrézia, like Sophie, first becomes pregnant at the age of fifteen and subsequently bears several illegitimate children to several different fathers.

Although Sophie Delaborde was actually twenty-seven when she met the twenty-two-year-old Maurice Dupin in Milan, where he was stationed with his regiment, Sand recorded in a letter to a friend: "My father met her when she was already thirty years old, and in the midst of quite a disordered life. He had a good heart; he understood that this beautiful creature was still capable of loving." Sand attributes the same age of thirty to Lucrézia at the time of her meeting the twenty-four-year-old Prince Karol on Lake Iseo, in northern Italy, not far from Milan. Maurice's sympathy for Sophie's goodness in the face of life's adversity is echoed in Karol's esteem for Lucrézia: "He saw her throughout as great by nature and degraded by life."[6]

As Sophie was the common-born daughter of a bird seller, Lucrézia, who, like Sophie, "retained an element of savage pride against society," is the daughter of a simple fisherman.[7] Both Sophie, albeit on a more modest scale, and Lucrézia perform on stage and are therefore associated with the tainted world of women and theater. In an apologia reminiscent of Sand's defense of Sophie's life, Lucrézia exhorts Prince Karol:

> The artist and in particular the dramatic artist always comes
> from the poorest and humblest ranks of society. It is women
> above all who suffer most in the world of art. This would be
> reasonable if it did not take shameful advantage of their
> strength, their health, and what is worst, alas! their honour,
> in order to make quicker profits, and by means of prostitution
> protect them from failure before their audiences. In this
> case the theatre also serves as a showcase, and more than one
> stupid and beautiful young woman pays for the privilege
> of showing herself—if only for a moment—on the boards,
> wearing provocative clothes, so as to make herself known
> and find clients.[8]

Sand's struggle in *Story of My Life* to absolve Sophie of blame for her wayward past is similar to the situation and set of rationalizations she presents in *Lucrézia Floriani*. Lucrézia, who admits to having had "an uninterrupted succession of love affairs" and who laments, "Ah, the past, that is my enemy," is depicted not as a "courtesan" or a "wanton" but as a woman who loves from the fullness of her heart. "I yielded to the weakness of human nature, to dejection, and later to the wild hope of finding happiness with another," Lucrézia explains herself to her old friend Salvator. Sophie's self-defense is much the same: "I don't feel guilty for anything. It doesn't seem to me that I have ever knowingly committed a malicious act. . . . My only crime is to have loved." And much as Sand wrote of her mother: "She was chaste, no matter what people may have said and thought about her, and her morals were beyond reproach," Karol tells Lucrézia; "what would be wrong in others is right in you."[9]

Similarities and parallels apply, as well, to the male protagonists and the plot of their lives. The aristocratic Prince Karol, like Maurice Dupin, was raised by a doting, protective mother. In *Story of My Life*, we learn that Maurice Dupin, "a sickly and terribly spoiled child," was "lazy and in languishing health." In her novel, Sand describes the prince in similar terms: "As a child Karol was weak and ailing." Much as Maurice Dupin took poorly to his lessons, Karol's "delicate health had resisted the toil, rigour and harshness of classical studies." Karol's mother, like Madame Dupin with Maurice, "lavished on him the most constant care and devotion."[10]

What's more, both Maurice and Karol fall in love during their first sojourn in Italy. "For the first time, the young man had come to feel the effects of a durable passion," Sand wrote of Maurice Dupin. In the novel, Sand tells us that Karol "had never burned with the flame of love, he had never felt the heart of a woman beat against his, and the first emotions of this nature were sharper and deeper for him than for an adolescent at the first awakening of the senses."[11]

When Karol contemplates marrying Lucrézia ("A husband would be the rehabilitation of her whole life . . . would beat off calumny and defamation"), Salvator points out their incompatibilities: "But he proved to the young prince that the harmony of tastes, opinions, character and inclinations which are the basis of conjugal calm, could never exist between a man of his, Karol's age, rank and nature and a peasant's daughter who had become an actress, was six years older than he, a mother, a democrat in her instincts and early background, etc. etc."[12] Salvator could just as well have been describing the young Maurice Dupin and Sophie Delaborde.

Both Maurice and Karol, whom the author dubs, intriguingly, "a walking hieroglyph, a personified myth," are caught in a life-threatening conflict between mother and mistress. "Ever since Asola, that is to say, from the end of the year 1800 until the time of my birth in 1804," Sand writes in *Story of My Life*, "my father was also to suffer mortally from the division in his soul between a cherished mother and a passionately beloved mistress." During his convalescence and in the course of his love affair, Prince Karol struggles with suicidal impulses. When Lucrézia assures the prince it is his mother's will that he live, Karol protests: "You are wrong. . . . High in Heaven, my mother has been calling a long time and urging me to go and join her. I can hear her clearly, but I, in my ingratitude, haven't the courage to give up life." He then cries out ironically, "No, I haven't the strength to die. You are holding me back and I cannot leave you. May my mother forgive me, I want to stay with you."[13]

Later in the novel, when Karol becomes obsessed with jealousy, Sand describes the prince's desperation in terms that recapture, metaphorically, her father's sudden and tragic fall from a spirited stallion on a reckless (and suggestively suicidal) late-night ride: "Prince Karol had soared too high to descend by slow degrees. His fall had to be sudden and without apparent cause. The giant steeds of the sun were certainly very fiery and powerful, and the gadfly which made them bolt was a very poor and very small insect!"[14] Maurice Dupin and Prince Karol are doomed, respectively, to death and self-destruction by virtue of runaway passion.

As though inserting a secret code, Sand would have us know that Lucrézia Floriani retains a small plaster statuette of Joachim Murat (Maurice Dupin's commanding officer in Napoléon's army), sold to her by a peddler who claimed it was her patron saint Anthony, to whom she prayed for many years in good faith. The general's name comes up again when Lucrézia's father, Menapace, compares the young Prince Karol unfavorably with him: "I saw Prince Murat when I was young. He was stout, strong, healthy-looking and wore magnificent clothes, gold and plumes. *That* was a prince! But this one looks like nothing at all and I wouldn't even trust him with my oars."[15]

There is another character who figures prominently in the novel and plays a role reminiscent of an important person from George Sand's past.

Count Salvator Albani in his relationship with Lucrézia—past, present, and imagined (by Prince Karol)—bears comparison with Sophie's long-time companion Pierret, nicknamed "Viconte" and described by Sand as her "oldest and best friend."[16] We know from Sand's correspondence that Pierret was still on the scene in the winter of 1843, when he attended the wedding of Hippolyte's daughter, and that Pierret died in an accident in Paris in October 1844. As Sand gathered inspiration for a new novel in the months that followed, it is not unlikely that her thoughts may have returned to this much beloved person from her past.

Like the "vicomte" Pierret in Sophie's life, Count Salvator Albani ("steadfast," "frankness itself") is a loyal and admiring friend from Lucrézia's past. Like Pierret, who tended to the Dupin household accounts and made himself generally indispensable, Salvator Albani "had become necessary to the young prince." But despite Pierret's involvement with the family, Sand would have us believe that he "was too conscientious and too upright not to have kept his distance from [Sophie], had he felt himself in danger of betraying, even mentally, the trust of which he was so proud and zealous." Likewise, when Karol suspects that Lucrézia may have been his friend's mistress, Salvator takes pains to clear himself of suspicion: "No, Karol, I have not been her lover; and as I was the friend of the man she loved when we knew one another . . . and I knew her to be loyal and faithful, I never dreamed of desiring her."[17]

But Sand takes the liberty in her fiction (that she was careful to avoid in her account of her life) to fantasize about a more intimate connection between Lucrézia and Salvator, who confesses, "Oh, if she were only living alone today as they told me in Milan. . . . And if she wished to love me." She thus prepares the way for the obsessive jealousy and suspicion that Karol subsequently develops: "He thought that Salvator had not renounced the idea of being Lucrézia's lover after him and that, treating him as a spoilt child, he had permitted him to precede him so as to claim his rights in secret as soon as he saw him satiated. . . . Or else . . . Karol told himself that Salvator had thought of marrying Lucrézia even before he had had the same idea and that by mutual consent she and he, tied by an affection consistent with their characters, had agreed to be united one day."[18] We know that after Maurice Dupin's death in 1808, Sophie and Pierret became companions, living together until Sophie's death, in 1837. Was Sand projecting onto the character of Prince Karol some of her own suspicions about her mother and Pierret's past association, or perhaps even imagining what Maurice Dupin, had he lived, might have come to fear?

In a further adaptation of the romantic triangle, Lucrézia brings her former lover Vandoni, father of her young son, and Prince Karol together under a common roof, thereby inciting Karol's jealousy and exacerbating Vandoni's pain in not being recognized as the father of his own child: "Never to hear the word father uttered by the lips of my son."[19]

As we have seen, Pierret may have suffered a similar fate vis-à-vis the young Aurore, with whom he played a surrogate paternal role. "When it came to me," Sand wrote of Pierret, "he assumed a paternal right which would have verged on tyranny, if his threats could possibly have been realized."[20]

As the novel progresses and emotional pressures mount, Lucrézia becomes more volatile, indeed more like Sophie: "Although usually mild-tempered she had had great outbursts of indignation in her life. At such times she had abandoned herself to the violence of her distress, she had cursed, she had broken things, she may even have used coarse language. . . . She was a fisherman's daughter."[21]

As Sand peels away the defensive layers of the fictional character she is forging, she also seems to be baring the soul of her mother; the description of Lucrézia sounds much like the scrappy, streetwise Sophie that Sand frequently evokes in Story of My Life.

Toward the end of the novel Lucrézia announces to Prince Karol: "I am now going to tell you what obligations weigh upon my real life, what considerations I must retain, what duties my conscience traces out for me." There follows a scene in which Lucrézia lays bare the facts and conditions of her past. And just as Aurore was overwhelmed by Sophie's scene of confession, Karol, "trembling like a child," tells Lucrézia, "I haven't nor will I perhaps ever have the strength to hear it." Karol's plaint, "But is it life that I shall find with Lucrézia? Will it not be death—this attachment whose circumstances make me blush and in which doubt will poison everything?" is an echo of Aurore's when she wonders, "Will I blush to be my mother's daughter?"[22]

If, then, a case has been made for a likeness between Sophie Delaborde Dupin and Lucrézia Floriani, there is, nevertheless, much of George Sand in the portrait of this heroine. It is Sand, after all, not Sophie, who enjoyed a successful and self-sustaining professional life. Although Sophie only

"spoke of nothing less than going far away with the children and supporting them on her own," George Sand and Lucrézia Floriani actually accomplish this.[23] It is as though Sand has projected onto Lucrézia the unlived
possibilities of a bigger, better, more developed life than Sophie was able
to create for herself. And in this sense the portrait of Lucrézia serves
double duty, standing in for both the unfortunate, beleaguered mother
(the fallen woman) as well as for the sturdy, successful daughter (her apologist and redeemer).

Sand would write in *Story of My Life*, "Some have claimed because
they thought they recognized a few of his characteristics, that in one of
my novels I described and analyzed [Chopin] in great detail. They were
wrong."[24] But beware: Sand is parsing again. "A few of his characteristics"
doesn't mean none and still leaves room for lots of someone else's. And
if not in "great detail," Sand still managed to spike her story with enough
telltale clues to convince her readers that the novel was actually about her
life with Chopin.

Despite her adamant denial, Sand must have known how a contemporary audience would respond. After all, from the beginning of her writing
career almost twenty years earlier, readers had been combing her publications for hints and revelations about her private life. As usual, Sand is ob-
fuscating. Had she really meant to distract her readers from identifying
Chopin with Prince Karol, she would never have made the association so
obvious. It was not her relationship with Chopin that Sand was hiding—
her letters abundantly chronicled their life together; it was the far murkier
matter of Sophie Delaborde Dupin's mysterious past and her relationship
with the man who claimed paternity of the child who grew up to tell the
tale. This was what lurked behind the tightly sealed door that Sand's roman
à clef sets ajar.

PART FIVE WAR AND PEACE

CHAPTER TWENTY-TWO

Revolution and Reverberations

Equality will always be an exception.

I therefore prefer men to women, and I say this without malice,
seriously convinced that the goals of nature are logical and
complete.

THE FEBRUARY REVOLUTION OF 1848 and the advent of the Second
Republic roused George Sand from the dejection into which the nightmare
of family events had cast her. She had spent the waning months of 1847
reliving the sordid saga of her recently married daughter. Adding to her
torment, Sand's much coddled son, Maurice, had recently moved to Paris
to participate in the overthrow of King Louis Philippe, leaving her fearful
and bereft. "Your place is here if there are serious disturbances," she wrote
him on the eve of the revolution. "Come home right away unless calm is
restored."[1] But Maurice stayed on, and as soon as news of the popular uprising of 24 February and the abdication of the king reached the provinces,
Sand headed for Paris, where she moved in with Maurice on rue Condé
and took up the cause of the dawning republic.

Soon after her arrival in the capital, Sand proclaimed, "The Republic
is the best of families, the people are the best of friends. One mustn't
think of another thing." If personal relations with Solange ("another thing"
that mustn't be thought about) had nearly destroyed her, Sand's political
relationship with France would now revive her. "Devotion and loyalty aren't
enough," she declared of her new vocation, "what's called for is fanaticism."
In the early morning hours of 5 March, Sand wrote a letter recording two
poignant events of the previous day. The first was the surprise meeting
with Chopin, in which he informed her of the birth of Solange's daughter.
The second was the glorious procession that followed the dead of February
through the streets of Paris. That these two momentous experiences, the

one painful and private, the other proud and public, converged on the same day is one of the abiding ironies of Sand's life. She reacted with characteristic resilience: "Personal worries disappear when we become absorbed in public life."[2]

Sand's report of the birth of Solange's baby, Jeanne-Gabrielle Clésinger, was brief and breezily delivered, no doubt to suppress the shock of her unexpected encounter with Chopin (it would be Sand's last) and the humiliation of having to learn through him that she had become a grandmother. Sand had always counted motherhood among her most important accomplishments—"I believe deep down that I was the best of mothers . . . the most caring, the most indulgent and the most good-natured"—and for her own daughter not to have notified her immediately of the birth of her first child hurt Sand to the quick. But public events held sway over this lesser, private matter, and Sand swiftly moved on to an exuberant description of the funeral procession: "This morning from Guizot's window, while chatting with Lamartine, I saw the cortege pass by. It was beautiful, simple and touching . . . a throng of four hundred thousand people between the Madeleine and the July Column; not a single policeman, not a single constable, yet so much order, decency, calm and mutual consideration that not one foot was stepped on, not one cap crushed. It was admirable. The people of Paris are the best in the world."[3]

How gentle and civil the people of Paris must have seemed after the violent scene Sand had suffered the previous July with Solange and her brute of a husband. The confrontation left Sand physically as well as spiritually depleted. Plagued by fever, exhaustion, and a continuous round of ailments, she confided in a friend, "There's no cure for my grief." She told another, "It's Solange who's eating me up alive and killing me." (*C'est Solange qui déchire mes entrailles et qui me tue.*) Sand's complaint against her daughter lodged itself in her body, and she wrote her doctor friend Gustave Papet, "It's only intestinal discomfort that still plagues me [*Il n'y a plus que les entrailles qui me fassent souffrir*]. . . . One doesn't recover overnight from such a blow to one's soul."[4] The French *entrailles,* which links Sand's reflections on her daughter and her health, translates (in this instance nonidiomatically) as "womb," which heightens the psychological resonance of Sand's maternal wound.

Even the weather played a part in the sinister scheme of things, as torrential rains at the end of July flooded central France, sealing off Nohant from outside visits and further socking Sand into a sense of desolation. In letter after letter she rehearsed the sordid events of the past July and the history of her relationship with Solange, groping for perspective and searching for a way to absolve herself of blame.

"She's nineteen years old, beautiful, very smart," Sand wrote Charles Poncy. "She was raised with love, in an environment that fostered happiness, development, and morality that should have made of her a saint or a heroine. But this century is damned and she is the child of her century. She has no religion in her soul; and to the extent that seductive wiles have provided her with the evil pleasures of pride and vanity, she has sacrificed everything to this inebriation. Especially in the last two years, she has followed a deplorable course and blamed me for trying to restrain her. You would be astonished by her willfulness, and by the unrelenting intensity of this terrible nature."[5]

Sand was still suffering from bad health in September: palpitations and constant fever, which the quinine sulfate she was taking did nothing to relieve. Compared with her usual production, the number of letters that date from the fall of 1847 is markedly reduced. In one of the few notes she wrote in October, she described her condition: "I can't budge, I've been sick for two months, and I do practically nothing but lose weight and tremble with fever." But Sand was determined to get on with her life. In another letter posted on 5 March, following the February revolution, this one to a close family member, she jettisoned the news of Jeanne-Gabrielle's birth and dwelled, instead, on her own centrality to public events: "I came to witness all of this with my own eyes, for I am intimately connected with several. . . . I write you in haste to reassure you in case you have fears about the present. I know *better than anyone* what is happening in the corridors of government and among the working-class population on the sidelines."[6]

With a *laissez-passer* from the minister of the interior, Alexandre-Auguste Ledru-Rollin, Sand was granted unrestricted access to members of the provisional government. Proud of her newly acquired political influence, she boasted to a friend that it was she who confirmed his nomination as commissioner for the department of Nièvre: "For the Minister has effectively put me in charge of my friends, of rallying them and reassuring them."[7]

To oversee the establishment of the republic in the Berry, as well as

Le Beau Candidat. George Sand and Ledru-Rollin.
Anonymous engraving. (Courtesy Bibliothèque Nationale
de France)

Maurice's installation as mayor of Nohant (his doting mother's influence
had secured him a safer haven than the barricades of Paris), Sand would
shortly return home. "The Republic has been saved in Paris; it's a matter
of saving it in the provinces where its cause is not yet won." That accomplished, she would return to Paris "to fully devote myself to the new duties imposed by our situation." Sand assured her friends that "all my physical ailments, all my personal pain are forgotten. I'm alive, I'm strong, I'm
active, I feel twenty years old."[8]

Her new duties would include writing articles commissioned by Ledru-
Rollin for the provisional government's *Bulletin de la République*, as well
as launching a journal of her own, *La Cause du Peuple*. Sand lost no time
establishing herself as the "Muse of the new Republic," and on 7 March,
the day she left Paris, she published a letter exhorting the people to take

seriously their newly gained suffrage: "The right to vote and to elect representatives is the source of all other rights." Keenly aware that the fate of the new republic turned on the outcome of the forthcoming elections, she declared: "The desire, the principle and the fervent wish of the members of the provisional government is that we send to the National Assembly men who represent the people, and as many as possible who come from within its ranks."[9]

Sand was back in Paris on 6 April, when *La Voix des Femmes* circulated the news that she had been proposed as France's first female candidate to the newly formed National Assembly. The decision, taken the previous day by the Club de la rue de Taranne, was reported by the journal's director, Eugénie Niboyet: "The representative who uniformly earns our sympathy embodies the essence of man and woman: the virility of the male, the divine intention and poetry of the female; we wish to nominate *Sand*."[10]

Neither Niboyet, nor Jeanne Deroin, the secretary-general of the Société de la Voix des Femmes, nor any of the other women whose advocacy of Sand was predicated on the principle of "equality for all members of society" were prepared for Sand's response.[11] The woman who was known throughout France, indeed across the European continent and in the New World, as the most powerful female figure of the century was enraged. As far as Sand was concerned, these women had not asked her permission to be put up for office, and even if they had, she would have flatly turned them down. She had no interest in standing for election, and the women who put her up had no business going behind her back and second-guessing her. Sand didn't sympathize with their concern that "universal" suffrage excluded women; she believed that given the vote, wives would figure merely as their husbands' rubber stamps. Before political emancipation, the more pressing problem of women's civil rights within marriage and the sticky business of property rights had to be resolved, issues that had poisoned her own marriage and engendered a lengthy legal battle won only after years of embittered struggle.

Sand sharpened her quill and drafted a letter to the editor, not to the editor of *La Voix des Femmes* but to the men at the helm of *La Réforme* and *La Vraie République*, in which it appeared on 9 and 10 April, respectively:[12]

Sir,

A journal directed by women has announced my candidacy

to the National Assembly. If this foolishness only wounded my
pride by attributing to me a ridiculous presumption, I would
let it pass, like so much else of what each of us is subjected to
in this life. But my silence could lead to the belief that I adhere
to the principles for which this journal stands. I therefore
kindly request that the following statement be made known:

1) I hope that no elector wastes his vote by foolishly writing
my name on his ballot.

2) I don't have the honor of knowing any of the women who
form clubs and direct journals.

3) The articles that may be signed with my name or initials
in these journals are not mine.

I apologize to these women who, to be sure, have treated me
with much goodwill, for protecting myself against their zeal.

I don't presume to protest in advance against the ideas that
these women or any other women care to discuss among
themselves; freedom of opinion belongs equally to both sexes,
but I cannot allow myself to be used without my consent as the
token of a female coterie with which I've never had the slightest thing, agreeable or disagreeable, in common.

I remain, kind sir, respectfully,

George Sand[13]

The members of the Club de la rue de Taranne hastened to publish
an apology and to clear up the matter of articles printed in their journal
under the initials G. S. (which stood not for George Sand but for a regular
contributor named Gabrielle Soumet), but Sand's proposed nomination
had been received with such enthusiasm that her name was already inscribed on dozens of lists submitted to the central selection committee
for approval.

Sand was indignant. What kind of foolish whim would propel these
women to take political action when they hadn't even realized personal
independence? Shackled between their husbands and their lovers, how
on earth could they dream of being free to represent themselves? "I haven't
come to thank you for placing my name on forty some odd lists for the
Central Committee," Sand began the draft of what originally must have
been intended as a direct address before the members of the Central Com-

mittee. In response to the fundamental question raised by her unsolicited nomination, "Should women one day participate in politics?" Sand summed up her position vis-à-vis the place of women in public life:

> Yes, one day, I believe as you do, but is this day near? No, I don't think so, and in order for the condition of women to be thus transformed, society must be radically transformed.
>
> We are perhaps already in agreement on these two points. But there's a third point. Several women have raised this question: in order for society to be transformed, shouldn't women begin to participate in public affairs?—I daresay they should not, because social conditions are such that women would not be able to respond honorably and loyally to the public mandate.
>
> Being under the tutelage of men on whom they are dependent in marriage, it's absolutely impossible for women to guarantee their own political independence without severing the very bond, the tutelage, which is consecrated by morality and law.[14]

After indicting the women who by dint of misplaced admiration had provoked her wrath, Sand proceeded to prosecute her case against them. "How do these women understand female emancipation? Like Saint-Simon, Enfantin or Fourier?" Early on, Sand had sympathized with their theories ("I love these men and admire their foray into the world"), but she soon became disenchanted. "Saint-Simonism for women is far from offering me this solution, because it has yet to be invented," she wrote in 1834. "Women still have nothing to say, as far as I'm concerned."[15]

"Do they presume to destroy marriage and to proclaim promiscuity?" Sand scoffed at the women who proposed her candidacy, accusing them of having fallen for the idea that free love was a means of liberation and, even more ludicrous, that committing adultery was a form of social progress: "What freedom does woman acquire by fraud? Adultery. What power does a woman brag about behind her husband's back? The power as ridiculous for herself as well as for him of supposedly having the upper hand."

Had Sand forgotten that she herself took a lover behind the backs of her husband, brother, children, and maid? The morning after Jules Sandeau climbed clandestinely into her bedroom at Nohant, Sand boasted to a male friend: "We had more exquisite pleasure than I think we've ever experienced. Come, come, how can you scold such reasonable and happy people? . . . I want him to come again tonight. Twice is not too much. More would be excessively imprudent, my husband couldn't fail to find out that he's within rifle range of Nohant. But for now he [my husband] is unaware. He gathers his grapes. He sleeps through the night like a pig."[16]

But Sand was apparently in a different mood now. Disgusted, she would have no truck with women who had insulted her dignity by identifying with her: "I hold myself completely aloof from their cause . . . which is odious and repellent to me. I therefore have nothing more to say. Nothing to reply, nothing to dispute." But Sand was far from finished speaking her mind. She still had much more to say to these women whom she chided for believing that power could be gained by banding together and forming clubs. Never mind that they had led respectable and responsible lives; Sand was hell-bent on waging warfare. "These abuses must cease," she self-righteously declared, closing ranks with scores of men in high places who, like herself, viewed these women with condescension, "and the good husband must no longer be seen as a ninny who gets duped and mocked by his wife and friends." Had Sand forgotten that while she sported with Sandeau in her bedroom at Nohant, their friend had served as sentinel to alert the lovers in case husband or household staff should stir? "Gustave didn't scold us! He supported us, he risked his neck for our folly. He bivouacked about the garden moat the whole time Jules was in my room."[17]

Had Sand paused to consider that her own daughter was the illicit offspring of her affair with Stéphane? As Solange grew, her paternal lineage should have become obvious—the set of her jaw, the tawny golden hair, the slightly uneven slice of smile—although no one seems to have suspected the truth. But never mind that Sand had borne an adulterous child; she was still not finished breathing fire on the women of the Club de la rue de Taranne. "Your house is burning," she warned them. "Your domestic lives are in shambles and yet you dream of entering the political fray, which would only expose you to public mockery and insult." Sand's sweeping denunciation helped make it so. In the courtroom of public opinion where only powerful men presided, her ruthless conviction of the women of the Club de la rue de Taranne was designed not just to humiliate but to destroy them: "You are guilty of having set back the emancipation of women by twenty years of preaching without discernment, taste and enlightenment, because of which the question has been put off and indefinitely adjourned."[18]

The victims of Sand's vicious attack were subsequently ridiculed by the press, their public meetings were infiltrated and disrupted, and by the end of July, the government closed down their clubs and issued a decree banning public debate by women. In *Only Paradoxes to Offer,* Joan Wallach Scott reports that beginning in April 1848, organizers of women's clubs were publicly taunted and physically attacked. Scott refers to "a bogus feminist society called the Vésuviennes," about which Deroin complained: "[They] burlesqued everything we said and did in order to cast ridicule and contempt on our meetings and our acts." In *La Démocratie à l'épreuve des femmes,* Michèle Riot-Sarcey describes in detail the harassment to which Deroin and her circle were subjected: "On June 4th, at the théâtre du Vaudeville, *les clubbistes* were dramatized by Messieurs Clairville and Jules Cordier in a production evocatively titled *Le Club des maris et le Club des femmes.* The characters were given nicknames familiar to the Parisian 'quarante-huitards' [forty-eighters]: Madame Bonnivet (a veiled allusion to Eugénie Niboyet), Madame Trinquart, Madame Chapotin, and the inevitable Madame Lampion. The tone is intentionally buffoonish."[19]

Eugénie Niboyet's appeals to officials went unheeded, and she eventually left Paris for Lyons, where she formed an association to assist women workers. Her badly damaged reputation never recovered from Sand's denunciation. The backlash of Sand's response to her unsolicited candidacy hit Jeanne Deroin perhaps the hardest. Her own bid to become a candidate in the legislative elections of 1849 was derailed largely through the efforts of P. J. Proudhon, serving as finance minister, who published the following notice in *La Liberté:* "A *very serious event* about which we cannot keep silent took place at a recent socialist banquet. A woman seriously proposed her candidature to the National Assembly. We cannot let such intentions and principles prevail without energetically protesting in the name of public morality and of justice itself. It is essential that socialism not accept solidarity. Political equality of the sexes, which is to say the presumption by women of the male prerogative of public office, is one of the fallacies that defy not only logic but even more so human conscience and the nature of things."[20]

Deroin, along with her socialist friend Pauline Roland, was imprisoned for subversive activity. We can only imagine what Sand was thinking when, soon after, she glowingly described Proudhon to Théophile Thoré, the founding editor of *La Vraie République:* "But what a useful and vigorous champion of democracy! What immense service he has rendered for the past year!" As history would have it, Sand would get as good as she gave: "She earned the distinction of being classed by Proudhon among women enemies of their own sex whose mistreatment of women was worse than the most misogynous philosophers and theologians." (Those who throw stones should not live in glass houses; Proudhon was ultimately jailed for his political views.)[21]

The draft of Sand's address to the members of the Central Committee stops in mid-sentence with the words "But this . . . ," and then the page goes blank. Perhaps she was distracted by a window blown open by a gust of wind. She may have been exhausted by the force of her own emotion. But why, we are left to wonder, did she not complete what she set out to say?[22] The piece was never published in Sand's lifetime, although its destructive intent was carried out by the dissemination of its malicious content.

The good women who advocated Sand's candidacy were dumbfounded by her response, which not only rebuked them for their principled resolutions but also ran roughshod over their private lives. They had not only lived and worked well but had also meant well; it had never occurred to them that the woman they so admired could hold them in such utter contempt. Sand had publicly positioned herself at the forefront of what she referred to as the "cause of women," and it was altogether logical that female reformists looked to her as an inspiration and identified her as a potential leader. "For the larger public, the female emancipation movement between 1830 and 1850 consisted of a single name, George Sand," writes Marguerite Thibert in *Féminisme dans le socialisme français de 1830 à 1850.* "The freedom of expression enjoyed by Madame Dudevant, even before her legal separation, and the wave of revolt against matrimonial constraint that animated a large number of her novels, identified this great writer as the essence of the *emancipated woman* and the brilliant advocate of women's liberation." Nothing but good faith, reasonable expectations, and high hopes were at work when her followers conferred upon her the honor of representing them in the National Assembly: "It is [Sand] whom we must call by unanimous vote. We are convinced of it; from the day that our interests are in her hands, she will live within us and as we live! Make way for undying principles, for genuine talent, and for immortal genius."[23]

Of course Sand had every right not to stand for election to public office, but she had other options than the one she hastened to exercise upon learning of her unsolicited candidacy. Dissatisfied with her advocates' designated platform of political action—specifically, women's suffrage —Sand was well positioned to offer alternative proposals. Sand was persuaded that civil rights for women within the institution of marriage was paramount, and since the government minister Adolphe Crémieux was already waging a legislative campaign to reinstate divorce (Sand's banner issue), why not have joined ranks with the already organized power base of women activists to spearhead these reforms? Jeanne Deroin was soon to become, in her own right, a staunch advocate of divorce, and it is not likely that she or the other women who publicly declared Sand's word to be "religious and sacred" would have turned Sand down had she prevailed upon them to modify their strategy for reform.[24]

But Sand wasn't interested in joining forces with women reformists of any stripe. Her hostile reaction to her nomination has nothing to do with ideological differences. Clearly, something else, some form of destructive malice was at work in her denigration of the women's movement, whose greatest crime, it would seem, was to have sought her support. If there is a single issue that separates Sand from the women whom she attacked so fiercely, it is not women's suffrage, which Sand envisioned as a future goal ("Yes, one day, I believe as you do"). Rather, it was her aversion to female solidarity. "You will understand, fellow citizens, that I do not wish to accept the slightest appearance of solidarity with an effort about which I was not consulted," Sand wrote in her undelivered address to the Central Committee. Ironically, despite Sand's nonadherance, Eugénie Niboyet understood that female solidarity was indispensable to the cause of women: "Woman will not be truly strong until she becomes, in good faith, the friend of her own sex. . . . She [presently] lacks esprit de corps."[25]

Wendy Deutelbaum and Cynthia Hugg, writing in The (M)other Tongue, agree: "What Sand neither experienced in her family nor imagined in her work was a world in which women themselves, women of all social classes, could join forces to end their own oppression." And in her introduction to Sand's novel Le Dernier Amour (The Last Love), Mireille Bossis also grapples with this problem: "George Sand did not participate in solidarity with the socialist feminism of her era. Should one go so far as to suggest that the 'cause of women,' their emancipation, didn't really interest her, except to justify her own conduct? Her novels provided her, nonetheless, with an excellent vehicle that she either didn't know how to use or didn't want to. Her plots and denouements are 'gentle and moderate,' as she herself told Buloz in 1866, which is to say they were essentially conformist."[26] To be sure, it was the presumption of her solidarity with the women who proposed her candidacy, rather than not having been consulted, that angered Sand the most.

Underlying Sand's resistance to female solidarity is her sense of being unlike other women, which is to say her sense of herself as exceptional: "I saw clearly that an education somewhat different from that of other women, owing to fortuitous circumstances, had modified me; that my small bones had been hardened by fatigue, or else that my will, developed by the Stoic theories of Deschartres on one hand, and Christian mortification on the other, had grown accustomed to compensate for limits set by nature. I also felt that the stupid vanity of adornment, as well as the suspect desire to please all men, had no hold on my mind, schooled to scorn them by the lessons and example of grandmother. Therefore, I was not a woman completely like those whom some moralists censure and mock; I had in my soul an enthusiasm for the beautiful, a thirst for the true."[27]

Surely, there were other women who thirsted after truth and beauty. Although Sand would deny it, her proponents represented many of the ideals for which she, too, stood: among them, the sanctity of motherhood, the need for women's education, and the economic right to work for compensation and to own property. Coming close in style as well as substance to Sand's own formulations (perhaps too close for comfort), the Société de la Voix des Femmes subscribed to a moderate and "essentialist" view of women: "What men have in physical force, we are equal to in moral force." Sand would not have disagreed: "That women are different from men, that the heart and mind have a particular sex, I have no doubt."[28]

Sand's attack was not only divisive; it was unfounded. Well attuned to the problem of female dependency, the editors of *La Voix des Femmes* had published views entirely consistent with those expressed by Sand in her harsh critique: "There can be no sound and fertile emancipation for our sex if we do not overcome ignorance. . . . What accounts for the fact that our free will is practically always subjugated to the will of a master, of a liberating despot? . . . It's that our captive intelligence is unfamiliar with any serious reasoning, it's that in general our minds are filled with only words, limited knowledge and wavering opinions." Hence, the Société's advocacy of instruction for women, especially for women of the lower social classes. Having rejected "the indolent odalisque, the ignorant and sensual woman" imagined by Enfantin, the collaborators of *La Voix des Femmes* had followed an ideological trajectory not unlike Sand's.[29]

Sand's accusation that these women engaged in adulterous affairs was equally gratuitous. Eugénie Niboyet was separated from her husband, and Jeanne Deroin's marriage to her fellow Saint-Simonian, "in a civil ceremony in 1832 [in which] their exchange of vows eliminated the husband's promise to protect and the wife's to obey," conformed to the very standards Sand would idealize the following year in her novel *Jacques,* in which the eponymous protagonist tells his fiancée on the eve of their wedding, "You must not promise to obey me because that would be to degrade both of us."[30] If Deroin's model of marriage had, in fact, inspired this passage, Sand's bilious treatment of Deroin seems all the more hypocritical.

Indeed, Sand's attack on the women who proposed her candidacy reverberates with the moralistic reproach of critics of her early writings. In an article on *Jacques,* which appeared in the *Revue de Paris* in 1834, Granier de Cassagnac accused Sand of vulgarizing the doctrines of Saint-Simon: "He reproached her for writing saint-simonian novels and for celebrating the free woman; for vaunting free, unlimited, wanton and wayward love affairs; for advocating reform of domestic and social values in accordance with this new position of women."[31]

Théobald Walsh's *George Sand,* which appeared in 1837, bore the following dedication: "Author of *Jacques* and *Lélia,* I wish to expose the scandal and the degrading immorality of your depressing doctrines and your uncivilized refutations." The violence of Sand's attack on contemporary feminists mirrors this and other similar assaults that she herself sustained. Sand's behavior is therefore susceptible to interpretation as identification with the aggressor.[32] In the preface to the 1842 Perrotin edition of her works, Sand described the harsh criticism to which she had been subjected:

> Never had a novel [*Lélia*] unchained such anathemas, or excited
> such savage indignation. I had a perverse mind, an odious
> character, an obscene pen, for having sketched the portrait of
> a woman who seeks in vain for love in the heart of the men
> of our time, and who retires to the desert there to dream of the

love with which Saint Theresa burned. Still I was not convinced that the fathers of the church, with whom my head
was filled at that period, had inspired me with the thought
of an abominable book.

I wrote a new novel entitled *Jacques,* in which, taking a man
for the principal type, I asked again, and this time in the name
of the man, as I had before in the name of the woman, what
was the ideal of love in marriage. This time, it was still worse,
I was the enemy of marriage, the apologist of licentiousness,
the condemner of fidelity, the corrupter of all women, the
scourge of all husbands.[33]

Various rationalizations for Sand's rejection of the women who proposed her candidacy have been advanced. Taking their cue from Sand herself, some critics discern a class distinction between the pro-proletarian
Sand and the "bourgeois feminists" whom she trivialized as "ladies who
form clubs and edit journals." In fact, Jeanne Deroin and Suzanne Voilquin,
among Sand's most prominent targets, were from working-class backgrounds.[34] But regardless of their origins, in their ministrations on behalf
of the working women of France, undertaken in the spirit of human justice
and with the intention of effecting important social reforms, these activists bore no allegiance to the bourgeoisie.

Ironically, on the very day *La Voix des Femmes* published the report of
Sand's proposed candidacy, Sand (anonymously) published a *Bulletin de
la République,* aimed at the very women who would shortly come forward
as her proponents: "In recent times, some women of sectarian mentality,
in the name of intelligence, have clamored for the privileges of intelligence.
The question was wrongly posed. In asserting that society would have
benefited if certain gender traits were represented in the administration
of public affairs, the great mass of poor and uneducated women would
have gained nothing. These personal demands have no general resonance.
. . . We have no hesitation in saying that the liberated saint-simonian
women's agenda is aristocratic in character. Since men are not free, how
can women aspire to even greater freedom?"[35]

Thus, even before Sand's proposed candidacy was announced, this
Bulletin betrays a desire to stigmatize the women who were acting on behalf of female workers. Sand accused them of agitating for political power

for self-serving reasons ("personal demands") and predicted, as though it were a fait accompli rather than her personal opinion (or worse, her wish), that their actions would be of no benefit to working women. Pejorative buzzwords like *sectarian, saint-simonian,* and *aristocratic* were deployed to incite liberal Republican antagonism. In her final rhetorical flourish, which lacks any semblance of logic, Sand suggested that by claiming what she deemed disproportionate rights, these women activists posed a serious threat to society; as though what they would take would deprive the other half of humanity of its fair share. Surely, the misogyny of Sand's thinly veiled vituperation was aimed at fomenting fear of female competition. The gambit succeeded brilliantly. In an unprecedented gesture of political solidarity (or was it merely male bonding?) Sand's beloved "peuple" joined forces with the Provisional Government in general protest against women's right to representation.

There has been a tendency among Sand scholars to chalk up Sand's belittlement of the contemporary women's movement as an inglorious glitch or a momentary lapse, an *"occasional* lack of a feminist perspective." But Sand's unconscionable conduct was about more than just having a bad day, and though it has not been altogether deleted from the record, it has been diluted by distinctions between Sand's alleged brand of feminism—"difference" or "essentialist" feminism—and "equality" feminism. But this stratagem fails to account for Sand's turn against those who believed, as she did, that for women to be equal to men did not mean that they were identical with men. Niboyet and her circle also emphasized women's unique attributes and, like Sand, advocated complementarity rather than fusion of men's and women's roles.[36]

Since the short form of difference feminism fails to explain away Sand's revilement of the contemporary women's movement, Naomi Schor invokes a longer form that throws in public- versus private-sphere theory: "What is for Sand the true aporia: the opposition between public and private; in other words, the great Enlightenment opposition ratified by the French Revolution that structures Sand's thought, her theorization of sexual difference. What is not so much the unthought as the unthinkable for Sand is the transgression by woman (as well as by man) of the bar that separates the two spheres. For Sand, the separation of the spheres is sacred, inscribed in nature, and must be maintained, for social order depends on it."[37]

It is true that the women reformists who chose Sand to represent them in their quest for political rights were bumping up against the boundary separating public and private spheres. And it is equally true that Sand articulated a more conservative agenda: "Those women who profess that they will have time to be deputies and to raise their children haven't raised them by themselves; otherwise, they would know that it's impossible. . . . At some point surely woman can assume a social and political role, but not a function which deprives her of her natural mission, the love of family." But true to form, Sand contradicts herself and expresses the opposite point of view: "There is no logical classification by which a woman can be placed in a particular sphere . . . [and] any concept of classification which detracts from these (natural) laws seems arbitrary and artificial to me. I shall not say that I reject it, I go even further, I don't acknowledge it."[38]

Even though Sand never exercised the right to vote, or cared that she couldn't, and even though she turned down the nomination to run for elective office, there's no doubt that she savored her privileged place at the table of public policy. After spending an hour discussing public affairs with her in May 1848 at a dinner party at the home of Richard Monkton-Milnes, Alexis de Tocqueville observed: "Madame Sand was a kind of political man. . . . [She] described for me in great detail and with singular vivacity the state of the Parisian workers, their organization, their number, their weapons, their preparations, their thoughts, their terrible determination. I thought her depiction was exaggerated and it was not; what followed demonstrated this."[39]

However overworked this observation may be, Sand was hardly one who practiced what she preached. Although she may well have believed that woman's place was in the home and that motherhood was her primordial role, and even though she's on record for having stated that "maternal instinct is stronger and more beautiful than all men's ancient and modern philosophies," Sand nevertheless left her young children behind to join her lover in Paris and to earn a living as a writer. "Almost all the friends of whom she gives portraits towards the end of [Story of My Life] are male —Delacroix, Sainte-Beuve, Calamatta, Gustave Planche, Charles Didier," Janet Hiddleston observes, "and she clearly ungenders the friendship by concentrating more on their ideas than on their personalities or their lives. . . . It is as though Sand wishes to present herself as beyond her sex, an honorary man."[40]

The theoretical distinction between public and private spheres, like the distinction Sand drew between political and civil rights for women, like that which is drawn between difference and equality feminism, therefore flies in the face of her exceptional status ("She made the freedom of one woman separate from the freedom of other women"). Her fame made possible significant participation in public life, as well as conspicuous indulgence in libertinage. These distinctions, designed to water down Sand's unconscionably destructive behavior, distract from the true meaning of her (mis)conduct toward other women. Nor do such distinctions hold up to the scrutiny of careful analysis, which betrays Sand's conflict about women in general and her own female identity in particular: "With very few exceptions, I cannot stand the company of women for long, not because I feel they are inferior to me in intelligence . . . but woman is, in general, a nervous, anxious being who communicates to me her eternal confusion about everything, in spite of myself. I begin by listening reluctantly, then I let myself take a natural interest, and, finally, I discover that all the infantile disturbances narrated to me do not amount to a row of beans."[41]

In a letter of commiseration to the writer Hortense Allart de Méritens, Sand revealed the extent of her cynicism: "I have suffered like you, my dear Hortense, for all our stories of being women are first cousins. It's our destiny, admit it, there's no way around it. I'm not convinced that we love better than men in general, but being more vulnerable by nature, we're more needy, and we can't help ourselves from being unhappy. Do you believe that this will change, and that better education, more activity, more importance accorded our sex will modify our instincts, our aptitude for grief, our jealousies, our miseries? I'm not at all sure, because those others of us, women artists, who can live practically like men, we remain women in spite of it all."[42]

Sand's position on the woman question was based, then, not on a feminism of difference, in which women are considered distinct from but equal to men but rather on a view of the female sex as fundamentally insufficient. "You believe in the grandeur of women and you consider them better than men," Sand wrote Charlotte Marliani. "I don't share this opinion. Having been more demoralized, it's inevitable that [women] have the mentality of slaves."[43]

Sand's ambivalence toward women and her hypocrisy in relations with them are duly captured in her comment to another friend: "I think of Madame [Hortense] Allart [de Méritens], a woman of letters who has a boring style and who had written books which are somewhat elevated but badly developed. She's not worthy of her books, she's a vulgar pedant, she's cutting, manipulative, manly, a *woman author* to beat the band. She pretends to admire me, I think, in order not to seem jealous, which would be in bad taste, she's ill at ease, without grace and, I believe, without heart. I don't care for her." But alas, to suppress the record of her duplicity toward an ostensible friend, Sand airbrushed her portrait of Hortense Allart de Méritens in her autobiography: "A writer of lofty sentiment and poetic form, an erudite woman 'all pretty and pink,' as Delatouche used to say —a courageous, independent spirit, a brilliant, serious woman who brought as much serenity to her life in seclusion as she brought grace and brilliance to society, a strong and tender mother, with a woman's compassion and a man's firmness."[44]

In her novel *Gabriel* (1839), Sand tells the story of a girl (Gabrielle), who is raised as a boy. Gabriel relates a dream to "his" tutor: "I had wings, and I soared over worlds, toward some ideal world . . . and I was a girl crowned with flowers and dressed in a long, flowing gown." When the tutor, who's charged with instructing his student as a boy, responds: "Then you were an angel, and not a woman," Gabriel declares: "I was a woman; for suddenly my wings collapsed, ether closed in around my head like an impenetrable crystal vault, and I fell, fell . . . and I had around my neck a heavy chain the weight of which dragged me toward the abyss; and then I awakened, overwhelmed with sadness, lethargy and fear."[45]

The message is clear in Sand's feminized adaptation of the Icarus myth: a woman who aspires to transcending her gender is doomed. "I feel sorry for woman, but I love man. He is my son, my brother, my father, my friend; I love everything about him, even his authority when he doesn't abuse it." Straightforward and sincere, this poignant late-life explanation dispenses with the self-effacing contortions of Sand's more characteristic comments on being a woman in a man's world. At the age of sixty, she still hadn't shed her desolation about the female sex: "I see woman as eternally enslaved by her own heart and womb. I've written this many times and still think it is so." With menopause and her last major love affair well behind her, Sand wrote Flaubert: "Now that I'm no longer a woman, if the good Lord were just, I would become a man."[46]

Despite the many attempts that have been made to construe a theory of Sand's feminism, Sand's relationship to the woman question neither derives from nor devolves to theoretical principles, much less to a systematic resolution of the problem of women's rights and roles. Sand provides no answers to the questions raised by feminist theoreticians, because she was not, in fact, a theoretical feminist. Sand would not have disagreed: "The desire to reconcile some sort of theory with my feelings has been my life's great project as well as its great disappointment. Feelings have always been stronger than reason, and the curbs I've applied to my nature have never done me any good. I've changed my mind twenty times." And in a letter to Flaubert some thirty years later, Sand wrote: "As for me, I have no theories, I spend my life asking questions and hearing how they're resolved in one way or another without ever having come up with a satisfactory conclusion or an answer."[47]

If not a systematic feminist, Sand was nonetheless a woman who, with equal parts bravery and bravado, posed the problem of being female. Sand's relationship to the woman question remains a subjective one, and the beliefs she propounded (which did not always correspond to her behavior) have to do not with theory but with her personal life, which is why Sand did not apply the rules by which she lived to the lives of other women. Scholarly objections (and objectivity) notwithstanding, Sand's formulations on the "cause of women" should be read against her subjective experience of being a woman. If, as Schor eloquently asserts, "Sand's feminism is the pons asinorum of Sand studies," then being female is the fault line that underlies the story of George Sand's life.[48]

CHAPTER TWENTY-THREE

Coming to Writing

You have betrayed me, you have lied to me, my mother. . . . You have
broken my heart.

FLOWERS ON THE WALLPAPER, folds of a window curtain, buzzing
flies, and objects seen as though doubled in the flickering candlelight are
George Sand's earliest memories of her cradled infancy on the fourth floor
of the rue Meslée apartment where her life began. Benign though these
memories may be, Sand shouldn't be taken at her word when she writes
nostalgically in her autobiography that life's "beginnings are so sweet and
childhood such a happy time." In fact, as we have seen, Sand's childhood
was dominated by a cruel and divisive contest between her mother and
grandmother, who represented different eras, different classes, and different moral systems. Sand's dilemma as a child was her inability to reconcile these differences so as to make harmony out of dissonance; hence,
the treatment of childhood in *Story of My Life,* which is designed to soften
the edges of many of the conflicts and deceptions with which, in reality,
early life, as well as the rest of life, was riddled:[1]

> At fifty years of age, I am exactly as I was then. I love reverie,
> contemplation, and work; but beyond a certain point, sadness
> takes over, because contemplation turns to melancholy, and
> if perforce reality appears in a sinister form, either my soul is
> obliged to succumb, or gaiety must come to my rescue. . . .
>
> I need to hear around me a vital exchange which does not
> remind me of the emptiness and horror of human existence.
> Accusations, blame, suspicions, meanness, mockery, condem-
> nations—these are what wait at the end of all political or liter-
> ary discussions, because understanding, confidence, and
> admiration are unfortunately more concisely expressed than

are aversion, criticism, and gossip. Saintliness is not my natural condition in life, but poetry is my reason for being, and everything that extinguishes the dream of the good, the simple, and the true, a dream which alone sustains me against the terrors of the century—is torture I avoid as much as possible.

In all situations where I have been able to choose my style of living, I have looked for ways to idealize the reality around me and transform it into an illusionary oasis, where the wicked or idle would not be tempted to enter or remain. A dream of a golden age, a mirage of pastoral innocence, artistic and poetical, took possession of me in childhood and has followed me into maturity.[2]

Although Sand casts her inclination toward idealization against the political backdrop of the "terrors of the century," what she describes of her need to combat the "emptiness and horror of human existence" could be said just as well about her personal and creative life. "Art is not a study of reality; it's a quest for ideal truth," Sand declared in the foreword to *La Mare au diable* (*The Devil's Pool*).[3] The purpose of her fiction, among other things, was to attenuate the terrors of her own existence.

Sand's penchant for storytelling began early in life. While attending to cooking and other household chores, her mother constructed a makeshift playpen out of four chairs surrounding an unlit foot warmer for Aurore to sit on when she became tired. The child would climb onto the chafing dish of the foot warmer, lean her elbows on the seats of the chairs, and claw away at the straw stuffing while she wove long, meandering tales that her mother referred to as "novels between four chairs."

Spontaneous and unpredictable, Sand's fiction, which is far less studied than her nonfiction, emanates from the privileged place within four chairs where her earliest impressions and fantasies found free rein. "Fiction! We can no sooner do without it," Sand would one day declare, "than we can do without bread."[4] The finite, physical containment of four chairs, out of which Aurore fashioned a free and open mental space, is paradigmatic of Sand's emotional impasse in life and the eventual escape route she followed in writing fiction, which, far more than wearing men's clothes, adopting a male name, or taking lovers, was Sand's true and perhaps only real means of liberation.

In *Story of My Life,* Sand describes how, after her father's death, her powers of invention took a spiritual turn:

> As my grandmother had taken only one precaution, that of
> fighting my penchant for superstition, I could not believe in
> miracles, nor could I believe in Jesus' divinity. But I loved the
> figure, nevertheless, and said to myself, "Since all religion is
> fiction, let me create a novel which might be a religion, or a
> religion which might be a novel. I don't believe in my novels,
> but they give me as much happiness as if I did. Anyhow, if
> I happen to believe in them once in a while, no one will know.
> No one will foil my illusion by proving that I'm dreaming."
>
> And behold, while dreaming one night, there came to me
> a shape and a name. The name had no meaning that I know of;
> it was the kind of fortuitous collection of syllables that is some-
> times formed in dreams. My phantom was called Corambé,
> and it kept that name. It became the title of my novel and the
> god of my religion.[5]

Rather than with romantic love, Aurore's novel of Corambé was pre-occupied with "friendship, filial or fraternal love, understanding, the purest attractions." Sand explained in her autobiography: "My heart, as well as my imagination, was entirely wrapped up in that fantasy, and when I was un-happy about something or someone in real life, I would think of Corambé with almost as much faith and consolation as of a demonstrated truth."[6]

Subsequently, as a by-product of her grandmother's revelation about her mother, which, as we have seen, took place during Aurore's adoles-cence, her childhood deity Corambé fell silent: "In effect, I no longer made any plans, I gave up my sweet reveries. No more novel, no more daydreams. Corambé was silent. I lived like a machine. The harm was deeper than anyone thought."[7] Thus, Corambé died when Aurore was confronted with the truth of her mother's past and, by extension, the suspected truth of her own identity. From the loss of her mother ideal and in conjunction with her compulsion to tell stories, Aurore's vocation as a writer was born.

"Sand's evocation of her childhood through memories of her mother," Marilyn Yalom notes, "has a unique cathexis; the urgency of these memo-ries, linking the adult Sand with herself as a girl, reminds us of Virginia Woolf's assertion that we think back through our mothers. It seems to lend credence to the belief, held by Sand long before Sigmund Freud, that one's relationship with one's mother provides the template for future inter-personal relationships." Pam Hirsch alludes to the English poem "Aurora Leigh" in her observation that "George Sand's novels are shot through with what Elizabeth Barrett Browning identified as 'mother-want.'"[8]

When the fledgling author wonders for whom she should write in the slight but seminal *Voyage en Auvergne*, one of the earliest literary forays of the future George Sand, her mother comes instantly to mind ("to my mother, oh God!"), and she composes the following text: "Oh my mother, what have I done to you? why do you not love me? I'm good, nevertheless. . . . Oh how I would have loved you, my mother, if you had wanted it. But you have betrayed me, you have lied to me, my mother, is it possible that you lied to me? Oh how guilty you are! You have broken my heart. The wound you've inflicted on me will bleed for the rest of my life. You've made me bitter and uncertain. You've instilled in me a brittleness and bitterness that I find in all things."[9]

As soon as Aurore has recorded these feelings, she realizes she will never show them to her mother. "Dear mother. Poor mother! How much grief this would cause you! You're fickle, but you're not evil. . . . Oh, I'll never reproach you. I'll cry in silence." Instead of baring her soul to her mother, Aurore fills her pages with descriptions of the resort she had vis-ited in Mont-Dore two summers earlier, and, remarkably, with a rough outline of a memoir she would write some twenty years later.

There is also another brief but significant passage in *Voyage en Au-vergne*. Aurore presents "Manuscrit trouvé" ("Found Manuscript") not as her own text but in quotation marks as an unidentified work of some other author. "Paging through my book," Aurore explains in *Voyage en Auvergne*, "here is what I found on a loose leaf of paper: who did it? I have no idea. It was written in pencil and was practically illegible." Georges Lubin pro-vides an elucidating footnote: "Reader beware, for this little piece appears to be by the young Madame Dudevant."[10] He further informs us that "Manu-scrit trouvé" was written sometime before *Voyage en Auvergne* and after October 1828. Solange's birth in September 1828 may well have rekindled Aurore's misgivings about the conditions of her own birth. The fragment consists of half a dozen quoted paragraphs plus a final paragraph in which Aurore comments on the found manuscript, noting the trace of tears that has been left on the page.

What does the manuscript contain? The author begins by addressing a crow that appears in the sky above an autumn landscape: "Why are you perched on my favorite tree, prophetess of bad omen? Your raucous, mournful song saddens and frightens me. I like all those fables I was once told about the science of prognostics and those melancholy tales that comforted me in childhood." The terrifying myth of Procne and Philomela is then invoked: "Sing, sing old companion of winter. Wasn't it you who sung over my cradle? What did you predict, the day of my mother's labor? Ah, if you told of sorrows worse than those of Philomela and Procne, you were truly a seer. But what do these sad cries, like a death rattle, announce today? Are you going to call me? And what does the mystery of my destiny matter to me? I who have tolerated life, what's to be afraid of in death? Come, even if this faraway cry which still echoes in my ear meant I would spend my days like you, in misery as in my youth, I wouldn't shy away."

The mysterious manuscript moves from despair to hope and concludes optimistically. "Tireless traveler, I will get there. I'll get there even if it means only reaching the house of peace in time to die on its threshold." Aurore takes note of the tear-stained page and speculates on what sort of person could have written such an ambiguous text: "How could someone who had the bravado to do this, to challenge fate in this way, how could he shed tears and be defiant at the same time? Did this inexplicable soul harbor contrary passions, was it some sort of Daedalus winding his way in vain through a labyrinth of mysterious meanings? or rather, as the unhappy author proudly and boldly took revenge for the wrongs foist upon him by fate, was his forsaken heart not still bleeding at the memory of the past? Alas, who will tell us the torture, who will explain the contradictions of a heart broken by grief, embittered by injustice, in despair over the past, menaced by the future?"

According to Greek mythology, Philomela's tongue was cut out to silence her from divulging the story of her rape by Tereus, the husband of her sister, Procne. Philomela is shut away and weaves an elaborate tapestry that depicts what has befallen her. A messenger delivers the tapestry to Procne, who decodes her sister's fate and arranges for her liberation. "'Let us weep hereafter,' Procne told her sister. 'I am prepared for any deed that will make Tereus pay for what he has done to you.' At this moment her little son Itys ran into the room and suddenly as she looked at him it seemed to her that she hated him. 'How like your father you are,' she said slowly, and with the words her plan was clear to her. She killed the child with one stroke of the dagger. She cut the little dead body up, put the limbs in a kettle over the fire, and served them to Tereus that night for supper." When Tereus tries to kill the fleeing sisters, the gods turn them into birds, "Procne into a nightingale and Philomela into a swallow, which, because her tongue was cut out, only twitters and can never sing. . . . The wretched Tereus too was changed into a bird, an ugly bird with a huge beak, said sometimes to be a hawk."[11]

Although the myth does not correlate literally with George Sand's life, the figure of the silenced Philomela, who weaves a tapestry of her experience, is highly resonant. In *Writing for Her Life*, Isabelle Naginski observes: "A dark myth, then, lies at the bottom of Sand's mind, a myth of male violence and silencing." Although Naginski associates Sand's fear of being silenced with a different myth, she concludes that "the terror that [Sand] might be silenced was what incited her to write novel after novel. . . . She wrote because she needed to talk."[12] Naginski relates this phenomenon to Sand's fiction:

> *Indiana, Lélia, Spiridion,* and *Consuelo* . . . end in a very comparable way, with the silencing of the hero or heroine. . . . The four novels, through four images of the broken voice—a mysterious case of muteness, a broken neck, a murder, the mysterious loss of a singing talent—express a central Sandian phobia. We might wonder at the fear of silence in a writer who produced over eighty novels, thirty volumes of letters, numerous plays, critical articles of every description, a significant body of journalistic writing, and approximately three thousand pages of memoirs. And we remember the prophetic words pronounced by her first artist: "My voice is my life" (*Histoire du rêveur*). But perhaps one of Sand's motivating forces is revealed here; the only way not to be silenced was to continue to write. Unlike her dark heroine Lélia, unlike Indiana, Alexis-Aurore, and Consuelo, Sand never ceased to give voice to her inner life through her writing.

The pain against which the writer of "Manuscrit trouvé" rails, which relates to the "mystery" of its author's fate, began, we are told, with her birth. Although we know that Aurore believed herself to have been betrayed,

this text further suggests that she suffered the burden of having been silenced. In addition to identifying with Philomela, Aurore may have identified with the small child sacrificed by his own mother. The transformation
of the mythological characters into birds, the privileged form of animal
life for Aurore–George Sand ("But the bird, I insist, is the superior being
in all creation"), would also have stirred her imagination.[13]

Voyage en Auvergne provides a glimpse of the transition Sand effected
between autobiography and fiction. The frame of Voyage constitutes the
autobiographical tract (indeed it comprises an abbreviated outline of the
eventual Story of My Life), and the inserted "Manuscrit trouvé" takes the
place that fiction comes to occupy in the Sandian oeuvre. The invocation
of Aurore's mother is the catalytic element of transition, for when the author realizes she will never send the text she has written to her mother,
she must find another way to give voice to her inner pain. Instead of addressing her mother, Aurore (in the guise of anonymous authorship) addresses the mythological crow (Tereus transformed), who has presided
over her birth and presaged her future.

Like Aurore, who found herself unable to send her mother the text
she addresses to her in Voyage en Auvergne, Sand felt constrained from
telling the full story of her life in her autobiography. Instead, she wove a
deeper, more complex version of her life story into her many works of
fiction. In a notice to her novel Valentine, Sand explained, "By a phenomenon that accompanies all deep emotions, moral as well as intellectual, it
is that which one wishes to reveal most that one dares least bring up in
public."[14] Story of My Life, written with an eye trained on public image and
posterity, is ultimately less confessional than Sand's fiction, which abounds
in the themes that riddled her life: adultery, adoption, the struggle for
identity, and the quest for authenticity.

The disparity between the story of Sand's life as told in her autobiography and the version(s) of it that she encodes in her fiction reprises
the early technical maneuver of Voyage en Auvergne, in which the writer-
memoirist disclaims authorship of the very text, the "Manuscrit trouvé,"
which confesses, albeit in the form of a mythical riddle, the deepest, most
personal story of the writer's life. The text within the text, or the device of
a narrative frame in which the story of someone other than the narrator
is told, is a form to which Sand frequently reverted in future works of

fiction. Like Philomela's tapestry, fiction would provide the means by which Sand was finally able to weave the untold fragments of her past into a whole piece of cloth.

As Naomi Schor has observed, "Much of Sand's oeuvre can be seen as driven by a constant struggle to overcome the pull of the discredited maternal idealization, in favor of the more prestigious paternal."[15] This tug-of-war is played out with much poignancy and drama in Sand's earliest writings. As I noted earlier, writing in her autobiography in 1848, at the age of forty-four, George Sand makes the startling admission that until two or three years earlier she did not know for sure who she actually was. According to what she was told by certain individuals who claimed to have seen her born, Sand tells her readers: "I would have been born in Madrid in 1802 or 1803, and the birth certificate that bears my name really belonged to another child who was born after me and died shortly thereafter."[16] Sand goes on to tell us that recently, while reading her father's letters to his mother, she discovered the truth: "I was indeed born in Paris on July 5, 1804; I am indeed *myself*, in a word."

How much of the Spanish-born hypothesis was based on fantasy and how much on having been misguided by unreliable sources we shall never know. But apparently Sand internalized this theory of her Spanish birth at least partially in response to her early life experience of traveling with her mother to join her father in Madrid. "One can imagine the enormous disturbance that this misfortune created in the life of the child and her family," Christian Abbadie notes. "But it would take a psychoanalytic study to measure the impact of this shock, and the emotional compensation that it entailed, in this four-year-old child."[17]

Who was this other child who Sand imagined herself to have been? Clues can be found in Sand's writings on her trip to Spain in 1808. In the brief piece originally titled "Souvenirs d'Espagne," which has come down to us as *Voyage en Espagne,* Aurore Dudevant, aged twenty-five, begins: "I left the apartment on rue Grange-Batelière. I was four years old, but I remember very well."[18] In his introduction, Lubin convincingly dates this draft to August 1829, following Aurore's brief trip to Mont-Dore, in the Pyrenees, with Casimir and young Maurice. Revisiting the same era some twenty years later, Sand takes up the same material in *Story of My Life,* augmenting the earlier recollection.

But preceding either of these formal compositions is a letter dated 11 June 1829, in which Aurore asks her mother for information about the storm and the shipwreck in which they nearly lost their lives en route home from Spain.[19] This letter to Sophie Dupin that precedes *Voyage en Espagne*, breezy and anecdotal though it seems, contains an urgent agenda: unhappily married, in the throes of what appears to be a postpartum depression, uncertain of who she is and where she is headed in life, Aurore is paving her way toward an emotional (and eventually literary) breakthrough. But before this can occur, she must undergo the process of separation from her mother that will enable her to consolidate an identity of her own.

Aurore's letter to Sophie begins with a formulaic apology for not having written for so long. "It's entirely the fault of my behavior and not my heart." This is followed by a slew of self-blame (replete with references to "guilt," "fault," "insolence," "vice") that for the moment masks Aurore's underlying feelings of dissatisfaction with her mother. In a move more wish fulfilling than sincere, Aurore then reflects, "There's so much mercy and forbearance in a mother's heart." But we know, and she knows, that this has hardly been Aurore's experience with her own mother.

After this preamble, Aurore gets to the point: "Tell me," she writes her mother from Bordeaux, "all about this shipwreck business that happened in my childhood and, if I recall correctly, took place where I am now." A description follows of what Aurore remembers: her mother afraid, her father jumping in the water to save his sword, the sailors swearing, the boat taking water. She wants her mother to recall all the details for her, because in the sea voyage she has just made with friends to the Cordouan tower in the Bay of Biscay, everything was, by contrast, simple and safe: "They say this is a difficult and dangerous voyage, which is curious, because when we were there the winds were favorable, the sea superb with mild currents, and the sailors excellent! And added to this humiliation, none of us was seasick; we returned as healthy and happy . . . in a word, as comfortable as if we had taken a stroll on the *boulevard de Gand*." It's as though she's saying to her mother: Look at me, when I take a sea voyage with friends, I don't become shipwrecked and nearly die. Aurore's competitive dander has obviously been raised. To top off her glowing account, she boasts, "Such an easy success fills me with desire to take a ship around the world and to sail to China the way one takes a snuff of tobacco."

Aurore's exorbitant self-confidence only thinly veils the blame she lays not on her father, whom she heroizes ("I remember my father throwing himself into the water to save his sword, after having rescued us"), but on her mother: "I do not know why my mother got the notion of wanting to return by sea to Bordeaux . . . yet another risk to venture out in a launch along the coast of Gascony in the Bay of Biscay, which is always so choppy." In the concluding paragraph of *Voyage en Espagne,* Aurore describes the catastrophic effects of her mother's decision: "On the way back, I remember nothing, absolutely nothing, until Nohant. I was dying when I arrived." And again, in *Story of My Life:* "What I remember best was the suffering, thirst, voracious heat, and the fever I experienced during the whole trip."[20] Because of Sophie's irresponsible decision to undertake the Spanish voyage, Aurore had been subjected to soup made from candlewicks, to wretchedly unhealthy conditions that gave her scabies, to a coach ride over cadavers strewn in the wake of the Spanish uprising of 1808—in sum, to traumas that would haunt her throughout life.

Sophie's greatest failing, however, lay not in the details of the trip. Rather, Aurore's complaint concerns her mother's lack of memory: "She was truly weak with regard to her memory and had never been able to link two ideas in her mind." Sophie is repeatedly cast in the role of unreliable witness: her memory fails, her stories are confused, her perceptions and interpretations are distorted and subject to doubt. When Sand speaks of her mother's failure of memory, she reveals her underlying fear, like every daughter's fear, that she will be just like her imperfect mother: "This weakness in me, which in many respects has been inherited."[21] Consequently, a double-pronged problem—that of *amnesia,* or lack of memory, and of *anamnesis,* or recollection—persists throughout Sand's struggle to recall and record the Spanish journey. Although Sand keeps protesting in *Story of My Life* that she remembers nothing ("I have no recollection of my father until we reached Bayonne"), she contradicts herself by elaborating memories in remarkable detail ("It comes back to me now that my father must have been with us") and launches into an impressive reconstruction of past events.

While writing *Voyage en Espagne,* Sand discovers a peculiar property of memory: "The farther away things are, the closer they seem to me." In February 1848, on the verge of rewriting the Spanish journey in *Story of My Life,* Sand sends Hetzel a letter that records her progress: "I've begun my second part, in which I have much to tell. . . . I think it will work out well. It's amazing how my memories of childhood awaken as I approach the era when I will speak of myself."[22] Although *Voyage en Espagne* is a mere three-page sketch, by the time Sand develops the same material in *Story of My Life*, she has recovered enough memories to fill some thirty minutely detailed pages. Where did this additional material come from?

It appears that Sophie did not take the trouble to respond to her daughter's letter requesting information about the past. According to George Lubin, "There are very few letters from George Sand's mother that have been saved, and none that recount the shipwreck."[23] Assuming that Sophie did not respond, how did Sand develop her material? By what mechanism did she unleash the lost memories of this distant past? The thematic and imagistic content of Sand's writing reveals how she may have liberated herself from the impasse of not knowing.

Both the early and later drafts of the Spanish journey are infused with images of enclosure, containment, and entrapment. In the 1829 text, Aurore writes: "In the Pyrenees there were roads lined with mountains which seemed to entrap us. When we had left their enclosure [*leur enceinte*], I was unable to figure out how we had gotten out." Later, in *Story of My Life*, Sand goes back over the same territory: "The abrupt turnings of the road in the midst of this amphitheater, whose peaks enclosed the horizon, brought me a surprise filled with anguish at every instant. It seemed to me we were imprisoned in these mountains, that there was no longer a road, and that we could neither continue nor return."[24]

The French word *enceinte*, when used as a noun translates as "enclosure," whereas the same word used as an adjective means "pregnant." The image of the "enceinte" of the mountains brings to mind both the mother in whose womb the unborn baby is contained and held back—Sophie was in a very advanced stage of pregnancy at the time—as well as the process, or passage, of breaking through and being born. Just as Aurore was once trapped in a confusing and confining landscape, Sand is at first blocked from remembering by her containment within, that is, by her identification with her un-remembering mother. To be born into herself—"I am myself, in a word"—Sand must break through the barrier of forgetting.

In August 1829, following her trip to Mont-Dore, Aurore sent a letter to a friend containing a draft of what we now know as *Voyage en Espagne*.

Lubin has argued convincingly that this friend was, in all likelihood, Félicie Molliet. Aurore tells her: "As you know I only have *one copy* of this work that I'm sending you. . . . Of everything I've written in my life, this is the only thing I value because it took a lot of concentration to gather *all these memories.*" Aurore suspected that Félicie Molliet was her half sister, Madame Molliet having been Maurice Dupin's mistress. It is possible that Aurore harbored a special kinship for this older female, and possible half sibling. Although Maurice Dupin is conspicuously absent in this early text, entrusting her treasured memories to someone in whom a part of him may have lived on might represent Aurore's attempt to build a bridge to her lost father.[25]

In addition to the change in size and scope of the Spanish journey in *Story of My Life,* a major shift of focus occurs. In the earlier piece, Aurore's memories are confined almost entirely to her mother. Her father is evoked more in terms of absence than of presence. He's mentioned in connection with a soldier who has lost an arm in battle and with the German serving man who attends Aurore in the palace where she stayed in Madrid: "Wèpres was with my father in the allée of poplar trees in La Châtre the night he was killed." The father's only active presence in the early text is when he responds to the four-year-old Aurore in exotic dress—"My father thought I looked Spanish"—no doubt feeding into Sand's fantasy of her Spanish identity.

Aurore's mother, on the other hand, is depicted as fearful, unhappy, a victim of misfortunes that culminate in the birth of the blind baby, the younger brother who died shortly after birth. In drafts of the Spanish journey, the repeated use of the verb "to see" and the frequent juxtaposition of Aurore's sightedness and the baby brother's blindness are remarkable. Whenever Aurore evokes the baby's blindness, she conspicuously endows herself with the power of heightened visual memory: "I still *see* . . . the crimson bed where my mother gave birth to a blind son"; "I *see* my mother who cried every day because her child was born blind."[26]

Once again in *Story of My Life,* Sophie is consistently portrayed as victim of malevolent external circumstance. She imagines, no doubt paranoically, that the stallion, Leopardo, conceals a death wish, that the surgeon who attended her delivery maliciously blinded her baby at birth. Sophie believes that the world is out to get her, and, tragically, her self-fulfilling prophecy comes true: she loses not only a baby but also her beloved husband.

Sand even goes so far as to suggest that Sophie may be partially responsible for her husband's demise. Sand tells us: "[The stallion] was a sinister present and one which my mother, given her fatalism or intuition, mistrusted and feared. But she was not able to persuade my father to get rid of it in time, even though he admitted it was the only horse he could not mount without a certain degree of apprehension. For him this was all the more reason to want to master the horse, and he took pleasure in vanquishing him. Nevertheless, he did reach the point of saying one day, 'I'm not afraid of him, but I don't ride him well because I don't trust him, and he knows it.'"[27]

We have nothing to fear but fear itself, Sand seems to be saying, and it is Sophie's fear that undermines Maurice's relationship to his mount. Lacking the power to prevent her husband from riding the horse, she proceeds to contaminate him with doubts that may have cost him his life. By incriminating her mother, Sand has found the means of maintaining her father's infallibility, of absolving him from responsibility for his own death.

In the embellished version of the Spanish saga, Sand is now conspicuously concerned with her father's presence and participation. In dramatic contrast with Sophie's passivity and inadequacy, Sand displays Maurice in high heroic gear: "Once, when we were following a rather narrow mountain road, we saw an enormous snake which stretched almost all the way across the road in a black line. My father called for a halt, ran forward, and cut it in two with his saber." And the familiar refrain: "My mother had tried in vain to restrain him; as usual she was fearful."[28]

Revisiting the sea voyage to Bordeaux, Sand once again contrasts her mother's fearfulness and passivity with her father's active, able engagement. "My mother was frightened again, and my father got busy helping the crew." Sand proceeds to a description of Maurice's courageous rescue of his family: "It took several hours, during which my mother would not leave the shore, for my father, after having assured our safety, had gone back to the launch to save our things, then our carriage, and finally the launch. I was struck by his courage, his speed, and his strength. Experienced as were the sailors and the local people, they nonetheless admired the skill and resolution of this young officer, who . . . directed the whole salvage operation more deftly than they could have done. . . . In everything he acted with calm and sangfroid."[29]

The penultimate gesture of the shipwreck in *Story of My Life* is Maurice's rescue of the famous Spanish sword—a symbol of power, courage, and conquest—the same sword with which he killed the snake, and no doubt the same African saber about which he writes his mother in his final letter before leaving Spain. As her own final gesture of the shipwreck, Aurore salvages the bouquet of roses she was given before setting sail: "As for me, I had saved my wilted bouquet of roses with as much love as my father had shown in saving us all. I had been very careful not to let go of it while getting out of the half-submerged carriage and climbing the rescue ladder. It was my first concern, just as my father's was his saber."[30]

Memory, too, is a kind of retrieval, if not of a material object, then of the past itself. The act of remembering therefore provides a symbolic equivalent to the retrieval of the sword and the bouquet of roses. By actively seeking and retrieving information, Sand repeats once again the saving of the sword, thereby passing from the state of not knowing and not remembering (amnesia) to that of recollection (anamnesis) and retelling. In a transfer mediated by the roses, the power of the sword passes to the power of the pen. It is the writer George Sand, who, by remembering and recording, supersedes the mother without memory: "I do not remember my mother ever using flowery phrases with me. I do not believe she had the means to do it, for if she knew how to write at this time, it was with difficulty, and she did not pride herself on a vain and useless orthography."[31]

Identification with the powerful, phallic father and separation from the inadequate, incomplete mother are firmly established in the reflections with which Sand concludes the Spanish journey in *Story of My Life*: "I do not recall having felt the least fear in all of these encounters. There are two kinds of fear: one relates to temperament and the other to imagination. I have never known the first kind, my constitution having endowed me with a sang-froid just like my father's. (The word 'sang-froid' expresses very precisely that composure we get from our physical disposition. . . .) As for the fear which results from an overly excitable imagination and is fed only by fantasy, I was tormented by that kind all through my childhood. But when age and reason had chased away the ghosts, I recovered my equilibrium and never suffered any kind of fear."[32]

Sand has firmly established herself as her father's daughter. She has remembered and gained mastery over the past. In discovering her identity, she has established her calling: she now knows not only who she was born but who she was meant to be. Aurore Dupin Dudevant's writings on her early journey to and from Spain chart the course of her self-discovery and of her self-possession. In a word, she has become herself, George Sand.

CHAPTER TWENTY-FOUR

Confession of a Young Girl

I have brought up the subject of appearance so as to be finished
with it. . . . I hope, however, in the future, one can avoid this
demand of curiosity, or if absolutely required, the portrait should
be limited to the description on one's passport, drawn up by
the local police chief in an unemphatic, uncompromising style.
Mine is as follows: dark hair, dark eyes, average forehead, light
skin, pronounced nose, receding chin, average mouth, four feet
ten inches tall, no particular distinguishing marks.

IN *STORY OF MY LIFE*, Sand makes a compelling statement about the
reason for writing her autobiography: "I have always promised myself not
to die without having done what I have always advised others to do for
themselves: a sincere study of my own nature and a careful examination
of my own existence." Seventeen years later, in 1864, Sand would write
Confession of a Young Girl, a novel in which the protagonist, Lucienne de
Valangis, makes a similar pronouncement: "I want to give you an account
of my life and myself with the most scrupulous sincerity." This similarity
in itself would not be particularly meaningful but for the special context
in which it occurs: *Confession of a Young Girl*, the first novel George Sand
wrote in the first-person voice of a woman, constitutes a deeply personal
fictional account of what Sand believed was her life story.[1]

Lucienne de Valangis is ostensibly the daughter of a French émigré
who remains in England following the Revolution of 1789. When he learns
from his wife that Lucienne is not his child, he arranges for the ten-month-
old baby to be kidnapped. Grief-stricken, Lucienne's mother dies. Several
years later, a four-year-old girl is returned to the paternal grandmother in
France. Although the identity of the child is uncertain, the grandmother
claims to recognize her as Lucienne de Valangis and, despite knowing
otherwise, raises her as her biological granddaughter.

Following the death of the father and grandmother, the father's English widow (the father had remarried) disputes Lucienne's legitimacy in order to protect her son's inheritance and hires a lawyer named Mac Allan to investigate the situation. He discovers that Lucienne is, in fact, illegitimate, the product of "an unplanned, unfortunate, and misguided impulse" between her mother and an unidentified Spaniard, and, according to the man who turns out not to have been her father, merely "a random child that Mme de Valangis happened to have taken a whim to raising as her granddaughter to console herself for the one she lost."[2]

There are striking parallels between Sand's *Story of My Life* and *Confession of a Young Girl*. In the former, as we have seen, Sand tells us that she did not know the date or place of her birth until she was fifteen and that until recently she had lived not knowing who she was: "It was only two or three years ago that I learned with certainty who I was . . . there is always something disturbing in having doubts about your name, your age, and your nationality." In the novel, Lucienne declares, "I was without a name, an age, a family, a past, a future, without protection and without responsibility." Aurore Dupin and Sand's fictional Lucienne de Valangis share the birth year of 1804. Both Aurore and Lucienne are physically small, dark, and sturdy, with untamed hair. They are fearless and capable equestrians. Dreamy and prone to fantasy and the fabrication of interminable stories, Lucienne, like Aurore, is given a masculine education. "I have looked for ways to idealize the reality around me and transform it into an illusionary oasis," Sand wrote of herself in *Story of My Life*. Like Aurore-Sand, Lucienne is also prone to idealization: "I wasn't a liar, I was a romantic. Reality didn't satisfy me, I was seeking something stranger and more brilliant in the realm of dreams. I haven't changed: this was the cause of all my misfortunes and perhaps the source of all my strengths, as well."[3]

The paternal grandmothers, to whose care both girls are conferred at age four, have much in common. Like Madame Dupin, Madame de Valangis escaped the "vicissitudes of the Revolution," married late, lost her husbands early, and lived out her life single and celibate. Her clothing and coiffure seem strange and imposing to Lucienne, as Madame Dupin's similar ancien-régime style seemed to Aurore. Both grandmothers are described as sedentary, verging on paralytic. Lucienne articulates the central trauma of her life in ways that poignantly recall Sand's pronouncements about her own difficult past: "The one thing I have not forgotten is the despair I felt when [my mother] left me with my grandmother."[4]

Just as Sand's father died of a fall from a horse near his home in the Berry, Lucienne's father dies of a fall from a horse in his native Yorkshire. While the grandmothers grow old and weak and relax their vigil over their granddaughters, both Aurore and Lucienne become voracious readers and avid students of natural science and philosophy. In adolescence, both girls cause their elderly guardians concern because of their independence, unusual education, boyish proclivities, and general unconventionality. As a remedy, both grandmothers form marriage plans for their reluctant granddaughters. Lucienne's cousin Marius proposes marriage in much the same unromantic manner that Casimir proposed to Aurore during their stay at Le Plessis. Both relationships are depicted as friendly, more sisterly and brotherly than passionate.

There is another key character in *Confession of a Young Girl:* Jennie, the nurse who attends Lucienne from her earliest childhood and who returns her to her paternal grandmother after she has been kidnapped. Like Sand's mother, Jennie is described as "a small brunette woman whose charming face pleased me at first. Although she was slender and petite, she had an indescribably vigorous and active manner." But there are significant ways in which Jennie differs from Sophie, who could barely read or write and was deficient in memory, as we have seen. Lucienne reports that Jennie "read and wrote better than I. . . . She was very observant with an astonishing memory. . . . Nothing was unfathomable to her active and alert mind." Another nurse, Denise, who also attends Lucienne as a young girl, is described in terms that are more reminiscent of the Sophie of Sand's childhood. Denise is volatile and unpredictable, given to sudden shifts of mood and spontaneous outbreaks of anger and jealousy. "What a difference between them, and how superior Jennie was in every way to my poor crazy one!" Lucienne exclaims after enumerating her beloved Jennie's many attributes.[5]

One is tempted to argue that Jennie represents an idealization of Sophie, "the mature writer's reflections on what she would have wished her mother had been like," suggests Marielle Vanderkerkhove. But the doubling of the mother surrogate role in the novel yields another interpretation, one that involves an enigmatic, little-discussed figure from Sand's early life. In addition to Sophie, the baby Aurore was attended and nursed by

Pierret. In *Story of My Life,* Sand prefaces her portrait of Louis-Mammès Pierret with a stirring tribute: "It is time for the story and portrait of this priceless man, whom I shall miss for the rest of my life." The son of a modest landowner from Champagne, Pierret is described as a "high-strung," "irritable" man of "prosaic tastes." Sand devotes a lengthy passage to his appearance, emphasizing his extreme homeliness to the point of repugnance: "heavy," with a "big flat nose, a wide mouth, and tiny eyes . . . his face . . . constantly furrowed with frightful grimaces because of a nervous tic," Sand dubs Pierret "the ugliest of men." She paints quite a different moral portrait, however: "I do not believe that there was ever a man more pure, loyal, generous, and to the extent that he was unaware of its beauty and rarity, his soul was that much more beautiful. Convinced of the goodness of others, it never occurred to him that he might be exceptional. . . . The notion of evil never touched his honorable and simple soul."[6]

When Pierret was not working at the treasury in the position alternately described as "superintendent" and "employee," a post he had held since the age of eighteen, or spending time at his favorite tavern, the Cheval Blanc, on rue du Faubourg-Poissonnière, he was a regular in the Dupin household, frequently standing in for Aurore's absent father. When Aurore displayed fear of fire trucks on walks through Paris with her mother and Pierret, it was Pierret who would take her in his arms, hold her head to his chest, and reassure her. It was from her secure perch on Pierret's shoulders that Aurore glimpsed the emperor Napoléon, who returned her gaze with a warm smile as he marched through Paris at the end of 1807. Such anecdotes, lovingly related by Sand in her autobiography, testify to Pierret's special place in her early life.

Sand contradicts herself in her account of how Pierret became part of her family's life. Only a few paragraphs after informing us that Pierret witnessed her birth, she changes her story: "[Pierret] had become acquainted with my parents during the earliest days of my existence, and in a way that united all of them instantly. A relative of his lived on Rue Meslée on the same block as my mother. This woman had a child my age whom she neglected and who, deprived of milk, cried all day. My mother entered the room where the unfortunate little one was dying from want, nursed it, and continued to rescue it in this way without saying a word. But Pierret, when coming to see his relative, caught my mother in this act, was duly moved, and pledged himself evermore to her and her kin."[7]

The official certificate of Aurore Dupin's birth divides the list of witnesses into those who were there from the father's side and those who were there on behalf of the mother. Louis-Mammès Pierret's name does, in fact, appear (along with Maréchal, the fiancé of Sophie's sister), as witness for the wife, which would indicate an acquaintance that antedates Aurore's birth. Sand's account that Pierret became acquainted with Sophie as she nursed a neighbor's baby places him in Sophie's life after Aurore's birth, for Sophie could not have nursed a baby if she wasn't lactating. (Caroline was already well beyond nursing age.) Apparently, Sand was eager to establish the impression that Pierret had not been a part of her mother's life before she (Aurore) was born.

Having told us that Pierret "was not the least bit what we call bright," Sand contradicts herself by claiming elsewhere that he was "juster and more intelligent than my mother," and by her description of the role he played in her father's life: Pierret "took care of all his affairs, put them in order, got rid of disreputable creditors, and . . . finally delivered him of all material concerns from which my father could hardly have extricated himself without the help of someone trained in the details of business."[8]

Adding to the impressive list, Sand informs us, "It was Pierret who chose [Maurice's] domestic help, kept his accounts, paid his bills, and insured that he received his money in whatever unforeseen place the war might take him." To accomplish all of the above, Pierret could not have been a dunce. By diminishing Pierret's physical and mental attributes while augmenting his moral virtues, Sand positions Pierret as "an excellent family friend." Clearly, she wants us to believe that his relationship with Sophie was entirely unambiguous. Sand dismisses the possibility that during her early childhood Pierret and Sophie were more than just friends, rationalizing that he "was too conscientious and too upright not to have kept his distance from her, had he felt himself in danger of betraying, even mentally, the trust of which he was so proud and zealous." As for Sophie, Sand contends that Pierret "was not attractive enough to have rendered my mother unfaithful even in thought." But this argument loses ground when we consider that after Maurice's death, in 1808, Sophie and Pierret, whom Georges Lubin refers to as "le sigisbée [gallant] de Madame Dupin," kept constant company and, for some years at least, a common living arrangement until Sophie's death in 1837.[9]

But the most compelling argument against an intimate relationship between Sophie and Pierret is Sand's invention that Pierret "Eventually . . . married the daughter of a general of no great fortune, and they were very happy together." Sand's narrative of her mother and Pierret's bond in later life leaves no place for such a marriage. After Sophie died, Sand tells us,

> Pierret did not weep. . . . He seemed not to comprehend that
> two people could be separated forever. He accompanied her to
> the cemetery the next day, and returned laughing uproariously.
> Then he abruptly stopped laughing and melted in tears. Poor
> Pierret, excellent man, he was never consoled. He went back to
> his beer and pipe at the Cheval Blanc. He was always cheerful,
> brusque, oblivious, noisy. He came to see me at Nohant the
> following year. On the surface he was still the same Pierret.
> But suddenly he said to me, "Let's talk a little about your
> mother. Do you remember . . ." and then he recalled again
> all the details of her life, all the singularities of her character,
> all the outbursts of which he had been the willing victim;
> he quoted her words, he recalled the inflections of her voice,
> and he laughed wholeheartedly. And then he picked up his
> hat and went out with a joke. I followed him closely, since
> I could see that he was overcome with nervous excitation,
> and I found him sobbing in a corner of the garden.[10]

It is true that Pierret, who died in 1844, survived Sophie by seven years and that after her death he could have married someone else. But Sand's presentation of Pierret's ostensible marriage, of which no documentation has ever been found, implies that it was coextensive with his relationship with Sophie and is clearly intended to distract the reader from deducing an intimate relationship between them.[11]

Sand surprises us with her report that this unlikely individual, Pierret, "witnessed my birth . . . weaned me . . . [and] assumed a paternal right which would have verged on tyranny, if his threats could possibly have been realized." Finding Sophie exhausted by the ten-month-old Aurore's nocturnal crying, "Pierret came one evening of his own accord, took me in my cradle and carried me to his home, where he kept me for fifteen or twenty nights, hardly sleeping, so fearful was he for me, and making me drink milk and sugared water with as much solicitude, care, and tidiness as a nanny would have."[12]

Note the coincidence between dating this event in Aurore's life and the kidnapping of Lucienne at the same age, ten months. In the mornings, Pierret returned Aurore to her mother, "clean, fresh, and in good humor," much as Jennie returns Lucienne to her grandmother. Sand acknowledges that Pierret's proprietary role in her infancy caused tension within the family: "Each evening he came to fetch me again, carrying me on foot, in full view of the entire neighborhood, a grown fellow of twenty-two or twenty-three years, hardly caring if he was noticed. When my mother seemed to show resistance or anxiety, he grew red with anger, reproaching her for 'imbecilic weakness,' for he was reckless with his epithets."

Reckless or righteous? And for what other possible reason would Sophie be upset unless Pierret's prideful performance caused speculation about the baby's true father? Sand's depiction intentionally casts him as a sort of swashbuckling older brother in the family, "a grown fellow of twenty-two or twenty-three," rather than as a possible rival for Sophie's affection. Pierret's frequent bouts of bad temper seem to have been connected with his proprietary attitude toward Aurore. "He was very demanding . . . of affection," Sand explains, "and when you tested him by asking why he wanted so much to be loved, he would merely reply, 'It's just that I love you.' And he spoke these tender words with a furious tone and nervous spasm that made him grind his teeth. . . . My mother, who was familiar with his nervous condition, would say to him, 'Be quiet now, Pierret, you're not making sense.' And she would even give him a sharp pinch to get it over with more quickly."[13]

What could have caused such physical contortions and emotional flare-ups? It sounds as though Pierret was suppressing something, as though he was laboring under a burden of silence, the pressure of which induced these eruptions. If we follow this line of thinking, a curious comparison can be made between Pierret's plight and that of a character who figures in a theatrical adaptation of *Confession of a Young Girl*. Some five years after writing the novel, Sand transposed it into a much simplified play titled *L'Autre,* which was staged at the Odéon Theater in February 1870. The lawyer Mac Allan, who in the novel is hired to determine Lucienne's legitimacy, is replaced in the play by a Dr. Maxwell, who turns out to be Hélène's (Lucienne's name in the play) true father. But he's constrained from identifying himself as her father because to do so would be to dishonor her mother, whom he loves, to wound her putative grandmother, and to deprive his daughter of her name and inheritance. Much of the dramatic tension in the play is generated by the frustration Dr. Maxwell feels at being constrained to silence. "As occurs with extraordinary frequency in George Sand's novels," Helene Deutsch observes, "the father figure is split into two, a foster father and a real father. Common to both is their great fondness for the little girl."[14]

Considering that Sophie and Pierret became lovers after Maurice's death, nothing precludes the possibility that they may also have been lovers during Sophie's liaison with and marriage to Sand's father. Pierret's paternalism, temperamental nature, and proprietary attitude toward Aurore may have derived from a conviction that he was her unacknowledged father. The enigmatic sum of so many contradictions, Pierret emerges as a far more central player than either Sand's manipulative account or her biographers' commentaries would lead us to believe. (Despite her insight into the role of the split father, Deutsch dismisses Pierret as a family "servant.")[15] When a husband was sought for Aurore after her grandmother's death, prospective partners presented themselves not only to her cousins the Villeneuves, from Maurice Dupin's side of the family, but also to Pierret. After Sophie died, Sand drew even closer to Pierret, who helped her manage and oversee her Narbonne town house, loyally attended productions of her plays, and regularly participated in family occasions and celebrations, serving as a witness to the marriages of both Caroline and Hippolyte.

René's brother, Auguste de Villeneuve, warned her that a "good match" ("a man of wealth and good breeding") would not be possible if she continued to associate with "your mother, her daughter, her daughter's husband, with Monsieur Pierret. You've been seen on the street with all those people. It's an impossible society. I don't speak for myself—it wouldn't matter to me—but for my sister-in-law, and for women from those honorable families to which we could have gotten you entry via a good marriage."[16]

"I wept over my relatives' desertion," Sand recorded in her autobiography. "I loved them. They were the sons of my father's [half] sister, my father had adored them, my grandmother had blessed them, they had smiled on my childhood. . . . But I quickly made up my mind about what had to be severed between us—certainly not affectionate family ties, but rather those of shared beliefs and status."[17]

Sand's lifelong correspondence is dotted with affectionate allusions to Pierret, whom she referred to as "Pierrot," "l'ami Pierrot," "Piérotard," and, in a nod to his role as stand-in for Maurice Dupin, "le vicomte" or "le vicomte de la Pierrotière." If by chance Sand failed to acknowledge Pierret in a letter to her mother, she would have to answer to them both for her oversight. Ever grateful to Pierret, who "treated me with the affection of a father and the concern of a mother," Sand recruited him as surrogate grandfather to Maurice, and Solange would pay Pierret regular visits until his death. Pierret had tenderly ministered to Sophie during her final illness, and when she died, Sand pronounced him her own "oldest and best friend."[18]

In 1832, Sand wrote an enigmatic passage dedicated simply to L ("A L . . ."), which is part of a collection of posthumously published fragments provocatively titled *Sketches and Hints*.[19] In it, Sand addresses an unnamed individual who has committed some terrible, secret misdeed (she says it is not a crime) and who has threatened to seek revenge by destroying someone whose loss would only add to his misery. "You are aware, unhappy man," says Sand, "that there is a cloud over your head that will inevitably break into a storm." She continues: "How do you hope to prevent the moral, physical, and social consequences of what you have done? You claim that no one knows about it, that no one can tell people about it. Well then, you will tell it yourself. A day will come when you feel hopeless or faint-hearted and when you will make the cowardly confession of your misfortune."

The plot thickens as Sand narrates the conditions of this person's misdeed: "You have picked a beautiful fruit, but remember that to search for it you fell into an abyss where no one can descend without leaving his ineradicable footsteps. Remember that you found it among brambles and thorns and in soil which produces only bitter fruit." Sand proceeds from this abstract, poetic evocation drawn from nature to an analogy drawn from human behavior: "If you had assassinated a man on a desert island in the tropics, if you had given him a watery grave where no trace of remains can be found, where there are no bloodstains, where there are no footprints, you would still be in danger within society. In the midst of society you've dug a grave in which to bury not the body of a man, but the peace you've thus forsaken for as long as you shall live!"

Sand implicates herself in the universal condition of human guilt— "No one among us is exempt from a crime of commission or intention, we have all been homicidal"—and counsels L to curb his anger and resentment, to think in terms of divine judgment, not in terms of human retribution. "You were neither vicious nor culpable," she tells him, "but you were imprudent and unfortunate."

Revisiting this passage some years later, Sand added a curious note: "If I leave this page it's because no one will ever guess to whom it was addressed (1845)." Georges Lubin accompanies the text with an explanatory footnote: "It was impossible for us to identity to whom these mysterious pages were addressed. However much we wanted to take on George Sand's own challenge to her researchers in the note she added to this passage in 1845, our attempts were foiled by a heavy, snake-like cross-out."[20]

If we bear in mind that Pierret's full name was Louis-Mammès Pierret, an interesting possibility for this unexplained passage emerges. Might Sand have been addressing Pierret, certain that her future readers would not associate him with the initial *L*? Pierret was frequently out of sorts with Sophie, who had a tendency to go off in a huff when they had disagreements. And he was highly sensitive to any sign, real or imagined, of neglect on Sand's part. During the time frame in which "A *L* . . ." was written (1832), Pierret had paid an early morning call on Aurore in Paris and was turned away at the door by a friend, but not before glimpsing the sleeping figure of Jules Sandeau inside her apartment. A volley of apologies and the pretext of a case of cholera were required before Aurore was able to appease Pierret's upset over the incident.[21] Could Sand have been concerned that Pierret, his feathers ruffled at having been slighted, was threatening to divulge the secret of his paternity? And were this the case, might it not have been construed by Sand as a form of destruction of human life commensurate with the metaphoric murder invoked in the passage to *L*? As noted, in the play *L'Autre*, Sand raises the problem of the harm Dr. Maxwell would do were he to divulge the truth of Hélène's identity.

Lubin conjectures that a following selection in *Sketches and Hints*, titled "Byron's Secret," "should perhaps be considered in juxtaposition with the mysterious 'A *L* . . .' with which it is altogether contemporaneous."[22] This subsequent passage is also concerned with secrecy and guilt: "Sainte-Beuve was telling me the other day that it's beautiful to have a big secret in life, an emotional secret which could be revealed but which remains undisclosed, that is a secret which in itself wouldn't be at all shameful, and which would remain enclosed in one's soul like a precious perfume that's exuded upon contact with air."

Sand goes on to refer to Byron's "alleged crime" of having fathered an illicit child by his own sister, for which Sand grants him absolution. Even incest doesn't rise to the level of a genuine crime according to Sand's forgiving view of human nature, which inclines all people, herself included, toward moral transgression of one kind or another: "None of us who live lackluster, unpersecuted bourgeois lives are untainted or unencumbered or without some unknown flaw or some hidden misfortune." Here again, as in the previous passage, Sand counsels discretion and secrecy as the best way to protect oneself from the slings and arrows of a malevolent world: "In our sad and somber life, nothing glorious, nothing enlivening offsets this insurmountable weight which burdens one side of our fate. We must endure this in silence and without false pride, for society applies horrible punishments and insulting taboos to those of us who dare defy it by subjecting ourselves to its judgment. Sincerity, far from absolving us in the eyes of our fellow men, would be another blemish inflicted upon us. . . . As you well know, we all have a smudge of dirt on our forehead, a great dread of the future, a great humiliation in the past."

Despite her deep attachment to Pierret, Sand is curiously silent on the subject of his death. We only learn of it through a letter from Chopin, who was living with Sand when Pierret died. On 31 October 1844, Chopin wrote his sister, Ludwika: "You remember how I once got out of the carriage in the square by the column, in Paris, and went to the Treasury, about some business, to a very old friend of this household. He called on me the next day. He was a good friend, the oldest friend of the father and mother of the Lady of the House. He was present at her birth, he buried her mother, and really belonged to the family. Well, returning from dining at the house of a certain deputy, a friend of his, he fell downstairs, and died in a few hours. It was a great blow here, for they were devotedly fond of him."[23] It was shortly after Pierret died that Sand revisited the passage written years before "A *L* . . ." Perhaps the message she added at this time was her private eulogy.

At the close of the lengthy court battle in which Sand won legal separation from her husband, she wrote her mother, "Hug Pierret for me, he's a good friend. He has not betrayed my father's memory by siding with those who persecute me: and my father's son has done so! How shameful." At the trial, Hippolyte apparently raised scandalous allegations concerning Sand's relationship to Maurice Dupin. Perhaps, like the English wife in

Confession of a Young Girl, who disputes Lucienne de Valangis' identity in order to protect her son's inheritance, Hippolyte was disgruntled by his half sister's privileged status within the Dupin family. Pierret, on the contrary, must have held his peace. Once again, several weeks after the Dudevant trial had concluded, Sand sent her mother a message for Pierret: "You can sleep in peace about everything. I give you a thousand kisses, as well as dear Pierret. I depend upon him in life and in death." Sand's love for and devotion to this man, though intentionally understated and therefore little noted, is movingly inscribed in the letter she wrote Pierret at the time of her mother's final illness: "And you, my dear old friend, if anything could make me love you more, it would be your devotion to my mother during her illness and the kind letters you wrote me. But the friendship which binds us goes back so far that it has neither a beginning nor an end."[24]

If Louis-Mammès Pierret was George Sand's father, or even if Sand merely believed he was, the story of their connection has remained outside the bounds of time and retelling. *Confession of a Young Girl,* on the other hand, comes to a clear and happy resolution, in which Lucienne marries Mac Allan, the lawyer who has helped her discover who she is. The novel's final image, "the bright light of daybreak [*l'aurore*] which dissipates all the shadows," suggestively underscores the novel's autobiographical connection: Lucienne-Aurore has finally emerged from the shadow of not knowing into the light of her true identity.[25]

CHAPTER TWENTY-FIVE

The Art of Loving

The old woman, yes, it's true, is another woman, another me that's
just beginning and that I can't yet complain about. This woman
is ignorant of her past mistakes. She's unaware of them because she
wouldn't know how to explain them and isn't capable of making
them again.

George Sand

Love is an activity, not a passive affect; it is a "standing in," not
a "falling for." In the most general way, the active character of love
can be described by stating that love is primarily giving, not
receiving.

Erich Fromm, The Art of Loving

WHEN SAND WAS FIFTY-TWO, her handwriting changed. In a study
devoted exclusively to this midlife transformation, *George Sand Under the
Magnifying Glass,* Frédéric Dubois interprets this phenomenon as a sign
of personal growth and development: "Liberation, serenity, these states
of mind concur with the graphologist's findings: straightening [signals]
independence in relation to the environment; the garland instead of the
arch and the angle, [which signaled] feminine receptivity and benevolence,
makes way for virility and resistance; freer use of graphic space and primacy
of movement over form [signals] freedom of feeling, spontaneity. Enlarge-
ment adds a note of self-confidence which goes along with a positive, more
peaceful personality." According to the Müller-Enskat curve, which Dubois
uses to track Sand's writing from 1822 until 1870, she seems to be "progres-
sively lifting the veil, revealing her true face to the world."[1]

There were other changes that accompanied age and maturity. From the petite, wasp-waisted young woman who passed as a male university student in the Paris of the 1830s, by midlife Sand had attained a full, matronly figure that she clothed in simple, comfortable dresses rather than the trousers, cutaway jacket, and high hat of her youthful, more rebellious years. From 1849 on, Sand spent most of her life at Nohant, eschewing Paris for a more tranquil country life.

"I'm spending less time on my writing, but I'm working faster and with more facility," Sand told Pierre-Jules Hetzel. Although she continued to write and produce at an impressive rate, in her later years Sand devoted increasing amounts of time to the study of nature, taking over the room once occupied by Chopin for her collections of rock specimens, minerals, plants, and butterflies. When her much loved friend of later years, Gustave Flaubert, convalescing on doctor's orders in Switzerland, wrote Sand, "I'm no man of Nature. And I'm baffled by countries that have no history. I'd give all the glaciers of Switzerland for the Vatican Museum," Sand shot back: "You don't want to be a man of nature. That's your loss. It means you attach too much importance to the details of human affairs and don't reflect that even in yourself there's a *natural* force that defies the ifs and buts of human chitchat. . . . Talent, will and genius are just as much natural phenomena as lakes, volcanoes, mountains, winds, stars and clouds."[2]

The changes registered themselves in her writing. Sand gradually turned away from her socialist agenda, which had begun to cost her her bourgeois readership, and toward the cycle of rustic novels: *Jeanne, La Mare au diable* (*The Devil's Pool*), *François le champi* (*The Little Waif*), *La Petite Fadette* (*Little Fadette*), published on the cusp of the 1848 revolution, and *Les Maîtres sonneurs* (*The Bagpipers*). "This is the strength of George Sand and of her second movement," Matthew Arnold exulted, "after the first movement of energy and revolt was over, towards nature and beauty, towards the country, primitive life, the peasant."[3]

Despite the passing years and the changes they brought, Sand grew younger in spirit. "I have white hairs, but that doesn't mean a thing," she told a friend. "Old women are loved better than young ones, I now know. It's not the person who must last, it's the love; may God make this one last, for it is good."[4] Sand was referring to her nascent love affair with Alexandre Manceau, an engraver thirteen years her junior whom her son had met in Delacroix's studio. Maurice introduced Manceau to his mother without any thought that he was presenting her with the loyal and loving

companion who would remain by her side for the next fifteen years, until
Manceau's death from tuberculosis, in 1865. Indeed, it was with this modest, unassuming, and altogether unillustrious younger man that Sand
would enjoy the longest lasting, most harmonious relationship of her life.

"This one sees to my every need and puts his whole self in the glass
of water he brings me or the cigarette he lights for me," Sand boasted to
Hetzel. "He never keeps me waiting! He's precise, he has a watch, and he
looks at it. Nor have I ever wanted for the glance or the word that would
set everything straight."[5] Following a visit, Théophile Gautier chronicled
his impressions: "But I must say Manceau has really turned Nohant into
a writing factory. She cannot sit down in any room without pens, blue ink,
cigarette papers, Turkish tobacco and lined writing paper suddenly material-
izing for her."[6] The attentions Manceau lavished on his mistress earned
him her enduring love and loyalty.

If past relationships were overburdened and undermined by feelings
of deprivation, with Manceau, Sand finally found the undistracted, "motherly" devotion that healed her wounds. "He's attentive the way a woman
is, an able, active, clever woman," Sand explained. "When I'm sick, I'm
cured, it takes no more than seeing him plump my pillow and bring me
my slippers. I, who never ask for or accept help, I rely on his, as though
it were my nature to be petted. . . . In sum, I love him, I love him with my
whole self; finally, in spite of terrible distrust which has plagued me to
the depths of my being in all my love affairs despite the superhuman
efforts I've made to overcome it. It's as though I've been transformed: I'm
healthy, I'm peaceful, I'm *happy*, nothing is too much for me, *even his absence*, which says it all for me who have never been able to bear that."

New construction was undertaken at Nohant, including a studio for
Maurice and installation of central heating. The château gardens were re-
designed and enlarged. With more time spent at Nohant and with Maurice's
and eventually Manceau's help, Sand developed a theater that, much to
Solange's chagrin, replaced her childhood bedroom. "When I returned
home after I was married," Solange complained to her former headmistress,
Madame Bascans, "my childhood room where I had left my bed, my furnishings, and many personal and meaningful objects was changed over. In place
of the bed and furnishings, I found a theatre, stage sets, and costumes."[7]

Sand would rewrite many of her novels as plays, which were staged at
Nohant, often before being produced professionally in Paris. Ever concerned

Alexandre Manceau. Drawing by Auguste Lehman.
(© Photothèque des musées de la ville de Paris.
Photo: Lifermann)

with the problem of illiteracy in France, Sand welcomed the opportunity
to write for the theater, which enabled the nonreading population to experience her work. Members of the family, château staff, and Sand's house-
guests were cast as characters, and the locals were invited to attend performances. "Enclosed in our Thébaïde," Sand wrote her friend Pauline
Viardot, "we're leading the life of ham-actors. Nohant is no longer Nohant,
it's a theater; my children are no longer children, they're actors; my inkwell
is no longer a fount of novels, it's a cistern of plays; I'm no longer Mad[ame]
Sand, I'm a leading lady."[8] Maurice constructed elaborate stage sets for
their productions and devoted himself with much passion and artistry to
a marionette theater, carving scores of exquisite wooden figures for which
Sand sewed costumes.

As rail lines were cut through the French countryside, the provinces became increasingly accessible. In 1841, the overnight trip by mail coach between Paris and Nohant took eighteen hours. If one stayed over in Orléans, Châteauroux, or Vierzon and continued by coach the following morning, the same trip could take two full days. By 1847, trains ran as far as Châteauroux (six to seven hours from Paris), shortening travel time to Nohant to only nine or ten hours. Sand could lure friends from the capital with the promise that "one leaves Paris around nine and dines at Nohant at seven."[9] Sand's table was graced by Flaubert, Dumas fils, Delacroix, Turgenev, Heinrich Heine, Napoléon Jérôme, to name but a few of her many illustrious guests.

Visits from Solange and her daughter, Jeanne-Gabrielle Clésinger (the second), born in May 1849 and nicknamed Nini, were welcome, but only on the condition that Clésinger not accompany them. As Solange and Clésinger struggled through the unraveling of their miserable marriage, Sand's bond with her granddaughter was sealed. Who better than this grandmother could understand the torment of being in the middle of feuding loved ones whose conflicting claims compete for one's love?

During the several years in which the Clésingers' marriage settlement was in litigation, Solange depended increasingly on her mother and virtually relinquished Nini's care to her. For her part, Sand relished the opportunity to relive some of the happy experiences of her own childhood, in particular the magical grotto that her mother had built with her at Nohant. Together, Sand and Nini toiled at the construction of their own little "Trianon." "I'm working the land four or five hours a day in a passionate stupor," Sand wrote Hetzel. "I've made a fantasy garden in my little woods . . . moss, ivy, vaults, shells, grottoes. It defies common sense, but all the stones, stumps, watering cans, barrowloads of sand and soil that I'm moving around, all the daydreaming about plays and novels and unimportant things, all this intellectual idling is fabulous." If she had it to do over again, Sand tells the publisher, she would live differently: "I'd like to forget that I was an author and immerse myself in a physical life, with a spiritual life of revery, contemplation, moderate and carefully selected reading: one or two hours a day for the mind, ten or twelve hours of movement."[10]

The longer Nini remained in Sand's care, the more responsibility Sand assumed for the child's needs, often in defiance of and competition with Solange, in whose absence Sand reported, "We're inseparable; family life couldn't be better."[11] Sand gave Nini her lessons and taught her to read by the Bourrousse de Laffore method, which she had used with much success with Luce Caillaud, her serving girl. But the strain of caring for such a young child while attending to other commitments—domestic, social, and professional—weighed heavily on Sand. When Nini became ill with dysentery and soiled the bed and herself from tip to toe, Manceau's note in the daily diary ("Agenda") that he and Sand kept suggests that his exhausted mistress was beginning to feel burdened by her child-care responsibilities.

"Solange is completely dependent upon me," Sand complained to Pauline Viardot after one of her daughter's visits. "She's bored to tears when no one's around her. She's unbelievably lazy and cares for nothing but riding and dressing up. When we gather in the evening, she's gay and sweet; all done up for dinner in white, in red, her lips and brows painted, ribbons in her hair, and for a couple hours she's in a good mood, laughing and chatting away."[12]

Word of Solange's relationships with men who returned her favors by contributing to her upkeep had reached Sand. She was, understandably, appalled. When Solange looked into renting a home in the Berry near Nohant, Sand cited practical problems with the property to dissuade her. But her reasons only barely disguised her essential motive, which was to keep her increasingly difficult daughter at a distance.

As the Clésingers' separation proceedings became more acrimonious, Nini was sent away to neutral ground, to a pension far from her warring parents. To wait out the court decision, Solange retired to a pension for single women in Paris, from which she wrote her mother in April 1852:

> I'm here at the pension since yesterday. It already feels like
> a long time. Is this how I'm to spend the most beautiful years
> of my life? Without family, friend, child, without even a dog to
> interrupt the emptiness. . . . Being alone in Paris between four
> dirty walls, with a sputtering candle and a wilting flower that
> seem to say: and I, too, would have been beautiful, loved,
> sought after, if I hadn't been shut in and abandoned. To be all
> alone amidst movement and noise, among people who are hav-
> ing fun, horses galloping, women singing, children playing in
> the sun, people who love one another and are happy—it isn't
> boredom, it's despair. It's no wonder that poor girls without

talent and education succumb to pleasure and vice. Do even reasonable and good women always know how to avoid it? Ah, how much courage it takes still to be standing![13]

Sand was enraged by Solange's self-indulgence, all the more so having just learned that the court had awarded Solange a tentative victory that would allow her to keep her daughter until the next stage of the trial: "It would seem that since you've won the first round . . . since in just a few days you'll have your daughter back and will bring her here where you can stay if you like until the next court decision, there's no longer need to despair of several days spent in a depressing room; for I see that that's the great misery of the moment. This is not the end of the world; I've lived a lot, worked a lot *alone*, between four *dirty walls*, in the *most beautiful years of my youth*, as you say, and it is not the worst thing that has happened to me."[14] Sand accused Solange of being the cause of her own misfortune: had she not been so precipitous in pressing for a separation from Clésinger, she would not have disrupted so many lives, including her own. "You swallow rods of steel and are shocked that they remain stuck in your gut. I'm surprised you're not worse off than you are for having consumed them."

There was still more on Sand's mind as she drafted the longest letter she would ever write her daughter. She blamed Solange for pushing away those who would have supported her and of disdaining loyal family friends for not being rich and important enough. "I wasn't born a princess like you, and I've chosen my friends according to my simple tastes and my preference for a quiet, retiring life. Your greatest misfortune is to be my daughter, but I can't do anything to change that, and you must take responsibility once and for all for yourself."

The next item on Sand's agenda was Solange's penchant for luxury. "It would take money, lots of money, to console you. In luxury, laziness, giddiness, the emptiness within you would be obliterated. But in order to give you what you'd need, I would have to double my work, which in six months' time would be the end of me, for the work I'm doing is already more than I can bear. To sum up our financial situation: for the three of us we have seven thousand francs income. The rest comes from my brain, my late-night vigils, from blood, sweat, and raw nerves."[15]

Sand was just coming to her core complaint: "Truly, you find it difficult to be poor, alone, and not to *succumb to vice*? You're having a hard time *standing up* because you've been between *four walls* for twenty-four hours and because you hear *women laughing* and *horses galloping outside? Qué malheur,* as Maurice says. The real misfortune is to have a brain which reasons the way yours does: *I must have happiness or vice.* Since when is the absence of happiness an excuse for the loss of dignity?"

Sand's next gambit was a dangerous one that ultimately backfired. "I defy you to give it a try, then, the life of vice and prostitution. It's not quite as easy as you think to dishonor oneself. You have to be more exceptionally beautiful and witty than you are to be pursued or even sought after by buyers. Or else you'd have to be more cunning, to make yourself desirable, to feign passion or libertinage and all sorts of *appealing things,* which, thank God, you don't know the first thing about! Men with money want women who know how to earn it, and this knowledge would fill you with so much disgust that in no time you'd be begging off."

And finally, Sand took Solange to task on maternal grounds. "Do you know that if I were the *judge* of your trial and I read your present aphorisms, I would surely not award you your daughter?" Sand closed by beseeching Solange to read this letter carefully, to reflect on its contents, and to examine her conscience. But Solange did not follow her mother's advice. Upon arriving at Nohant, she found the letter that her mother had left for her and threw it away. Sand retrieved it and saved it in an envelope marked for posterity: "From me, to be kept. 1852. In response to Solange's letter of the 23rd, reply to Solange dated 25 April '52, which didn't reach her in Paris the following Tuesday and which she read here and left to be swept up on the floor of her room."[16]

The letter may have gone unheeded (or unread) by Solange, but Sand did well to preserve what Henry James would later commemorate as "a document of the highest psychological value and a practical summary of all the elements of the writer's genius, of all her indefeasible advantages; it is verily the gem of her biographer's collection."[17]

The Clésingers' separation proceedings were further complicated when Clésinger seized Solange's correspondence with her cousin and lover René Gaston de Villeneuve, burst in on them, and reported the evidence to his lawyer in Paris. Clésinger and Solange engaged in a tug-of-war over Nini, who left Nohant with her father for the last time on 7 May 1854. By August, having won guardianship of Nini on appeal, Clésinger sent her away to a pension in Paris. In December, the court pronounced

Solange Dudevant-Sand. Drawing by Jean-Baptiste Clésinger. (© Photothèque des musées de la ville de Paris. Photo: Joffre)

the separation of the Clésingers and, reversing the earlier custodial arrangement, awarded Nini to George Sand.

But Nini would never make it back to Nohant and her beloved grandmother. Clésinger appealed the court decision, which delayed by two weeks Nini's release from the poorly run pension where she was boarded. Ill and underdressed for a bitter-cold winter outing with her father, Nini died of scarlet fever during the night of 13–14 January 1855, attended by Solange, who had raced to her bedside. Her description of Nini in her final hours —swollen and disfigured, packing her toys away in boxes, pulling off the locket that contained a clipping of her mother's hair, and smiling up at her before drifting away—is searing.[18]

On 16 January 1855, Nini was buried in the cemetery at Nohant, and Solange sank into a depression from which she never emerged. Racked with grief following her daughter's death, Solange composed an extraordinary confession: "I was seized by a furious strength, a stubborn desire to destroy everything in myself: health, youth, mind, heart, reputation, my very existence. I used it all up, smashed everything to smithereens with vigor, energy, determination, persistence that were truly admirable in a woman." As though addressing a matter of wayward diction rather than untoward destiny, Sand's devoted editor, Georges Lubin, responded unsympathetically to Solange's animus: "This last sentence, a manifestation of foolish vanity, detracts from the rest and undercuts the emotion."[19] In his overweening attachment to the mother, Lubin lapses into editorial *obiter dicta*, ruling in favor of her denigration of the daughter.

After Nini's death, Sand referred to her in letters as "the child" or "Jeanne," no longer as Nini, the name she had always used for her in life. In referring to Jean Reynaud's *Terre et ciel* (*Earth and Heaven*), which greatly solaced her grief, Sand reversed the title, calling it *Ciel et terre*, as though she had already set her sights on an afterlife with her cherished granddaughter. "[Jeanne] isn't dead, I know," Sand wrote Hetzel following the funeral, "but we must be separated for this life, which isn't long."[20]

In the wake of her disastrous marriage and Nini's death, Solange became the mistress of a series of wealthy men who provided her with considerable and conspicuous financial support. Self-destructive though it was, Solange had found an ingenious way of getting back at her mother, whose self-sustaining style of life had been created in reaction to the lives of her mother and great-grandmother, both of whom had been kept women.

In addition to Gaston de Villeneuve, Solange's lovers, whom Sand referred to as "les beaux-frères payants" (brothers-in-law who pay or, idiomatically, "sugar daddies"), included Count Alfred d'Orsay, an English socialite named Alfred Seymour, the Italian statesman Count Carlo Alfieri, Edouard Pissavy (a local doctor from La Châtre), and an official from Egypt, Wacy Pacha, who had been posted to Paris from Alexandria.[21]

Solange flaunted her extravagant lifestyle, which far exceeded her modest allowance. She wore expensive gowns and fine jewelry, rode in costly carriages drawn by teams of horses, built a villa in Cannes, and resided over an elaborately furnished Paris salon on rue Taitbout, whose lavish soirées were the subject of café gossip the following day. Currying her mother's favor, Solange sent plants for her garden from the south of France; Sand wrote back that she didn't want them. Solange offered to send cuttings for a herbarium; Sand told her not to bother. "I don't have time for this."[22]

"Your life is outrageous, my dear, and the more it goes on, the less I understand," Sand scolded Solange, whose exhibitionism and promiscuity had succeeded at embarrassing her. Resentful at being trumped by the high drama of her daughter's life, Sand's response was competitive: "It wasn't worth it for me to write so many novels, only to see myself surpassed by the novelistic existence you are leading." Ever controlling, Sand concluded, "I am sad not to be able to arrange for you another way of being." She had apparently forgotten (or chosen not to remember) that it was she who had cast her tiny daughter in the role of seductress: a carefully if unconsciously designed strategy to recycle her unresolved animosity toward her loose-living mother.[23]

On the eve of the first anniversary of Nini's death, Solange informed her mother that she planned to return to Nohant to visit her daughter's grave. Sand wrote back from Paris, where she was spending the winter, to advise Solange against the trip. "Our beloved child's soul is with us, everywhere and always. Her grave is but an object to be respected. Respect for graves, yes, but not a cult." Solange was not dissuaded, and after her visit she reported to her mother: "The Berry was under snow and the road was practically impassable. . . . I went to the cemetery today to put the flowers that I brought on the grave. I saw that you placed a stone on the place where I grieve. The idea of a stone crushing her and preventing her from ever getting up again is onerous to me. As I asked you on my last visit to let me replace it with a cross, I brought one with me this time. It's perfectly simple, without any ornament, in white marble with the name Jeanne-Gabrielle engraved on it. . . . Won't you let me have it set at my daughter's head?" Sand responded hastily: "Leave things as they are. Leave the cross that you brought nearby. I'll have it set properly when I'm home. Until then the workers and the gardener aren't to do anything without my permission."[24]

The following January when Solange alerted her mother that she would be visiting Nini's grave, Sand again discouraged her from making the trip. "My dear mother, I don't wish to displease you or to cause you pain," Solange wrote back on black-bordered paper. "Nevertheless, I don't intend to forego my visit to the cemetery on January 13th. I don't recall having asked you for anything; it seems to me that all I said was that I'd be in the Berry on January 13th and that I was going to spend an hour at my daughter's grave. . . . You won't see me or even hear about me. If it annoys you even to have me cross your garden to get to Her, I'll go by way of the cemetery and throw the flowers that I bring. Alas, I could hardly have imagined when I brought her there to be buried that this grave would become a source of discord between us. I wish your heart would be less bitter and more just toward me."[25]

When Solange arrived at the cemetery on the second anniversary of her daughter's death, the cross she had left the year before was gone and had been replaced by a stone block. Even more than anti-Catholic sentiment, unmitigated anger toward Solange ("My worst enemy in this world is my daughter") explains Sand's cruelty in ordering the cross removed.[26] By 1861, relations between Sand and Solange had further deteriorated. Four years would go by with no communication between them.

In general, scholars have tended to corroborate Sand's hostility toward Solange. In thrall to Sand's greatness and impervious to flaws in her character and conduct, biographers have judged her troubled daughter without compassion. André Maurois describes Solange as "by nature cold and odd. Whatever she did was apt to be inspired by a spirit of contradiction. Slightly unbalanced, she had her mother's daring without her mother's genius." Elizabeth Schermerhorn is no less forgiving: "From birth [Solange] had been destined to be a thorn in her mother's flesh. From her cradle she had been naughty, mischievous and disobedient, just as Maurice had always been good and quiet and affectionate. She appeared to have inherited all the family weaknesses; the frivolity and vanity of Sophie Delaborde, the stinginess and prosaicness [sic] of her father, her mother's imagination without her genius and warmth." As though her failure to thrive were not punishment enough, Solange gets blamed for her own misery: "The principal reason for her suffering, and to a certain extent for her unhappiness," Samuel Rocheblave believes, "was her own doing, due to her own character."[27]

Nearly forty years old, Maurice was still unmarried, and Sand began to express concern. "I'm always worried about his lack of commitment," she told a friend. "He needs to make a choice, otherwise he will have lost the chance forever, and what kind of old age would he have when he no longer has me?"[28] In June 1861, Maurice accompanied Prince Napoléon Jérôme on a trip to America. Sand would suffer throughout their separation and complained once their ship set sail from Portugal that her son was out of letter range. Perhaps this was part of Maurice's purpose in undertaking the lengthy journey.

"Maurice is with me and working on his notes on America," Sand wrote Armand Barbès in January of the new year, when Maurice had returned to the fold. "He saw a lot in a very brief time, including, with good reason, this false democracy that proclaimed *liberté* and *égalité* while forgetting only one thing: *fraternité*, without which the other two are sterile and destructive." To a French attaché in Algiers, Sand reported that Maurice "much prefers Africa to the United States" and the slower pace of French civilization to the "furor over material progress that makes Yankees insufferable."[29]

In April 1862, after several years of procrastination, Maurice married Lina Calamatta, the daughter of the distinguished engraver Luigi Calamatta, a longtime friend of Sand. She was ecstatic about the union and made it a collective family affair. To her future daughter-in-law, Sand exulted, "Yes, I'm certain of it, you will make us happy," and sealed their union with her blessing: "God will hold all three of us responsible for our faith, for marriage is an act of faith in Him and in ourselves."[30] Indeed, Maurice, Lina, and their two daughters, Aurore ("Lolo"), born in 1866, and Gabrielle ("Titite"), two years later, would remain at Nohant for the rest of their lives, with Sand joyously assuming the role of personal tutor as well as doting grandmother.

But beneath the seemingly tranquil surface of communal family life at Nohant, tensions reigned. Maurice bridled with resentment as Manceau increasingly assumed responsibility for administration of the château, in particular for the theater that Maurice had founded with his mother. Manceau "is our lead actor now," Sand boasted to a friend. "He plays serious and comic, and when it comes to costumes, billing, stage sets, he runs the show." Adding salt to an open wound, Sand wrote Maurice when he was away visiting his father: "Manceau . . . is taking care of your animals, your collections—and above all your mother."[31]

The cottage that Manceau bought for Sand in 1857 may have been the couple's first step away from the incipient conflict between a jealous and possessive son and the man who had won his mother's favor. "My life turns toward Gargilesse with an irresistible pull," Sand wrote in 1858. "This truly *rustic*, pell-mell village life seems much more normal to me than my complicated château life."[32] Although Sand would tell people that the cottage in the Creuse valley served as her escape from Nohant, it was more than the constant flow of visitors (which for years Sand had welcomed without objection) and the demands of running a country estate (which Sand had always managed with finesse) that drove her to seek refuge at "Algira," the cottage she named for a species of butterfly that inhabited the region.

By 1864, tensions between Maurice and his mother and Manceau had become intolerable, and Sand made an extraordinary decision that was no doubt influenced by her earlier experience with Chopin and her regrets about the way this central relationship in her life had ended. Like Chopin, Manceau was suffering from advanced tuberculosis, and Sand was painfully aware that he would not live for many more years. Without apparent regret, despite her lifelong attachment to the château where she was raised and where she had meant to grow old, Sand left Nohant and moved with Manceau to Palaiseau, a suburb of present-day Paris that at the time was on its rural outskirts. There they took up residence in a comfortable country house set in the center of a graciously landscaped park. At Palaiseau Sand tended her beloved companion in his decline, returning the love and care he had selflessly lavished on her.

The first person Sand informed of Manceau's death, on 21 August 1865, was her son. "Our poor friend's suffering has ended," she wrote Maurice. "He was entirely lucid when he fell asleep at midnight. He slept the night through, and when we wanted to awaken him at five o'clock to give him something, his speech was all confused as in a dream. He held his cup, he wanted to be raised, and he died unaware and seemingly without suffering." Sand hastened to reassure Maurice that she was fine. "Although heartbroken, after dressing and arranging him on his deathbed, I still have enough energy and willpower not to cry. Rest assured that I won't be sick, I don't want to be, I want to come join you as soon as I've attended to his poor remains and organized his affairs and my own, which are yours."[33]

To her nephew Sand showed a fuller measure of her grief: "He's here, this poor friend, calm, pale and as though rejuvenated by death. I'm keeping him until tomorrow. I have a terrible fear of premature burial! I've covered him with flowers. I've chosen a beautiful place in the cemetery. I'm holding up by taking care of him until the very last minute. But I'm overwhelmed with exhaustion, having taken care of him all by myself day and night since the beginning, for three months!"[34] In a quiet moment following the funeral, Sand made an entry in the *Agenda:* "Here I am at home *alone* forever. . . . My son is my very soul. I will live for him. . . . Yes, yes, but *you* who have loved me so much, you will never be replaced."[35]

With Manceau put to rest, Maurice's fears of dispossession were quelled, and when Sand sold Palaiseau, she resumed her role as chatelaine at Nohant, where she would live in harmony with Maurice and his family until her own death ten years later. Apparently, Maurice's resentment toward Manceau endured nonetheless, for when it came time to publish his deceased mother's correspondence, Maurice edited out Sand's beloved companion, replacing all references to Manceau with the impersonal pronouns "one" and "he."[36]

Sand's relations with Solange became increasingly strained, and in October 1865, Sand arranged to have Solange's pension cut off. "Personally, I don't accept prostitution, and nothing can any longer exist between me and a person who has followed this path, laughing, her head held high; a person of education, raised in a most respectable milieu with a name she should have honored and sufficient resources to live nobly in retirement, study, and modesty," Sand wrote Charles Poncy shortly before terminating Solange's support. "She preferred libertinage and its profits. I repeat that I no longer know her, especially since she has neither affection nor respect for me, nor does she show any regret for her deplorable life."[37] Sand would reinstate Solange's pension in May 1866, only to cut it off, once again, several years before her (Sand's) death.

In addition to family life at Nohant, Sand's later years were devoted to a modified renaissance of the early Bohemian life she had led as a young woman in Paris in the 1830s. She took up what she called a "vie de garçon" (a bachelor life), occasionally returning to Paris for biweekly dinners at the restaurant Magny attended by Flaubert, Sainte-Beuve, Gautier, Taine, Renan, the Goncourt brothers, Turgenev, and others among the French intellectual élite that prevailed in the last quarter of the nineteenth century. Sand was the only woman included. The photographer Félix Nadar left a description of the way Sand was living: "I found her in the rue des Feuillantines, in a student apartment that she was renting for six hundred francs a year."[38] A late-life affair with the painter Charles Marchal, whom Dumas fils had taken to Nohant some years earlier, seems to have sustained Sand after Manceau's death. They dined frequently at Chez Brebant and regularly attended the theater.

*

In 1869, at the age of forty-one, single and childless after her separation from Clésinger and the death of her second daughter, Solange began writing a novel titled *Jacques Bruneau,* which is narrated in the first-person voice of Marie Tasca, the grown daughter of a celebrated opera singer named Paolina Tasca. When the novel's eponymous protagonist Jacques Bruneau is seventeen and about to enter the African army, he asks the great Paolina Tasca for a free ticket to hear her sing. "My mother was forty-two-years-old," Tasca's daughter tells us, "but she was still extremely beautiful. On stage, she could pass for any age she wanted." Marie's narration continues: "At this time I was in a pension in Neuilly: reports of this [her mother's] triumph reached the schoolroom and I was questioned, sought after, complimented by my teachers and classmates."[39]

After hearing Tasca sing, the young Jacques Bruneau carries a copy of her portrait by Mercure with him on his military campaigns. Twenty-two years later, still enamored of the opera diva, Captain Bruneau is living in Algeria, where he runs an office. During the last year of his African sojourn, he receives the visit of a foreign prince, who recognizes the Mercure portrait, which Bruneau has prominently displayed, and confides his love for her twenty-four-year-old daughter, Marie Tasca: "She has an admirable voice; but laziness, a taste for the good life, the possibility of living without doing anything have kept her from working seriously enough to follow her mother's career."[40] He goes on to explain that this daughter of the distinguished opera legend married a Lombard gentleman who ate up most of her dowry and left her alone in the world. Jacques Bruneau, then thirty-six, returns to Paris, where he meets Marie Tasca and falls in love with her.

The novel, which amounts to an unrelentingly cynical meditation on women and their woeful lot in life, wends its way through a sadomasochistic relationship between Bruneau (who ultimately takes his own life) and Marie Tasca, who's caught in conflict between the choice of marriage and career: "I would rather marry the public, with whom the contract is not so long."[41]

Spurning marriage, Marie fails nevertheless to establish a successful stage career: "I don't have the strength to go before the public with the name that I carry. They will expect from me more than from another and will scoff at me for not being at the level of my mother." She finally succumbs to the scandal of becoming Bruneau's mistress. In the conclusion to Solange's first draft of the novel, Marie, who retreats to a convent after Bruneau's suicide and her mother's death, declares: "Finally, my strength was sapped. . . . I lost my will and had but one desire: to want nothing, to decide nothing, to conclude nothing, to do nothing."[42]

Solange's lethargy mirrored her protagonist's. In June 1869, after sending her mother a first draft of the novel, Solange wrote Charles Alfieri, the married Italian statesman with whom she had been involved for many years, "I'm detained in Paris with the business of my manuscript. My mother took it with her to Nohant this week and will reread it and let me know what corrections to make. It won't be until two weeks after she gets there that she'll be able to attend to it. I won't get back the work to be done until the end of June at the earliest. I'll have to rewrite three hundred pages from beginning to end, go to see Girardin or someone else, etc. It will all take time."[43]

Delighted that her daughter was finally applying herself to some higher purpose ("the life of the mind is the remedy for everything," Sand had advised), in mid-July she returned the marked-up manuscript with her comments.[44] Her response leaves no doubt of her sincere desire that Solange's foray into literature meet with success. Remarkably, in the correspondence that ensued between mother and daughter, no allusion is made to the startling similarities between Solange's fictional narrative and her life. Whether from personal discretion or by dint of professionalism, Sand refrained from commenting on the poignant literary replication of a celebrated and successful artistic mother and a daughter who struggles in her shadow. Instead, in unstinting compliance with her own high standards of grammar and diction, Sand assumed the role of line editor and shot bullets through her daughter's draft:

"Page 2, one doesn't say *en proie à une résolution,* because a resolution is the opposite of an anxiety;—page 43, one doesn't write *des candeurs qui viennent se briser contre;*—page 63, *opérer une fin* is not found in any language;—page 137, *avoir l'air d'une houri* is laughable. How do Moslem nymphs seem? Has anyone ever seen them?"[45]

Sand's most serious criticism was reserved for Solange's first-person narrator, whom she accused, among other shortcomings, of lacking the will to act decisively and with dignity. "Your heroine is truly odious. You clearly chose to give most of the interest to Jacques; this is nevertheless not a reason for Tasca to be an accomplished *carogne* [slut]." Sand advised her daughter to "feminize" and "humanize" her female protagonist and further suggested that the "logical and natural conclusion" to her story should be for Marie "to reconnect to life through some form of commitment." Instead of retreating to a convent, as per Solange's first draft, Marie should accept responsibility for raising the two daughters of the actress Nina Grossi while the latter pursues her career in the theater. (This plot twist eerily echoes Sand's gesture toward her dear friend Marie Dorval, after whose death Sand assumed responsibility for her daughters.)

Not content with merely suggesting a conclusion, Sand actually drafted one in Marie's voice, which Solange adopted in its unrevised entirety as the new ending to her novel, in which Marie Tasca declares: "I accepted this commitment. I fulfill it zealously, joyously, and with a heavy heart. I would like nothing more than to make these children happy and wise. But suddenly I feel despair for their future and mine. What is woman's happiness? a mutual love, and nothing can assure or even bring about this ideal goal of our existence! I who have been well loved, I have only found love to which I could respond in a troubled, hopeless, suicidal soul." In a final, cynical flourish, Solange added two brief lines. Nina Grossi declares: "How about religion? Faith saves and consoles one for everything." And Marie Tasca replies: "That's so, but you can't have it just because you want it."

When *Jacques Bruneau* was serialized in *La Liberté* in December 1869 and January 1870, Sand wrote Solange encouraging her to pursue publication of the novel in book form: "When the time comes, I'll let you know, and I'll speak to Lévy, who will offer you the same terms he offered Maurice. It's not much; a lot of work needs to be done to make a living. But you're young, you're getting off to a good start, and you're willing to work."[46] Sand's pronouncement was more wish than reality, and although Michel Lévy Frères did publish *Jacques Bruneau* in 1870, as well as a much later second novel, *Carl Robert* (1887), Solange seems to have shared Marie Tasca's lack of resolve in the shadow of her mother's renown.

In correspondence that sheds retrospective and perhaps prophetic light on Solange's state of mind when she undertook the composition of *Jacques Bruneau,* she wrote Alfieri on 19 August 1868: "I've produced nothing. I lack perseverance: the *idée fixe* that creates greatness. I know that in spite of every wish to pursue an intellectual occupation, I'm blocked, broken by something that defies my will, that prevents me from finishing what I start. It's a form of impotence. My female nature has corrupted the race from which I hail. Daughter of an illustrious line, I'm degenerating into irreversible mediocrity."[47]

The pleasurable pastimes of Sand's later years were interrupted by the Franco-Prussian War and the advent of the Paris Commune that followed in 1871. Although Sand had continually bemoaned the French people having voted for an emperor in 1852 in the wake of the 1848 revolution, she was nevertheless dismayed by the violence and destruction of human life that resulted from the fall of the Second Empire.

"This human butchery reduces me to tatters," she wrote Flaubert in August 1870 after an unprecedented period of bloodshed. "I tremble, too, for all my children and friends who may get cut to pieces." Sand's spirits were temporarily lifted when the defeat of the French in Sedan in September 1870 brought the collapse of the Bonaparte dynasty and declaration of the Third Republic. Even though she patently deplored the ravages of war, Sand never lost faith in human progress and the possibility of a better world: "In the middle of it all my soul revives and even has flashes of faith. We need these harsh lessons in order to realize our own foolishness, and we must make good use of them." Somewhat naively, to be sure, she added a prediction that would sadly go unfulfilled: "Perhaps this is our last relapse into the errors of the past. Some clear principles that are evident to all should emerge from this turmoil."[48] When Gambetta called for elections in October, Sand had further reason for delight: a blimp that was baptized "G. Sand" airlifted a group of Americans caught in the political fray to safety.

Flaubert was having none of Sand's optimism: "The vile things I witnessed in the capital are enough to add years to a man's life," he wrote her. "And we're only in the first act, because soon we'll be moving into 'la sociale' [current slang for Socialist Republic]. Which will be followed by a vigorous and lengthy reaction! This is what we've been brought to by Universal Suffrage, the new God I consider as stupid as the old."[49]

But even Sand's optimism was sorely tried by the "bloodbath that marked the repression of the Paris Commune in May 1871." In *Paris: Capital of the World*, Patrice Higonnet puts the violence of the Commune in historical perspective: "Within a few days, roughly 20,000 Parisians were court-martialed and shot. In the long Franco-French war that began, tragically enough, with the euphoric unity of the Parisian Fête de la Fédération

Gustave Flaubert. Photo by Nadar. (Courtesy Bibliothèque
Nationale de France)

on July 14, 1790, nothing—from the 1793 Vendée massacres of (peasant)
whites by (republican) blues and blues by whites to the tortures inflicted
by the Vichy-fascist *milice* during the Second World War or the beating
and killing of collaborators in 1944—can rival the vindictiveness that the
soldiers of Versailles showed toward the city they recaptured in May 1871."[50]

Flaubert was unstinting in his disgust. "I hate democracy (at least as
it is understood in France), because it is based on 'the morality of the
Gospels,' which is immorality itself. . . . The Commune is rehabilitating
assassins, just as Jesus forgave thieves; and they are looting the houses
of the rich because they have learned to curse Lazarus—who was not a
bad man, but simply a rich man." Flaubert's next gambit was clearly designed to strike at the very heart of Sand's sentimental populism: "The
only rational thing . . . is a government of Mandarins, provided the Mandarins know something—in fact, a great many things. The *people* never come
of age, and they will always be the bottom rung of the social scale because
they represent number, mass, the limitless. It is of little importance that

many peasants should be able to read and no longer listen to their priests; but it is infinitely important that many men like Renan or Littré be able to live *and be listened to.*"[51]

When Sand let her guard down and communicated her own bitter disappointment with the bloody turn of events, Flaubert shot back, "Why are you so sad? Mankind is displaying nothing new. . . . I believe that the crowd, the mass, the herd, will always be detestable. . . . Ah, chère bon maître, if you could only hate! That is what you lack: Hate."[52]

Sand found Flaubert's cynicism and disdain infuriating. When it came to matters of the human heart, she was unyielding. "So you want me to stop loving? You want me to say that I've been wrong my whole life, that humanity is contemptible and detestable, that it was always and will always be so?" Despite the unconscionable waste of human life and property, Sand once again, as in the past, took the side of the people, arguing that those responsible for the devastation were not representative of the true "peuple de Paris":

> The people are ferocious? No! They're not stupid, either; their
> real shortcoming is that they're uninformed and foolish. It's
> not the people of Paris who massacred the prisoners, destroyed
> the monuments, and tried to burn down the city. The people
> of Paris are what remained in Paris after the siege, because
> anyone who was the least well off raced off to breathe the coun-
> try air in the provinces and to embrace their families after the
> physical and moral suffering induced by the blockade. What
> remained in Paris are the merchant and the worker, these two
> agents of work and commerce without which Paris would no
> longer exist. These are the true people of Paris; a single and
> united family for whom political misunderstandings cannot
> undermine their relationship and solidarity.

The long letter that follows stands out as perhaps Sand's most power-fully articulated expression of love for country and faith in humanity. Be-cause of its length, instead of sending it directly to Flaubert, Sand sent it to *Le Temps*, in which it appeared as a letter "To a Friend," in compliance with her contract to produce an article every two weeks. "I don't want to believe that this sacred country, that this beloved race whose harmonies and discordances vibrate within my soul, whose qualities and faults I love in spite of everything, for whom I accept the good and the bad responsibilities rather than detaching myself through disdain, no, even in my suffering, in my grief, even in my moments of greatest defeat, I refuse to believe that my country and my race have been beaten to death. I love, therefore I live; let us love and live."[53]

Although Sand did all she could to prevent the purchase, Solange bought Hippolyte Chatiron's former residence at Montgivray in June 1873 and installed herself in the shadow of her mother's château. If ingratiating herself with family was Solange's intention, her geographic rapprochement was unsuccessful. Solange's last visit to Nohant before Sand's final illness two years later took place on 13 July 1874, after which Solange made the following entry in her journal: "Lina and my mother alone in the salon playing Bézique. Lina in a dress of blue toile without a corset. Ugly bosom. Sagging nipples like fried eggs fall below her waist. Her stomach sticks out, enormous, and covers all the rest. Not very nice this little negligee. Marie [Sand's servant] broke the lantern. Returned home at ten thirty." Sand's entry in the *Agenda* for the same date is terse—"Well during the day, upset in the evening"—but Solange's hostility apparently hit home: the following day Sand terminated her daughter's pension.[54]

"A single-minded obsession has consumed her entire life: to undo what I have done," Sand had said of Solange some years before. The time had finally come to let her daughter go. "Antoine, René and the doctor are coming to dinner. Sol[ange] is off traveling God knows where," Sand recorded in the *Agenda* on 2 August. "We're running races with the children. Then dominoes and drawing. Lolo is sleeping in my room for a special treat." "We're well," she wrote Eugène Lambert on 9 August 1874. "Sol[ange] no longer visits. It seems we bore her." Sand wrote Edmond Plauchut the same day: "I send kisses from me and from everyone. . . . Except for Sol[ange], who has cut us loose. It's raining cats and dogs. . . . A beautiful harvest has just been brought in."[55]

Although Sand never did resolve her relationship with Solange, in her twilight years she resolved her relationship with herself, leaning toward nature and a comfortable sort of androgyny, learning how to live without writing, and then writing about that: "A certain person called G. Sand is well," Sand wrote Flaubert, "enjoying the marvelous Berry winter, picking flowers, communicating interesting botanical anomalies, making dresses

Solange Dudevant. Portrait by Jean-Baptiste Clésinger.
(© Photothèque des musées de la ville de Paris. Photo:
Briant)

and coats for her daughter-in-law and costumes for puppets, cutting out
stage sets, dressing dolls and reading music—but above all spending
hours with little Aurore."[56]

Flaubert was "struggling like five hundred devils" with his writing
and was in political despair: "France is sinking slowly, like a rotten hulk.
Any hope of salvage seems chimerical, even to her most solid citizens.
One has to be here, in Paris, to have an idea of the universal degradation,
the stupidity, the senility, in which we're floundering." Sand sprang back:
"I'm not *saying* humanity is on its way to the heights. But I *believe* it is, in
spite of everything."[57]

"How you fret, and how sensitive you are to life!" she scolded Flaubert.
"For what you complain about *is* life. Yet it's never been any better, for anyone, ever. We feel it to a greater or lesser degree, we understand it more
or less, and the more we're in advance of our own time the more we suffer.
We move like shadows beneath a layer of clouds through which the sun

George Sand. Photo by Nadar. (Courtesy C. O. Darré, Musée George Sand, La Châtre)

shines but faintly and fitfully, and we keep appealing to the sun, which is helpless. It's up to us to clear away our own clouds."[58]

Sand began writing for her grandchildren, for children in general. Working and remaining useful were the keys, she believed, to growing old well. "You admire my serenity," she wrote Flaubert. "It doesn't come from my character, but from my need, now, to think only of others. It's about time. Old age is creeping on, and death has got me by the shoulders. But I'm still, if not necessary, at least very useful to my family, and as long as I have breath I shall go on thinking, speaking and working for them."[59]

Sand's writing arm, which had recently been paralyzed with rheumatism, was better, and she began a new novel, *Marianne Chevreuse* (*Marianne the Goatherd*), which would be her last. "Spring is exquisite, in spite of the dryness," Sand wrote her friend Henri Amic.[60] She spent the season reading the *Iliad* with her granddaughter Aurore and bathing in the shade of alder trees in the cool, fresh water of the Indre River.

During the winter of 1876 Flaubert was deeply depressed about the poor reception of his writing. "This desire to depict things as they are, and the events of life as they appear, seems to me to be based on unsound arguments," Sand told him. "Everyone sees things from his own point of view, which I acknowledge should be chosen freely. I can summarize my own point of view in a few words: not to stand in front of a misted window which shows one nothing but the reflection of one's own nose. And to see as much as possible—good, evil, near, far, around, about; and to perceive how everything, tangible or intangible, constantly gravitates towards the necessity of goodness, kindness, truth and beauty."[61] Sand's idealism, and her turn away from realism—"My hair would turn white if I didn't rid myself of this *realism*"—would cost her her place at the forefront of French literature.[62]

For the New Year, the countryside of central France was covered in a blanket of snow. "How beautiful Nohant is," Sand wrote Charles-Edmond, "with the pines and cedars white to the tips of their branches. Every night brings a clear, moonlit sky. When one's eyes, filled with the warm candle glow of indoors gaze outside at the softness of the stark blue sky, one is refreshed and enchanted by this other magical world which is separated by a window pane."[63]

Sand knew that her dear Flaubert was drowning in sorrow and that even her sunny optimism could not lift his spirits. All the same, she did her best to reassure and encourage her younger friend: "Before long you will gradually be entering upon the happiest and most propitious part of life: old age. It's then that art reveals itself in all its sweetness; in our youth it manifests itself in anguish."[64]

Coming surprisingly close to the cultural, constructionist view of gender famously articulated a century later by Simone de Beauvoir ("Women are not born; they are made"), Sand seems finally to have reversed herself on the woman question. "Men and women are so much alike," she told Flaubert, "it's hard to understand all the subtle distinctions and theories on the subject that have coloured our various human societies." And in an article published in 1872, four years before she died, Sand wrote, "*There is but one sex*. When we examine the thesis, at present upheld or contested by some very great minds, that man and woman, male and female, are essentially dissimilar beings subject to different laws, in my opinion we enter a world of conventional ideas, a world fabricated entirely of human conceits."[65]

It is tempting to consider the possibility that in her later, calmer years, no longer "enslaved by her heart and womb," George Sand experienced relief from the stigmata of female insufficiency she had felt so acutely as a younger woman: "There's no one in the world so inwardly calm and happy as this old retired troubadour who sings a little serenade to the moon every now and then without bothering much if it's sung well or ill so long as it expresses what he has in mind; and who, the rest of the time, is deliciously idle. He hasn't always been as comfortable as this. He was foolish enough, once, to be young, but as he didn't do any harm, or have any 'unwholesome passions,' or seek just to satisfy his vanity, he's lucky enough now to be peaceful and easily amused."[66]

Epilogue

IT BEGAN RAINING in the morning of 10 June 1876. Church bells sounded the death knell that beckoned people from miles around to trudge down muddy roads leading to the tiny French village where the Good Lady of Nohant had lived and died. Posted at the château gate, her two young granddaughters distributed alms to the poor, a traditional gesture of gratitude for the bountiful life that had come to a close. Journalists milled around the courtyard, eager to record their impressions of George Sand's funeral.

The intestinal blockage from which Sand had been suffering was inoperable, and a week before she died, she had taken to her bed, knowing this was the end.[1] When Solange received word that her estranged mother's condition was terminal, she promptly left Paris to minister to her in her final hours. It was she who closed George Sand's eyes.

Prince Napoléon Jérôme and Gustave Flaubert were among those who journeyed overnight by train from Paris to attend the funeral. The lead coffin that had been sent down from the capital was too small to contain Sand's bloated body, and the new one that was ordered arrived only hours before she was buried. Decked with a silver cross, it was carried into the town church by local country folk clad in blue smocks. A young Catholic priest preceded the cortege, followed by an old man who held a candle and recited psalms. Prince Napoléon Jérôme, son of Napoléon III, walked beside the old man, bearing a laurel branch betokening Sand's love of nature. "She gives us the wild-flowers by their actual names— snowdrops, primrose, columbine, iris, scabious," Matthew Arnold would lovingly recall in his commemoration of her writing. The last words she uttered were "laissez verdure."[2]

Sand had not intended to be buried according to the rites of the Catholic church. Free-spirited and fiercely independent, she had ceased formal religious observance when she left convent school in her teens. Following her death, her son and daughter had argued over the matter of their mother's funeral rites. The strong-willed daughter won out over the mild-mannered, much beloved son: a final and formidable act of revenge against the woman who had declared, "Anything that has to do with reconstruction of the cult of Catholicism will find in me an adversary."[3]

Flaubert later wrote a friend: "You want to know the truth about Mme Sand's last moments. It is this: she did not have any priest attend her. But as soon as she was dead, her daughter, Mme Clésinger, asked the bishop of Bourges to authorize a Catholic burial, and no one in the house (except perhaps her daughter-in-law, Mme Maurice) stood up for our poor friend's ideas. Maurice was so prostrated that he had no energy left, and then there were outside influences, miserable considerations inspired by certain bourgeois. I know no more than that. The ceremony was immensely moving: everyone was in tears, I along with the rest."[4]

The cortege entered the church overflowing with local men and women, loyal and humble folk whom Sand had taught to read, nursed in illness, provided for in financial and material need, fed at her kitchen table in exchange for their tales and legends out of which she wove the stuff of some of her best-known novels. Everyone else had to stand outside the church. Some two hundred people had gathered to pay their respects. Flaubert was among those who stood outside, bareheaded, in the wind and rain.

Victor Hugo had not made it from Paris, but his oration was read aloud by Paul Meurice: "I mourn for one who has died and I pay tribute to an immortal soul." Hugo commemorated Sand's greatness and goodness, her strength and gentleness. He acknowledged that admiration often spawns envy as well as adulation. "George Sand has a unique place in our time," he proclaimed. "There are others who are great men: she is *the* great woman."[5]

Napoléon Jérôme and Alexandre Dumas had planned to deliver remarks but deferred to Hugo, whose eulogy Flaubert found sublime. Auguste Renan judged it formulaic and recorded his own testimony to her legacy: "Her works are truly the echo of our age . . . [which] has not had a wound with which her heart has not bled, not an ailment of which she has not harmoniously complained."[6]

Flaubert wept throughout Sand's funeral service and on the way to the cemetery, recalling his dear friend's immense love of nature, gestured toward the broad horizon with a generous sweep of his arm and declared, "It's just like her."[7] The mourners filed by the open grave and lovingly let drop their laurel branches onto the coffin.

"I believe that in fifty years I'll be completely forgotten," Sand wrote Flaubert several years before her death.[8] Matthew Arnold disagreed: "The immense vibration of George Sand's voice upon the ear of Europe will not soon die away," he predicted after she was laid to rest.[9] Translated on seven continents, her voice has, indeed, been heard around the world. Elizabeth Barrett Browning, Charlotte Brontë, George Eliot, Willa Cather, Heinrich Heine, Ivan Turgenev, and Marcel Proust, among other celebrated literary figures, have acknowledged the influence of Sand's work on their own.

"Let us not forget," Sand's editor Georges Lubin reminded the twentieth century, "her work was the great Trojan horse in which liberal ideas travelled for the first time into Tzarist Russia."[10] And, indeed, upon her death, Dostoevsky intoned: "Women of the whole world should now don mourning garb in her memory, because one of their loftiest and most beautiful representatives has passed away, and, in addition, an almost unprecedented woman by reason of the power of her mind and talent—a name which has become historical and which is destined not to be forgotten by, or to disappear from, European humanity."[11]

Oscar Wilde remembered Sand for her compassion and generosity: "For the aristocracy of the intellect she had always the deepest veneration, but the democracy of suffering touched her more. Of all the artists of this century she was the most altruistic." "She needs no defense," Margaret Fuller wrote after visiting Sand in Paris, "but only to be understood, for she has bravely acted out her nature, and always with good intentions."[12] The year after Sand's death, the English critic Frederic W. H. Myers summed up her life:

> Through all her dealings with the ordinary literary and political world around her, this difference between her and them is discernible. She is free from their effusive self-assertion, their uneasy vanity; she is indifferent to luxury and to fame; there is about her a tranquillity like that of the Sphinx, to which her baffled admirers so often compared her—something steadfast, disdainful, and serene. The very length and vigour of her life seemed to attest the potency of her race. She had, as it were, the power of living down everybody and everything—enemies, partisanships, scandals, loves—whole schools of thought and whole generations of men. These pass away and leave her in

Château de Nohant. By Eugène Lambert. (Courtesy C. O. Darré, Musée George Sand, La Châtre)

great old age sitting beneath the roof that sheltered her earliest years, and writing for her grandchildren stories in which her own childhood lives anew.[13]

Maurice's grief was greater than he could bear. "After the death of this beloved mother," his daughter Aurore would recall, "my father was so devastated that he wanted to leave, to flee the empty nest. Then he changed his mind and, impelled by the need to transform what he no longer valued because she was no longer there to enjoy it, he cut and slashed. The elms fell to the ground. Even the huge lime tree, with a great rustling of its leaves and a giant crack, came crashing down. My father was possessed of the desire to sacrifice what was most beautiful among the foliage that she had woven around the house to shroud in mystery her peaceful retreat. There was something classical and awe-inspiring in this destructive impulse."[14]

Solange's animosity toward her mother must have mellowed after Sand's death, for some years later she wrote a friend: "Nohant is mournful. . . . There's nothing that can be done. Years go by and one is struck by the immense emptiness left in the wake of this gigantic personality. An immense, incommensurate sadness fills this house, this garden, these meadows. Behind every door, one expects to see. . . . Especially in the evening, one's heart breaks in despair over the pitiful *néant* that has swallowed up so precious a being, a soul so vast and so elevated, a life lost for all time, a genius that has forever disappeared."[15]

But Solange was mistaken; her mother has not been lost or disappeared. George Sand is still out there, two centuries after she was born, a force of nature on the horizon of historical memory.

NOTES

Translations are mine, unless otherwise noted. Unattributed epigraphs at the beginning of chapters are drawn from Sand's writings.

ABBREVIATIONS

BN n.a.f.: Bibliothèque Nationale, Paris, Manuscript Department, nouvelles acquisitions françaises.

Corr.: Correspondance. Edited by Georges Lubin. 25 volumes. Paris: Garnier Fréres, 1964–1991. Volume numbers are given in uppercase roman. Dates that are either uncertain or have not been entered by Sand appear in brackets.

OA: Oeuvres autobiographiques. Edited by Georges Lubin. 2 vols. Paris: Gallimard, 1970, 1971. On editorial notes see below, p. 320, n. 8.

SML: Story of My Life. A group translation, edited by Thelma Jurgau. Albany: State University of New York Press, 1991. In citations of this volume, parts are indicated in uppercase roman, chapters in lowercase roman, and page numbers in arabic. E.g., III, ii, 237. On editorial notes see below, p. 320, n. 8.

EPIGRAPHS

p. v: *Corr.* X, to Pierre Bocage, 16 Mar. [18]51, 147.

p. vi: *Corr.* XI, to Caroline Cazamajou, 13 June 1852, 213: "Maternal love is but a weave of joy and grief of the first order." Rich, *Of Woman Born*, 225–226.

INTRODUCTION

Epigraph: *SML* III, x, 635.

1. Beauvoir, *Le Deuxième Sexe*, 2:235.
2. Cate, *George Sand*, xii.
3. Martin Malia, *Alexander Herzen and the Birth of Russian Socialism* (New York: Grosset and Dunlop, 1965), 211. Arnold, "George Sand," 197. Johnson, "She Had It All," 9–12. Hofstadter, *The Love Affair as a Work of Art*, 122.
4. Martin Walker, UPI Hears for 17 Oct. 2003, Mwalker@upi.com.
5. Arnold, "George Sand," 196. *SML* I, i, 76.
6. Rabine, "Sand and the Myth of Femininity," 8, 15. Sand, "Souvenirs de 1848" (Paris: Editions d'Aujourd'hui, 1977), cited by Vermeylan in *Les Idées politiques et sociales de George Sand*, 97.
7. André-Maurois, *Correspondance inédite*, 11.
8. "Eau de George Sand" won a medal of honor in 1859, according to a report in *L'Opinion Nationale*, cited by Lubin in *Corr.* XV, note 1, 604. Sand wrote its inventor, Henri Rafin, the following acknowledgment: "The result is very light and very distinguished, very salutary for people like me who resist perfumes that are too strong." [Balzac]: *Corr.* II, note 1, 820.
9. Sand first mentioned difficulty hearing when she was thirty-five, in *Corr.* IV, to Edouard de Pompéry [29 Jan. 1840], 855: "My deafness makes it very difficult for me to engage in conversation, for which I have little aptitude." *SML* V, ii, 936. André-Maurois, *Correspondance inédite*, 73.
10. Baudelaire, "Mon coeur mis à nu" in *Oeuvres complètes*, ed. Théophile Gautier (Paris: Michel Lévy Frères, 1868), 633, cited and translated by Barry, *Infamous Woman*, 331. Friedrich Nietzsche, *Beyond Good and Evil*, trans. Marianne Cowan (New York: Gateway, 1955), 164–165. Edgar Allan Poe, *The Unknown Poe*, ed. Raymond Faye (San Francisco: City Lights, 1980), 69. Edmond de Goncourt, *Journal*, vol. 3, 8 Dec. 1893.
11. Margaret Fuller to Elizabeth Hoar, 18 Jan. and 17 Mar. 1847, in Chevigny, *Woman and the Myth*, 360–362.
12. Maurois, *Lélia*, 10. Trilling, *Matthew Arnold*, 29.
13. *SML* I, ii, 82. In *George Sand and Idealism*, 87, Naomi Schor notes: "The product of a unique alliance between a mother issued from the lowest popular classes and a father born into an illegitimate but distinguished branch of the aristocracy, no major nineteenth-century French writer was more oddly and uncomfortably inserted into the class structure than was Sand, and the issue of class difference was to mark her writings as forcefully as that of gender difference, though it is the more colorful embodiments of her gender ambivalence that popular legend has retained."
14. In "Women's Autobiography in France," 272–273, Nancy K. Miller proposes "a dialectical practice of reading which would privilege *neither* the autobiography *nor* the fiction, but take the two writings together in their status as text. . . . The historical truth of a woman writer's life lies in the reader's grasp of her intratext: the body of her writing and not the writing of her body."

15. Woolf, "A Sketch of the Past," 72.
16. *Corr.* II, to Emile Regnault, [13 Aug. 1832], 135–136: "It's not, as you think, the mental work that tires me out. I'm so used to it that I now write with as much facility as I sew a hem." [Scrawl notes]: *Corr.* VI, to Pierre Bocage, [20 July 1843], 202. Myers, "George Sand," 232.
17. [*Indiana*]: *SML* IV, xv, 927. [*Château des désertes*]: *Corr.* VII, to Emmanuel Arago, [6 May 1847], 681. [Poor memory]: *Corr.* III, to François Buloz, [25 Dec. 1835], 176. [Forgetfulness]: *SML* IV, xv, 927. [Defect]: ibid., II, xi, 426. Helene Deutsch makes the following observation in "George Sand," 449: "There are mental disturbances in which the patient falls into so-called twilight states, in which he experiences things that are normally cordoned off from his conscious life. . . . Something similar, though quantitatively different, evidently took place in George Sand. In her creative periods she relapsed into a kind of somnambulant state, into a communion with herself in which she was completely withdrawn from reality and committed her internal experiences to paper in the form of novels. . . . She herself says that she never knew what she wrote in her novels, so far was she from her ordinary, conscious life in the act of writing them. But they contain situations and characters that plainly and obviously correspond with the descriptions of real situations and characters that her conscious, critically controlling personality dictated in her autobiographical works."
18. *SML* IV, viii, 819.
19. Mozet, *Ecrivain de romans*, 94. The complete citation reads: "The daughter destroyed herself, and the mother prevailed. It's true that if we take into account the sum total of suffering that accumulated over the years, Solange was the great failure of Sand's life." Chambaz-Bertrand, "Paradoxes de la maternité," 423–424, 430, cited by Rosalien Van Witzen in "Une relation pervertie: George Sand et Solange," *Les Amis de George Sand* 18 (1996): 15.
20. *Corr.* VIII, to Charles Poncy, [27 Aug. 1847], 77.
21. *SML* IV, xiii, 888; V, xiii, 1104; IV, xiii, 890.
22. *Corr.* VII, to Anténor Joly, 21 Oct. [1845], 145, cited by Mary Rice-Defosse, in "Jocasta Vanishes: Maternal Absence and Narrative Desire in *Le Péché de Monsieur Antoine*," in *George Sand Studies* 19 (2000): 52. Sand, Notice to *Valentine* (1852) in Szabo, *Prefaces* 1:176, cited by Crecelius, *Family Romances*, 93. In "A Female Genealogy: The En-gendering of George Sand," 67, Marie Maclean observes: "Hers [Sand's] is not a revolutionary stance; rather than change society she wants to infiltrate and exploit it. The delegitimatory movement in her life and work is always accompanied by a compensatory relegitimation."

CHAPTER 1: HER FATHER'S DAUGHTER
Epigraph: *SML* I, vii, 169.
1. Sand was actually born on 1 July, 12 messidor, which she later acknowledges when her misinformation is rectified. *SML* II, viii, 375.

2. Ibid., II, vii, 373.

3. Sand tells us in *SML* II, iv, 327, that before she was born, Maurice and Sophie's "irrecusable bond brought about the birth of several children, one of whom lived only for a few years and died, I believe, two years after my birth."

4. *Encyclopaedia Britannica* 4:978: "French republican calendar, dating system adopted in 1793 during the French Revolution, intended to replace the Gregorian calendar with a more scientific and rational system and to avoid Christian associations. The Revolutionary Convention established the calendar on Oct. 5, 1793, setting its beginning (1 Vendémiaire, year I) on the Gregorian date of Sept. 22, 1792. The 12 months of the French republican calendar each contained three decades (instead of weeks) of 10 days each; at the end of the year were grouped five (six in leap years) supplementary days. The months in order were Vendémiaire, Brumaire, Frimaire, Nivôse, Pluviôse, Ventôse, Germinal, Floréal, Prairial, Messidor, Thermidor, and Fructidor. For the saints' names that had been attached to the Gregorian days, there were substituted names of seeds, trees, flowers, and fruits. The Gregorian calendar was reestablished in France by the Napoleonic regime on Jan. 1, 1806." *SML* II, viii, 379; 382.

5. In personal correspondence, 24 May 2001, Anne Chevereau informed me: "In a regularly repeated error concerning Maurice Dupin, the rank of lieutenant-colonel is attributed to him (even on his grave). He only reached the rank of major, accorded on 2 March 1807." *SML* II, viii, 380.

6. Ibid., 381.

7. Ibid., ix, 397–398.

8. Ibid., note 45, 398/1128 (in such citations, the number preceding the slash indicates the page in the text on which the note number appears, and the number following the slash, the page on which the full note is given).

9. Ibid., II, viii, 375: "I resume this work on June 1, 1848," following the February Revolution.

10. *Corr.* IV, note 1, 496. James, *Notes on Novelists*, 232.

11. Chalon, *Chère George Sand*, 23. In "A Female Genealogy," 67, Maclean shows considerably less credulity: "[Sand's] critics have accepted rather too easily her own version of her upbringing, the mythologized struggle which figures in *Story of My Life* (1854–5), and which enables the child Aurore to play such a saintly role."

12. *SML* II, ix, 394; *OA*, vol. 2, note 2, 493/1367. "Dernière lettre de mon père à sa mère," Bibliothèque Historique de la Ville de Paris, E281. *Corr.* VII, to René Vallet de Villeneuve, Nov. 1845, 173.

13. *Sketches and Hints*, in *OA*, 2:589.

14. *Corr.* III, to Mme. Maurice Dupin, [18 Feb. 1836], 280.

CHAPTER 2: THE IMPORTANCE OF BEING MARIE-AURORE DE SAXE
Epigraph: *Corr.* VIII, to René Vallet de Villeneuve [7 Oct. 1847], 97.

1. Gailly de Taurines, *Aventuriers et femmes de qualité,* 280. Maugras, *Les Demoiselles de Verrières,* 29. Marmontel, in Taurines, *Aventuriers,* 280.
2. Goncourts, *La Femme au XVIIIᵉ siècle,* 297–298. Maugras, *Les Demoiselles de Verrières,* 57–58.
3. Taurines, *Aventuriers et femmes de qualité,* 280.
4. *SML* I, ii, 86.
5. Maugras, *Les Demoiselles de Verrières,* 74.
6. Ibid.
7. *SML* I, ii, 91.
8. Ibid., 92.
9. Louis Petit de Bachaumont, *Mémoires secrets,* 36 vols. (London: J. Adamson, 1780–89), 1:247, cited by Barry, *Infamous Woman,* 7. Taurines, *Aventuriers et femmes de qualité,* 302.
10. *SML* I, ii, 90–91.
11. Ibid., 90.
12. Maurois, *Lélia,* 24. *SML* I, iii, 104.
13. Ibid., I, iv, 120.
14. Ibid., 121.
15. Ibid.
16. Ibid., I, v, 138.
17. Ibid., I, vi, 160; I, iv, 139.
18. After George Sand's death, in 1876, Nohant passed to her son, Maurice, and eventually to her granddaughter Gabrielle Palazzi-Sand, who bequeathed it to the Académie française with the understanding that her sister, Aurore, could live out her life there. In 1951, the Académie française transferred the legacy of Nohant to the Service des Monuments historiques, and following Aurore Sand's death, in 1961, Nohant was opened to the public as a museum commemorating the life of George Sand.
19. *SML* I, v, 154–157.
20. Ibid.
21. Ibid., I, x, 224–229.

CHAPTER 3: SOPHIE VICTORIOUS
Epigraph: *SML* I, i, 77. In Bell and Yalom, *Revealing Lives,* Yalom observes, 7: "George Sand acknowledged a crucial maternal influence at a time when mothers were rarely present in autobiographies and biographies."

1. This and the following references to the Lafayette anecdote are from *SML* I, iv, 114–115.
2. *OA,* vol. 1, note 3, 73/1255; note 1, 342/1324.
3. *SML* I, iv, 115. *Corr.* VI, to Charles Poncy, 23 Dec. 1843, 328.
4. *SML* I, iv, 117.

5. *Corr.* VI, to Charles Poncy, 23 Dec. 1843, 327–328.

6. *SML* II, ii, 296–297.

7. Ibid., 293–294.

8. Ibid., II, iii, 305.

9. Ibid., 307. *OA,* vol. I, note 1, 361/1328–1329.

10. *OA,* vol. I, note 2, 428/1348.

11. *SML* II, vi, 350–351.

12. In his memoir, Marmontel tells of having been wrongfully accused of being Marie-Aurore's father. Had the allegation proved correct, it could have had very serious consequences because the Dauphine would no longer have felt compelled to support Mademoiselle Verrières and her daughter after the death of the marshal de Saxe. In point of fact, Marmontel could not have been Marie-Aurore's father because he did not become Mademoiselle Ver-rière's lover until the year following the child's birth. Marmontel rectifies the misunderstanding and correctly reports that the Dauphine continued her support for mother and child. *SML* II, ix, 396.

13. Ibid.

14. Ibid., 397.

15. Ibid., II, viii, 381.

16. Frappier-Mazur, "George Sand et la généalogie," 3–4. The citation continues: "As Balzac writes in *Physiologie du mariage,* 'The merchandise goes with the household.' When the adulterous origin of the child is known, it produces conflict between its legal and moral status, which is false, as well as family strife and conflicts of interest. One can consider that the French Revolution's abolition of the right of inheritance of the first born added a new dimension to this theme. After the Revolution, in principle, all legitimate children inherited equally."

17. *SML* II, viii, 383.

18. Ibid., 377. In *OA,* vol. I, note 2, 469/1360–1361, Lubin writes: "This isn't altogether correct. The certificate was in no way irregular, and the municipality was thereby relieved of responsibility." However, the certificate contained false information that pertained to Marie-Aurore de Saxe, who was said to have been missing and unheard from since Year VIII.

19. *SML* II, ix, 397. Lubin informs us in *OA,* vol. I, note 2, 498/1369: "The Andrezxel abbey also interrogated a jurist from Limoges named Reculès-Poulouzat, certain of whose letters, which were very compromising for Sophie-Victoire, had been saved (E25 to 28). One signals a memoir which was supposedly full of specific and devastating details, but which must have been destroyed. We can well understand the reasons which led to the suppression of such a document."

20. *SML* II, ix, 398.

21. Ibid., 388.

22. Ibid., 398.

CHAPTER 4: SPANISH SOJOURN

Epigraph: Sand, *Voyage en Espagne*, 471.

1. *SML* II, xii, 434.
2. Ibid.
3. Ibid., II, x, 402–407.
4. Ibid., II, xii, 437. In *Les Idées politiques et sociales de George Sand*, 198, Vermeylan points out: "The psychologist Pierre Janet attributes to Pierre Leroux the
   discovery of involuntary memory that Sand evoked and suggested to Proust."
   Vermeylan's observation is based on the article "Pour George Sand et pour
   Pierre Leroux," in *La Nouvelle Revue des Deux Mondes* (Oct. 1975): 246–247,
   in which Jacques Viard writes: "Janet, Freud's mentor, admired Leroux, the
   theorist (before Proust) of involuntary memory."
5. Sand, *Voyage en Espagne*, 473.
6. *SML* II, xiii, 439.
7. *SML* II, xiii, 444.
8. The name that appears on the death certificate is Auguste, but he was
   referred to by Sand as Louis (*OA*, vol. 1, note 1, 575/1381). It's possible that
   Maurice named his son with his own father, Claude-Louis Dupin de Francueil, in mind. It's also possible, as Sand biographers have frequently conjectured, that the baby was named for the dauphin Louis-Auguste, who became
   Louis XVI. Maurice may have wanted to emphasize his relationship with
   the Bourbon line via the marshal de Saxe, illegitimate son of Auguste II
   of Poland, father of Auguste III of Poland, who fathered Marie-Josèphe de
   Saxe, who married the son of Louis XV, the dauphin who died before becoming king but fathered the eventual dauphin Louis-Auguste, who became
   Louis XVI. *SML* II, xiv, 451.
9. Personal communication from Dr. Benjamin Silverman, Professor of Clinical
   Pediatrics, UCLA, Harbor School of Medicine, 24 Oct. 2000: "There are
   many causes of dislocated lens and cataracts and blindness in newborns. . . .
   Some of these babies have congenital metabolic defects (galactosemia is an
   example); others have congenital infections (ex.: toxoplasmosis); others had
   been exposed to maternal infections (rubella); others had postnatal infection
   (gonorrhea, chlamydia); others have ophthalmic tumors (retinoblastoma);
   others have congenital defects in the formation of parts of the optic pathway
   (from brain through lens). A number of these conditions can be associated
   with premature birth, but it may be the underlying condition resulting in the
   prematurity, rather than the prematurity causing blindness. . . . Poor prenatal
   care, as we understand it today, and poor maternal nutrition, and poor maternal health can certainly result in premature termination of the pregnancy.
   Some of those prematures who survived in those days [the early nineteenth
   century] . . . might have multiple neurological defects related to the prematurity . . . [and] sensory (including visual) deprivation. . . . Extreme multiparity
   in a woman who had not had reasonable obstetrical care might result in a

boggy, dilated uterus which is unable to sustain a pregnancy to term." *SML* II, x, 415. Murat's regiment accompanied Napoléon to Italy, departing Paris on 16 Nov. 1807, and returning on 1 Jan. 1808. Sand includes in *SML* (II, x, 416) two letters from Maurice Dupin to Sophie from this period, one dated 29 Nov. 1807, from Venice, the other dated 11 Dec. 1807, from Milan.

10. *SML* II, xiv, 451.
11. Ibid.
12. Ibid., 451–452.
13. Ibid., 453.
14. Ibid.
15. Ibid.
16. Ibid., 454.
17. Ibid.
18. Ibid.
19. Ibid., 456.
20. Ibid., 456, 455.
21. Ibid., 468–469.
22. Ibid., 457.
23. Ibid., 460.
24. Ibid., 463.
25. *OA*, vol. 1, note 1, 594/1382–1383.
26. *SML* II, xiv, 463.
27. Ibid.
28. Deutsch, "George Sand," 456. The tutor Deschartres will later tell Aurore of a suicidal impulse that her father manifested as a young man while crossing a river on horseback (*SML* IV, vi, 794). *Corr.* VII, to René Vallet de Villeneuve, [18 or 19 Nov. 1845], 173.
29. Brée, "George Sand," 439. Crecelius, *Family Romances*, 5.

CHAPTER 5: SOPHIE'S CHOICE
Epigraph: *SML* II, xiv, 468.
1. Ibid., 463.
2. Ibid., 491.
3. Ibid., 466.
4. Ibid., II, xv, 472, 474; II, xiv, 466; II, xv, 476.
5. In *OA*, vol. 1, note 3, 600/1384, Lubin informs us that Sand is mistaken when she tells us in *SML* that Ursule was six months older than she.
6. Ibid., *SML* II, xv, 482.
7. Ibid., II, xiv, 469–470.
8. Ibid., 487–488.
9. Ibid., II, xv, 475, 474.
10. Ibid., 479.
11. Ibid., 478.

12. In *George Sand and Autobiography*, 56, Hiddleston points out that in *SML*, Aurore's separation from her mother "is made to appear far more protracted than it was in reality. To begin with, Sand extends to two or three years the few months during which she was torn between her mother and grandmother in Nohant." *SML* II, xv, 479.

13. *SML* II, xiv, 476, 468.

14. Ibid., 490; III, v, 561.

15. Ibid., II, xvi, 490.

16. Ibid.

17. Ibid., III, ii, 512.

18. *Corr.* I, to Mme. Maurice Dupin, [1812], 13.

19. *SML* III, vi, 570.

20. Ibid., 573.

CHAPTER 6: ENIGMA OF THE SPHINX
Epigraph: *SML* II, xvi, 484.

1. This and the following references to Marie Dupin's scene of revelation are drawn from *SML* III, x, 633–636.

2. In her chapter "Sand: Double Identity," in *Maternal Fictions*, 69, Lukacher points out: "Sand's grandmother, in order to ensure that all links between Aurore and her mother were severed once and for all, told Aurore that her mother had been a prostitute, which was in fact the truth. Among the highly disruptive effects this had on Aurore was the shock it presented to her notion of her own legitimacy. Whose daughter might she actually be? This is an issue that as we will see later, looms large in Sand's narrative imagination." In addition: "In suspecting 'some mysterious link between her mother and somebody,' Sand is addressing the problem of adultery and procreation."

3. Corambé was Aurore's self-invented deity. See *SML* III, viii, 605, and reference in chap. 23, "Coming to Writing."

4. *Corr.* VI, to Charles Poncy, 23 Dec. 1843, 327.

5. *SML* I, i, 77.

CHAPTER 7: CONVENT AND CONVERSION
Epigraph: *SML* III, xiii, 689.

1. In *Un Couvent de religieuses anglaises à Paris*, 1–3, Cédoz informs us that the school was founded in 1634, when Catholicism was abolished in England and convent schools were relocated abroad. During the Terror, in 1793, the five residences of the Dames anglaises in Paris were converted to jails (273). We have already noted the ironic coincidence of both Aurore's grandmother and mother having been simultaneously incarcerated in the same institution where she was subsequently sent to school. *SML* III, x, 637.

2. Mme. Dupin to Dr. Decerfz, 23 Dec. 1817, cited by Varilhe, *Les Années d'adolescence*, 47.

3. *SML* III, xi, 643, 645–646.

4. Ibid., 659.

5. Ibid., 649.

6. Ibid., 649–650. Pierrette Daly provides a compelling analysis of "Sexualité et mutisme" in the context of the convent in her article "De Sand à Cixous," in *George Sand*, 153–155.

7. Moers, *Literary Women*, 130.

8. *SML* III, xi, 647.

9. Ibid., 647, 660; III, xii, 669, and the following citation.

10. Ibid., 679.

11. Ibid., 680.

12. Ibid., III, xiii, 690–691.

13. Ibid., 694.

14. Ibid., 696.

15. Ibid., IV, i, 707.

16. Hamburg, "The Lie," 751.

17. *SML* III, xiii, 696, and the following paragraph.

18. Ibid., 689.

19. Ibid., IV, i, 708, 716.

20. Ibid., IV, ii, 719.

21. Ibid., 727.

22. Ibid., 728, 729.

23. Ibid., 734.

CHAPTER 8: COMING OF AGE

Epigraph: *SML* IV, iv, 752.

1. Ibid., IV, iii, 740.

2. Ibid., IV, iv, 753.

3. Ibid.

4. In *Corr.* III, to Maurice Dudevant, [3 January 1836], 221, Sand told her son: "It was only when I was sixteen, back at Nohant, ashamed of myself for writing French so poorly, that I made myself relearn grammar."

5. *SML* IV, iv, 763–765, 757.

6. *Corr.* XXII, to Gustave Flaubert, [25 Oct. 1871], 594–595.

7. In *OA*, vol. 1, note 1, 1075/1443, Lubin informs us that the question of Aurore's sexual involvement at this time with Stéphane has never been definitively resolved. Ajasson's son, however, has confirmed the existence of a now missing correspondence, in which proof supposedly exists that the young couple engaged in intimate sexual relations during the winter of 1820–21.

8. *SML* IV, v, 783.

9. *Corr.* I, to Emilie de Wismes, [July 1821], 69–70.

10. *SML* IV, vi, 796.

11. *Corr.* I, to Emilie de Wismes, 28 May 1821, 67.

12. *SML* IV, vi, 792–793, including the citation in the following paragraph.

As we have seen in chap. 4, "Spanish Sojourn," note 28, Maurice Dupin manifested a similar suicidal impulse while crossing a river on horseback.

13. *OA*, vol. I, note I, 594/1383. "I myself had a rather serious fall in the same spot, a coincidence where fate plays a part. . . . My father was distracted, and I was, too, as I well should have been, all the more so in this place that I could never pass without emotion."

14. *SML* IV, vi, 799, 801.

CHAPTER 9: *PATER SEMPER INCERTUS EST* (THE FATHER IS ALWAYS UNCERTAIN)

Chapter title: "When Sand learned of her mother's numerous sexual relations, she realized that *pater semper incertus est,* while the mother is *certissima.*" Lukacher, *Maternal Fictions,* 102.

Epigraph: *Corr.* VI, to Charles Poncy, 23 Dec. 1843, 328.

1. *SML* IV, vii, 815.

2. References to Sophie's scene of revelation are from *SML* IV, viii, 815–817, unless otherwise noted.

3. Didier, *George Sand écrivain,* 458.

4. *Corr.* VI, to Clarles Poncy, 23 Dec. 1843, 328.

5. *SML* II, iv, 327.

6. I noted in chap. 3, "Sophie Victorious," that records indicate Sophie bore a child to a man named Saint-Charles and another child, Caroline, to a different father.

7. In *OA*, I:xviii, Lubin notes: "And to undertake the project of obtaining the information that she lacks, of piecing together her memories, of clarifying her father's letters. On several occasions the Villeneuve cousins, who were friends from Maurice Dupin's youth, will be asked to supply their memories. She interrogates other contemporaries. . . . In order to resuscitate this father who disappeared so soon, who was so little known, she displays a true filial and novelistic passion." *Corr.* VIII, to René Vallet de Villeneuve, 8 Feb. 1848, 278; to Maurice Dudevant-Sand, 18 [Feb. 1848], 297.

8. *SML* II, viii, 375.

9. Ibid., 377, and the citations in the following paragraphs.

10. In *OA*, vol. I, note 2, 468/1359, Lubin inquires: "What letter? George Sand didn't take the trouble to clarify this."

CHAPTER 10: MARRIAGE AND MOTHERHOOD

Epigraph: *SML* IV, iv, 752.

1. Ibid., IV, viii, 823, 821, 822.

2. Ibid., 824.

3. Ibid., 825.

4. Ibid., 823.

5. Ibid., 829.

6. Ibid., 833.

7. *Corr.* VI, to Hippolyte Chatiron, [mid-Feb. 1843], 43.

8. Ibid., XXV, to Jane Bazouin, [mid-Dec. 1822], 53. Letter from Sophie Dupin to Mme. Casimir Dudevant, Bibliothèque municipale, La Châtre, 1822–23.

9. *Corr.* I, to Emilie de Wismes, 30 Jan. [1823], 103; XXV, to Jane Bazouin, 7 Feb. 1823, 55.

10. *SML* IV, ix, 836.

11. *Corr.* I, to Emilie de Wismes, 30 Jan. 1823, 104; to the viscountess de Cornulier (Emilie de Wismes' married name), 4 Nov. [1823], 115.

12. *SML* IV, ix, 838.

13. *Corr.* I, to Casimir Dudevant, [29 July 1823], 108–109. In "The Cult of True Womanhood: 1820–1860," in *The American Quarterly* 18 (Summer 1966): 151–174, Barbara Welter describes a phenomenon that applied to France as well as to the New World: "Woman in the cult of True Womanhood presented by the women's magazines, gift annuals and religious literature of the nineteenth century was the hostage in the home."

14. *Corr.* I, to Casimir Dudevant, 19 Aug. 1824, 144.

15. *SML* IV, ix, 838–839.

16. *Corr.* I, to the viscountess de Cornulier, 4 Nov. [1823], 115, including excerpt in the following paragraph.

17. Letter from Sophie Dupin to Mme. and M. Dudevant, 6 Jan. 1824, Bibliothèque municipale, La Châtre. Cited by Holland, *"Mademoiselle Merquem:* De-Mythifying Woman by Rejecting the Law of the Father," in Datlof, Fuchs, and Powell, *World of George Sand,* 178.

18. *SML* IV, ix, 841.

19. Ibid.

20. Ibid., 843.

21. Ibid., 846.

CHAPTER 11: PASSION IN THE PYRENEES
Epigraph: *SML* IV, x, 854.

1. *Corr.* I, to Mme. Maurice Dupin, 29 June [1825], 160.

2. *SML* IV, x, 852.

3. Ibid.

4. Ibid., 854. *Corr.* I, to Mme. Maurice Dupin, 28 Aug. 1825, 161.

5. Sand, *Le Roman d'Aurore Dudevant et d'Aurélien de Sèze,* 40.

6. Ibid., 107–108.

7. Ibid., 110–111.

8. *Corr.* I, to Casimir Dudevant, [15] Nov. 1825, 268.

9. Ibid., 268–269.

10. Ibid., 269.

11. Ibid., 280.

12. Ibid., 291–292.

13. Spoelberch de Lovenjoul Collection (now held by the Bibliothèque Historique de la Ville de Paris), Group E868, ff214, cited by Maurois, *Lélia,* 86.

CHAPTER 12: READY, SET, GO

Epigraph: *SML* IV, xii, 882.

1. *Corr.* XXV, to Laure Decerfz, 19 [Jan. 1827], 131.
2. Ibid., to Jane Bazouin. 27 Apr. [1827], 138; 3 July [1827], 145.
3. Ibid., I, to Louis-Nicolas Caron, 29 Nov. [1828], 478; to Madame Gondoüin Saint-Agnan, 23 Mar. [1830], 618–619.
4. Ibid., to Madame Gondoüin Saint-Agnan, 3 Apr. [1830], 624.
5. Ibid., 620.
6. Ibid., to Zoé Leroy, [10 Oct. 1826], 363.
7. Ibid., to Casimir Dudevant, [17 Oct. 1827], 402.
8. While Solange's illicit birth wasn't acknowledged in Sand's lifetime, recent research has effectively resolved the issue of Stéphane Ajasson de Grand-sagne's paternity. See Lubin's note 1 in *Corr.* III, 499, recapping the Dudevant separation trial in which incriminating allegations raised by Casimir's lawyers were not refuted by Sand's.
9. *Corr.* I, to François Duris-Dufresne, [19 July 1830], 674–675; to Jules Boucoiran, 31 July [1830], 685.
10. Ibid., to Charles Meure, [17 Sept. 1830], 705–706.
11. Ibid., to Madame Gondoüin Saint-Agnan, [Sept. 1830], 710–711.
12. Ibid., Lubin, note 1** [asterisked note], 561.
13. Ibid., to Countess de Fenoyl (Jane Bazouin), [Nov. 1829], 561–563.
14. Ibid., to Jules Boucoiran, [1 Dec. 1830], 737.
15. Ibid., to Charles Duvernet, [2 Dec. 1830], 743.
16. *SML* IV, xii, 882.

CHAPTER 13: "OUR MOTTO IS FREEDOM"

Epigraph: *Corr.* II, to Franz Liszt, 21 Apr. [1835], 871.

1. *Corr.* I, to Casimir Dudevant, [8 Jan. 1831], 773.
2. Ibid., to Mme. Maurice Dupin, 21 Jan. [1831], 786.
3. *SML* IV, xiii, 892.
4. Ibid.
5. Ibid.
6. Richardson, *The Bohemians*, 40–41, citing Auguste Barbier, *Souvenirs personnels*, 323–324.
7. *SML* IV, xiv, 904–905.
8. The opera by Puccini was based on the well-known book by Henri Murger, *Scènes de la vie de bohème* (Paris: Garnier, 1851).
9. Seigel, *Bohemian Paris*, 9–11.
10. Sand, *Valentine*, 48.
11. Winegarten, *Double Life of George Sand*, 97.
12. In *OA*, vol. 2, note 2, 149/1338, Lubin attributes Stendhal's description of Kératry to an article that appeared in *London Magazine* in September 1825. *SML* IV, xv, 915.
13. *Corr.* I, to Jules Boucoiran, [4 Mar. 1831], 818.

14. Ibid.

15. Ibid., 817–818.

16. *SML* IV, xv, 918.

17. *Corr.* I, to Maurice Dudevant, 2 Mar. [1831], 816.

18. Ibid., to Jules Boucoiran, [4 Mar. 1831], 817.

19. Ibid., 824; to Charles Duvernet, 6 Mar. [1831], 821.

20. Ibid., to Emile Regnault, [12 Apr. 1831], 835–836.

21. Ibid., to Charles Meure, 14 Apr. [1831], 844; to Mmm. Maurice Dupin, 31 May [1831], 886–888, including citations from the same letter in the following paragraph.

22. Ibid., to Emile Regnault, [2 May 1831], 854.

23. Ibid., [28 June 1831], 906.

24. Ibid., to Maurice Dudevant, [11 July 1831], 914–915.

25. Ibid., 20 Aug. [1831], 931.

26. Ibid., [30 July 1831], 891; [toward 10 Nov. 1831], 977.

27. Ibid., to Emile Regnault, [before 13 June 1831], 891; 13 June 1831, 896.

28. Ibid., [toward 25 May 1831], 875.

29. *SML* IV, xiii, 891.

30. *Corr.* I, to Gustave Papet, [20 Sept. 1831], 944.

31. Ibid., to Charles Duvernet, [27 June 1831], 904; to Emile Regnault, [18 Sept. 1831], 941.

32. Ibid., to Charles Duvernet, [15 Nov. 1831], 984.

33. Karénine, *George Sand* 1:339.

34. *Corr.* I, to Emile Regnault, [3 Oct. 1831], 955.

35. Ibid., [8 Oct. 1831], 962.

36. Ibid., 963. The title of Balzac's novel *La Peau de chagrin* is translated as "The Magic Skin" or as "The Fatal Skin."

37. Ibid., to Maurice Dudevant, [30 Dec. 1831], 993.

CHAPTER 14: GEORGE SAND IS BORN

Epigraph: *Corr.* III, to Charles Didier, [13 June 1836], 433–434.

1. *SML* IV, xiv, 909.

2. Ibid., IV, xv, 921.

3. In *George Sand: Writing for Her Life*, note 31, 245, Naginski writes: "Georges Lubin speculates that 90 percent of the text of the second edition is Sand's. Cf. a lecture he delivered at the Collège de France, 23 Oct. 1976, 'Rose et Blanche ou le roman renié,' as well as an unpublished article, 'Autour de *Rose et Blanche*.' Lubin thinks that if Sand disowned the novel in 1855 and again in 1867 in her correspondence with her editor, it was because Jules Sandeau was still alive at the time. Significantly, neither Sand nor Sandeau included the novel in their respective lists of complete works."

4. *OA*, vol. 2, note 1, 174/1342–1343.

5. Maurois, *Lélia*, 132, citing Balzac's review in *Caricature* and Planche from *La Revue des Deux Mondes*.

6. *Corr.* II, to Emile Regnault, [27 Feb. 1832], 47–48.

7. *SML* IV, xv, 921. Moers, *Literary Women*, 32. Sand, *Indiana*, trans. Ives, 206.

8. *SML* V, ii, 941.

9. Schor, *George Sand and Idealism*, 53.

10. After the break with Sand in 1833, Sandeau went on to write a novel titled *Marianne* about their relationship, which was published in 1839. He was better known for a subsequent novel, *Mademoiselle de la Seiglière* (1848), which he adapted as a play. Sand would later support Sandeau's candidacy for the French Academy and was present at his reception.

11. In Sand's novel *The Miller of Angibault*, the miller tells Lémor: "If you weren't so stubborn about drinking nothing but water with your meals . . . I'd think you'd get yourself into the right state for catching sight of the *Great Beast, the white lurcher bitch,* or *Georgeon the wolf-drover.*" Cited and translated by Donna Dickenson, *George Sand*, 191. And in *SML* III, ix, 619, Sand tells of spending time with the shepherds of her region: "I confess their terror had pervaded me and that, without exactly believing in fairies, ghosts, or in Georgeon, the devil of the Vallée Noire, my imagination had been deeply influenced by these phantoms." In *George Sand, l'amoureuse*, 80, Douchin, speculates that Sand's association with George Podiebrad, king of Bohemia, was a possible source of her choice of name. In *Les Amis de George Sand* 1 (1980): 12–13, Lubin notes that although Sand was descended from Podiebrad, she was unaware of this during her lifetime, rendering unlikely Douchin's supposition.

12. *Corr.* II, to Laure Decerfz, [3, 6, 7 July 1832], 120.

13. *Corr.* II, to Emile Regnault, [15 June 1833], 326.

14. Moers, *Literary Women*, 32.

15. *SML* V, ii, 937.

16. Lubin, *OA*, vol. 2, note 3, 146/1337. Douchin, *George Sand*, 95, citing Henri Amic, *Le Figaro*, 2 Nov. 1896. Balzac, *Lettres à l'étrangère* 1:19–20, cited by Maurois in *Lélia*, 143.

CHAPTER 15: A DAUGHTER IS BORN

Note: An earlier version of some of the material on Solange in this chapter and elsewhere in the book was published in an article entitled "Ghosts in the Nursery: My Mother, My Subject, Myself," which I contributed to *American Imago* 54, no. 4 (Winter 1997): 417–436.

Epigraphs: *SML* IV, xi, 875. Solange Clésinger-Sand, *Carl Robert*, 98.

1. *SML* IV, ix, 838. *Corr.* XII, note 1, 480; I, to Zoé Leroy, 2 Feb. [1828], 438.

2. Ibid., to Mme. Maurice Dupin, [2 Aug. 1828], 454; to Jane de Fenoyl, 18 [Sept. 1828]. *SML* IV, xi, 875.

3. *Corr.* I, to Casimir Dudevant, [17 Oct. 1828], 461.

4. Ibid., to Mme. Maurice Dupin, [27 Dec. 1828], 491; to Casimir Dudevant, 1 [Nov. 1828], 470; II, to Emile Regnault, [20 Mar. 1832], 57.

5. Ibid., I, to Jules Boucoiran, 20 July [1830], 677. Sand, "Le Grillon."

6. *Corr.* II, to Emile Regnault, [23 Feb. 1832], 43.

7. Ibid., to Maurice Dudevant, [20 June 1832], 107.

8. Ibid., to Emile Paultre, [18 Nov. 1832], 181; to Emile Regnault, [2 Mar. 1832], 51.

9. *Corr.* II, to Emile Regnault, [18 Feb. 1832], 37.

10. *Corr.* II, to Emile Paultre [3 Sept. 1832], 155, cited by Chovelon, "L'Education des filles," 35–36.

11. *Corr.* II, to Maurice Dudevant and Léontine Chatiron, [after 25 May 1832], 93–94. *SML* V, vii, 1019–1020.

12. *Corr.* I, to Casimir Dudevant, 1 [Nov. 1828], 470; to Jules Boucoiran, [1 Dec. 1829], 566.

13. Chovelon, "L'Education des filles," 65.

14. *Corr.* III, to Sosthènes de la Rochefoucauld, [around 5 Mar. 1836], 305; IV, to David Richard, May 1838, 424.

15. *SML* V, x, 1069.

16. Sand, *Lettres d'un voyageur,* letter 10, 261–262. After being serialized in *La Revue des Deux Mondes* (1834–36), the original edition of *Lettres d'un voyageur* was published by Bonnaire in 1837.

17. Thurer, *The Myths of Motherhood,* 193, 183.

18. Chovelon, "L'éducation des filles," 72.

19. *Corr.* XII, to Maurice Dudevant-Sand, 29–30 June 1854, 480. Ibid., III, to Michel de Bourges, 30 April 1837, 825.

20. Marie d'Agoult's observation dates from 9 June 1837 and is recorded in her *Mémoires,* 82–83, cited in *Corr.* IV, note 2, 157.

21. *Corr.* IV, to Alexis Duteil, 8 Oct. 1837, 218–219.

22. Sand, *Entretiens journaliers,* 1000.

CHAPTER 16: THE AUTHOR AND THE ACTRESS
Epigraph: Sand, "Marie Dorval," in *Questions d'art,* 93.

1. *Corr.* II, to François Buloz, [29 Dec. 1832], 202.

2. Ibid., to Maurice Dudevant, [29 Dec. 1832], 204.

3. Ibid., [9 Jan. 1833], 222.

4. Ibid., to Emile Regnault, [16 Sept. 1832], 161.

5. *SML* V, iv, 966–967. Sand, "Mars et Dorval," in *Questions d'art,* 42–44.

6. *SML* V, iv, 962–964, including citation in previous paragraph.

7. *Corr.* II, to Marie Dorval, [26 Jan. 1833], 242; [22 June 1833], 339.

8. *Corr.* II, to Marie Dorval, [2 Feb. 1833], 249. André-Maurois, *Correspondance inédite,* 23–27.

9. *Corr.* II, note 2, 241.

10. André-Maurois, *Correspondance inédite,* 27–28, citing Houssaye, *Les Confessions* 2:13–14.

11. Barry, *George Sand,* 248–249, citing from Sand, *Lélia* (1833).

12. *SML* III, xiii, 689.

13. *Corr.* II, note 3, 62. Garber, *Vice Versa,* 191.

14. *SML* IV, xiii, 898–899, citing Montaigne, *Essays.*

15. André-Maurois, *Correspondance inédite,* 15.

16. Douchin, *George Sand,* 88–89, 93.

17. Barry, *Infamous Woman*, 155. *Corr.* II, to Sainte-Beuve, [24 July 1833], 375.

18. Ibid., to Marie Dorval, [15 Feb. 1833], 258–259; note 3, 301.

19. Ibid., note 1, 401, citing Chateaubriand's letter from Paris, dated 16 Aug. 1833. *SML* IV, xii, 879.

20. Naginski, *George Sand*, 113, citing *La Revue des Deux Mondes* 3 (15 Aug. 1833): 353. Naginski, 108, citing Sainte-Beuve, *Portraits contemporains*, 1: 497, 501, 502–503.

21. Ibid., 115, citing Sand's "Préface de 1839," *Lélia*, 350.

22. Ibid., 108, citing from *La Revue des Deux Mondes* 2 (15 May 1833): 460.

23. In her seminal study *George Sand: Writing for Her Life*, Naginski has titled her chapter on the *Lélia* of 1833 "Novel of the Invisible," 105–137. The citation in this paragraph is on p. 110.

24. *Corr.* II, note 1, 406 citing *L'Europe Littéraire*, 24 Aug. 1833.

25. Schor, *George Sand and Idealism*, 58.

26. Barry, *George Sand: In Her Own Words*, 253–254, citing from Sand, *Lélia* (1833), reprinted by Indiana University Press, 1978.

27. Maurois, *Lélia*. Cate, *George Sand*, 232. Naginski, *George Sand*, 115, citing Didier, preface to *Indiana*, 14.

28. *Corr.* I, to Emile Regnault, [20 Sept. 1831], 945–946.

29. *SML* V, ii, 945.

CHAPTER 17: SONS AND LOVERS

Epigraph: *Corr.* II, to Sainte-Beuve, [toward 10 Mar. 1835], 825.

1. Hofstadter, *The Love Affair as a Work of Art*, 135.

2. *Corr.* II, note 2, 368, citing Sand, *Correspondance: Sand-Musset*, ed. Decori, 8–10.

3. Cate, *George Sand*, 263.

4. James, cited by Hofstadter, in *The Love Affair as a Work of Art*, 163. In *Le Plus Grand Amour de George Sand*, note 1, 80, Toesca recounts his experience of discovering the pertinent journals: "I discovered these notebooks in the attic at Nohant when I was working on my thesis. . . . Of course I returned them straight-away to my host, Madame Aurore Lauth-Sand, the granddaughter of George Sand; she kept them in her possession. No one has seen them since."

5. Cate, *George Sand*, 264–265.

6. *Corr.* II, to Sainte-Beuve, 25 Aug. [1833], 408–409.

7. Douchin, *George Sand*, 84, citing Maurois, *Lélia*, and the Goncourt brothers' citation of Janin.

8. *Corr.* II, to Casimir Dudevant, [30 Nov. 1833], 446.

9. Ibid., to François Buloz, [5 Dec. 1833], 450; *SML* V, i, 932.

10. Ibid., to Mme. Maurice Dupin, [12 Dec. 1833], 459.

11. Ibid., 20 Jan. 1834, from Casimir Dudevant, 465–466.

12. *Corr.* II, to Alfred de Musset, 12 May [1834], 590.

13. This and the material in the following two paragraphs is from *SML* V, iii, 951.

14. Pommier, *Autour du drâme de Venise*, 37, based on the account of Antoine Quadri, *Huit jours à Venise* (Venice: Antoine Bazzarini, 1842).

15. *Corr.* II, to Pietro Pagello, [beginning of Mar. 1834], 525.

16. Ibid., to Mme. Maurice Dupin, 29 Jan. [1834], 482.

17. Ibid., to Pietro Pagello, [Feb. 1834], 501–503; to Hippolyte Chatiron, 6 March [1834], 526.

18. Ibid., to Jules Boucoiran, 6 Apr. [1834], 553–554.

19. Ibid., note 2, 561–562.

20. *Corr.* II, to Alfred de Musset, 15 Apr. [and 17 Apr. 1834], 561–562.

21. Ibid., [24 May 1834], 597. Cf. note 14, chap. 14. *Corr.* II, to Adolphe Guéroult, [toward 12 Apr. 1835], 857.

22. Ibid., note 1, 637, based on Pierre-Jules Hetzel's transmission of a conversation with Musset, in Juliette Adam, *Mes premières armes littéraires et politiques* (Paris: Lemerre, 1904).

23. *OA*, vol. 2, *Histoire de ma vie*, 293–294, cited by Barry, *George Sand*, 416–417.

24. *Corr.* II, to Alfred de Musset, 12 May [1834], 589.

25. Belluno Luigia Codemo, unpublished letter, 8 Feb. 1877, Bibliothèque de Trévise, cited by Poli in *L'Italie*, 389–390.

26. *Corr.* II, to Hippolyte Chatiron, 6 Mar. [1834], 528.

27. Ibid., to Alfred de Musset, 15 Apr. [and 17 Apr. 1834], 564.

28. Ibid., 12 May [1834], 588.

29. *Corr.* II, to Hippolyte Chatiron, 6 Mar. [1834], 528; to Jules Boucoiran, 7 Mar. 1834, 535; to Maurice Dudevant, [8 May 1834], 577.

30. Ibid., note 2, 577.

31. Ibid., 578.

32. Ibid., note 1, 578; to Maurice Dudevant, [8 May 1834], 579.

33. Ibid., to Alfred de Musset, [30 May 1834], 602–603; to Hippolyte Chatiron, 1 June [1834], 606–607.

34. Ibid., to Maurice Dudevant, [14 June 1834], 619.

35. Ibid., to Alfred de Musset, [30 May 1834], 604; to Solange Dudevant, 1 June 1834, 605.

36. Ibid., to Casimir Dudevant, 8 July [1834], 654.

37. *SML* V, iii, 953.

38. *Corr.* II, note 2, 673: Pagello's observation is from a manuscript titled *Da Parigi a Genova*, cited by Poli, *L'Italie*.

39. Ibid., note 2, 681–682, citing Musset. Abeylard is Musset's spelling of Abélard.

40. *Corr.* II, note 1, 369, citing Vigny, *Le Journal d'un poète*.

41. According to *Corr.* II, note 2, 747. The Delacroix portrait, originally done on canvas and frequently reproduced, passed to Robert Bourget-Pailleron, a descendant of François Buloz. Calamatta published an engraving of it in *La Revue des Deux Mondes* 7 (1 July 1836): n.p. (follows title page).

42. *Corr.* II, to Alfred de Musset, [beginning of Jan. 1835], 786; [22 or 23 Feb. 1835], 811–812.

43. Ibid., 12 May [1834], 589.

44. Musset, *On ne badine pas avec l'amour* (*Don't Fool with Love*), act 2, scene 5, cited in *Corr.* II, note 2, 589.

45. Anne E. McCall, "Une nouvellle héroïde: Les lettres de George Sand à Michel de Bourges," in Mozet, *Une Correspondance*, note 7, 122.

CHAPTER 18: MOTHER LOVE

Epigraph: *SML* V, xii, 1092.

1. Marie-Paule Rambeau, *Chopin dans la vie et l'oeuvre de George Sand* (Paris: Les Belles Lettres, 1985), 36.
2. This portrait, no. 155, appears in Lubin, *Album Sand*, 86.
3. In *Corr.* IV, to Albert Grzymala, [end of May 1838], 430, Sand referred to Mallefille as "soft wax on which I've placed my seal."
4. West, *Mortal Wounds*, 275–276.
5. Szulc, *Chopin in Paris*, 208–213.
6. Sand, *Un hiver au midi de l'Europe: Majorque et les majorcains,* was first published in serial form in the *Revue des Deux Mondes* between January and March of 1841, and subsequently in book form, as *Un hiver à Majorque,* in January 1842 with Hippolyte Souverain.
7. Sand, *Winter in Majorca,* 24. Robert Graves, who lived on Majorca, published an annotated translation of *Winter in Majorca* in which he vehemently rebuts Sand's interpretation of the islanders, xi: "George Sand (Baroness Aurore de Dudevant, *née* Dupin), the child of a *mésalliance* between an aristocrat and an ex-milliner, was the uncrowned queen of Romantics. She came to show the Majorcans by precept and example that the world had now changed, and that, by paying attention to her, they could shake themselves free from their intellectual and moral shackles, and become modern men and women. But her own house was not in order, and after a campaign of three months she retired in confusion. The precise nature of the defeat, however, is not so apparent as the bitterness it left in her heart."
8. *Corr.* V, to Dr. Paul Gaubert, 28 Aug. 1840, 110. Liszt, *Correspondance* I, 19 Nov. 1840, 290, cited in *Corr.* IV, note 1, 871.
9. *Corr.* V, to Ferdinand Bascans, [2 and 3 May 1841], 295, cited in Chovelon, "L'Education des filles," 152.
10. Ibid., 181.
11. BN n.a.f. 14279, ff74–75, cited in Chovelon, "L'Education des filles," 12.
12. *Corr.* V, to Solange Dudevant-Sand (Solange had by then adopted her mother's chosen name), 14 May 1841, 305. Chovelon, "L'Education des filles," 181. Later in life, Solange recorded the following journal entry: "Ah jealousy! Who will inflict it? Enigma without explanation, a bottomless pit. . . . How can I loose myself from your dizzying grasp? To suffer, suffer, and suffer more is the fate reserved for the one you possess!—no relief, no rest for the jealous—the poor people who are condemned to a preview of hell on earth." Clésinger-Sand, "Journaux de Solange," BN n.a.f. 26215, Sept. 1860.
13. *Corr.* V, to Solange Dudevant-Sand, [13 Aug. 1841], 398; [end of June 1841], 341. Chovelon, "L'Education des filles," 185, 192. *Corr.* V, to Marie de Rozières, [18 Nov. 1841], 501.

14. *Corr.* V, to Ferdinand Bascans, [29 Sept. 1841], 433; [toward 20 Mar. 1842], 618.
15. Ibid., VI, note 1, 160; to Solange Dudevant-Sand, [13 June 1843], 167.
16. Sand, *La Mare au diable*, 5, 12.
17. Sand, *La Confession d'une jeune fille*, 1:8.
18. *Corr.* VI, note 1, 160.
19. Solange was away at the Bascans pension in May 1843 when she read *Mauprat*. When the novel was originally published in 1837, Solange, then only nine years old, would have been too young to read it. *Corr.* VI, note 2, 158; to Solange Dudevant-Sand, [13 June 1843], 168.
20. Ibid., [6 June 1843], 159. Sand, *Mauprat*, 158, contains a reference to this plant: "All he managed to get from me was to slip into my precious box a very pretty little plant, which he claimed to have discovered and to which I only gave the right of asylum beside my fiancée's letter and ring on condition that it was called *Edmea sylvestris*." Ibid., 118.

CHAPTER 19: LIAISON DANGEREUSE

Epigraph: Laclos, *Liaisons dangereuses*, 256. "L'auteur au lecteur," in Sand, *Préfaces de George Sand*, 1:117.

1. In *Mortal Wounds*, West notes, 302: "George finally called her [Solange] back into their game-playing by writing a novel at her. Called *Mademoiselle Merquem*, it consists quite simply of an exceedingly ill-natured account of Solange's broken engagement with the Vicomte de Preaulx and of her capture by Clésinger hung on a portrait of her daughter which can only be described as a vicious caricature."
2. Laclos, *Liaisons dangereuses*, 100–101. *Corr.* VII, to Eugène Delacroix, [6 May 1847], 678–679.
3. Ibid., note 4, 293.
4. Ibid., note 1, 615–616.
5. Ibid., to Jean-Baptiste Clésinger, [19 Feb. 1847], 615–616.
6. Ibid., [12 Mar. 1847], 623.
7. Ibid., to Charlotte Marliani, [6 May 1847], 683.
8. Gautier, cited by Emile Fourquet in "Les Hommes célèbres et les personnalités marquantes de Franche-Comté du IVe siècle à nos jours" (1929), in *French Biographical Index* (Munich: Saur, 1998), 424. Estignard, *Clésinger*, 50. (Clesinger's *Femme piquée par un serpent* is in the Musée d'Orsay.)
9. Ibid., 51.
10. *Corr.* VII, to René Vallet de Villeneuve, [10 May 1847], 697.
11. Ibid., to Charles Poncy, [18 Apr. 1847], 663; to René Vallet de Villeneuve, [10 May 1847], 697.
12. Ibid., to Théodore Rousseau, 15 May 1847, 708.
13. Ibid., to Eugène Delacroix, 6 May 1847, 679.
14. Ibid., to Emmanuel Arago, [6 May 1847], 681.
15. Ibid., to Charles Poncy, 18 Apr. [1847], 662–663.

16. Ibid., 662, note 2.

17. Ibid.

18. In a personal e-mail communication, 4 Oct. 2000, Catharine R. Stimpson offered an interpretation: "It is a version of the father giving the son his mistress as sexual introduction."

19. *Corr.* VII, note 4, 623.

20. Ibid., IV, to Charlotte Marliani, [15 Feb. 1839], 570.

21. Ibid., VII, to Albert Grzymala, [12 May 1847], 700.

22. Ibid., to René Vallet de Villeneuve, 31 Mar. [1847], 638.

23. Ibid., 639.

24. Ibid., to Charles Poncy, [15 June 1847], 752–753.

25. Ibid., to Jules Dupré, 22 June [1847], 657.

26. Ibid., to Pierre-Jules Hetzel, 29 [Apr.] 1847, 668.

27. Owing to conflicts with Maurice, Chopin hadn't been at Nohant since November 1846. *Corr.* VII, to Maurice Dudevant-Sand, [16 Apr. 1847], 659–661.

28. Ibid., note 2, 661–662, and note 2, 662.

29. Ibid., to Emmanuel Arago, [6 May 1847], 681.

30. Ibid., to Charlotte Marliani, [11 Feb. 1847], 613.

31. Ibid., to René Vallet de Villeneuve, [10 May 1847], 697; VI, to Eugène Delacroix, [17 September 1843], 234.

32. Ibid., VII, to Pierre-Jules Hetzel, 15 Nov. [1845], 165. The wedding scene in Sand's future *La Noce de campagne* (*The Country Wedding*) was inspired by Solange Biaud's wedding.

33. The only other instance of such ambulatory debilitation that Sand experienced occurred in 1865, as Alexandre Manceau was dying. In *SML* V, viii, 1024, Sand commented on the connection between psychology and physiology: "I am convinced that negligence of one's body must have some correspondence with negligence of one's mind, and should serve as a warning." And in *Corr.* XVI, to Alexandre Dumas fils, 11 Dec. 1860, 192, Sand observed: "For as long as I've lived, I know and I also sense that when I think of sickness, I get sick. I have had in the past some serious bouts of hypochondria that are completely alien to my nature, and this was owing to friends and doctors who gratified me ten times over with illnesses I didn't have." Annabelle M. Rea, "Healers in George Sand's Works," in Datlof, Fuchs, and Powell, *The World of George Sand*, 182, cites "La Maladie comme ressort dramatique dans les romans de George Sand," *Revue d'Histoire Littéraire de France* 4 (July–Aug. 1976): 598–613, in which Mireille Bossis "surveys the types of illnesses treated in Sand's earlier works. She shows the rarity of infectious diseases and the frequent use of characteristically romantic fainting spells, brain fevers, and general listlessness, all physical manifestations of psychological stress. For Bossis, illness in Sand is never gratuitous; it always has a narrative function."

34. Clésinger-Sand, "Journaux de Solange," 31 July 1858, 233, BN n.a.f. 26216.

CHAPTER 20: BROKEN BONDS

Epigraph: *Corr.* VI, to Pierre Bocage, [23 Feb. 1845], 897; VII, to Pierre-Jules Hetzel, 15 Nov. [1845], 167.

1. Solange trumps Sand's masterplot: in *Les Liaisons dangereuses*, Madame de Merteuil seeks revenge on Gercourt, who has spurned her, by having Valmont despoil his fiancée, Cécile de Volanges. Solange retaliates against Sand by casting Augustine in the role of Cécile de Volanges, thereby destroying Augustine's engagement to Théodore Rousseau on the grounds that she has been despoiled by Maurice!

2. *Corr.* VII, to Marie de Rozières, [28 Sept. 1845], 102.

3. Ibid., VIII, to Chaix d'Est-Ange, [25 July 1848], 553: "Mother Brault is a former prostitute ["fille entretenue"], a close relative of my mother."

4. Ibid., VII, to Hippolyte Chatiron, [Jan. 1846], 263.

5. Ibid., to Théodore Rousseau, 15 May 1847, 708; to Adèle Brault, [autumn 1845], 149–150.

6. When Maurice Dudevant-Sand became engaged, Sand wrote her future daughter-in-law, Lina Calamatta, *Corr.* XVI, 31 Mar. 1862, 872: "I have a strong sense that I will be a true mother, for I have need of a daughter." And in *Corr.* XX, to Gustave Flaubert, 24 July [1867], 468–469, Sand wrote, "My daughter Lina is still my true daughter. The *other one* is beautiful and is behaving well, which is all I ask of her." Ibid., VI, [6 June 1843], 159; note 1, 160.

7. Ibid., VI, to Solange Dudevant, [13 June 1843], 169.

8. Ibid., V, to Solange Dudevant, [13 Aug. 1841], 398.

9. Karénine, *George Sand*, 3:453, cited in *Corr.* X, note 2, 289.

10. *Corr.* VIII, to Marie de Rozières, 25 July 1847, 18.

11. Ibid., to Emmanuel Arago, 26 July 1847, 47.

12. Ibid.

13. In 1851 Sand burned all her letters to Chopin, which Alexandre Dumas fils had brought back to her from Myslowitz. André-Maurois, *Correspondance inédite*, 181. *Corr.* VIII, to Emmanuel Arago, 26 July 1847, 47–48.

14. Ibid., IV, to Charlotte Marliani, [15 Feb. 1839], 570.

15. Ibid., VI, to Pierre Leroux, 10 Jan. 1844, 376.

16. *Corr.* VIII, to Emmanuel Arago, 26 July 1847, 47. Salomon, "Un amour de Chopin," 265. Salomon comments, 268: "Chopin loved Solange Sand, not with a burning passion, but with a deep, devoted tenderness that derived from an involuntary carnal attraction that was barely conscious."

17. *Corr.* VIII, to Frédéric Chopin, [28 July 1847], 54.

18. Ibid., to Emmanuel Arago, 26 July 1847, 21.

19. Ibid., 22.

20. Ibid., to Pauline Viardot, 8 Dec. 1848, 727; to Emmanuel Arago, 26 July 1847, 48.

21. Ibid., note 1, 49. Chopin, *Chopin's Letters*, to Ludwicka at Christmas, 1847, 337–338.

22. Ibid.

23. Brault pamphlet: *Une contemporaine.* Seized by police on 1 July 1848.

24. Chopin, *Chopin's Letters,* to his family, 19 Aug. 1848, 377.

25. *Corr.* VIII, to Chaix d'Est-Ange, [25 July 1848], 565.

26. D'Heylli, *La Fille de George Sand,* 63. Solange to Samuel Rocheblave in 1896, cited by Chovelon, "L'Education des filles d'après George Sand," 383.

27. *Corr.* VIII, to Pierre-Jules Hetzel, 1 Feb. [1848], 265.

28. Chopin, *Chopin's Letters,* to his sister Ludwika, Christmas 1847, 336.

CHAPTER 21: COLLATERAL DAMAGE AND *LUCRÉZIA FLORIANI*
Epigraph: *Corr.* XII, to Emile Aucante, [1 Apr. 1854], 378.

1. Sand, *Lucrézia Floriani,* 229. All references to *LF* are from the English translation by Eker, 1985.

2. Ibid., xi. Eisler, *Chopin's Funeral,* 151–152.

3. *Lucrézia Floriani,* jacket copy. In *George Sand,* note 18, 152, Powell writes: "Pierre Salomon, Marie-Thérèse Rouget, Marie Jenny Howe, Francis Gribble, William Atwood, Joseph Barry, Curtis Cate, and several others identify Chopin as the inspiration for Prince Karol. See *Histoire de ma vie, OA,* 2: 443–444, and Lubin's note 3, 443. Sand is not entirely wrong to point out that Karol's character and Chopin's are quite dissimilar; and Karol has no artistic talents, which makes him totally incomparable to Chopin. Still, a sickly man with aristocratic pretensions and Catholic guilt as a result of cohorting with a marked woman could easily describe both Karol and Chopin. Marie-Paule Rambeau brings new and convincing evidence to confirm the identity of Karol and Chopin in her well-documented and well-presented *Chopin dans la vie et l'oeuvre de George Sand* (Paris: Les Belles Lettres, 1985), pt. 2, chap. 1, esp. 229–233.

4. Eisler, *Chopin's Funeral,* 153.

5. *Lucrézia Floriani,* 49, 144.

6. *Corr.* VI, to Charles Poncy, 23 December 1843, 328. *Lucrézia Floriani,* 66.

7. *Lucrézia Floriani,* 105.

8. Ibid., 127–128.

9. Ibid., 25, 63. *SML* IV, viii, 818; IV, viii, 817. *Lucrézia Floriani,* 124.

10. *SML* I, iii, 103. *Lucrézia Floriani,* 1.

11. *SML* II, ii, 293. *Lucrézia Floriani,* 99.

12. *Lucrézia Floriani,* 168–169.

13. Ibid., 154. *SML* II, ii, 296. *Lucrézia Floriani,* 78–79.

14. *Lucrézia Floriani,* 115.

15. Ibid., 122, 146.

16. *Corr.* IV, to Louis-Mammès Pierret, [25 Jan. 1838], 332.

17. *Lucrézia Floriani,* 8–9. *SML* II, xii, 434. *Lucrézia Floriani,* 22.

18. *Lucrézia Floriani,* 22–23, 172.

19. Ibid., 193.

20. *SML* II, xii, 432.

21. *Lucrézia Floriani,* 199.

22. Ibid., 203, 150. *SML* III, x, 635.

23. *SML* II, viii, 378.

24. Ibid., V, xiii, 1106–1107.

CHAPTER 22: REVOLUTION AND REVERBERATIONS

Epigraph: *SML* IV, xiii, 899; V, iv, 963.

1. *Corr.* VIII, to Maurice Sand, [23 Feb. 1848], 304–305. When Maurice expressed his desire to participate in the Crimean War, Sand intervened by requesting of Prince Napoléon Jérôme that he not draft Maurice: "My son tells me every day that if I were not such a foolish mother, he would have asked to follow you [to war]. But he is my only son, and how could I live without him?" *Corr.,* XII, to Prince Napoléon (Jérôme), [16 July 1854], 510.

2. Ibid., VIII, to Frédéric Girerd, Paris, [6 Mar. 1848], 324. In *Corr.* XV, to Prince de Villafranca, [29 Aug. 1859], 495, Sand reprises the theme of political engagement as consolation for personal loss: "There's no remedy for a broken passion but another passion, and patriotic passion would have been the only kind worthy of succeeding a great affection."

3. *Corr.* VIII, to Emmanuel Arago, 26 July [18]47, 21; to Augustine Brault, 5 Mar. 1848, 319.

4. Ibid., to Charles Poncy, [27 Aug. 1847], 78; to Emmanuel Arago, 26 July [18]47, 21; to Gustave Papet, [mid-Aug. 1847], 74.

5. Ibid., to Charles Poncy, [27 Aug. 1847], 78.

6. Ibid., to Pierre Bocage, [4 Oct. 1847], 96; to René Vallet de Villeneuve, [4 Mar. 1848], 316.

7. Ibid., to Frédéric Girerd, [6 Mar. 1848], 324–326.

8. Ibid., to Charles Poncy, 8 Mar. [1848], 331.

9. Sand, "Lettre au peuple," in *Politique et polémiques,* 241. Sand published her first "Lettre au peuple" at the beginning of Mar. 1848. Jules Hetzel immediately republished it as a brochure entitled *Hier et aujourd'hui,* 7 Mar. 1848, Paris. It was reprinted in *La Cause du Peuple* on 9 Apr. 1848. *Corr.* VIII, to Charles Poncy, 8 Mar. [1848], 330.

10. *La Voix des Femmes* 16 (6 Apr. 1848), cited in Riot-Sarcey, *La Démocratie,* 202.

11. Riot-Sarcey, *La Démocratie,* 199.

12. Sand's letter was also published in *La Ruche de la Dordogne* on 16 Apr. 1848.

13. *Corr.* VIII, to the editors of *La Réforme* and *La Vraie République,* [8 Apr. 1848], 391–392.

14. Sand, *Politique et polémiques,* 534.

15. *Corr.* II, to Adolphe Guéroult, [6 May 1835], 879; to Marie Talon, 10 [Nov. 1834], 741. In *The Miller of Angibault* [1844], 113, Sand's aversion to Saint-Simonism is unequivocal. The novel's virtuous protagonist, Marcelle, who parts graciously with fortune and social status, declares: "My good instincts require me to reject those systems bandied about today, rather too arrogantly, under various titles. I have yet to see one in which moral freedom is toler-

ated, in which atheism and ambition to dominate do not creep in somewhere. Perhaps you have heard of the Saint-Simonians and the Fourierites.
Those are systems without religion or love, abortive philosophies, roughly
sketched, in which the spirit of evil seems to lurk beneath the appearance of
philanthropy. I shall not judge them absolutely, but they repel me, as a new
trap laid for the simplicity of humanity."

16. *Corr.* I, to Emile Regnault, [20 Sept. 1831], 945.

17. Ibid., VIII, to members of the Central Committee, [mid-Apr. 1848], 400–
408, including subsequent references. Sand scratched out the words *odieuse*
and *répugnante* and replaced them with *étrangère*, note 1, 401. Although never
completed, this letter was published in 1904 by Sand's granddaughter Aurore
Sand in the posthumous collection titled *Souvenirs et idées. Corr.* I, to Emile
Regnault, [20 Sept. 1831], 945.

18. Sand, *Politique et polémiques,* 542. In *Ecrivain de romans,* 88, Mozet comments: "On this particular point, Sand was no doubt mistaken, because it's
often better to demand too much rather than too little. But it would have
been suicidal on her part to accept the proposition of *La Voix des femmes.*
In turning it down, she displays a very acute awareness of 'symbolic capital,'
to use Bourdieu's term, which is essential to public discourse and to the way
Sand herself was perceived. [*Qui fait toute l'efficacité d'une parole publique,
à commencer par la sienne.*] Having only her prestige as a writer, she's already
taking a risk by contributing to the *Bulletin de la République* editorials which
she doesn't sign but which are recognized as her own."

19. Scott, *Only Paradoxes to Offer,* 80–81. Riot-Sarcey, *La Démocratie,* 216.

20. Riot-Sarcey, *La Démocratie,* note 285, 246.

21. *Corr.* IX, to Théophile Thoré, 26 May 1849, 176. P. J. Proudhon, *La Justice
dans la Révolution et dans l'église,* 3 vols., ed. Pierre-Joseph Lacroix (Paris:
Garnier Frères, 1858), 3:114–116, cited by Thibert, in *Féminisme dans le socialisme français,* 276–277. In "George Sand et le féminisme," 75, Chonez makes
the following observation: "If George Sand was detested by so many men,
it's less because of her political or social ideas (among the 'left' were staunch
defenders, including Marx), than because of her seemingly aggressive
feminism—aggressive in appearance, above all. Other women were, in fact,
ahead of her, in the same era, only one of whom I need mention: the
admirable Flora Tristan, whose critical analysis of patriarchal society goes
so much farther, is so much denser and more coherent."

22. In Sand, *Politique et polémiques,* 530, Perrot observes: "What is most surprising is the absence of direct communication between these women who were,
after all, engaged in the common cause of female emancipation. Why didn't
Eugénie Niboyet first approach Sand? Why did Sand neither complete nor
subsequently send the letter 'to the Members of the Central Committee,'
which is ultimately one of her most cogent texts on her fundamental conviction: priority of civil equality, reform of marriage, the key to women's
enslavement . . ."

23. Thibert, *Féminisme dans le socialisme français*, 264. Niboyet in Riot-Sarcey, *La Démocratie*, 202.

24. Divorce was decreed in France on 20 Sept. 1792, and abolished on 8 May 1816. It was not reinstated in 1848, despite several propositions, among them Adolphe Crémieux's, a lawyer and politician (1796–1880).

25. Riot-Sarcey, *La Démocratie*, note 32, 133.

26. Deutelbaum and Hugg, "Class, Gender, and Family System," 277–278. Sand, *Le Dernier Amour*, 17. In "George Sand and Her Sisters: Women Writers in the *Société des Gens de Lettres* (1838–1848)," *George Sand Studies* 16, nos. 1 and 2, (1997): 97–108, Elisabeth-Christine Muelsch notes, 99: "Sand, who had joined the SDGL also because she was intrigued by the term, 'association,' was condemned for selfish and inconsiderate behavior, unworthy of an 'association' member. The note in the *Bulletin* would represent her as a member who insisted on authorial rights while neglecting the other two goals of the association, solidarity and support among writers. Wiping out the emergency fund would ultimately hurt her own sex the most as destitute women writers were always supported very generously through it. This portrayal of George Sand in the *Bulletin* might very well have aimed at driving a wedge between Sand and the other female members of the SDGL."

27. *SML* IV, xiii, 899. Even while insisting on her exceptionality, Sand reverts to feelings of female insufficiency. The citation continues: "And yet I was a woman like others—dependent, nervous, prey to my imagination, childishly susceptible to the emotionalism and anxieties of motherhood."

28. Riot-Sarcey, *La Démocratie*, note 43, 136, citing Niboyet. *SML* IV, xiii, 899.

29. Riot-Sarcey, *La Démocratie*, notes 71 and 70, 195.

30. Scott, *Only Paradoxes to Offer*, 71–72. Sand, *Jacques*, in *Romans 1830*, 852–853.

31. Granier de Cassagnac, "*Jacques* de George Sand," *La Revue de Paris* 10 (1834): 80, cited by Jeanne Goldin in "Le saint-simonisme," 163–191, in Mozet, *Une Correspondance*, 178.

32. Théobold Walsh, *George Sand* (Paris: Hivert, 1837). In "Paradoxes de la maternité," 424, Chambaz-Bertrand makes the following observation about Sand's psychology in relation to her daughter, which perhaps sheds light, as well, on Sand's behavior with the women activists whom she attacked with so much animus: "Solange is the shadow part of George Sand, an anomaly in a woman whose maternal feeling was so well established. . . . Isn't it so that we always develop at the expense of those who are weak, particularly within a family? Hadn't George Sand, who belongs to the conquering class, without being aware of it, without having wished for it, flourished at her daughter's expense?"

33. Sand, preface to the 1842 Perrotin edition of her works, in *The Companion of the Tour of France* (also published as *The Journeyman Joiner*), trans. Francis Geo. Shaw (New York: William H. Graham, 1847), viii.

34. Schor, *Idealism*, 71. In *Joyous Greetings*, 55, Anderson notes: "Deroin wrote that 'when she was too young to appreciate her social position' she dreamed

of a brilliant future. But by her early teens 'the necessity of labor' led her to understand 'without money, I had to give up.'"

35. Sand, *Politique et polémiques*, 393.

36. Naginski, *George Sand*, note 30 (emphasis added), 252: "The most distressing evidence of Sand's occasional lack of a feminist perspective is the letter she wrote to the 'Comite-central de la Gauche' in 1848, in which she states her opposition to women's suffrage." Schor, *Idealism*, 71: "The very fact that the bourgeois feminists gathered at the Club de la Rue Taranne could have misunderstood the nature of Sand's involvement, the extent of her *representativity* clearly demonstrates how difficult it is to classify Sand when it comes to what she calls, 'the women's cause.'"

37. Schor, *Idealism*, 78.

38. *Corr.* XVIII, to Edouard de Pompéry, 23 Dec. 1864, 628–629. In "Paradoxes de la maternité," 379–380, Chambaz-Bertrand comments on Sand's remark: "Once again, the text surprises us by its contemporaneity and once again George Sand's position is clear: motherhood is woman's destiny. We had already seen this attitude in response to Solange and Clésinger's separation in 1848. We had asked ourselves if in the nineteenth century George Sand, in her capacity as George Sand, could have raised her daughter differently. There were at this time women who had other conceptions: the Saint-Simonians—whom George Sand specifically rejected—Flora Tristan, the pariah. . . . And before them, during the Revolution, Olympe de Gouges who died for her ideas, Théroigne de Méricourt. George Sand lives the life of a liberated woman, but her ideas are not the same as those of a liberated woman. Or are we to believe that her lifelong assertion of the primacy of motherhood is merely denial, a cover-up for woman's indulgence in free love? Should we attribute to her correspondence the role Mireille Bossis fondly describes as literature of denial?" Sand, *Impressions et souvenirs*, 259–260.

39. *Corr.* VIII, note 1, 590–591, citing A. de Tocqueville, *Souvenirs* (Paris: Calmann-Lévy, 1893), 204.

40. *Corr.* XIX, to Lina Dudevant-Sand, [28 May 1865], 218. Hiddleston, *George Sand and Autobiography*, 22. Hiddleston further notes, 27: "She refused in her life to allow her motherhood to constrain her freedom, and in her autobiography she largely omits both the joys and the pains which motherhood brings. These are specifically the emotions of a woman, and therefore at odds with the universal image Sand wished to project and the male tradition within which she was writing." The above notwithstanding, in *Corr.* VI, to Edouard de Pompéry, [Jan. 1845], 789, Sand was highly critical of Flora Tristan, whom she accused of sacrificing her daughter's well-being for her socialist apostleship: "Did her mother love her? Why were they separated? What apostolate could thus result in forgetting and sending so far away . . . such a charming and adorable being?" In "Motherhood and Politics in George Sand and Flora Tristan," *George Sand Studies* 16, nos. 1 and 2, (1997): 83–96, Annie

Smart observes, 83: "Born a year apart—Sand in 1804 and Tristan in 1803—these two independent women writers shared much in common, in spite of their mutual distrust and probable dislike. Both were unhappily married, both saw women as society's outsiders, and were seen as liberated women *par excellence.*" Sand may well have harbored resentment toward Tristan for what she wrote about Sand in *Pérégrinations d'une paria (1833–1834)*, in *Dieu, franchise, liberté* (Paris: Arthur Bertrand, 1838), cited by Moses and Rabine, in *Feminism, Socialism, and French Romanticism*, 207–208: "One woman who has become famous from her first writings, for her elevated thought, dignity, and purity of style, has used the form of the novel to put into relief the misery arising from the situation into which our laws have placed woman. But she has put so much truth into her portrayal that her own misfortunes were divined by the reader. But this writer, who is a woman, not content with the veil behind which she has hidden herself in her writings, has signed them with the name of a man. What reverberations can there be from protests enveloped in fictions? What influence could they exert when the facts that prompt them are stripped of their reality? Fictions amuse and occupy the mind for a moment but are never the driving force behind men's actions."

41. Rabine, "Sand and the Myth of Femininity," 15. *SML* V, iv, 963.
42. *Corr.* X, to Hortense Allart de Méritens, [beginning of July 1851], 349.
43. Ibid., IV, to Charlotte Marliani, 3 June 1839, 664.
44. Ibid., II, to Laure Decerfz, 1 Apr. [1833], 291. *SML* V, xiii, 1103.
45. Sand, *Gabriel*, 60, cited by Naginski, in "La Comédie féminine," 231–239, in *George Sand et l'écriture du roman*. Naginski, 238, relates *Gabriel* to the novel *Lélia*, in which "the heroine conducted herself like a fallen angel—reproaching God for having taken away her wing, the angelic member, for having condemned her to an earthbound life of the body. . . . The rejection of the female sexed body as obstacle to the life of the mind is clear."
46. *Corr.* XXIII, to Emile de Girardin, 7 Sept. [18]72, 219; XVIII, to Edouard de Pompéry, 23 Dec. 1864, 628–629; XX, to Gustave Flaubert, [1 Oct. 1866], 138.
47. Ibid., IV, to Albert Grzymala, [end of May 1838], 434; XX, to Gustave Flaubert, 29 Nov. [1866], 206. In *George Sand and Autobiography*, Hiddleston, 71, observes: "The transformations that took place in Sand almost always appear as the result of emotional stimulation rather than rational deliberation, and so fit in with the different way a woman is said to determine her destiny." In *Idealism*, 76, Schor argues that Sand's credential as a feminist is based on her self-contradictions: "The apparently irreconcilable debate that currently opposes essentialists and constructionists is false, in that neither of the warring forces has an exclusive hold on the truth. *Feminism is the debate itself.* If Sand is a feminist, it is in the sense that she bodies forth and articulates these contradictions and not to the extent that she resolves them in a more or less satisfactory fashion." In *Joyous Greetings*, 81, Anderson considers solidarity a defining element of mid-nineteenth century feminism: "The antifeminism

of Sand and other women of achievement undercut attempts to form organizations to work for women's interests. . . . What distinguished feminists from nonfeminist activists was their willingness to keep trying to form connections to other women like themselves."

48. Schor, *Idealism*, 71. The complete passage reads: "In fact, considering the enormity of the stakes, Sand's feminism is the pons asinorum of Sand studies. It would not be exaggerated to say that, sooner or later, all those interested in Sand are led to wonder about her feminism and take a position pro or con. Sand's feminism is an obligatory and unavoidable theme of reflection for all Sand scholars." *Webster's New Universal Unabridged Dictionary* (New York: Simon and Schuster, 1983), 1399, lists the following (modified) meaning for *pons asinorum:* "any problem that is hard for beginners."

CHAPTER 23: COMING TO WRITING

Epigraph: *OA*, vol. 2, *Voyage en Auvergne*, 504. An earlier version of some of the material in this chapter was published as "Voyage en Espagne: From the Foreign to the Familiar," in *Le Chantier de George Sand: George Sand et l'étranger*, Actes du Xe colloque international George Sand (Debrecen, Hungary: Kossuth Lajos Tudományegyetem, 1993), 265–272.

1. *SML* II, xi, 418. In "Le Mythe des origines et l'autoportrait chez George Sand et Colette," *Studies in Honour of Wallace Fowlie*, ed. Marcel Tetel (Durham: Duke University Press, 1978), 108, Germaine Brée observes: "The 'I' of the autobiographer Sand, such as she acknowledges it, is linked to her victory over the personal social conflict into which she was born. The 'mothers' have been reconciled and transcended, not rejected, in these scenes of intense auto-dramatization in which self-justification is conspicuous." Cited by Hiddleston, *George Sand and Autobiography*, 36–37.

2. *SML* IV, ix, 840.

3. Sand, *La Mare au diable*, 12.

4. *Corr.* XIX, to Charles Marchal, 18 Mar. 1866, 767–768.

5. *SML* III, viii, 605. In response to Sand's account of her persistent omission of the letter B when she recited the alphabet as a child, the psychoanalyst Helene Deutch, in her 1928 paper "George Sand: A Woman's Destiny," as well as, more recently, Maryline Lukacher (*Maternal Fictions*) have explored this parapraxis in connection with the absent father and Aurore's invention of the deity Corambé.

6. *SML* III, ix, 622.

7. Ibid., x, 635.

8. Yalom, "George Sand's Poetics of Autobiography," in Datlof, Fuchs, and Powell, *The World of George Sand*, 90. Pam Hirsch, "Charlotte Brontë and George Sand: The Influence of Female Romanticism," 214, in *Brontë Society Transactions* 21, pt. 6 (1996): 209–218.

9. Sand, *Voyage en Auvergne*, 504–505, including the citation in the following paragraph.

10. *OA*, vol. 2, note 3, 517/1419. "Two other copies can be found in the collection Lovenjoul: E841, f154, also a signed, first draft; E842, f99–100, a copy. They show serious differences with E850, a final, more fully worked draft. E841 bears the date: 'Oct. 1828. Nohant.'" "Manuscrit trouvé," in *Voyage en Auvergne*, 518–520.

11. Hamilton, *Mythology*, 271.

12. In *Writing for Her Life*, 217–220, Naginski associates Sand's fear of being silenced specifically with the myth of Cyane, "one of Proserpina's nymphs who was metamorphosed and thereby lost the power of speech. She was the only one to witness Proserpina's abduction by the lord of the underworld. When she came forth to help, Pluto changed her into a fountain so that she would not be able to reveal what she had seen."

13. *SML* I, i, 79.

14. Szabo, Notice to *Valentine* (1852), in *Prefaces* 1:176, cited by Crecelius, *Family Romances*, 93.

15. Schor, *Idealism*, 174.

16. *SML* II, viii, 377.

17. Abbadie, "George Sand et les relations franco-espagnoles," 54.

18. Sand, *Voyage en Espagne*, 471. Lubin, Introduction to *Voyage en Espagne*, 469.

19. *Corr.* I, to Madame Maurice Dupin, 11 June 1829, 531–534.

20. *SML*, II, xiv, 454. *Voyage en Espagne*, 474. *SML*, II, iv, 451–452.

21. *SML* II, xii, 437. Sand, *Voyage en Espagne*, 474. *SML*, II, xiv, 452.

22. *Corr.* VIII, to Pierre-Jules Hetzel, 1 Feb. 1848, 264.

23. Personal correspondence from Georges Lubin, 26 Apr. 1992.

24. *SML* II, xii, 436.

25. *Corr.* I, to [Félicie Molliet], [16 Aug. 1829], and note 1, 543–544. In *Corr.* IV, note 1, 425, Lubin informs us: "Rose-Félicité Fontaine (Mme Molliet), was in fact Maurice Dupin's mistress; we have found the proof in a letter by her to her mother. But the dates fail to corroborate that he was Félicité's father. She was born on . . . 31 May 1800; nine months earlier, Maurice Dupin was at Thionville and about to leave for Switzerland to chase the Russian army."

26. Sand, *Voyage en Espagne*, 472–473 (emphasis added).

27. *SML*, II, xiv, 451.

28. Ibid., 452.

29. Ibid., 455, including citation in the following paragraph.

30. *OA*, 1:578, "From my father to my mother," 12 June 1808. *SML*, II, xiv, 455.

31. *SML*, II, xii, 437.

32. Ibid., II, xiv, 455.

CHAPTER 24: *CONFESSION OF A YOUNG GIRL*
Epigraph: *SML* II, viii, 376.

1. *SML* I, i, 71. Sand, *La Confession d'une jeune fille* (*Confession of a Young Girl*), 1:1. In "George Sand," 447, Brée notes: "*Confession of a Young Girl* reactivates in fictional form the material presented in the autobiography." And in "La

Comédie féminine," 232, Naginski comments on *La Confession d'une jeune fille:* "Confession thus becomes, in the Sandian oeuvre, the privileged place for self-analytic discourse. A superior form than the intimate journal because it is spoken in dialogue with an Other, confession puts to work the polyphony so dear to its author."

2. Capasso, "Female Voice in *Confession of a Young Girl,*" 58–59.

3. *SML* II, viii, 377. *Confession of a Young Girl,* 1:310. In "La Comédie féminine," 236, Naginski observes: "Lucienne's crisis concerns . . . the quest for her true self. When her grandmother dies and she's divested of her name, her title, her fortune, and a home, she defiantly trades in her identity as Lucienne de Valangis for 'Yvonne from nothing' [t.II, 205]. . . . Under conditions of such utter deprivation, Lucienne will probe as deeply as possible the question of 'who am I?'" In "George Sand et la généalogie," 11, Frappier-Mazur notes, "Lucienne owes her dark beauty to her real father's Spanish origin, which does not preclude a certain resemblance to Aurore." *SML* IV, ix, 840.

4. *Confession of a Young Girl* 1:2, 1:143–144.

5. Sand, *La Confession,* 1:101–102.

6. Vanderkerkhove, "Romanesque et autobiographie dans *La Confession d'une jeune fille,*" 26. *SML* II, xii, 432.

7. *SML* II, xii, 433.

8. Ibid., IV, viii, 817.

9. *Corr.* I, note 1, 129.

10. *SML* V, xi, 1080.

11. In *Corr.* III, 894, Lubin notes: "[Sand] says that [Pierret] had married the daughter of a general without fortune: we were unable to find a record of this marriage in the Archives de la Seine, and there is no mention of Madame Pierret in any letter."

12. *SML* II, xii, 432–433, including the citation in the following paragraph.

13. Ibid., 433.

14. Karénine, *George Sand,* 4:590, notes: "Of the plays that appeared after *Le Marquis de Villemer,* this is the only one that Mme Sand wrote without collaboration." Deutsch, "A Woman's Destiny," 451. Deutsch further notes: "The doubling of the mother role in Sand's life and fiction is often noted, but the doubling of the father role hasn't received the attention that's warranted. In 'l'Autre,' an extension or evolution of *La Confession,* as well as in the novel *La Filleule,* where Stéphane is the foster or stepfather and the duke turns out to be Morénita's real father: Morénita in her diary: 'Why must I always think about him? He was so fond of me when I was smaller. He rocked me so lovingly on his knees and always spoke to me like a father to his child. Now I shall seriously try not to think about him any longer and to stop being fond of him. I shall think about my beloved duke. Who knows . . . whether he is not my father?'"

15. Deutsch, "A Woman's Destiny," 454.

16. *SML,* IV, vii, 812.

17. Ibid., 814.

18. "Affection of a father": *SML* II, xii, 432; "oldest and best friend": *Corr.* IV, to Louis-Mammès Pierret, [25 Jan. 1838], 332.

19. Sand, "A L . . ." in *Sketches and Hints,* 595–596.

20. *OA,* vol. 2, note 1, 595/1426.

21. *Corr.* II, to Madame Maurice Dupin, [14 Apr. 1832], 65, including note 1.

22. *Sketches and Hints,* 597–599, and note 2, 597/1426.

23. Chopin, *Chopin's Letters,* to Ludwika, 31 Oct. 1844, 277.

24. *Corr.* III, to Madame Maurice Dupin, [14 June 1836], 436; [30 July 1836], 502; IV, to Louis-Mammès Pierret, [22 July 1837], 160.

25. *Confession of a Young Girl* 2:317. See Naginski, "La Comédie féminine," 239, for an excellent analysis of the conclusion of this novel.

CHAPTER 25: THE ART OF LOVING

Epigraphs: Sand, *Isidora* (1846), cited in *Corr.* XIII, 673. Erich Fromm, *The Art of Loving* (New York: Harper and Row, 1962), 22.

1. *Corr.* XIII, appendix, "Le Changement d'écriture," 674.

2. *Corr.* XII, to Pierre-Jules Hetzel, 12 Jan. [1854], 248. Sand, *Flaubert-Sand Correspondence,* to Sand, 3 July [18]74, 350; to Flaubert, 8 July [18]74, 351.

3. Arnold, "George Sand," 199–200. In *Idealism,* 25, Schor notes: "Already in 1887, Emile Faguet had written: 'Hers was the genius of the idyll.' According to him it is the . . . peasant idylls situated in her home region, the Berry, that are destined for immortality."

4. *Corr.* IX, to Pierre-Jules Hetzel, [7 July 1850], 609.

5. Ibid., [end of April, 1850], 545, including following paragraph.

6. Gautier's description was published by Edmond and Jules de Goncourt, in *Journal* 2:144–146, cited by Barry, *Infamous Woman,* 334.

7. D'Heylli, *La Fille de George Sand,* 58.

8. Sand also welcomed the income that theatrical productions could generate. In *George Sand's Theatre Career,* 53, Manifold notes: "In addition to her eight percent author's share of the first run's net receipts [for plays], Sand could expect two or three thousand francs for a first edition, depending on the length; publishers paid Sand one centime per letter (which helps to explain why she did not edit her novels more severely). *Corr.* X, to Pauline Viardot, 16 Oct. [18]51, 496.

9. *Corr.* XXI, to Louis Ulbach, [26 Nov. 1869], 711.

10. Ibid., XII, to Pierre-Jules Hetzel, 12 Jan. [1854], 248.

11. Ibid., to Solange Clésinger, 9 Feb. [18]54, 284.

12. Ibid., XI, to Pauline Viardot, [25 July 1852], 265–266.

13. Ibid., note 1, 58.

14. Ibid., to Solange Clésinger, [25 Apr. 1852], 58–65, including further citations from this letter.

15. In addition to Solange and Sand, "the three of us" refers to Maurice, as well.

16. *Corr.* XI, note 1, 58–59.

17. James, "George Sand, 1914," 243.

18. Chovelon, *George Sand et Solange*, 389.

19. *Corr.* XV, note 1, 43–44.

20. Ibid., XIII, to Pierre-Jules Hetzel, [17 Jan. 1855], 31.

21. According to Chambaz-Bertrand, in "Paradoxes de la maternité," 370, Solange's testament mentions a gift of an allowance to a Mlle. Nazy Azair, daughter of Wacy Pacha, leading to speculation that Solange bore Wacy Pacha a child.

22. *Corr.* XXIII, to Solange Clésinger, [1 Sept. 1872], 208.

23. Ibid., XII, to Solange Clésinger, [22 Jan. 1854], 273. In "Solange ou la déchirure," in *Ecrivain de romans*, 99, Mozet observes: "Like parents who were beaten in their childhood and who beat their children, Sand repeated the family pattern. Some forty years later, the child who had become a writer and a grandmother sentenced her daughter to the same fate of prostitution. The nightmare goes on, enlarged by time."

24. *Corr.* XIII, to Solange Clésinger, [9 Jan. 1856], 498–499. Ibid., note 1, 505; to Solange Clésinger, [15 Jan. 1856], 505.

25. Ibid., XIV, note 1, 173.

26. Ibid., XV, to Emile Aucante, [30 Oct. 1858], 129.

27. Maurois, *Lélia*, 301. Schermerhorn, *The Seven Strings*, 194–195. Rocheblave, *George Sand et sa fille*, 223.

28. *Corr.* XV, to Emile Aucante, [11 May 1859], 410.

29. Ibid., XVI, to Armand Barbès, 8 Jan. 1862, 727; to Fortuné Lapaine, 7 Feb. [18]62, 772.

30. Ibid., XVII, to Lina Calamatta, [10 Apr. 1862], 22.

31. Ibid., IX, to Augustine de Bertholdi, [15 Jan. 1850], 427; XVI, to Maurice Dudevant, 11 Aug. [18]61, 516.

32. Ibid., XIV, to Solange Clésinger, [16 June 1858], 773.

33. Ibid., XIX, to Maurice Dudevant-Sand, [21 Aug. 1865], 361.

34. Ibid., to Oscar Cazamajou, [22 Aug. 1865], 370.

35. *Agenda* III, 23 Aug. 1865, 299.

36. *Corr.* XVI, note 2, 512, and note 1, 516.

37. Ibid., XIX, to Charles Poncy, [14 Oct. 1865], 458.

38. Ibid., "Notes sur les domiciles parisiens," 911.

39. Solange Clésinger-Sand, *Jacques Bruneau*, 6. Mozet's analysis of this novel is found in chap. 5, "Solange ou la déchirure," in *Ecrivain de romans*, 93–129.

40. Clésinger-Sand, *Jacques Bruneau*, 18.

41. Ibid., 121.

42. Ibid., 95, 272.

43. BN n.a.f. 16267, Solange Clésinger–Charles Alfieri Correspondence, vol. 1, 12 June 1869.

44. *Corr.* XV, to Solange Clésinger, [4 Oct. 1859], 521.

45. Ibid., XXI, to Solange Clésinger, [17 July 1869], 539–541, including references in two following paragraphs. Sand also used the word *carogne*, which is

related to the contemporary French word *charogne*, meaning "carrion," "spoiled meat," or, by idiomatic extension, "slut," to devalue promiscuous female protagonists in her novels *Jacques* (1834), *Mademoiselle Merquem* (1868), and *Le Dernier Amour* (*The Last Love*, 1866).

46. *Corr.* XXI, to Solange Clésinger, 30 Dec. 1869, 741.
47. Solange Clésinger–Charles Alfieri Correspondence 1:19, Aug. 1868, BN n.a.f. 16267.
48. Sand, *Flaubert-Sand Correspondence*, Sand to Flaubert, 15 Aug. [1870], 210.
49. Ibid., Flaubert to Sand, [17 Aug. 1870], 211.
50. Higonnet, *Paris*, 109.
51. Sand, *Flaubert-Sand Correspondence*, Flaubert to Sand, 30 Apr. [1871], 228.
52. Ibid., 8 Sept. [1871], 240–241.
53. *Corr.* XXII, to Gustave Flaubert, 14 Sept. 1871, 545–555.
54. Solange Clésinger, *Nouvel Agenda de 1874*, 13 July, BN n.a.f. 15556. Sand, *Agenda*, vol. 5, 13 July 1874, 221.
55. *Corr.* XV, to Ernest Périgois, 19 and 10 [Nov. 1858], 156. *Agenda*, vol. 5, 13 July and 2 Aug. 1874. *Corr.* XXIV, to Eugène Lambert, [9 Aug. 1874], 83; to Edmond Plauchut, [9 Aug. 1874], 84.
56. Sand, *Flaubert-Sand Correspondence*, Sand to Flaubert, 17 Jan. [18]69, 131.
57. Ibid., Flaubert to Sand, 2 Dec. [1874], 358. *Corr.* XXIV, to Gustave Flaubert, [12 and 15 Jan. 1876], 510 (emphasis added).
58. Sand, *Flaubert-Sand Correspondence*, Sand to Flaubert, 8 Dec. [18]74, 359.
59. Ibid., 16 [Jan. 18[75], 362.
60. Sand's last novel, *Marianne* (1876), first appeared as *Marianne Chevreuse* in *La Revue des Deux Mondes*, 1 and 15 Aug. 1875. *Corr.* XXIV, to Henri Amic, [1 May 1875], 251.
61. Sand, *Flaubert-Sand Correspondence*, Sand to Flaubert, 12 Jan. 1876, 386.
62. *Corr.* XIV, to Pierre-Jules Hetzel, [23 Nov. 1857], 529. In a letter to Ernest Feydeau, *Corr.* XV, [16 Aug. 1859], 479–480, Sand commented: "I suspect, in effect, that there is a way of envisioning the reality of things and beings, which marks great progress, and you are providing the triumphant proof of this. But the name *realism* isn't appropriate, because art is a multifarious, infinite interpretation. It is the artist who creates the real within himself, his own real, and not that of another."
63. *Corr.* XXIV, to Charles-Edmond, [9 Jan. 1876], 507.
64. Sand, *Flaubert-Sand Correspondence*, Sand to Flaubert, 12 Jan. 1876, 384.
65. Beauvoir, *The Second Sex* 2:235. Sand, *Flaubert-Sand Correspondence*, Sand to Flaubert, 15 Jan. [1867], 57. Sand, *Impressions et souvenirs*, 258–271, cited by Lubin in *Corr.* XX, note 2, 297. Tracing the split between "difference" and "equality" feminism, in "French Feminism Is a Universalism," 19, Schor observes: "The persistence of certain aspects of the Enlightenment model of the universal pervades both equality and difference feminists who followed in Beauvoir's wake. Or rather: the ambiguity built into the Enlightenment ideal of the universal produced the split between those feminists (*e.g.* Woll-

stonecraft and Beauvoir) who revindicated equal rights for women and un-masked feminity as a male construct, and those (*e.g.* George Sand and Luce Irigary) who while sharing the same aspirations to education and economic independence as equality feminists, subscribe to the notion of an inalienable female difference."

66. Sand, *Flaubert-Sand Correspondence*, Sand to Flaubert, 17 Jan. [18]69, 131.

EPILOGUE

1. Sand died at 9:00 A.M. on 8 June 1876.

2. Arnold, "George Sand," 199–200. "Laissez verdure" ("Leave the greenery"): *Corr.* XXIV, Annexe IV, 664.

3. *Corr.* VI, to the Abbey***, curate of . . . , [13 Nov. 1844], 696–697. The citation continues: "Since the spirit of liberty has been extinguished in the Catholic church, since its doctrine is no longer based on discussion, or coun-cils, or progress, or enlightenment, I view Catholic doctrine as something obsolete that has served as a political brake on governments and the people. As far as I'm concerned it's a mendacious cover-up of the true word of Christ, a false interpretation of the sublime Gospel, and an insurmountable obstacle to the sacred equality that God promises, that God will bestow upon men on earth as in heaven."

4. In *Corr.* XIII, to Emile Aucante, [18 Jan. 1856], 509, Sand had made clear her aversion to Catholic burial rites when Solange wanted to place a cross on her daughter's grave at Nohant: "I've had enough of Solange's stories about this grave which is profaned by the way she's carrying on. My ancestors are also there and don't need to be decorated with Catholic symbolism. Let her take her cross away, for there is a cross there and it's a *cross* which she wants to place on the patch of earth where I shall be sooner or later. I personally do not want this. She was wrong to insist and to try to force Catholicism on me by effigy. I won't let this happen." In Sand, *Flaubert-Sand Correspondence*, Flaubert to Mademoiselle Leroyer de Chantepie, [17 June 1876], 399. See also Gustave Flaubert, *Oeuvres complètes*, ser. 7, 1873–76 (Paris: Louis Conard, 1930), 304.

5. Paul Meurice, Tribute, cited in Henry Harisse, "Derniers moments et obsèques de George Sand," in *Souvenirs d'un ami*, in the *Berry Médical*, coll. Bibliothèque municipale de La Châtre, note 2, 127.

6. Auguste Renan, *Le Temps*, cited by Henry James, *Parisian Sketches*, ed. Leon Edel and Ilse Dusoir Lind (New York: New York University Press, 1957), 182.

7. In Henry Harisse, "Derniers moments et obsèques de George Sand," note 3, 123.

8. *Corr.* XXIII, to Gustave Flaubert, 8 Dec. [18]72, 332.

9. Arnold, "George Sand," 204.

10. *Corr.* I, ii–iii.

11. F. M. Dostoevsky, *The Diary of a Writer*, trans. Boris Braso (New York: Scribner's, 1949), 34.

12. Oscar Wilde, cited in Cate, *George Sand*, xvi. Margaret Fuller, cited in Miller, *American Romantic*, 264.

13. Frederic W. H. Myers, "George Sand," *The Nineteenth Century* 1, no. 2 (Apr. 1877): 225.

14. Toesca, *Le Plus Grand Amour de George Sand*, 319.

15. Solange Dudevant Sand to Emile Aucante, 25 July 1883, in Lovenjoul E962, ff154–155, cited by Chambaz-Bertrand, "Paradoxes de la maternité," 15.

SELECT BIBLIOGRAPHY

WORKS BY GEORGE SAND

Agendas. 5 vols. Paris: Jean Touzot Libraire-Editeur, 1990–1993.

The Companion of the Tour of France. Translated by Francis Geo. Shaw. New York: William H. Graham, 1847.

La Confession d'une jeune fille. 2 vols. Paris: Calmann-Lévy, 1888. Reprint, Geneva: Slatkine, 1979.

Consuelo. Paris: Aurore, 1985.

Consuelo. Translated by Fayette Robinson. Greenwich, Conn.: Fawcett, 1961.

Correspondance. Edited by Georges Lubin. 25 vols. Paris: Garnier, 1964–1991.

Correspondance. Vol. 26. Edited by Georges Lubin. Tusson: Du Lérot, 1995.

Correspondance: Sand-Musset. Edited by E. Decori. Brussels: E. Deman, 1904.

Le Dernier Amour. Edited by Mireille Bossis. Paris: des femmes, 1991.

Entretiens journaliers avec le très docte et très habile docteur Piffoël. In *Oeuvres autobiographiques,* vol. 2. Edited by Georges Lubin. Paris: Gallimard, 1971.

Flaubert-Sand: The Correspondence. Translated by Francis Steegmuller and Barbara Bray. New York: Knopf, 1993.

Gabriel. Paris: Des Femmes, 1988.

George Sand: In Her Own Words. Translated by Joseph Barry. London: Quartet, 1979.

George Sand: Politique et polémiques (1843–1850). Edited by Michelle Perrot. Paris: Imprimerie Nationale Editions, 1997.

"Le Grillon." In *L'Histoire du rêveur.* Paris: Montaigne, 1931.

Histoire de ma vie. In *Oeuvres autobiographiques.* Edited by Georges Lubin. 2 vols. Paris: Gallimard, 1970, 1971.

Un Hiver à Majorque. Paris: Hippolyte Souverain, 1842.

Impressions et souvenirs. Paris: Michel-Lévy, 1869.

Indiana. Paris: Garnier Frères, 1962.

Indiana. Edited by Béatrice Didier. Paris: Folio, 1984.

Indiana. Translated by George Burnham Ives. Chicago: Academy Chicago Publishers, 1992.

Lélia. Paris: Dupuy, 1833. 2d version, Paris: Bonnaire, 1839. Reprint, Paris: Garnier Frères, 1960.

Lélia. Translated by Marie Espinosa. Bloomington: Indiana University Press, 1978.

Lettres d'un voyageur. Paris: Garnier-Flammarion, 1971.

Lettres d'un voyageur. Translated by Sacha Rabinovitch and Patricia Thomson. Harmondsworth, Middlesex: Penguin, 1987.

Lucrézia Floriani. Paris: Calmann-Lévy, 1880.

Lucrézia Floriani. Translated by Julius Eker. Chicago: Academy Chicago Publishers, 1985.

La Mare au diable. Edited by P. Salomon and J. Mallion. Paris: Garnier Frères, 1962.

Mauprat. Paris: Gallimard/Folio, 1981.

Mauprat. Translated by Sylvia Raphael. New York: Oxford University Press, 1997.

Le Meunier d'Angibault. Paris: Livre de Poche, 1985.

The Miller of Angibault. Translated by Donna Dickenson. New York: Oxford University Press, 1995.

Oeuvres autobiographiques. Edited by Georges Lubin. 2 vols. Paris: Gallimard, 1970, 1971.

Préfaces de George Sand. Edited by Anna Szabó. 2 vols. Debrecen, Hungary: Kossuth Lajos Tudományegyetem, 1997.

Questions d'art et de littérature. Edited by Henriette Bessis and Janice Glasgow. Paris: Des Femmes, 1991.

Le Roman d'Aurore Dudevant et d'Aurélien de Sèze. Paris: Editions Montaigne, 1928.

Romans 1830. Paris: Presses de la Cité, 1991.

Sketches and Hints. In *Oeuvres autobiographiques,* vol. 2. Edited by Georges Lubin. Paris: Gallimard, 1971.

Story of My Life. A group translation. Edited by Thelma Jurgau. Albany: State University of New York Press, 1991.

Valentine. Paris: Hetzel, 1853.

Voyage en Auvergne. In *Oeuvres autobiographiques,* vol. 2. Edited by Georges Lubin. Paris: Gallimard, 1971.

Voyage en Espagne. In *Oeuvres autobiographiques,* vol. 2. Edited by Georges Lubin. Paris: Gallimard, 1971.

Winter in Majorca. Translated by Robert Graves. Chicago: Academy Press Limited, 1978.

OTHER SOURCES

Abbadie, Christian. "George Sand et les relations franco-espagnoles." *Europe* 587 (March 1978): 48–74.

Agoult, Marie d'. *Mémoires, 1833–1854.* Paris: Calmann Lévy, 1987.

Anderson, Bonnie S. *Joyous Greetings: The International Women's Movement, 1830 to 1860.* New York: Oxford University Press, 2000.

André-Maurois, Simone, ed. *Correspondance inédite: George Sand–Marie Dorval.* Paris: Gallimard, 1953.

Arnold, Matthew. "George Sand." *Littell's Living Age* 134, no. 1728 (28 July 1877): 195–204.

Barry, Joseph. *Infamous Woman: The Life of George Sand.* New York: Doubleday, 1977.

Beauvoir, Simone de. *Le Deuxième Sexe.* 2 vols. Paris: Gallimard, 1949.

Bell, Susan Groag, and Marilyn Yalom, eds. *Revealing Lives.* Albany: State University of New York Press, 1990.

Brault, Joseph. *Une contemporaine. Biographie et intrigues de George Sand.* Pamphlet seized by police on 1 July 1848.

Brée, Germaine. "George Sand: The Fictions of Autobiography." *Nineteenth-Century French Studies* 4 (Summer 1976): 438–449.

Capasso, Ruth Carver. "Female Voice in *Confession of a Young Girl.*" *George Sand Studies* 13 (Spring 1994): 55–62.

Cate, Curtis. *George Sand: A Biography.* Boston: Houghton Mifflin, 1975.

Cédoz, F.-M.-Th. *Un Couvent de religieuses anglaises à Paris.* Paris: Victor Lecoffre, 1891.

Chalon, Jean. *Chère George Sand.* Paris: Flammarion, 1991.

Chambaz-Bertrand, Christine. "Paradoxes de la maternité dans la vie et l'oeuvre de George Sand." Dissertation, Université de Paris VIII, St.-Denis, 1991.

Chevigny, Bell Gale. *The Woman and the Myth: Margaret Fuller's Life and Writings.* Old Westbury, N.Y.: Feminist Press, 1976.

Chonez, Claudine. "George Sand et le féminisme." *Europe* 587 (March 1978): 75–79.

Chopin, Frederik. *Chopin's Letters.* Collected by Henryk Opienski. Translated by E. L. Voynich. New York: Dover, 1988.

Chovelon, Bernadette. "L'Education des filles d'après George Sand." Dissertation, University of Grenoble, 1982.

———. *George Sand et Solange: Mère et fille.* Saint-Cyr-sur-Loire: Christian Pirot, 1994.

Clésinger-Sand, Solange. *Carl Robert.* Paris: Calmann Lévy, 1887. BN n.a.f. 8.Y2 40927.

———. *Jacques Bruneau.* Paris: Michel Lévy Frères, 1870. BN n.a.f. Y2 23205.

———. "Journaux de Solange." Gift of Ryuji Nagatsuka, BN n.a.f. 26215, 1852–1860, 125 ff. BN n.a.f. 26216, 1857–1862, 33 ff.

———. Nouvel Agenda de 1874, 1889. BN n.a.f. 15556.

———. Solange Clésinger–Charles Alfieri Correspondence. Vol. 1. 24 October 1857–30 January 1896. 492 ff. BN n.a.f. 16267.

Crecelius, Kathryn J. *Family Romances: George Sand's Early Novels.* Bloomington: Indiana University Press, 1987.

Daly, Pierrette. "De Sand à Cixous: La 'Venue à l'écriture' au féminin." *George Sand.* Colloque de Cerisy. Paris: Editions C.D.U. SEDES, 1983.

Datlof, Natalie, Jeanne Fuchs, and David A. Powell, eds. *The World of George Sand.* Westport, Conn.: Greenwood Press, 1991.

Deutelbaum, Wendy, and Cynthia Hugg. "Class, Gender, and Family System: The Case of George Sand." In *The (M)other Tongue: Essays in Feminist Psychoanalytic Interpretation.* Edited by Shirley Nelson Garner, Claire Kahane, and Madelon Sprengnether. Ithaca: Cornell University Press, 1985.

Deutsch, Helene. "George Sand: A Woman's Destiny." *The International Review of Psycho-analysis* 9, no. 4 (1982): 445–460.

D'Heylli, Georges [Edmond Poinsot]. *La Fille de George Sand.* Paris: 1900. (Two hundred copies printed but not published commercially.)

Dickenson, Donna. *George Sand: A Brave Man—The Most Womanly Woman.* Oxford: Berg Publishers, 1988.

Didier, Béatrice. *George Sand écrivain: "Un grand fleuve d'Amérique."* Paris: Presses Universitaires de France, 1998.

Douchin, Jacques-Louis. *George Sand, l'amoureuse.* Paris: Ramsay/J.-J. Pauvert, 1992.

Eisler, Benita. *Chopin's Funeral.* New York: Knopf, 2003.

Estignard, A. *Clésinger, sa vie, ses oeuvres.* Paris: H. Floury, 1900.

Frappier-Mazur, Lucienne. "George Sand et la généalogie: Adultère, adoption et légitimation dans *La Confession d'une jeune fille* (1864)." *George Sand Studies* 17 (1998): 3–16.

Gailly de Taurines, Charles. *Aventuriers et femmes de qualité: La Fille du maréchal de Saxe.* Paris: Hachette, 1907.

Garber, Marge. *Vice Versa: Bisexuality and the Eroticism of Everyday Life.* New York: Simon and Schuster, 1995.

Gautier, Théophile. *Etudes baudelairiennes.* Neuchâtel: A la Baconnière, 1985.

Goncourt, Edmond de, and Jules de Goncourt. *La Femme au XVIIIᵉ siècle.* Paris: Charpentier, 1905.

———. *Journal.* 3 vols. Edited by Robert Ricatte. Paris: Fasquelle and Flammarion, 1956.

Hamburg, Paul. "The Lie: Anorexia and the Paternal Metaphor." *Psychoanalytic Review* 86, no. 5 (October 1999): 745–769.

Hamilton, Edith. *Mythology.* New York: Mentor, 1969.

Hiddleston, Janet. *George Sand and Autobiography.* Legenda. European Humanities Research Centre. Oxford University. Research monographs in French Studies 5, 1999.

Higonnet, Patrice. *Paris: Capital of the World.* Translated by Arthur Goldhammer. Cambridge, Mass.: Belknap Press, 2002.

Hirsch, Pam. "Charlotte Brontë and George Sand: The Influence of Female Romanticism." In *Brontë Society Transactions* 21 (1996): 209–218.

Hofstadter, Dan. *The Love Affair as a Work of Art.* New York: Farrar, Straus and Giroux, 1966.

Houssaye, Arsène. *Les Confessions.* 2 vols. Geneva: Slatkine, 1971.

James, Henry. "George Sand, 1914." In *Notes on Novelists*. New York: Scribner's, 1914.

Johnson, Diane. "Experience as Melodrama: George Sand." In *Terrorists and Novelists*. New York: Knopf, 1982.

———. "She Had It All." *New York Review of Books* 26, no. 15 (11 October 1979): 9–12.

Karénine, Wladimir. *George Sand: Sa vie et ses oeuvres*. 4 vols. Geneva: Slatkine Reprints, 2000.

Laclos, Choderlos de. *Les Liaisons dangereuses*. Paris: Gallimard, 1958.

Liszt, Franz. *Correspondance: Franz Liszt, Marie d'Agoult*. Paris: Fayard, 2001.

Lubin, Georges, ed. *Album Sand*. Paris: Gallimard, 1973.

———. "*Rose et Blanche:* Roman renié." *Revue des Sciences Humaines* 226 (April–June 1992): 13–20.

Lukacher, Maryline. *Maternal Fictions*. Durham: Duke University Press, 1994.

Maclean, Marie. "A Female Genealogy: The En-gendering of George Sand." In Maclean, *The Name of the Mother: Writing Illegitimacy*. London: Routledge, 1994.

Manifold, Gay. *George Sand's Theatre Career*. Ann Arbor, Mich.: UMI Research Press, 1985.

Maugras, Gaston. *Les Demoiselles de Verrières*. Paris: Calmann-Lévy, 1890.

Maurois, André. *Lélia: The Life of George Sand*. Translated by Gerard Hopkins. New York: Harper and Brothers, 1953.

Miller, Nancy K. "Women's Autobiography in France: For a Dialetics of Identification." In *Women and Language in Literature and Society*. Edited by Sally McConnell-Gonet, Ruth Borker, and Nelly Furman. Westport, Conn.: Praeger, 1980.

Miller, Perry, ed. *American Romantic*. New York: Doubleday, 1963.

Moers, Ellen. *Literary Women*. New York: Oxford University Press, 1963.

Montesquieu. *Persian Letters*. Translated by J. Robert Loy. New York: Meridian, 1959.

Moses, Claire Goldberg, and Leslie Wahl Rabine, eds. *Feminism, Socialism, and French Romanticism*. Bloomington: Indiana University Press, 1993.

Mozet, Nicole, ed. *George Sand: Une correspondance*. Saint-Cyr-sur-Loire: Christian Pirot, 1994.

———. *George Sand, écrivain de romans*. Saint-Cyr-sur-Loire: Christian Pirot, 1997.

Muelsch, Elisabeth-Christine. "George Sand and Her Sisters: Women Writers in the *Société des Gens de Lettres* (1838–1848)." *George Sand Studies* 16 (1997): 97–108.

Murger, Henri. *Scènes de la vie de Bohème*. Paris: Garnier Frères, 1851.

Myers, Frederic W. H. "George Sand." *The Nineteenth Century* 1, no. 2 (April 1877): 221–241.

Nagatsuka, Ryuji. "Une Education manquée: George Sand et sa fille." Communication au XXVIIe Congrès de l'Association Internationale des Etudes Françaises, 30 July 1975.

Naginski, Isabelle Hoog. "La Comédie féminine: Constance et mouvance dans l'oeuvre sandienne." In *G. Sand et l'écriture du roman*. Actes du XIe colloque international George Sand. Montreal: Librairie de l'Université de Montréal, 1996.

———. *George Sand: Writing for Her Life*. New Brunswick: Rutgers University Press, 1991.

Poli, Annarosa. *L'Italie dans la vie et dans l'oeuvre de George Sand*. Paris: Armand Collin, 1960.

Pommier, Jean. *Autour du drâme de Venise: G. Sand et A. de Musset au lendemain de "Lorenzaccio."* Paris: Nizet, 1958.

Powell, David A. *George Sand*. Boston: Twayne, 1990.

Rabine, Leslie Wahl. "Sand and the Myth of Femininity." In *Women and Literature* 4 (1976): 2–17.

Rea, Annabelle M. "Healers in George Sand's Works." In *The World of George Sand*. Edited by Natalie Datlof, Jeanne Fuchs, and David A. Powell. Westport, Conn.: Greenwood Press, 1991.

Riot-Sarcey, Michèle. *La Démocratie à l'épreuve des femmes: Trois figures critiques du pouvoir, 1830–1848*. Paris: Albin Michel, 1994.

Rice-Defosse, Mary. "Jocasta Vanishes: Maternal Absence and Narrative Desire in *Le Péché de Monsieur Antoine*." In *George Sand Studies* 19 (2000): 52–61.

Rich, Adrienne. *Of Woman Born*. New York: Norton, 1976.

Richardson, Joanna. *The Bohemians*. London: Macmillan, 1969.

Rocheblave, Samuel. *George Sand et sa fille*. Paris: Calmann-Lévy, 1906.

Sainte-Beuve, Charles Augustin. *Portraits contemporains*. 5 vols. Paris: Calmann-Lévy, 1881.

Salomon, Pierre. "Un amour de Chopin: Solange Sand." *Revue des Sciences Humaines* 60 (October–December 1950): 261–269.

Schermerhorn, Elizabeth W. *The Seven Strings of the Lyre: The Romantic Life of George Sand*. Boston: Houghton Mifflin, 1927.

Schor, Naomi. "Le Féminisme de George Sand: *Lettres à Marcie*." *Revue des Sciences Humaines* 226 (1992): 21–35.

———. "French Feminism Is a Universalism." *Differences: A Journal of Feminist Cultural Studies* 7 (spring 1995): 15–47.

———. *George Sand and Idealism*. New York: Columbia University Press, 1993.

Scott, Joan Wallach. *Only Paradoxes to Offer: French Feminists and the Rights of Man*. Cambridge: Harvard University Press, 1996.

Seigel, Jerrold. *Bohemian Paris: Culture, Politics, and the Boundaries of Bourgeois Life, 1830–1930*. New York: Viking, 1986.

Smart, Annie. "Motherhood and Politics in George Sand and Flora Tristan." *George Sand Studies* 16 (1997): 83–96.

Spoelberch de Lovenjoul, Charles de. *La Véritable Histoire de "Elle et Lui."* Paris: Calmann-Lévy, 1897.

Szulc, Tad. *Chopin in Paris*. New York: Scribner, 1998.

Thibert, Marguerite. *Féminisme dans le socialisme français de 1830 à 1850*. Paris: Marcel Giard, 1926.

Thurer, Shari L. *The Myths of Motherhood: How Culture Reinvents the Good Mother*. New York: Houghton Mifflin, 1994.

Toesca, Maurice. *Le Plus Grand Amour de George Sand*. Paris: Albin Michel, 1980.

Trilling, Lionel. *Matthew Arnold*. New York: Harcourt Brace Javonovich, 1954.

Vanderkerkhove, Marielle. "Romanesque et autobiographie dans *La Confession d'une jeune fille*." *Les Amis de George Sand* 20 (1998): 20–29.

Van Witzen, Rosalien. "Une relation pervertie: George Sand et Solange." *Les Amis de George Sand* 18 (1996): 11–18.

Varilhe, Jean de. *Les Années d'adolescence de George Sand*. Guéret: Les Presses du Massif Central, 1956.

Vermeylan, Pierre. *Les Idées politiques et sociales de George Sand*. Brussels: Editions de l'Université de Bruxelles, 1984.

West, Anthony. *Mortal Wounds*. New York: McGraw-Hill, 1973.

Winegarten, Renée. *The Double Life of George Sand, Woman and Writer*. New York: Basic, 1978.

Woolf, Virginia. "A Sketch of the Past." In *Moments of Being*. New York: Harcourt Brace Jovanovich, 1985.

ACKNOWLEDGMENTS

I AM GRATEFUL for the research assistance graciously provided by the staff at the Bibliothèque Historique de la Ville de Paris and the Bibliothèque Nationale de France (both the venerable nineteenth-century site Richelieu and its extraordinary contemporary offspring at Tolbiac). I owe thanks, in particular, to Dr. John Logan at the Firestone Library of Princeton University, for his expert guidance and unstinting support.

With deep regret that he is no longer with us, I would like to acknowledge Georges Lubin, whose tireless fieldwork over the course of the twentieth century has laid the foundation of modern Sand studies. The Friends of George Sand, which was founded by Natalie Datlof at Hofstra University in 1976, is largely responsible for the interest and enthusiasm that George Sand's life and work continue to generate around the world.

At Yale University Press I take this opportunity to thank Lara Heimert, executive editor, for honoring me by her decision to publish this book; Susan Laity, for skillfully overseeing its production; and Keith Condon, for careful coordination of the illustrations. My thanks as well to Karen Gangel for the rigor and respect with which she edited my manuscript.

Louise DeSalvo, Brooke Kroeger, and Nancy Rubin Stuart are among the caring friends who have been kind enough to take time from their own work to read my pages and to offer invaluable commentary and encouragement.

I'm indebted to Louise Kaplan and David Hoddeson who invited me, in medias res, to contribute an article to *American Imago* on my experience of writing Sand's biography. This exercise in introspection enabled me to complete the book.

I owe a special expression of gratitude to Leonard Harlan, without whose generous support the many years of research and writing that have gone into this book would not have been possible.

And finally, to my partner of the past decade, John Patrick Diggins, fondest friend and passionate provocateur, go thanks for his faith in me and my work.

INDEX